MORE BLACK
AMERICAN PLAYWRIGHTS:
A Bibliography

by

ESTHER SPRING ARATA

with the assistance of

Marlene J. Erickson
Sandra Dewitz
Mary Linse Alexander

The Scarecrow Press, Inc.

Metuchen, N.J. & London

1978

Also by Esther Spring Arata

Black American Writers, Past and Present: A Bio-
graphical and Bibliographical Dictionary, by Theressa
Gunnels Rush, Carol Fairbanks Myers, and Esther Spring
Arata (Scarecrow Press, 1975, 2 vols.)

Black American Playwrights, 1800 to the Present:
A Bibliography, by Esther Spring Arata and Nicholas
John Rotoli (Scarecrow Press, 1976)

Library of Congress Cataloging in Publication Data

Arata, Esther Spring.
More Black American playwrights.

    Includes index.
    Bibliography: p.
    1. American drama--Afro-American authors--Bibliography
2. American drama--Afro-American authors--History and
criticism--Bibliography. I. Title.
Z1229.N39A73 [PS153.N5] 016.812'009'896073 78-15231
ISBN 0-8108-1158-8

Dedicated to

John, my husband

My Mother

Josie Spring Campbell, my sister

CONTENTS

ACKNOWLEDGMENTS

The editor wishes to express her appreciation to the following persons who, in one way or another, influenced and helped to make this bibliography possible:

The staff members at: The McIntyre Library, University of Wisconsin-Eau Claire; the Eau Claire Public Library; the Reference and Rare Books Rooms, Memorial Library, University of Wisconsin-Madison; and the Minneapolis Public Library. The editor was also privileged to use a new acquisition, The <u>Newsbank--Performing Arts</u>, at the Eau Claire Public Library, and many black periodicals and newspapers, unavailable elsewhere, at the Minneapolis Public Library.

Those special members of the English Department who were always encouraging and understanding: Dr. Kenneth H. Spaulding; Mr. Douglas Pearson, Jr., chairperson; and the Department secretary, Caryl Laubauch, who typed a portion of the book.

The assistants who performed various tasks which enabled the book to mature:

Marlene J. Erickson, co-worker; chief typist and proofreader.

Sandra Dewitz, research assistant who worked with the black American and general theater sources available at McIntyre Library.

Mary Linse Alexander, who utilized the Inter-Library Loan services, alphabetized entries, and did cross referencing.

The graduate student assistant, Dawn Marble Whited, whose services, retrieving and checking sources, and proofing the General Bibliography, were invaluable.

To each, a heartfelt thank you.

E. A.

PREFACE

Continuing interest in black drama as a vital creative force in writing and in the performing arts, produced the need for an additional source enabling instructors, students, researchers, and readers to locate information about black playwrights and their works. This bibliography attempts to make such information possible, and to expose the continued growth and success of this genre.

The policies established in the production of the earlier volume, Black American Playwrights, 1800 to the Present: A Bibliography, by Esther Spring Arata and Nicholas John Rotoli (Metuchen, N.J.: Scarecrow Press, 1976), were adhered to in the preparation of this book: the consultation, first, of the Black Theatre Directory, black journals, magazines, newspapers, and books for biographical information, critiques, and reviews about black dramatists before investigating other miscellaneous sources for related data; the inclusion of white writers who collaborated with black playwrights on a given work (see, for example, Hatch, Pinero, Weill, et al.); the restriction of research to local libraries--the William McIntyre Library at the University of Wisconsin-Eau Claire, the Eau Claire Public Library, Memorial Library at the University of Wisconsin-Madison, and at the Minneapolis Public Library (Downtown Branch).

Although the same format was observed, this volume, unlike the earlier, includes a listing of all periodicals and newspapers used in the compilation of the entries, and the author and titles of reviews.

There are three sections in the book: an alphabetized listing of black playwrights and their works, together with criticisms, reviews, and awards; a general bibliography; an index of play titles. For purposes of simplicity, abbreviated citations appear in the body of the authors' entries. For example, when an abbreviated entry reads "Mitchell. Voices of the Black Theatre, p. 10" the reader refers to the General Bibliography for complete bibliographical details of the Mitchell book.

Approximately 490 playwrights appear in this bibliography, of which 190 appeared in the 1976 edition. Since this volume proposes to offer More about black playwrights and their works, information published in the 1976 volume was not duplicated in this book. To alert readers that additional material on these dramatists exists in the 1976 edition, the symbol † was placed before the playwrights' names.

Frequently, current information located in periodicals and newspapers is unavailable at a given time for research. Periodical issues from the preceding year are systematically removed from library shelves to be either bound, microfilmed, or placed on microfiche cards. Some issues have been vandalized, some lost; some are in copying rooms, some in use by other researchers or readers. Much of the information inaccessible to Arata and Rotoli when they prepared the 1976 volume for publication, now appears in this book. The entries in the present volume span the years from 1970 to 1978, in an attempt to offer as much current material as possible.

While it is true that a bibliography of this nature offers a compilation of facts, and functions primarily as a starting-point for further investigations into black drama, there exists another aspect of this tool. As I see it, vision, that power in an artist which helps him/her to see life as it is, and then create something out of what he/she sees, can also be a power to the researcher as well. The researcher with vision will read the titles of the primary and secondary works herein, will see much--and perhaps create much. Careful reading of this bibliography, as well as of the 1976 volume, reveals that many black playwrights are less concerned with the portrayal of racial tensions, and more interested in black male/female relationships, the evolution of black heroes/heroines, the shaping of a culture, and the need to establish a medium of expression accessible to many members in the black community; that certain playwrights, and works, continue to pique the interest of critics; and most of all, that black women playwrights play strong, successful roles as creative innovators in the dramatic mode.

The possibilities for discovering new ideas and making them viable are limitless. Hopefully, More Black American Playwrights, along with the 1976 volume, will serve the readers well and enable each to envision the creative possibilities for research nestled within the various entries.

Esther Spring Arata
January 1978

x

PERIODICALS AND NEWSPAPERS USED

Periodicals

Action
Africa
African Report
After Dark
America
American Imago
American Libraries
American Literary Scholar-
    ship
American Quarterly
The Antioch Review
Antogionish Review (Nova
    Scotia)
Art in America
Arts in Society

Black Academy Review
Black Books Bulletin
The Black Collegian
Black Creation
Black Enterprise
Black Images
Black Lines
Black Scholar
Black Star
Black Theatre
Black World
Book World
Booklist
The Bookman
Books and Bookmen
Bookviews
Bulletin of the New York
    Public Library

CLA Journal
Cahiers Renauld--Barrault
California English Journal
Caribbean Literature
Caribbean Quarterly

The Carolina Play Book
Catholic World
Choice
Christian Scholar's Review
Christian Science Monitor
Christianity Today
College and Research Libraries
College English
Commentary
Commonweal
Community
Colored American Magazine
Crisis
Critical Digest
Cue
Current Biography

Dance Magazine
December
Dissent
Drama
Drama Review

Ebony
Edge
Educational Theatre Journal
Empirical Research in Theatre
Encore
English Journal
Esquire
Essence

Film Quarterly
First World
Freedomways

Half-Century Magazine
Harper
Hudson Review
Human Events

Iowa Review

Jet
Journal of American Studies
Journal of Black Studies
Journal of Broadcasting
Journal of Negro History
Journal of Popular Culture

Liberator
Library Journal
Life
Literature and Ideology
(Montreal)

Mademoiselle
Madheart Studies in Black
Literature
Massachusetts Review
Modern Theatre and Drama
More
Ms.

Nation
Negro American Literature
Forum
Negro Digest
The Negro Educational Review
Negro History Bulletin
New Boston Review
New Directions: The Howard
University Magazine
New Masses
New Republic
New Statesman
New York
New York Review of Books
New York Theatre Critics'
Reviews
New York Times Magazine
New Yorker
Newsweek
Notes on Contemporary Lit-
erature

Obsidian
The Ohio Review
Opportunity

Pan-African Journal
Partisan Review
People
Phylon
Playboy
Players

Plays and Players
Psychology Today
Publishers Weekly

Quarterly Journal of Speech
Quinzaine Littéraire

Race Relations Reporter
Record
Renaissance 2
Research Studies
Resources for American Lit-
erary Study
Rolling Stone

Saturday Review
Scripts
Senior Scholastic
Sepia
Seventeen
Social Problems
Soul Illustrated
Soundings
South Atlantic Quarterly
South Carolina Review
Southern Folklore Quarterly
Studies in Black Literature
Studies in Literary Imagination
Studies in the Twentieth Century

TV Guide
Theatre Documentation
Theatre News
Time
Transatlantic Review
Tuesday Magazine

Urban Life and Culture

Village Voice
Vogue

West Coast Review
Women's Wear Daily
World Theatre
Writer's Digest

Xavier University Studies

Yale Literary Magazine
Yale/Theatre
Zeitschrift für Anglistik und
Amerikanistik

Newspapers

The Afro-American (Baltimore)
Albuquerque Journal
American Statesman (Austin)
Amsterdam News (N.Y.)
Arkansas Gazette (Little Rock)
Atlanta Journal

Bay State Banner (Boston)
Birmingham (Ala.) News
Black Dispatch (Oklahoma City)
Boston Globe
Buffalo (N.Y.) Evening News

Call and Post (Cincinnati)
Chicago Daily Defender
Chicago Sun Times
Chicago Tribune
Cleveland Plain Dealer
Cleveland Press
Columbus Evening Dispatch
Commercial Appeal (Memphis)
Courier (Chicago)

Daily News (N.Y.)
Dallas Morning News
Denver Post
Denver Press
Detroit Free Press

Evening Bulletin (Philadelphia)

Hartford Courant
Houston Post

Ifco News

Kansas City (Mo.) Star

Long Island (N.Y.) Press
Los Angeles Herald Examiner
Los Angeles Times
Louisville Courier-Journal

Miami Herald
Milwaukee Journal
Minneapolis Tribune
Minneapolis Spokesman

New York Post
New York Times
News and Observor (Raleigh, N.C.)
Newsday (Long Island, N.Y.)

Oakland (Calif.) Tribune
Omaha World Herald

Philadelphia Tribune
Pioneer Press (St. Paul, Minn.)

Rocky Mountain News (Denver)

Sacramento Bee
St. Louis Argus
St. Louis Globe-Democrat
St. Louis Post-Dispatch
San Diego Union
San Francisco Examiner
Seattle Times
Star-Ledger (Newark, N.J.)
Sun (Baltimore)

Tennessean (Nashville)
Times-Union (Albany, N.Y.)
Times-Picayune (New Orleans)
Times-Society (Albany, N.Y.)
Trenton Times
Twin Cities Courier (Minneapolis/St. Paul)

Wall Street Journal
Washington Post
Washington Star-News

BLACK AMERICAN PLAYWRIGHTS

ABBOTT, GEORGE
    MUSICALS:
    [with Richard Adler and Will Holt] Music Is, an adaptation
        of Twelfth Night
    REVIEWS OF INDIVIDUAL MUSICALS:
    Music Is
        Farrow, Charles. "'Music Is' Witty and Colorful Adapta-
            tion of 'Twelfth Night'." Afro-American (Baltimore,
            Md.), 30 November-4 December 1976, p. 11

ABDALLAH, MOHAMMAD BIN
    PLAYS:
    Ananse and the Rain God

ABRAMSON, DOLORES
    PLAYS:
    The Light
    PLAYS PUBLISHED IN ANTHOLOGIES:
    The Light, in Sonia Sanchez Writers Workshop. Three Hun-
        dred and Sixty Degrees of Blackness Comin' at You

ACAZ, MBA
    PLAYS:
    The Ambassadors
    REVIEWS OF INDIVIDUAL PLAYS:
    The Ambassadors
        Kupa, Kushauri. "Close-up: The New York Scene--Black
            Theatre in New York, 1970-1971." Black Theatre, no.
            6 (1972): 48

ADDERLEY, CANNONBALL
    MUSICALS:
    Big Man--The Legend of John Henry
    CRITICISMS OF ADDERLEY:
    "Cannon Ball Adderley Medal." (N.Y.) Amsterdam News:
        Arts and Entertainment, 7 August 1976, D-2
    REVIEWS OF INDIVIDUAL MUSICALS:
    Big Man--The Legend of John Henry
        "World Premiere of the Adderley's 'Big Man'." (N.Y.)
            Amsterdam News: Arts and Entertainment, 3 July
            1976, D-6

1

†ADELL, ILUNGA (aka William Adell Stevenson, III) (b. November 27, 1948)
    TELEVISION SCRIPTS:
        Sanford and Son (Story Editor)
        [with John Forbes] Stone and Steel
    CRITICISMS OF INDIVIDUAL TELEVISION SCRIPTS:
        Sanford and Son
            Trubo, Richard. "A Cinderella Story for a Hollywood
                Writer." (Adell) Sepia 23 (December 1974): 30+

ADLER, RICHARD
    MUSICALS:
        [with Will Holt and George Abbott] Music Is, an adaptation
        of Twelfth Night
    REVIEWS OF INDIVIDUAL MUSICALS:
        Music Is
            Farrow, Charles. "'Music Is' Witty and Colorful Adapta-
                tion of 'Twelfth Night'." Afro-American (Baltimore,
                Md.), 30 November-4 December 1976, p. 11
            Taubman. The Making of the American Theatre, p. 122

AJAMU
    PLAYS:
        The Brass Medallion
    REVIEWS OF INDIVIDUAL PLAYS:
        The Brass Medallion
            "The Brass Medallion." Theatre News 8 (March 1976):
                2-3
            Coe, Richard. "'The Brass Medallion' of Manhood."
                Washington (D.C.) Post, 14 April 1976, in Newsbank--
                Performing Arts. March-April 1976, 29: F6
            Richards, David. "ACTF-Virtues in Brass." Washington
                (D.C.) Star News. 13 April 1976, in Newsbank--Per-
                forming Arts. March-April 1976, 29: F5

†ALDRIDGE, IRA (1807-1867)
    PLAYS:
        The Black Doctor, adapted for the English Stage. Originally
        written in French by Anicet-Bourgeois
        Titus Andronucus, 1849, an adaptation of Shakespeare's play
    CRITICISMS OF ALDRIDGE:
        Blum and Willis, eds. A Pictorial History of the American
            Theatre: 1860-1976, p. 13
        Geisinger. Plays, Players, and Playwrights, pp. 326-328
        Marshall, Herbert and Mildred Stock. Ira Aldridge--the
            Negro Tragedian. London: Rockliff, 1958; N.Y.: Mac-
            millan, 1958
        Olivia, L. J. "Ira Aldridge and Theophile Gautier." Jour-
            nal of Negro History 48 (July 1963): 229-231
        Shafer, Yvonne. "Black Actors in the Nineteenth Century
            American Theatre." CLA Journal 20 (March 1977): 387,
            397-398

ALI, JAMAL
    PLAYS:
        Dark Days and Light Nights
    FILM SCRIPTS:
        Black Joy, movie based on play, Dark Days and Light Nights
    REVIEWS OF INDIVIDUAL FILMS:
        Black Joy
            "At Cannes Film Festival." The Afro-American (Balti-
                more, Md.), 17-21 May 1977, p. 15

ALI, MUHAMMAD (Cassius Clay) (1939)
    PLAYS:
        Old Man Cassius
    PLAYS PUBLISHED IN ANTHOLOGIES:
        Old Man Cassius in David, Black Joy
        Hatch, James. "Speak to Me in Those Old Words, You
            Know, Those La-La Words, Those Tung-Tung Sounds."
            Yale/Theatre 8 (Fall 1976): 31

†ALLISON, HUGHES
    PLAYS:
        Trial of Dr. Beck, 1937
    CRITICISMS OF INDIVIDUAL PLAYS:
        The Trial of Dr. Beck
            Abramson, Doris. "The Great White Way: Critics and
            the First Black Playwrights on Broadway." Educational
            Theatre Journal 28 (March 1976): 53-55
            Hartnoll. The Oxford Companion to the Theatre, p. 677

†ALONZO, CECIL
    PLAYS:
        Beaulah Johnson, in soap opera
    CRITICISMS OF INDIVIDUAL PLAYS:
        Beaulah Johnson
            Todd, George. "Alonzo Players' New Comedy Applauded."
            (N.Y.) Amsterdam News: Arts and Entertainment, 25
            June 1977, D-17

AMOS, JOHN
    PLAYS:
        Truth and Soul
    CRITICISMS BY AMOS:
        "Truth and Soul." Soul Illustrated 3 (Spring 1972): 19, 64
    REVIEWS OF INDIVIDUAL PLAYS:
        Truth and Soul
            Fitz Bartley, G. "Soul-Stirrin' Theatre." Soul Illus-
            trated 3 (Spring 1972): 64

†ANDERSON, GARLAND
    PLAYS:
        Appearances, 1925
    CRITICISMS OF INDIVIDUAL PLAYS:
        Appearances

Abramson, Doris. "The Great White Way: Critics and the First Black Playwrights on Broadway." Educational Theatre Journal 28 (March 1976): 46-47
Edmonds, Randolph. "The Blacks in the American Theatre, 1700-1969." The Pan-African Journal 7 (Winter 1974): 303
Hall, Frederick Douglass, Jr. "The Black Theatre in New York from 1960-1969." Ed. D. Columbia University, 1973, Part I
Vacha, J. E. "Black Man on the Great White Way." Journal of Popular Culture 7 (Fall 1973): 293
"The Words of Dick Campbell." In Mitchell. Voices of the Black Theatre. p. 106

ANDERSON, THOMAS
PLAYS:
Crispus Attucks. New York: New Dimensions, 1970

ANDERSON, WALT
PLAYS:
Bitter Bread! A Dramatic Reading. New York: Seabury Press, 1964

†ANDREWS, REGINA M.
PLAYS:
Climbing Jacob's Ladder
CRITICISMS OF ANDREWS:
"The Words of Regina M. Andrews." In Mitchell. Voices of the Black Theatre, pp. 61-66, 67-81
CRITICISMS OF INDIVIDUAL PLAYS:
Climbing Jacob's Ladder
Mitchell. Voices of the Black Theatre, pp. 78-79

†ANGELOU, MAYA (b. April 4, 1928)
PLAYS:
Ajax (based on Sophocles' play)
And Still I Rise!
Encounters
FILM SCRIPTS:
Georgia! Georgia!
CRITICISMS OF ANGELOU
"Creative Directions." Essence 3 (May 1972): 76
CRITICISMS OF INDIVIDUAL PLAYS:
And Still I Rise!
Redmond, Eugene. "A Review of Maya Angelou's 'And Still I Rise!'" Crisis 83 (September 1976): 50-51
CRITICISMS OF INDIVIDUAL FILM SCRIPTS:
Georgia! Georgia!
Klotman. Another Man Gone, p. 148, ff. 26
Sloan, Margaret. "Film: Keeping the Black Women in Her Place." Ms. 2 (January 1974): 31
REVIEWS OF INDIVIDUAL PLAYS:

Ajax
 Willis' Theatre World.   vol. 30, 1973-1974, p. 197
And Still I Rise!
 Redmond, Eugene.   "The Black Scholar Reviews: 'And
  Still I Rise!' by Maya Angelou."   Black Scholar 8
  (September 1976): 50-51
Encounters
 Willis' Theatre World.   vol. 30, 1973-1974, p. 198
REVIEWS OF INDIVIDUAL FILM SCRIPTS:
 Georgia! Georgia!
  "'Caged Bird' Authoress Writes Script for Film."   Jet
   (26 August 1971): 57
  Higgins, Chester.   "People Are Talking About: Maya
   Angelou."   Jet (21 October 1971): 42
  Peterson, Maurice.   "Black Imagery on the Silver Screen."
   Essence 3 (December 1972): 34

ANTARAMIA, ANNA
 PLAYS:
  [with William Rolleri and Martin Zurla] Night Shift

†ANTHONY, EARL
 PLAYS:
  Charlie Still Can't Win No Wars on the Ground
  (Mis) Judgment
 REVIEWS OF INDIVIDUAL PLAYS:
  Charlie Still Can't Win No Wars on the Ground
   Kupa, Kushauri.   "Closeup: The New York Scene--Black
    Theatre in New York, 1970-1971."   Black Theatre no.
    6 (1972): 43-44
  (Mis) Judgment
   Kupa, Kushauri.   "Closeup: The New York Scene--Black
    Theatre in New York, 1970-1971."   Black Theatre no.
    6 (1972): 43

†ARANHA, RAY (b. May 1, 1939)
 PLAYS:
  The Estate
  My Sister, My Sister
 CRITICISMS OF INDIVIDUAL PLAYS:
  The Estate
   Fleckstein, Joan S.   "Theatre in Review--'The Estate'."
    Educational Theatre Journal 28 (October 1976): 409-410
  My Sister, My Sister
   Bailey, Peter.   "Annual Round-up: Black Theater in
    America--New York."   Black World 24 (April 1975): 20
   Engel.   The Critics, pp. 5, 31, 201
 REVIEWS OF INDIVIDUAL PLAYS:
  My Sister, My Sister
   Blum and Willis, eds.   A Pictorial History of the Ameri-
    can Theatre: 1860-1976.   p. 422
   Clurman, Harold.   "Theatre."   Nation 218 (18 May 1974):
    636-7

Feingold, Michael. "Cases Alter Circumstances." Village Voice 19 (9 May 1974): 80
"My Sister, My Sister." Milwaukee (Wis.) Journal, 25 April 1976, 2:14
Peterson, Maurice. "On the Aisle: Theater and Film." Essence 5 (September 1974): 24
Simon, John. "Ripe, or Merely Ready?" New York Magazine 7 (13 May 1974): 98
Willis' Theatre World, vol. 30, 1973-1974, pp. 89, 207

ARCHER, L. C.
PLAYS:
Crosswise, children's play
CRITICISMS OF INDIVIDUAL PLAYS:
Crosswise
Sandle. The Negro in the American Educational Theatre, p. 76

AREMU, ADUKE
PLAYS:
Babylon II, children's play
Ju Ju Man, children's play
Land of the Egyptians, children's play
The Liberation of Mother Goose, children's play
REVIEWS OF INDIVIDUAL PLAYS:
Babylon II
"'Babylon II' Has Cast of 50 Kids." (N.Y.) Amsterdam News: Arts and Entertainment, 13 November 1976, D-15
Grimes, Nikki. "'Babylon II': a triumph." (N.Y.) Amsterdam News: Arts and Entertainment, 27 November 1976, D-8

AUSTIN, ELSIE
PLAYS:
Blood Doesn't Tell: A Play About Blood Plasma and Blood Donors. New York: The Woman's Press, 1945

†AYERS, VIVIAN
PLAYS:
Hawk. Houston: The Hawk Press, 1957

†BALDWIN, JAMES (b. August 2, 1924)
PLAYS:
Amen Corner. New York: Dial, 1968
Blues for Mr. Charlie. New York: Dial, 1964; New York: Dell, 1965
Blues für Mr. Charlie. Trans. [Reinbek bei Hamburg, 1971] (NYPL)
Blues para Mister Charlie. Drana en Tres actos. Trans. Andres Bosch. Barcelona: Editorial Lumen, 1966
Giovanni's Room. Adapted for theatre; performed by Actor's Studio Workshop

One Day When I Was Lost: A Senario Based on "The Auto-
biography of Malcolm X". New York: Dial Press, 1972;
London: Joseph, 1972
FILM SCRIPTS:
The Inheritance, 1973
One Day When I Was Lost (based on the play by the same
title)
CRITICISMS BY BALDWIN:
"Sweet Lorraine." Esquire 72 (November 1969): 139-40
CRITICISMS OF BALDWIN:
Bigsby. Confrontation and Commitment, p. xix, passim
Bogle, Donald. "A Look at the Movies by Baldwin."
Freedomways, 16 (Second Quarter): 103-08
Brooks, Mary Ellen. "Reactionary Trends in Recent Black
Drama." Literature and Ideology (Montreal), no. 10
(1970): 46-48
Cohn. Dialogue in American Drama, pp. 188-92
Gresham, Jewell Handy, ed. "James Baldwin Comes Home."
Essence 7 (June 1976): 55, 80+
Hall, John. "James Baldwin." Transatlantic Review nos. 37-
38, (Autumn-Winter 1970-1971): n.p.
Littlejohn. Black on White, pp. 72-3
McGraw-Hill Encyclopedia of World Drama, vol. 1, p. 125
McWhirter, W. A. "Parting Shots: After Years of Futility
Baldwin Explodes Again." Life (30 July 1971): 63
Proffer. Soviet Criticism of American Literature in the
Sixties, pp. 84-85
Smiley. Playwrighting: The Structure of Action, pp. 19,
49, 50, 161
Tedesco, John L. "Blues for Mister Charlie: The Rhetori-
cal Dimension." Players Magazine 50 (Fall/Winter 1975):
20-23
"The Words of Frederick O'Neal." In Mitchell. Voices of
the Black Theatre, p. 181
"The Words of Regina M. Andrews." In Mitchell. Voices
of the Black Theatre, p. 72
CRITICISMS OF INDIVIDUAL PLAYS:
The Amen Corner
Anderson, Mary Louise. "Black Matriarchy: Portrayals
of Women in Three Plays." Negro American Literature
Forum 10 Fall (1976): 93+
Bigsby. Confrontation and Commitment, p. 136
Cohn. Dialogue in American Drama, pp. 188-89, 193
Edmonds, Randolph. "The Blacks in the American Theatre,
1700-1969." The Pan-African Journal 7 (Winter 1974):
306
Hartnoll. The Oxford Companion to the Theatre, p. 681
Littlejohn. Black on White, p. 73
Simmons, Bill. "Some Impressions of 'The Amen Corner'."
Black Theatre no. 2 (1969): 32-33
"The Words of Abram Hill." In Mitchell. Voices of the
Black Theatre, p. 146

Blues for Mr. Charlie

Adams, George R. "Black Militant Drama." American
Imago 28 (Summer 1971): 109, 115 passim
Bigsby. Confrontation and Commitment, pp. 122, 129-37,
166
"Black Theatre: A Bid for Cultural Identity." Black
Enterprise 2 (September 1971): 31
Brooks, Mary Ellen. "Reactionary Trends in Recent
Black Drama." Literature and Ideology (Montreal)
10 (1970): 47
Cohn. Dialogue in American Drama, pp. 189-92
Driver, Tom. "Blues for Mr. Charlie: The Review That
Was Too True to be Published." Negro Digest 13
(September 1964): 34-40
Edmonds, Randolph. "The Blacks in the American Theatre,
1700-1969." The Pan-African Journal 7 (Winter 1974):
306
Friedman. American Drama in Social Context, pp. 86, 98
Hartnoll. The Oxford Companion to the Theatre, p. 681
Hay, Samuel A. "African-American Drama, 1950-1970."
Negro History Bulletin 36 (January 1973): 5
Houghton. The Exploding Stage, p. 200
Inge, M. Thomas. "James Baldwin's Blues." Notes on
Contemporary Literature 2 (September 1972): 8-11
Keller, Joseph. "Black Writing and the White Critic."
Negro American Literature Forum 3 (Winter 1970): 103,
107
Littlejohn. Black on White, pp. 73-4
Nascimento, Abdias do. "The Negro Theatre in Brazil."
In Mezu, ed. Modern Black Literature, p. 172
Newman, Jill. "The Players the Thing at Clay Steven-
son's Workshop." Encore 6 (21 February 1977): 35
Proffer. Soviet Criticism of American Literature in the
Sixties, p. xxix
Roth, Phillip. "Channel X: Two Plays on the Race Con-
flict." New York Review of Books 2 (28 May 1964):
10-11
Scheller, Bernhard. "Die Gestolt des Farbigen bie Wil-
liams, Albee und Baldwin und ihre szenische Realisie-
rung in DDR-Aufführungen [The Concept of the Colored
Races in Williams, Albee and Baldwin and its Scenic
Realization in G. D. R. -Productions]. Zeitschrift für
Anglistik und Amerikanistik 20:2 (1972): 137-157
Simon. Uneasy Changes, pp. 47-51, 52
Smiley. Playwrighting: The Structure of Action, pp. 19,
51, 161
Sontag, Susan. Against Interpretation and Other Essays,
pp. 51-55
Stevenson, Robert Louis "The Images of the White Man
as Projected in the Published Plays of Black Ameri-
cans, 1847-1973." Ph. D. Dissertation, Indiana Uni-
versity, 1976

Taubman. The Making of the American Theatre, pp. 334-
35, 365

Tedesco, John Leonard. "Blues for Mister Charlie: The
Rhetorical Dimension." Players 50 (Fall 1974-Winter
1975): 20-23

_____. "The White Image as Second 'Persona' in Black
Drama, 1955-1970." Ph. D. Dissertation, University of
Iowa, 1974

REVIEWS OF INDIVIDUAL PLAYS:

The Amen Corner

"Beah Richards Combines Poetic Touch with Acting."
Chicago Daily Defender, 1 August 1977, p. 18

"Claudia McNeil Won Fame the Hard Way." The Afro-
American: Afro-Magazine (Baltimore, Md.), 15-19
March 1977, p. 1

Davis, Curt. "Isabel Is a Belly Laugh " Encore 6 (6
June 1977): 32

Blues for Mr. Charlie

"Avante Theater Presents 'Blues for Mr. Charlie'."
Philadelphia (Pa.) Tribune, 18 February 1975, in News-
bank--Performing Arts. January-February 1975, 13:B
12

Blum and Willis, eds. A Pictorial History of the American Theatre: 1860-1976, pp. 383, 386

Dougherty, Jim. "Blues for Mr. Charlie." Edge no. 5
(Fall 1966): 116-120

"Le Nore, Rosetta." In Parker. Who's Who in the
Theatre, p. 1076

Shere, Charles. "Baldwin's 'Blues for Mr. Charlie' a
Grabber." Oakland (Calif.) Tribune, 6 October 1975,
in Newsbank--Performing Arts. September-October
1975, 68:E 7

Willis. Theatre World, vol. 31, 1974-1975, p. 114

†BARAKA, IMAMU AMIRI (LeRoi Jones) (b. October 7, 1934)
PLAYS:

Arm Yourself or Harm Yourself. Newark, N.J.: Jihad,
1967

Baptism and the Toilet. N.Y.: Grove, 1967

Ba-Ra-Ka

A Black Mass

Death of Malcolm X

Dutchman and the Slave: Two Plays. N.Y.: Morrow, 1964

The Eighth Ditch, also known as Dante; taken from a section
of Jones' novel, The System of Dante's Hell

Experimental Death Unit #1

Four Black Revolutionary Plays. Indianapolis: Bobbs-Mer-
rill, 1969. (includes Experimental Death Unit #2, A
Black Mass, Great Goodness of Life: A Coon Show, and
Madheart)

Home on the Range

J-E-L-L-O. Newark, N.J.: Jihad, n.d.; Chicago: Third World, 1970
The Kid Poeta, Heroic
The Motion of History
Murderous Angels
Police
A Recent Killing
Roi
S-1: A Play
The Screamers
Sidney Poet Heroical
The Slave
The Slave Ship. Newark, N.J.: Jihad, 1969
The Toilet
Two Plays for L.A.
PLAYS PUBLISHED IN ANTHOLOGIES:
Ba-Ra-Ka in Owens, Spontaneous Combustion
Dutchman in Allen and Creeley, eds. The New Writing in the USA: Holmes and Lehman. Keys to Understanding: Receiving and Sending [Drama]; Schorer. The Literature of America: Twentieth Century
The Slave in Taylor and Thompson. Ritual, Realism, and Revolt: Major Traditions in the Drama
Slave Ship in Poland and Mailman. The Off-Off Broadway Book
The Toilet in Allison, Carr, and Eastman. Masterpieces of the Drama, 3rd ed.; Gassner and Barnes. Best American Plays, 6th Series, 1963-1967; Lahr, ed. Grove Press Modern Drama
CRITICISMS BY BARAKA:
"For Maulana Karenga and Pharoah Saunders." Black Theatre no. 4 (April 1970): 7
Guernsey, O. Jr. Playwrights, Lyricists, Composers, on Theater, pp. 199, 213, 420
"Jim Brown on the Screen." Black Theatre no. 4 (April 1970): 32
Jones, Le Roi. "The Revolutionary Theatre." In Dukore. Documents for Drama and Revolution, pp. 206-07
CRITICISMS OF BARAKA:
Allen and Creeley, eds. The New Writing in the USA, pp. 324-325
"Amiri Baraka Joins Yale University." Chicago Daily Defender 2 June 1977, p. 17
Anderson, Michael. Crowell's Handbook of Contemporary Drama. N.Y.: Crowell, 1971, p. 450
Benston. Baraka: The Renegade and the Mask. passim
Bentley. Theatre of War, pp. 404-406
Bermel. Contradictory Characters, pp. 243-55
Bigsby. Confrontation and Comment, pp. xix, passim
"Black Theatre: A Bid for Cultural Identity." Black Enterprise 2 (September 1971): 31, 33-34
Bloom, Arthur W. "The Theatre of Non-Mimetic Propaganda: Critical Criteria." Xavier University Studies 11

(No. 1): 29, 31
Bonin, Jane F. Major Themes in Prize-Winning American
Drama, pp. 72-76
_____. Prize-Winning American Drama: A Bibliographi-
cal and Descriptive Guide. Metuchen, N.J.: Scarecrow
Press, 1973, p. 178
Brooks, Mary Ellen. "The Pro-Imperialist Career of LeRoi
Jones." Literature and Ideology no. 11 (1972): 37-48
_____. Reactionary Trends in Recent Black Drama."
Literature and Ideology (Montreal) no. 10 (1970): 42-43
Brown, Lloyd W. "The Cultural Revolution in Black Theatre."
Negro American Literature Forum 8 (Spring 1974): 159
_____. "Dreamers and Slaves: The Ethos of Revolution
in Derek Walcott and LeRoi Jones." Caribbean Quarterly
16 (September 1971): 36-44
"Bush Mama." Trincontinental Film Center: 1977-78, p. 44
Cameron and Hoffman. A Guide to Theatre Study, pp. 202-
204
Cohn. Dialogue in American Drama, pp. 295-302
Cook and Henderson. The Militant Black Writer, p. 80
Dace, Tish. "LeRoi Jones/Amiri Baraka: From Muse to
Malcolm to Mao." Village Voice 22 (1 August 1977): 12-
14
Dace and Dace. The Student Theatre: Modern Theatre and
Drama, pp. 58-64
Daughtry, Willia A. "A Quarter Century of the Black Ex-
perience in the Fine Arts, 1950-1974." The Negro Edu-
cational Review 27 (January 1976): 27
Eckstein, George. "The New Black Theater." Dissent 20
(Winter 1973): 111
"Ed Bullins." Current Biography 38 (May 1977): 16
Edelin, Ramona. "Shirley Graham Du Bois." First World
1 (May/June 1977): 38
Edmonds, Randolph. "The Blacks in the American Theatre,
1700-1969." The Pan-African Journal 7 (Winter 1974):
306-307, 310
Erzsébet, Zombori. "LeRoi Jones: A Négerek Mozgalmának
Drámairója." Nagyvilág (Budapest). 15 (December 1970).
n.p.
Falb. American Drama in Paris, 1945-1970, pp. 6, 82-83,
133
Fauchereau, Serge, trans. "Des Figures interssantes rien
de plus" (Entretien avec M. L. Rosenthal). Quinzaine
Litteraire no. 126 (1-15 October 1971): 11
Freedman. American Drama in Social Context, pp. 86, 91,
oassun
Gaffney, Floyd. "Black Theatre: The Moral Function of
Imamu Amiri Baraka." Players 50 (Summer 1975): 122-
131
Geisinger. Plays, Players, & Playwrights, p. 742
Gilder, Rosmond. "Theatre As People: Book Report." In
Theatre 4: The American Theatre, 1970-1971, p. 187

12 / BARAKA

Glackin, William C. "American--More or Less Out of Focus."
Sacramento (Calif.) Bee, 1 May 1976, in Newsbank--Per-
forming Arts. May-June 1976, 40: E 1
Gottfried, Martin. "The New Ethnic Theater." New York
Post, 4 October 1975, in Newsbank--Performing Arts.
September-October 1975, 68:B 4
Guernsey, O. Jr. Playwrights, Lyricists, Composers on
Theater, pp. 213, 420
Haley, Elsie Galbreath. "The Black Revolutionary Theatre:
LeRoi Jones, Ed Bullins, and Minor Playwrights." Ph.D.
Dissertation, University of Denver, 1971
Haslam, Gerald W. "Two Traditions in Afro-American
Literature." Research Studies 36 (September 1969): 187,
190, 193
Hatch, James. "Speak to Me in Those Old Words, You Know,
Those La-La Words, Those Tung-Tung Sounds." Yale/
Theatre 8 (Fall 1976): 28-29, 30, 33
Hedley, Leslie Woolf. "Art vs. Society?" Arts in Society
9 (Winter 1972): 389
Hill, Errol. "LeRoi Jones." In Vinson. ed. Contemporary
Dramtists. vol. 5, pp. 423-27
Horton and Edwards. Backgrounds of American Literary
Thought. 3rd ed. p. 588
Hughes, Catharine. "Bicentennial Reflections." America
135 (24 July 1976): 31
Jackson, Esther M. "LeRoi Jones (Imamu Amiri Baraka):
Form and the Progression of Consciousness." CLA
Journal 17 (September 1973): 33-56
Jouffray, Alain. "LeRoi Jones, le Théâtre de la Révolution
Noire." Cahiers Renauld-Barrault 63 (October 1967): 44-
53
Kinnamon, Keneth. "The Political Dimension of Afro-Ameri-
can Literature." Soundings 58 (Spring 1975): 143
Klotman. Another Man Gone, pp. 108-109
Krans, Ted M. "Critical Thoughts." Critical Digest 21 (2
February 1970): 35
Lahr, John. "The Deli: Off-Broadway and Off-Off, 68-69." In
Theatre 2: The American Theatre, 1968-1969, p. 50
Lhamon, W. T. "Baraka and the Bourgeois Figure."
Studies in Black Literature 6 (Spring 1975): 18-21
McGraw-Hill Encyclopedia of World Drama. vol. 2, pp. 430-
431
Marvin X. "Everything's Cool: An Interview with LeRoi
Jones." Black Theatre no. 1 (1968): 16-23
Menchise, Don N. "LeRoi Jones and a Case of Shifting Iden-
tities." CLA Journal 20 (December 1976): 232-234
Michelman, Frederic. "American and African Blacks: A
Review of Alain Ricard's Théâtre et Nationalisme: Wole
Soyinka et Leroi Jones." Negro American Literature
Forum 8 (Winter 1974): 282-283
Miller, Jeanne-Marie A. "Images of Black Women in Plays
by Black Playwrights." CLA Journal 20 (June 1977): 504-
05

Mitchell. Voices of the Black Theatre, p. 224

Moser, Norman. "A Revolutionary Art: LeRoi Jones, Ed Bullins, and the Black Revolution." December 12 (1970): 180-190

Munro, C. Lynn. "LeRoi Jones: A Man in Transition." CLA Journal 17 (September 1973): 57-78

Ognibene, E. R. "Black Literature Revisited: 'Sonny's Blues'." English Journal 60 (January 1971): 36-37

Ogunbiyi, Yemi. "New Black Playwrights in America, 1960-1975." Ph.D. Dissertation, New York University, 1976, Chp. 1

Pennington-Jones, Paulette. "From Brother LeRoi Jones Through 'The System of Dante's Hell' to Imamu Ameer Baraka." Journal of Black Studies 4 (December 1973): 195-214

Poland and Mailman. The Off-Off Broadway Book, p. 527

Proffer. Soviet Criticism of American Literature in the Sixties, p. 85

Robbins. American Literary Scholarship: 1968, pp. 270, 309-310

_____. American Literary Scholarship: 1972, pp. 355, 369-370

Rowell, Charles H. "Teaching Black American Literature: A Review." Negro American Literature Forum 7 (Spring 1973): 17

Schechner. Public Domain, p. 40

Schorer. The Literature of America: Twentieth Century, pp. 853-854

Simon. Uneasy Stages, p. 452

Smiley. Playwrighting: The Structure of Action, pp. 72, 161, 244

Stevenson, Robert Louis. "The Image of the White Man as Projected in the Published Plays of Black Americans, 1847-1973." Ph.D. Dissertation, Indiana University, 1976

Taylor, Willene Pulliam. "The Reversal of the Tainted Blood Theme in the Works of Writers of the Revolutionary Theatre." Negro American Literature Forum 10 (Fall 1976): 88-90+

Turner, Darwin. "W. E. DuBois and the Theory of a Black Aesthetic." Studies in Literary Imagination 7 (Fall 1974): 1

Velde, Paul. "LeRoi Jones II: Pursued by the Furies." Commonweal 88 (28 June 1968): 440-41

Weales, Gerald. "The Day LeRoi Jones Spoke on the Penn Campus, What Were the Blacks Doing in the Balcony?" New York Times Magazine (4 May 1969): 38-40+

Woodress. American Literary Scholarship: 1973, p. 280

"Words of Frederick O'Neal." In Mitchell. Voices of the Black Theatre, p. 181

"Words of Regina M. Andrews." In Mitchell. Voices of the Black Theatre, p. 72

Zatlin, Linda G. "Paying His Dues: Ritual in LeRoi Jones' Early Dramas." Obsidian 2 (Spring 1976): 21-31

CRITICISMS OF INDIVIDUAL PLAYS:
Arm Yourself or Harm Yourself
>Benston. Baraka: The Renegade and the Mask, pp. 220-221
>
>Dace and Dace. "The Theatre Student: Modern Theatre and Drama, p. 60

Baptism
>Benston. Baraka: The Renegade and the Mask, pp. 49, 188, 198-202, 210, 222-225
>
>Cohn. Dialogue in American Drama, pp. 296-97
>
>Dace and Dace. "The Theatre Student: Modern Theatre and Drama, p. 58
>
>Edmonds, Randolph. "The Blacks in the American Theatre, 1700-1969." The Pan-African Journal 7 (Winter 1974): 307
>
>Willis, Robert. "Anger and Contemporary Black Theatre." Negro American Literature Forum 8 (Summer 1974): 214
>
>Zatlin, Linda G. "Paying His Dues: Ritual in LeRoi Jones' Early Dramas." Obsidian 2 (Spring 1976): 21-22, 27-30

A Black Mass
>Benston. Baraka: The Renegade and the Mask, pp. 49-50, 236-242
>
>Brown, Lloyd W. "The Cultural Revolution in Black Theatre." Negro American Literature Form 8 (Spring 1974): 161-162
>
>Dace and Dace. The Theatre Student: Modern Theatre and Drama, p. 62
>
>Hay, Samuel A. "African-American Drama, 1950-1970." Negro History Bulletin 36 (January 1973): 8
>
>Houghton. The Exploding Stage, p. 201
>
>McGraw-Hill Encyclopedia of World Drama. vol. 2, p. 431
>
>Marvin X and Faruk. "Islam and Black Art: An Interview with LeRoi Jones." Negro Digest 18 (January 1969): 4
>
>Miller, Jeanne-Marie A. "Images of Black Women in Plays by Black Playwrights." CLA Journal 20 (June 1977): 505
>
>Riley, Clayton. "Black Theatre." In Theatre 5: The American Theatre, 1971-1972, p. 62
>
>Salaam, Kalamu ya. "Making the Image Real." The Black Collegian 7 (March-April 1977): 56

Dante
>Pennington-Jones, Paulette. "From Brother LeRoi Jones through 'The System of Dante's Hell' to Imamu Ameer Baraka." Journal of Black Studies 4 (December 1973): 209-210

The Death of Malcolm X
>Brooks, Mary Ellen. "Reactionary Trends in Recent Black Drama." Literature and Ideology (Montreal), no. 10 (1970): 44-45

Cohn. Dialogue in American Drama, p. 302
Dace and Dace. The Theatre Student: Modern Theatre
and Drama, pp. 60-61
Munro, C. Lynn. "LeRoi Jones: A Man in Transition."
CLA Journal 17 (September 1973): 68

The Dutchman
Adams, George R. "Black Militant Drama." American
Imago 28 (Summer 1971): 109, 115 passim
Benston. Baraka: The Renegade and the Mask. passim
Bermel, Albert. Contradictory Characters, pp. 243-255
_____. "'Dutchman', or The Black Stranger in Ameri-
ca." Arts in Society 9 (Winter 1972): 423-434
Bigsby. Confrontation and Commitment, pp. 122, 142-
47, 148, 150-51, 154, 155
Billingsley, Ronald G. "The Burden of the Hero in Modern
Afro-American Fiction." Black World 25 (December
1975): 73
"Black Theatre: A Bid for Cultural Identity." Black Enter-
prise 2 (September 1971): 31
Bonin, Jane F. Major Themes in Prize-Winning American
Drama, pp. 72-75, 76, 90, 176
_____. Prize-Winning American Drama: A Bibliographi-
cal and Descriptive Guide. Metuchen, N.J.: Scarecrow
Press, 1973, p. 177
Brooks, Mary Ellen. "The Pro-Imperialist Career of Le-
Roi Jones." Literature and Ideology no. 11 (1972):
38-39
Cameron and Hoffman. A Guide to Theatre Study, pp.
202-203, 205
Cohn. Dialogue in American Drama, pp. 298-300, 302
Cook and Henderson. The Militant Black Writer, p. 80
Cosgrove, Wm. "Strategies of Survival: The Gimmick
Motif in Black Literature." Studies in the Twentieth
Century no. 15 (Spring 1975): 124-126
Dace and Dace. The Theatre Student: Modern Theatre
and Drama, p. 59
Dance, Darrell. "Contemporary Militant Black Humor."
Negro American Literature Forum 8 (Summer 1974):
217
Davis, Arthur P. From the Dark Tower, p. 50
_____. "Trends in Negro American Literature (1940-
1965): In Altenbernd. Exploring Literature, p. 678
Davis, Curt. "The Ever-Flying 'Dutchman'." Encore 6
(4 April 1977): 40
Falb. American Drama in Paris, 1945-1970, pp. 82-83,
133, 157, 166
Felgar, Robert. "Black Content, White Form." Studies
in Black Literature 5 (Winter 1974): 29
Freedman. American Drama in Social Context, pp. 86,
91, 98, 122, 126
Gaffney, Floyd. "Black Theatre: The Moral Function of
Imamu Amiri Baraka." Players Magazine 50 (Summer
1975): 122

Garland, Phyl. "The Prize Winners." Ebony 25 (July 1970): 36

Gassner and Dukore. A Treasury of the Theatre, 4th ed. vol. 2. p. 1247

Hartnoll. The Oxford Companion to the Theatre, p. 681

Haslam, Gerald W. "Two Traditions in Afro-American Literature." Research Studies 37 (September 1969): 187

Hay, Samuel A. "African-American Drama, 1950-1970." Negro History Bulletin 36 (January 1973): 5

Holmes and Lehman. Keys to Understanding: Receiving and Sending [Drama], pp. 393, 421-22

Houghton. The Exploding Stage, pp. 199-200

Jackson, Esther M. "LeRoi Jones (Imamu Amiri Baraka): Form and the Progression of Consciousness." CLA Journal 17 (September 1973): 47-50

Keyssar-Franke, Helene. "Strategies in Black Drama." Ph.D. Dissertation, University of Iowa, 1974

Klinkowitz, Jerome. "LeRoi Jones (Imamu Amiri Baraka): 'Dutchman' as Drama." Negro American Literature Forum 7 (Winter 1973): 123-26

Lindberg, John. "'Dutchman' and 'The Slave': Companions in Revolution." Black Academy Review 2 (Spring-Summer 1971): 101-108; also in Black Academy Review (Summer 1971): 101-07; in Mazu, ed. Modern Black Literature, pp. 101-07

Littlejohn. Black on White, pp. 75-9

McGraw-Hill Encyclopedia of World Drama. vol. 2, p. 431

Mandel, Oscar. "Notes on Ethical Deprivation with the Avant-Garde Drama." Antigonish Review (Nova Scotia) 8 (Winter 1972): 47

Meserve, Walter, J. "Black Drama." In Robbins. American Literary Scholarship--1970, p. 344

Munro, C. Lynn. "LeRoi Jones: A Man in Transition." CLA Journal 17 (September 1973): 66-67

"The Revolutionary Theatre." In Dukore. Documents for Drama and Revolution, p. 206

Robbins. American Literary Scholarship: 1972, p. 370

Robinson, Le Roy. "Black Theatre: A Need for the Seventies." Soul Illustrated 2 (February 1970): 39, 57, 64

Roth, Phillip. "Channel X: Two Plays on the Race Conflict." New York Review of Books 2 (28 May 1964): 11-13

Savory, Jerold J. "Descent and Baptism in Native Son, Invincible Man, Dutchman." Christian Scholar's Review 3 (1973): 33-37

Simon. Uneasy Stages, pp. 47, 51-52

Smiley. Playwrighting: The Structure of Action, p. 161

Taubman. The Making of the American Theatre, p. 334

Taylor, Willene Pulliam. "The Reversal of the Tainted Blood Theme in the Works of Writers of the Black

Revolutionary Theatre." Negro American Literature Forum 10 (Fall 1976): 88

Tedesco, John L. "The White Image as Second 'Persona' in Black Drama, 1955-1970." Ph.D. Dissertation, University of Iowa, 1974

Zatlin, Linda G. "Paying His Dues: Ritual in LeRoi Jones' Early Dramas." Obsidian 2 (Spring 1976): 21-22, 24-25, 30

Four Black Revolutionary Plays

Benston, Kimberly W. "'Cities in Bezique': Adrienne Kennedy's Expressionistic Vision." CLA Journal 20 (December 1976): 236

Dace and Dace. The Theatre Student: Modern Theatre and Drama, p. 61

Dance, Darrell. "Contemporary Militant Black Humor." Negro American Literature Forum 8 (Summer 1974): 217

Great Goodness of Life

Benston, Kimberly W. Baraka: The Renegade and the Mask, pp. 211-213, 223, 234, 247

————. "'Cities in Bezique': Adrienne Kennedy's Expressionistic Vision." CLA Journal 20 (December 1976): 241

Cohn. Dialogue in American Drama, p. 301

Dace and Dace. The Theatre Student: Modern Theatre and Drama, p. 62

Gaffney, Floyd. "Black Theatre: The Moral Function of Imamu Amiri Baraka." Players Magazine 50 (Summer 1975): 128-29

Hay, Samuel A. "African-American Drama, 1950-1970." Negro History Bulletin 36 (January 1973): 8

Jackson, Esther M. "LeRoi Jones (Imamu Amiri Baraka): Form and the Progression of Consciousness." CLA Journal 17 (September 1973): 45

The Eighth Ditch

Dace and Dace. The Theatre Student: Modern Theatre and Drama, p. 58

Edmonds, Randolph. "The Blacks in the American Theatre, 1700-1969." The Pan-African Journal 7 (Winter 1974): 307

Experimental Death Unit #1

Benston, Kimberly W. Baraka: The Renegade and the Mask, pp. 218-219, 223, 225

————. "'Cities in Bezique': Adrienne Kennedy's Expressionistic Vision." CLA Journal 20 (December 1976): 235

Brady, Owens. "Baraka's 'Experimental Death Unit #1': Plan for (R)evolution." Negro American Literature Forum 9 (Summer 1975): 57-61

Cohn. Dialogue in American Drama, pp. 300-01

Dace and Dace. The Theatre Student: Modern Theatre and Drama, p. 62

Edmonds, Randolph. "The Blacks in the American Theatre, 1700-1969." The Pan-African Journal 7 (Winter 1974): 307

Hay, Samuel A. "African-American Drama, 1950-1970." Negro History Bulletin 36 (January 1973): 8

Miller, Jeanne-Marie A. "Images of Black Women in Plays by Black Playwrights." CLA Journal 20 (June 1977): 505

Home on the Range

Brockett. The Theatre: An Introduction, p. 372

Cohn. Dialogue in American Drama, p. 301

Dace and Dace. The Theatre Student: Modern Theatre and Drama, p. 60

Gaffney, Floyd. "Black Theatre: The Moral Function of Imamu Amiri Baraka." Players Magazine 50 (Summer 1975): 127

J-E-L-L-O

Benston. Baraka: The Renegade and the Mask, pp. 188, 193-198, 209-210, 225, 250

Dace and Dace. The Theatre Student: Modern Theatre and Drama, p. 60

Dance, Darrell. "Contemporary Militant Black Humor." Negro American Literature Forum 8 (Summer 1974): 221

Edmonds, Randolph. "The Blacks in the American Theatre, 1700-1969." The Pan-African Journal 7 (Winter 1974): 307

Gaffney, Floyd. "Black Theatre: The Moral Function of Imamu Amiri Baraka." Players Magazine 50 (Summer 1975): 127

Houghton. The Exploding Stage, p. 201

Madheart

Benston. Baraka: The Renegade and the Mask, pp. 221-237

Cohn. Dialogue in American Drama, p. 301

Dace and Dace. The Theatre Student: Modern Theatre and Drama, p. 62

Dance, Darrell. "Contemporary Militant Black Humor." Negro American Literature Forum 8 (Summer 1974): 218

Hay, Samuel A. "African-American Drama, 1950-1970." Negro History Bulletin 36 (January 1973): 8

Meserve, Walter J. "Black Drama." In Robbins. American Literary Scholarship--1970, p. 344

Miller, Jeanne-Marie A. "Images of Black Women in Plays by Black Playwrights." CLA Journal 20 (June 1977): 505

Reavy, Charles D. "Myth, Magic, and Manhood in LeRoi Jones' 'Madheart'." Studies in Black Literature 1 (Summer 1970): 12-20

Police

Benston. Baraka: The Renegade and the Mask, pp. 220-221, 223, 225

Cohn. <u>Dialogue in American Drama</u>, p. 301
Dace and Dace. <u>The Theatre Student: Modern Theatre and Drama</u>, p. 60

A Recent Killing
Benston. <u>Baraka: The Renegade and the Mask</u>, pp. 203-209, 263
Dace and Dace. <u>The Theatre Student: Modern Theatre and Drama</u>, p. 59

The Screamers
Keller, Joseph. "Black Writing and the White Critic." <u>Negro American Literature Forum</u> 3 (Winter 1970): 107

Sidney Poet Heroical
Mackay, Barbara. "Studies in Black and White." <u>Saturday Review</u> 2 (12 July 1975): 52

The Slave
Benston. <u>Baraka: The Renegade and the Mask</u>. passim
Bermel, Albert. <u>Contradictory Characters</u>, p. 158 n
_____. "'Dutchman', or The Black Stranger in America." <u>Arts in Society</u> 9 (Winter 1972): 431, 433
Bigsby. <u>Confrontation and Commitment</u>, pp. 122, 140, 147-51, 152, 154, 155
"The Black Revolution--'The Slave'." In Dukore. <u>Documents for Drama and Revolution</u>, pp. 160-71
"Black Theatre: A Bid for Cultural Identity." <u>Black Enterprise</u> 2 (September 1971): 31
Bonin. <u>Major Themes in Prize-Winning American Drama</u>, p. 90
Brown, Lloyd W. "The Cultural Revolution in Black Theatre." <u>Negro American Literature Forum</u> 8 (Spring 1974): 163
Cohn. <u>Dialogue in American Drama</u>, pp. 297-98
Dace and Dace. <u>The Theatre Student: Modern Theatre and Drama</u>, p. 59
Edmonds, Randolph. "The Blacks in the American Theatre, 1700-1969." <u>The Pan-African Journal</u> 7 (Winter 1974): 307
Falb. <u>American Drama in Paris, 1945-1970</u>, pp. 82-83, 133, 157, 166
Freedman. <u>American Drama in Social Context</u>, p. 98
Gaffney, Floyd. "Black Theatre: The Moral Function of Imamu Amiri Baraka." <u>Players Magazine</u> 50 (Summer 1975): 122, 127
Hartnoll. <u>The Oxford Companion to the Theatre</u>, p. 681
Hay, Samuel A. "African-American Drama, 1950-1970." <u>Negro History Bulletin</u> 36 (January 1973): 6
Houghton. <u>The Exploding Stage</u>, p. 201
Jackson, Esther M. "Le Roi Jones (Imamu Amiri Baraka): Form and the Progression of Consciousness." <u>CLA Journal</u> 17 (September 1973): 45-47
Lindberg, John. "'Dutchman' and 'The Slave': Companions in Revolution." <u>Black Academy Review</u> 2 (Spring-Summer 1971): 101-108

_____. "'Dutchman' and 'The Slave': Companions in Revolution." In Mezu, ed. Modern Black Literature, pp. 101-07

Littlejohn. Black on White, pp. 74-75

McGraw-Hill Encyclopedia of World Drama. vol. 2, p. 431

Munro, C. Lynn. "Le Roi Jones: A Man in Transition." CLA Journal 17 (September 1973): 67-68

"The Revolutionary Theatre." In Dukore. Documents for Drama and Revolution, pp. 206-07

Robbins. American Literary Scholarship: 1972, p. 370

Simon. Uneasy Stages, pp. 69-70

Taylor, Willene Pulliam. "The Reversal of the Tainted Blood Theme in the Works of Writers of the Black Revolutionary Theatre." Negro American Literature Forum 10 (Fall 1976): 88-90

Woodress. American Literary Scholarship: 1973, p. 380

Zatlin, Linda G. "Paying His Dues: Ritual in Le Roi Jones' Early Dramas." Obsidian 2 (Spring 1976): 21-22, 25-27, 30

The Slaveship

Benston. Baraka: The Renegade and the Mask, passim

Bentley, Eric. "White Plague and Black Terror." In Theatre of War: Comments on 32 Occasions, pp. 404-405

Cohn. Dialogue in American Drama, pp. 301-02

Dace and Dace. The Theatre Student: Modern Theatre and Drama, p. 61

Eddy, Bill. "4 Directors on Criticism." Drama Review 18 (September 1974): 24-26

Hay, Samuel A. "African-American Drama, 1950-1970." Negro History Bulletin 36 (January 1973): 8

Lahr, John. "America: The Collapsing Underground." Gambit: An International Drama Quarterly. 17: 67-68

McGraw-Hill Encyclopedia of World Drama. vol. 2, p. 431

Meserve, Walter J. "Black Drama." In Robbins. American Literary Scholarship--1970, p. 344

Moses, Gilbert. "Hubert Humphrey Is to Politics...." In Theatre 2: The American Theatre, 1968-1969, p. 113

Quick, Paula N. "Black Theatre." Black Creation 2 (April 1971): 54

The Toilet

Benston. Baraka: The Renegade and the Mask, pp. 189-194, 223, 263

Bigsby. Confrontation and Commitment, pp. 109, 122, 138, 140

"Black Theatre: A Bid for Cultural Identity." Black Enterprise 2 (September 1971): 31

Brady, Owen E. "Cultural Conflict and Cult Ritual in Le Roi Jones's The Toilet." Educational Theatre

Journal 28 (March 1976): 69-77

Cohn. Dialogue in American Drama, pp. 294-96

Dace and Dace. The Theatre Student: Modern Theatre and Drama, p. 58-59

Edmonds, Randolph. "The Blacks in the American Theatre, 1700-1969." The Pan-African Journal 7 (Winter 1974): 307

Freedman. American Drama in Social Context, pp. x-xi, 100, 122, 126

Gaffney, Floyd. "Black Theatre: The Moral Function of Imamu Amiri Baraka." Players Magazine 50 (Summer 1975): 126

Hartnoll. The Oxford Companion to the Theatre, p. 681

Hatch, James. "Speak to Me in Those Old Words, You Know, Those La-La Words, Those Tung-Tung Sounds." Yale/Theatre 8 (Fall 1976): 33

Hay, Samuel A. "African-American Drama, 1950-1970." Negro History Bulletin 36 (January 1973): 5-6

Houghton. The Exploding Stage, p. 201

Lahr. Grove Press Modern Drama, pp. xvii-xix

Littlejohn. Black on White, p. 74

McGraw-Hill Encyclopedia of World Drama. vol. 2, pp. 430-431

Mandel, Oscar. "Notes on Ethical Deprivation with the Avant-Garde Drama." Antigonish Review (Nova Scotia) 8 (Winter 1972): 43, 44

"The Revolutionary Theatre." In Dukore. Documents for Drama and Revolution, p. 206

Robbins. American Literary Scholarship: 1972, p. 370

Robinson, Le Roy. "Black Theatre: A Need for the Seventies." Soul Illustrated 2 (February 1970): 39, 57, 64

Simon. Uneasy Stages, pp. 68-69

Taylor, Willene Pulliam. "The Reversal of the Tainted Blood Theme in the Works of Writers of the Black Revolutionary Theater." Negro American Literature Forum 10 (Fall 1976): 88

Tener, Robert L. "The Corrupted Warrior Heroes: Amiri Baraka's The Toilet." Modern Theatre and Drama 17 (June 1974): 207-215

Willis, Robert. "Anger and Contemporary Black Theatre." Negro American Literature Forum 8 (Summer 1974): 214-215

Witherington, Paul. "Exorcism and Baptism in Le Roi Jones's The Toilet." Modern Theatre and Drama 15 (September 1972): 159-163

Woodress. American Literary Scholarship: 1974, p. 185

Zatlin, Linda G. "Paying His Dues: Ritual in Le Roi Jones' Early Dramas." Obsidian 2 (Spring 1976): 2, 22, 24, 30

REVIEWS OF INDIVIDUAL PLAYS:

Dutchman

Blum and Willis, eds. A Pictorial History of the Ameri-
can Theatre: 1860-1976, p. 386
Dodds, Richard. "Dashiki '76 Finale." (New Orleans,
La.) Times--Picayune, 8 January 1977, in Newsbank--
Performing Arts. January-February 1977, 11: E 11
"Length of Run of American Plays in Paris" in Lewis W.
Falb. American Drama in Paris: 1945-1970, p. 166
Peterson, Maurice. "On the Aisle: Spotlight on Dianne
Oyama Dixon." Essence 7 (November 1975): 39
Robinson, Le Roy. "Black Theatre: A Need for the
Seventies." Soul Illustrated 2 (February 1970): 57, 64
Willis' Theatre World. vol. 31. 1974-1975. p. 197
Home on the Range
Jones, Charles E. "Soul-Stirrin' Theatre." Soul Illus-
trated 2 (July 1970): 18
The Motion of History
Dace, Tish. "Le Roi Jones/Amiri Baraka: From Muse
to Malcolm, to Mao." Village Voice 22 (1 August
1977): 12-14
Murderous Angels
Robinson, Le Roy. "Soul-Stirrin' Theatre." Soul Illus-
trated 2 (July 1970): 15-16, 63
A Recent Killing
Clurman, Harold. "Theatre." Nation 216 (12 February
1973): 218-219
Kroll, Jack. "Hopes, Dreams, Fantasies." Newsweek
81 (19 February 1973): 75
Oliver, Edith. "The Theatre: Off Broadway." New
Yorker 48 (10 February 1973): 75
Roi
Jones, Charles E. "Soul-Stirrin' Theatre." Soul Illus-
trated 2 (July 1970): 17-18
S-1: A Play
Peeples, Kenneth. "Baraka Dramatizes Senate Bill."
(N.Y.) Amsterdam News: Arts and Entertainment, 14
August 1976, D-7
Sidney Poet Heroical
Mackay, Barbara. "Studies in Black and White." Satur-
day Review 2 (12 July 1975): 52
The Slave
Atkinson, Brooks. "'The Slave' and 'The Toilet' by Le
Roi Jones." In Beckerman and Siegman. "On Stage:
Selected Theatre Reviews from the New York Stage,
1920-1970, pp. 472-73
"Length of Run of American Plays in Paris." In Lewis
W. Falb. American Drama in Paris: 1945-1970,
p. 166
Slaveship
"Cast of the 'Slave Ship' Quits Stage After Protests About
Conditions." New York Times, 24 January 1970, p.
24
Clurman, Harold. "Theatre." Nation 210 (2 February
1970): 125

Hewes, Henry. "Black Hopes." Saturday Review 53 (14 February 1970): 30

Kroll, Jack. "Dark Voyage." Newsweek 74 (1 December 1969): 86

"'Slave Ship' Closed Again by 14 Actors." New York Times, 25 January 1970, p. 70

The Toilet

Atkinson, Brooks. "'The Slave' and 'The Toilet' by Le Roi Jones." In Beckerman and Siegman. On Stage: Selected Theatre Reviews from the New York Stage, 1920-1970, pp. 472-73

Blum and Willis, eds. A Pictorial History of the American Theatre: 1860-1976, p. 386

McKensie, Vashti. "D'Urville Martin, Actor-Producer Came Up 'Hard Way'." The Afro-American: Dawn Magazine (Baltimore, Md.), 14 May 1977, p. 10

Robinson, Le Roy. "Black Theatre: A Need for the Seventies." Soul Illustrated 2 (February 1970): 57, 64

Two Plays for L. A.

Robinson, Le Roy. "Soul Stirrin' Theatre." Soul Illustrated 2 (July 1970): 15

BIBLIOGRAPHIES OF BARAKA:

Dace, Letitia. Le Roi Jones: A Checklist of Works by and About Him. London: Nether Press, 1971

Hudson, Theodore R. From Le Roi Jones to Amiri Baraka. Durham, N.C.: Duke University Press, 1973

AWARDS:

1961 Whitney Fellowship

1963-64 Obie Award for the Best American Play of the Season: Dutchman

1965 Guggenheim Fellowship

1966 Dakar Prize

BARKER, J. S.
PLAYS:
Bond of Matrimony
Vulnerable Doubled

BARNETT, MARGO
PLAYS:
Black Is a Beautiful Woman, a one woman show

BASCOMBE, RONALD D.
PLAYS:
The Unifier
PLAYS PUBLISHED IN ANTHOLOGIES:
The Unifier, in Sonia Sanchez Writers Workshop, Three Hundred and Sixty Degrees of Blackness Comin' at You

†BASS, GEORGE H. (b. April 23, 1938)
PLAYS:
The Booby, 1967

†BASS, KINGSLEY B., Jr. (pseudonym attributed to Ed Bullins)
    PLAYS:
        We Righteous Bombers
    CRITICISMS OF INDIVIDUAL PLAYS:
        We Righteous Bombers
            Brown, Lloyd W. "The Cultural Revolution in Black
                Theatre." Negro American Literature Forum 8 (Spring
                1974): 1963-1964
            Gant, Lisbeth. "The New Lafayette Theatre." Drama
                Review 16 (December 1972): 49-50
            Harris, Jessica B. "The New Lafayette: 'Nothing Lasts
                Forever'." Black Creation 4 (Summer 1973): 9
            Hay, Samuel A. "Alain Locke and Black Drama." Black
                World 21 (April 1972): 12-13
            "Lafayette Theatre Reaction to 'Bombers'." Black Theatre
                4 (April 1970): 16-25
            Marvin X. "The Black Ritual Theatre: An Interview with
                Robert Macbeth." Black Theatre no. 3 (1969): 23-24
    AWARDS:
        The Harriet Webster Updike Theater Award for literary ex-
        cellence

BASSHE, EM JO
    PLAYS:
        [with Hall Johnson] Earth
        [with Hall Johnson] Hoboken Blues (subtitle: The Black
        Rip Van Winkle)
    CRITICISMS OF INDIVIDUAL PLAYS:
        Earth
            Hartnoll. The Oxford Companion to the Theatre, p. 675
        Hoboken Blues
            Hartnoll. The Oxford Companion to the Theater, p. 675

BATSON, SUSAN
    PLAYS:
        Hoodoo Talkin'
    PLAYS PUBLISHED IN ANTHOLOGIES:
        Hoodoo Talkin', in Sonia Sanchez Writers Workshop, Three
        Hundred and Sixty Degrees of Blackness Comin' at You

†BATTLE, SOL (b. November 20, 1934)
    FILM SCRIPTS:
        Julie Loves a Mugger. N.Y.: Contemporary Classics (Im-
        print Panther House Ltd.) 1974

BERRY, DAVID
    PLAYS:
        The Freedom Bird
        G. R. Point
    REVIEWS OF INDIVIDUAL PLAYS:
        The Freedom Bird
            "Playwrights Conference Spotlights 12 New Dramas."

(N.Y.) Amsterdam News: Arts and Entertainment, 14
August 1976, D-14
G. R. Point
"Playwrights Conference Spotlights 12 New Dramas."
(N.Y.) Amsterdam News: Arts and Entertainment, 14
August 1976, D-14

†BERRY, KELLY-MARIE
PLAYS:
Alonzo Jason Jefferson Jones, children's play

BETTER, ANTHONY
PLAYS:
The Window of Our Dreams

BLACK, ISAAC J.
PLAYS:
Niggeramus

BLACK, JEANNE BELCHER
PLAYS:
The Pit
CRITICISMS OF INDIVIDUAL PLAYS:
The Pit
Sandle. The Negro in the American Educational Theatre,
p. 152

BLACK EXPERIENCE FAMILY
PLAYS:
A Blues, Jazz, Gospel, Revolutionary Thang
REVIEWS OF INDIVIDUAL PLAYS:
A Blues, Jazz, Gospel, Revolutionary Thang
Kupa, Kushauri. "Closeup: The New York Scene--Black
Theatre in New York, 1970-1971." Black Theatre no.
6 (1972), 39-40

BLACKWELL, DON
PLAYS:
The Has Been
REVIEWS OF INDIVIDUAL PLAYS:
The Has Been
Smith, Marian. "Black Theater Week Renews Basic Aim:
Reflect Community." Chicago (Ill.) Sun-Times, 23
May 1976, in Newsbank--Performing Arts. May-June
1976, 41:G 6

†BLAKE, EUBIE
MUSICALS:
[with Flournoy Miller, Andy Razaf and Noble Sissle] The
Blackbirds, 1929
[with Noble Sissle] The Chocolate Dandies
[with Flournoy Miller, Andy Razaf and Noble Sissle] O,
Sing a New Song

[with Aubrey Lyles, Flournoy Miller and Noble Sissle]
    Shuffle Along, 1921; 1933
CRITICISMS OF BLAKE:
    Birmingham. Certain People, p. 191
    "Birthday Party." New Yorker 52 (8 March 1976): 30-32
    Kimball and Bolcom. Reminiscing with Sissle and Blake,
        passim
CRITICISMS OF INDIVIDUAL MUSICALS:
    The Blackbirds
        Hatch, James. "Speak to Me in Those Old Words, You
            Know, Those La-La Words, Those Tung-Tung Sounds."
            Yale/Theatre 8 (Fall 1976): 27
    The Chocolate Dandies
        Bovosco, Carole. "Discovering Foremothers." Ms. 6
            (September 1977): 59
        Current, Gloster B. "Noble Sissle." The Crisis 83
            (March 1976): 87
        Kimball and Bolcom. Reminiscing with Sissle and Blake,
            passim
    Shuffle Along
        "Black Theatre: A Bid for Cultural Identity." Black
            Enterprise 2 (September 1971): 31
        Current, Gloster B. "Noble Sissle." The Crisis 83
            (March 1976): 87
        Gagey. Revolution in American Drama, p. 253
        Jackson. The Waiting Years, p. 171
        Kimball and Bolcom. Reminiscing with Sissle and Blake,
            passim
        McGraw-Hill Encyclopedia of World Drama. vol. 3, p.
            288
        Mitchell. Voices of the Black Theatre, pp. 30, 43, 103
        Turner, Darwin. "W. E. B. Du Bois and the Theory of
            a Black Aesthetic." Studies in Literary Imagination 7
            (Fall 1974): 3, 5
REVIEWS OF INDIVIDUAL MUSICALS:
    Shuffle Along
        Blum and Willis, eds. A Pictorial History of the Ameri-
            can Theatre: 1860-1976, pp. 188, 338
        Lewis, Barbara. "Metropolitan Museum Highlights Black
            Theatre." (N.Y.) Amsterdam News: Arts and Enter-
            tainment, 19 February 1977, D-8
        Peterson, Maurice. "On the Aisle: Focus on Avon Long."
            Essence 6 (January 1976): 28
AWARDS:
    Ellington Medal, October, 1972

BOND, HORACE J.
    PLAYS:
    Mother April's, a satire
    CRITICISMS OF INDIVIDUAL PLAYS:
    Mother April's
        "Mixed Blood Theatre Co." Twin Cities Courier (Minne-
            apolis/St. Paul, Minn.), 4 August 1977, p. 2

†BONTEMPS, ARNA (October 13, 1902-June 1973)
  PLAYS:
  God Sends Sundays, 1931
  MUSICALS:
    [with Countee Cullen] The Saint Louis Woman, 1946. Musi-
      cal Adaptation of God Sends Sunday, 1931. Revised for
      Federal Theatre Project by Langston Hughes
  CRITICISMS OF INDIVIDUAL MUSICALS:
    The Saint Louis Woman
      Davis. From the Dark Tower, p. 87
      Edmonds, Rudolph. "The Blacks in the American Theatre,
        1700-1969." The Pan-African Journal 7 (Winter 1974):
        .314
      "Pearl Bailey." In Parker. Who's Who in the Theatre
        15th ed., p. 491

BOURNE, ST. CLAIRE
  TELEVISION SCRIPTS:
  Let the Church Say Amen, a Documentary
  CRITICISMS OF BOURNE:
    "Images of the Eye." Soul Illustrated 3 (Fall 1971): 22-23
    Mitchell. Voices of the Black Theatre, p. 85

BOWEN, JOHN
  PLAYS:
  After the Rain
  CRITICISMS OF INDIVIDUAL PLAYS:
    After the Rain
      Lamele, Nina. "'After the Rain'." (Boston, Mass.) Bay
        State Banner, 10 July 1975, in Newsbank--Performing
        Arts. July-August 1975, 53: D 2, 3

†BRANCH, WILLIAM BLACKWELL (b. September 11, 1927)
  PLAYS:
  In Splendid Error, 1955, New York Public Library, Schom-
    burg Collection
  A Medal for Willie, 1951, New York Public Library, Schom-
    burg Collection
  A Wreath for Udomo, 1961. (Based on the novel by Peter
    Abrams)
  CRITICISMS OF BRANCH:
    "Hatch-Billops Archives Interviews with Playwrights."
      Negro American Literature Forum 10 (Summer 1976): 64
    Mitchell. Voices of the Black Theatre, pp. 23, 72, 217
    Robinson, Le Roy. "Black Theatre: A Need for the Seven-
      ties." Soul Illustrated 2 (February 1970): 57
  CRITICISMS OF INDIVIDUAL PLAYS:
    In Splendid Error
      Hartnoll. The Oxford Companion to the Theatre, p. 680
      Hay, Samuel A. "African-American Drama, 1950-1970."
        Negro History Bulletin 36 (January 1973): 8
      Jones, John Henry. "Great Themes for Black Plays

and Films." Freedomways 14 (Third Quarter 1974):
261
"The Words of Ruby Dee." In Mitchell. Voices of the
Black Theatre, p. 219
A Medal for Willie
    Evans, Donald T. "Playwrights of the Fifties: Bring It
       All Back Home." Black World 20 (February 1971): 45
    Hartnoll. The Oxford Companion to the Theatre, p. 680
    Hay, Samuel A. "African-American Drama, 1950-1970."
       Negro History Bulletin 36 (January 1973): 5
A Wreath for Udomo
    Hartnoll. The Oxford Companion to the Theater, p. 680
REVIEWS OF INDIVIDUAL PLAYS:
    A Wreath for Udomo
       "'A Wreath for Udomo' (at Karamu)." Jet (31 March
       1960): 60
       "'A Wreath for Udomo' (Broadway Preparation)." Jet
       (2 March 1961): 59

BROOME, BARBARA CUMMINGS
    PLAYS:
       The Fat Sisters
       Millie Brown, 1977
    REVIEWS OF INDIVIDUAL PLAYS:
       Millie Brown, 1977
       "Millie Brown, 1977." Chicago Daily Defender, 23 June
       1977, p. 17
    AWARDS:
       1976 John Clemmons Drama Award for Fat Sisters

BROWN, ARROW
    PLAYS:
       All for the Cause, 1972, one-act, Kuumba Workshop in
       Chicago reported in Black World 21 (April 1972): 38
    CRITICISMS OF INDIVIDUAL PLAYS:
       Bailey, Peter. "Annual Round-Up: Black Theatre in America
       New York City." Black World 21 (April 1972): 38

†BROWN, CECIL
    PLAYS:
       Real Nigger, 1969

BROWN, DONNA
    MUSICALS:
       [with James W. Durrah and Victor Willis] How Do You
       Spell Watergait?

†BROWN, JAMES N.
    PLAYS:
       The Barren Heritage
    CRITICISMS OF BROWN:
       Riley, Clayton. "Black Theatre." In Theatre 5: The
       American Theatre, 1971-1972, p. 65

CRITICISMS OF INDIVIDUAL PLAYS:
The Barren Heritage
    Sandle. The Negro in the American Educational Theatre,
        p. 61

BROWN, JIM
    PLAYS:
    Three the Hard Way

†BROWN, LENNOX JOHN
    PLAYS:
    A Ballet Behind the Bridge
    The Captive
    Winti-Train
    CRITICISMS OF BROWN:
    Chintoh, Jo Jo. "Lennox Brown: A Black Canadian Drama-
        tist." Black Collegian 1 (January 1972): 28-29
    Stephenson, Oliver. "Culture projected by Caribbean Ameri-
        can Repertory Theatre." (A Fog Drifts in the Night; A
        Trinity of Four) (N.Y.) Amsterdam News: Arts and En-
        tertainment, 18 September 1976, D-2
    CRITICISMS OF INDIVIDUAL PLAYS:
    A Ballet Behind the Bridge
        Chintoh, Jo Jo. "Lennox Brown: A Black Canadian
            Dramatist." Black Collegian 1 (January 1972): 28-29
        Stasio, Marilyn. "Off-Broadway." In Theatre 5: The
            American Theatre, 1971-1972, p. 38
    The Captive
        Chintoh, Jo Jo. "Lennox Brown: A Black Canadian
            Dramatist." Black Collegian 1 (January 1972): 28-29
    REVIEWS OF INDIVIDUAL PLAYS:
    Winti-Train
        Wadud, Ali. "'Winti-Train'." (N.Y.) Amsterdam News:
            Arts and Entertainment, 19 March 1977, D-13

†BROWN, OSCAR, JR.
    PLAYS:
    In De Beginnin'
    Summer in the City
    Sunshine and Shadows
    A Year
    MUSICALS:
    Buck White
    Kicks and Co.
    REVIEWS OF INDIVIDUAL PLAYS:
    In De Beginnin'
        Engstrom, Karen. "A Story of Sin on a Stage Full of
            Kin." Chicago (Ill.) Tribune, 19 November 1977, 2:12
        "'In De Beginnin' Opens August 3.'" Chicago Daily Defender,
            28 July 1977, p. 13
    REVIEWS OF INDIVIDUAL MUSICALS:
    Buck White

Blum and Willis, eds. A Pictorial History of the Ameri-
can Theatre: 1860-1976, p. 401
Kicks and Co.
"Oscar Brown, Jr. Home Again a Stronger Man." Chi-
cago Daily News, 25 January 1975, in Newsbank--Per-
forming Arts. January-February 1975, 13: C 1, 2
AWARDS:
Paul Robeson Award, 1976

BROWN, RHOZIER T. (Roach)
PLAYS:
Xmas in Time, 1969

†BROWN, ROSCOE LEE (b. 1925)
PLAYS:
A Hand Is on the Gate
CRITICISMS OF BROWN:
Parker. Who's Who in the Theatre, 15th ed., pp. 580-81,
872
Troupe, Quincy. "I Mimic No One--Roscoe Lee Brown."
Essence 7 (December 1976): 55, 57, 92-94, 112
"The Words of Vinnette Carrol." In Mitchell. Voices of
the Black Theatre, p. 198

BROWN, WESLEY
PLAYS:
And Now, Will the Real Bud Jones Please Stand Up
PLAYS PUBLISHED IN ANTHOLOGIES:
And Now, Will the Real Bud Jones Please Stand Up, in
Sonia Sanchez Writers Workshop, Three Hundred and
Sixty Degrees of Blackness Comin' at You

BROWN, WILLIAM F.
MUSICALS:
[with Charlie Smalls] The Wiz based on The Wonderful
Wizard of Oz by Frank Baum; originally conceived as a
television special by former disc jockey Ken Harper
CRITICISMS OF BROWN:
De Vine, Laurence. "New York Is Still Where It's At, As
Broadway Hits the Upbeat." Detroit (Mich.) Free Press,
17 March 1975, in Newsbank--Performing Arts. March-
April 1975, 28: D 4
CRITICISMS OF INDIVIDUAL MUSICALS:
The Wiz
Bailey, Peter. "Annual Round-up: Black Theater in
America--New York." Black World 24 (April 1975):
23
Davis, Curt. "People in the News--'Wiz'." Encore 6
(7 February 1977): 26
Douglas, Carlyle C. "The Whiz behind 'The Wiz'."
Ebony 30 (October 1975): 114-116+
Engel. The Critics, pp. 115, passim

Geisinger. Plays, Players, & Playwrights, pp. 241, il.; 742

Guernsey. The Best Plays of 1974-1975, pp. 10, 18, 335-36

Martin, Sharon Stockard. "Bring It Down Front: The Tanning of Oz--Reflections on the Usurpation of a Myth." Essence 6 (September 1975): 32, 35

Nachman, Gerald. "Who's Afraid of the Broadway Critics?" More 7 (July/August 1977): 22

Peterson, Maurice. "Rising Stars." Essence 7 (December 1976): 52, 89

Ribowsky, Mark. "'Father' of the Black Theater Boom." Sepia 25 (November 1976): 70

Taylor, Clark. "Fortune Smiles on Broadway's Gypsies." Essence 7 (August 1976): 78

Weathers, Diane. "Fantasy in Black Theatre: A Kind of New Freedom." Encore 4 (21 April 1975): 28, 32-34

Winer, Linda. "... the Stage is Set for a Hit Season." Chicago Tribune: Arts & Fun, 26 June 1977, sec. 6, p. 12

REVIEWS OF INDIVIDUAL MUSICALS:

The Wiz

Bellany, Peter. "'The Wiz' Musical a Whiz of a Show." (Cleveland, Ohio) Plain Dealer, 25 May 1975, in Newsbank--Performing Arts. May-June 1975, 38: G 8

Blum and Willis, eds. A Pictorial History of the American Theatre: 1860-1976, pp. 424, 426, 428

Calloway, Earl. "Kamal as the Wiz is Electrifying." Chicago Daily Defender, 7 June 1977, p. 20

Clurman, Harold. "Theatre." Nation 220 (25 January 1975): 94

Davis, Curt. "It's Happening for Mabel King." Encore 6 (20 June 1977): 51

_____. "Ken Page is Doing Nicely--Nicely, Thanks." Encore 6 (7 February 1977): 35

_____. "Welcome 'Arms'." Encore 6 (17 January 1977): 36

Drew, Michael F. "Critics Seem Unkind to Theater in Uneven Season." Milwaukee (Wis.) Journal, 26 February 1976, in Newsbank--Performing Arts. January-February 1976, 13: A 5

Flippo, Chet. "Broadway Rock: 'The Wiz' and the Worst." Rolling Stone 187 (22 May 1975): 18

Gilbert, Ruth, ed. "In and Around Town: On Broadway." New York 10 (2 May 1977): 20; (6 June 1977): 20; (20 June 1977): 20; (27 June 1977): 16; (4 July 1977): 14; (11 July 1977): 20; (18 July 1977): 14; (25 July 1977): 15; (1 August 1977): 15; (8 August 1977): 15; (15 August 1977): 16; (22 August 1977): 15; (29 August 1977): 14; (19 September 1977): 19; (26 September 1977): 16; (3 October 1977): 19

Gill, Brendan. "The Theatre: Tennis with the New Down." New Yorker 50 (13 January 1975): 64

Hanis, Jessica B. "Harper a Show Biz 'Wiz'." (N.Y. Amsterdam News: Arts and Entertainment, 29 March 1975, in Newsbank--Performing Arts. March-April 1975, 29: F 2

Hieronymus, Clara. "'The Wiz' a Wiz of a Show." (Nashville) Tennessean, 31 October 1975, in Newsbank--Performing Arts. September-October 1975, 66: G 4, 5

Higginsen, Vy. "Oh, Yeah." Essence 5 (November 1974): 12

Hodgson, Moira. "Warming Up on Broadway." Dance Magazine 49 (March 1975): 34+

Kalem, T. E. "Jumping Jivernacular." Time 105 (20 January 1975): 76

Kroll, Jack. "Oz with Soul." Newsweek 85 (20 January 1975): 82

Lewis, Barbara. "Mini-Wiz Captivates Rikers' Audience." (N.Y.) Amsterdam News: Arts and Entertainment, 30 April 1977, D-5

"Long Runs." Facts on File. 1976, 1015 A 3

McKenzie, Vashti. "The McKenzie Report: 'The Wiz' was a Wow ... Won Seven Tonys." Afro-American (Baltimore, Md.), 22 April 1975, in Newsbank--Performing Arts. March-April 1975, 31: D 12, 13

McMorrow, Tom. "Broadway Expects a Championship Season." New York Daily News, 7 September 1975, in Newsbank--Performing Arts. September-October 1975, 68: C-14-D1

Mancini, Joseph. "A Wiz." New York Post, 26 April 1975, in Newsbank--Performing Arts. March-April 1975, 27: A 4, 5

Meade, James. "Big Man Brings Elegance Back." San Diego (Calif.) Union, 20 October 1975, in Newsbank--Performing Arts. September-October 1975, 69: C 12

Murray, James P. "Blacks Invade Broadway in a Big Way ... with Soul Cheers, and Society Boos." St. Louis (Mo.) Argus, 17 April 1975, in Newsbank--Performing Arts. March-April 1975, 28: D 9

The New York Theatre Critics' Reviews--1975 36 (13 January 1975): 390-394; containing: Watt, Douglas, "Fine Cast and Splendid Looking in 'Wiz'" ([N.Y.] Daily News, 6 January 1975). Barnes, Clive, "Stage: 'The Wiz' of Oz" (New York Times, 6 January 1975). Gottfried, Martin, "Black Wizard of Oz Musical" (New York Post, 6 January 1975). Wilson, Edwin, "Jivey Dudes" (The Wall Street Journal, 9 January 1975). Kissel, Howard, "'The Wiz'" (Women's Wear Daily, 6 January 1975). Beaufort, John, "Broadway's All-New, All Black Musical 'Wizard of Oz'" (Christian Science Monitor, 10 January 1975). Kalem, T. E., "Jumping Jivernacular" (Time, 20 January 1975). Kroll, Jack, "Oz with Soul" (Newsweek, 20 January 1975). Probst, Leonard, "The Wiz" (NBC, 6 January 1975). "The Wiz" (WABC-TV, 5 January 1975)

Novick, Julius. "In Search of the New Consensus."
Saturday Review 3 (3 April 1976): 42
Peterson, Maurice. "On the Aisle." Essence 5 (March
1975): 11
_____. "The Wiz's Wizzes: Ken Harper and Geoffrey
Holder." Essence 6 (September 1975): 54-5, 83-4, 87
"Playboy After Hours--Theatre." Playboy 22 (June 1975):
41
Rich, Alan. "Broadway's Senior Musical--A Tourist's
Guide." New York 10 (27 June 1977): 114
Robinson, Major. "Invisible Stars Twinkle." (N.Y.)
Amsterdam News: Arts and Entertainment, 25 June
1977, D-15
Simon, John. "Music of the Squares." New York Maga-
zine 8 (27 January 1975): 51
Smith, Angela E. "All-Black, All Soulful and Very To-
gether." St. Louis (Mo.) Argus, 17 April 1975, in
Newsbank--Performing Arts. March-April 1975, 27:
A 6
Tapley, Mel. "Long Island 'Scarecrow' Gets Broadway
Break." (N.Y.) Amsterdam News: Arts and Enter-
tainment, 11 September 1976, D-2
Trescott, Jacqueline. "Robert Guillame: The Leading
Guy." Washington (D.C.) Post, 6 May 1976, in News-
bank--Performing Arts. May-June 1976, 40: D 5-6
Walker, Jesse H. "And Now a Word...." The Afro-
American (Baltimore, Md.), 19-23 July 1977, p. 11
Weales, Gerald. "Birthday Mutterings." Modern Theatre
and Drama 19 (December 1976): 420-21
"Welcome to the Great Black Way." Time 108 (1 Novem-
ber 1976): 75
Willis' Theatre World. vol. 31, 1974-1975, p. 35
_____. vol. 32, 1975-1976, p. 64, play bill
Winer, Linda. "The Boom in Black Theatre: Growing
Profits ... and Growing Pains." Chicago Tribune:
Arts & Fun, 30 May 1976, 6: 2-3
_____. "Here, It's Promises, Promises." Chicago
Tribune: Arts and Fun/Books, 23 January 1977, p. 3
_____. "Over the Rainbow, Into the Shubert." Chicago
Tribune: Arts & Fun, 7 November 1976, 6:3
MEDIA:
The Wiz
Soundtrack by Atlantic
AWARDS:
The Wiz
Antoinette Perry--Tony Award 1975 (7 awards)

†BROWN, WILLIAM WELLS
PLAYS:
The Escape; or, A Leap for Freedom: A Drama in Five
Acts. Boston: Wallcutt, 1858
Experience: Escape: Life at the South

Miralda, 1855
CRITICISMS OF BROWN:
Farrison, W. Edward. "The Kidnapped Clergyman and
Brown's Experience." CLA Journal 18 (June 1975): 507-
15
CRITICISMS OF INDIVIDUAL PLAYS:
The Escape; or, A Leap for Freedom
Davis, Arthur P. From the Dark Tower, p. 11
Edmonds, Randolph. "The Blacks in the American
Theatre, 1700-1969." The Pan-African Journal 7
(Winter 1974): 301
Farrison, W. Edward. "The Kidnapped Clergyman and
Brown's Experience." CLA Journal 18 (June 1975):
507-15
Hartnoll. The Oxford Companion to the Theatre, p. 673
Hatch, James. "Speak to Me of Those Old Words, You
Know, Those La-La Words, Those Tung-Tung Sounds
(Some African Influences on the Afro American Theatre)."
Yale/Theatre 8 (Fall 1976): 30
Miller, Jeanne-Marie A. "Images of Black Women in
Plays by Black Playwrights." CLA Journal 20 (June
1977): 494
Mitchell. Voices of the Black Theatre, pp. 20-21

†BROWNE, THEODORE
PLAYS:
Natural Man, formerly titled This Old Hammer
CRITICISMS OF BROWNE:
Hartnoll. The Oxford Companion to the Theatre, p. 677
Mitchell. Voices of the Black Theatre, pp. 23, 146
Walsh, Elizabeth and Diane Bowers. "WPA Federal Theatre
Project." Theatre News 8 (April 1976): 2
CRITICISMS OF INDIVIDUAL PLAYS:
The Natural Man
Goldstein. The Political Stage, p. 255
Hartnoll. The Oxford Companion to the Theatre, p. 677
Hatch, James. "Speak to Me in Those Old Words, You
Know, Those La-La Words, Those Tung-Tung Sounds."
Yale/Theatre 8 (Fall 1976): 33
"Words of Regina M. Andrews." In Mitchell. Voices of
the Black Theatre, p. 74, 115, 127

BROWNING, ALICE C.
MUSICALS:
How to be Happy Though, children's musical
How to Beat Old Age
How's Your Sex Life
It's Fun to be Black, children's musical
CRITICISMS OF BROWNING:
Edding, Cynthia. "Essence Woman: Alice C. Browning."
Essence 8 (May 1977): 6
Moore, Jacqueline. "Alice C. Browning: Realizes Deferred

Writing Dream." Chicago Daily Defender: Joy, 20 June 1977, p. 11
REVIEWS OF INDIVIDUAL MUSICALS:
How's Your Sex Life
 "Comedy on Sex Staged for Winter's Conference." Chicago Daily Defender, 20 June 1977, p. 19

†BRUCE, RICHARD
 PLAYS:
  Sodhji
 CRITICISMS OF INDIVIDUAL PLAYS:
  Sodhji
   Hatch, James. "Speak to Me in Those Old Words, You Know, Those La-La Words, Those Tung-Tung Sounds." Yale/Theatre 8 (Fall 1976): 27

†BRUNO, JOANNE
 PLAYS:
  Sister Selena's Got the Gift

†BULLINS, ED.
 PLAYS:
  The American Flag Ritual
  Black Commercial #2
  Clara's Old Man
  C'Mon Back to Heavenly House
  The Corner
  Daddy
  Death List
  The Duplex: A Love Fable in Four Movements. N.Y.: Morrow, 1971
  The Electronic Nigger
  The Fabulous Miss Marie
  The Gentleman Caller
  Goin' a Buffalo
  The Helper
  Home Boy
  The House Party
  How Do You Do? A Nonsense Drama. Mill Valley, Cal.: Illuminations Press, 1965: 1967
  I Am Lucy Terry
  In New England Winter
  In the Wine Time
  It Bees Dat Way: A Confrontation Ritual
  It Has No Choice
  Jo Anne!
  Malcolm: '71; or Publishing Blackness (Based upon a real experience)
  The Mystery of Phillis [sic] Wheatley
  Night of the Beast
  One-Minute Commercial
  The Pig Pen

The Play of the Play
The Psychic Defenders
The Rally
A Son Come Home
State Office Bldg. Curse
Street Sounds
The Taking of Miss Janie

PLAYS PUBLISHED IN ANTHOLOGIES:
The American Flag Ritual, in Bullins, The Theme Is Black-
ness; The Corner and Other Plays
Black Commercial #2, in Bullins, The Theme Is Blackness;
The Corner and Other Plays
Clara's Old Man, in Poland and Mailman, The Off-Off Broad-
way Book
Death List, in Bullins, Four Dynamite Plays
Dialect Determinism, in Bullins, The Theme Is Blackness;
The Corner and Other Plays
The Electronic Nigger, in Hoffman, New American Plays,
vol. 3
The Helper, in Bullins, The Theme Is Blackness
In the Wine Time, in Patterson, Black Theater
It Bees Dat Way, in Bullins, Four Dynamite Plays; in
Theatre 2: The American Theatre, 1968-1969
It Has No Choice, in Bullins, The Theme Is Blackness
Night of the Beast, in Bullins, Four Dynamite Plays
One-Minute Commercial, in Bullins, The Theme Is Blackness
The Play of the Play, in Bullins, The Theme Is Blackness
A Son Come Home, in Bain, Carl E., Jerome Beaty and J.
Paul Hunter, The Norton Introduction to Literature, 2nd
ed.; Clayes, Drama and Discussion
State Office Bldg. Curse, in Bullins, The Theme Is Blackness
The Taking of Miss Janie, in Guernsey, The Best Plays of
1974-1975

PLAYS PUBLISHED IN PERIODICALS:
In the Wine Time, in Black Theatre no. 3 (1969): 8-11
(synopsis)
Malcolm: '71, in Black Scholar 6 (June 1975): 84-86 (a scene)

MUSICALS:
[with Mildred Kayden] Absurdities in Black
[with Mildred Kayden] Storyville

FILM SCRIPTS:
Night of the Beast, 1971
The Ritual Masters, 1972

FILM SCRIPTS PUBLISHED IN ANTHOLOGIES:
Night of the Beast, in Bullins, Four Dynamite Plays

COLLECTIONS:
Black Quartet: Four New Black Plays (Bullins). N.Y.: New
American Library, 1970
As editor. "Black Theatre Group: A Directory." Drama
Review 4 (Summer 1968): 172-175
Four Dynamite Plays. N.Y.: Morrow, 1972
The New Lafayette Theatre Presents: Plays with Aesthetic

Comments by 6 Black Playwrights. N.Y.: Anchor Press/
Doubleday, 1974
The Theme Is Blackness: The Corner and Other Plays.
N.Y.: Morrow, 1973
CRITICISMS BY BULLINS:
"Black Revolutionary Commercial." Drama Review 13 (Sum-
mer 1969): 144-45
Guernsey, O., Jr. Playwrights, Lyricists, Composers, On
Theater, p. 344
"Introduction: Black Theater: The '70's--Evolutionary
Changes." In Bullins. The Theme Is Blackness, N.Y.:
Morrow, 1973, pp. 1-15
"Introduction: The Black Revolutionary Commercial." In
Bullins. The Theme Is Blackness, N.Y.: Morrow, 1973
CRITICISMS OF BULLINS:
Bentley, Eric. Theatre of War, pp. 406-407
Blackman, Brandon R., IV. "Black Hope of Broadway."
Sepia 24 (December 1975): 62-68
Brooks, Mary Ellen. "Reactionary Trends in Recent Black
Drama." Literature and Ideology (Montreal). no. 10
(1970): 43, 46-48
Brukenfeld, Dick. "Off-Off-Broadway." In Theatre 4: The
American Theatre, 1970-1971, p. 49
"Bush Mama." Tricontinental Film Center: 1977-79, p. 44
Cameron and Hoffman. A Guide to Theatre Study, pp. 202,
214
Clayborne, Jon L. "Modern Black Drama and the Gay
Image." College English 36 (November 1974): 381-82
Cohn, Ruby. "Theatre in Review." Educational Theatre
Journal 28 (October 1976): 406
Cook and Henderson. The Militant Black Writer, pp. 80-81
Current Biography 38 (May 1977): 15-18
Dace and Dace. The Theatre Student: Modern Theatre and
Drama, pp. 56-58
Daughtry, Willa A. "A Quarter Century in the Fine Arts,
1950-1974." The Negro Educational Review 27 (January
1976): 27
Davis, Curt. "People in the News." Encore 6 (23 May
1977): 31
Duckett, Alfred. "The Birth of a Screenwriter" (Wesley).
Sepia 26 (January 1977): 62, 64
Eckstein, George. "The New Black Theater." Dissent 20
(Winter 1973): 111, 112-113
_____. "Softened Voices in the Black Theater." Dissent
23 (Summer 1976): 308
Gaffney, Floyd. "A Hand Is on the Gate in Athens." Educa-
tional Theatre Journal 21 (May 1969): 196
Gant, Lisbeth. "The New Lafayette Theatre." Drama Re-
view 16 (December 1972): 52
Geisinger. Plays, Players, & Playwrights, p. 742
Gilder, Rosamond. "Theatre As People: Book Report." In
Theatre 4: The American Theatre, 1970-1971, p. 187

Gottfried, Martin. "The New Ethnic Theater." New York Post, 4 October 1975, in Newsbank--Performing Arts. September-October 1975, 68: B 4

Guernsey, O. Jr. Playwrights, Lyricists, Composers, On Theater, p. 421

Haley, Elsie Galbreath. "The Black Revolutionary Theatre: Le Roi Jones, Ed Bullins, and Minor Playwrights." Ph.D. Dissertation, University of Denver, 1971

Hall, Frederick Douglass, Jr. "The Black Theatre in New York from 1960-1969." Ed.D. Columbia University, 1973, Part III

Haslam, Gerald W. "Two Traditions in Afro-American Literature." Research Studies 37 (September 1969): 187, 190, 193

Hatch, James. "Speak to Me in Those Old Words, You Know, Those La-La Words, Those Tung-Tung Sounds." Yale/ Theatre 8 (Fall 1976): 33

Hord, Fred. "But We Need More." Black Books Bulletin 2 (1974): 10, 12, 14

Houghton. The Exploding Stage, pp. 202, 237, 251

Hughes, Catherine. "Bicentennial Reflections." America 135 (24 July 1976): 31

Jackson, Kennell Jr. "Notes on the Works of Ed Bullins and 'The Hungered One'." CLA Journal 18 (December 1974): 292-99

Lahr, John. "The Deli: Off Broadway and Off, 68-69." In Theatre 2: The American Theatre, 1968-1969, p. 50

Miller, Jeanne-Marie A. "Images of Black Women in Plays by Black Playwrights." CLA Journal 20 (June 1977): 502-04

Moser, Norman. "A Revolutionary Art: Le Roi Jones, Ed Bullins and the Black Revolution." December 12 (1970): 180-190

Nordel, Roderick. "Bullins and Black Theatre." Christian Science Monitor, 4 June 1969

Ogunbiyi, Yemi. "New Black Playwrights in America, 1960-1975." Ph.D. Dissertation, New York University, 1976, Chp. 2

O'Haire, Patricia. "Bullins: A Philadelphia Story." (N.Y.) Daily News, 7 June 1975, in Newsbank--Performing Arts. May-June 1975, 39: G 8

Oliver, Edith. "Report from 137th Street." In Theatre 5: The American Theatre, 1971-1972, p. 133

Poland and Mailman. The Off-Off Broadway Book, pp. 530

Reilly, John N. "Bullins." In Vinson. Contemporary Dramatists, pp. 126-128

Robinson, Le Roy. "Black Theatre: A Need for the Seventies." Soul Illustrated 2 (February 1970): 57

Simon. Uneasy Stages, p. 452

Smitherman, Geneva. "Everybody Wants to Know Why I Sing the Blues." Black World 23 (April 1974): 4-113

Stamper, Sam. "Playwright in Residence for One Week."

Bay State Banner, (Boston, Mass.) 30 January 1975, in
Newsbank--Performing Arts. January-February 1975,
13: C 4

"Talking of Black Art, Theatre, Revolution and Nationhood."
[interviews] Black Theatre no. 5 (1971): 23-24

True, Warren R. "Ed Bullins, Anton Chekov, and the 'Drama
Mood'." CLA Journal 20 (June 1977): 521-32

Turner, Darwin, T. "Afro-American Literary Critics."
Black World 19 (June 1970): 54

"The Words of Regina M. Andrews." In Mitchell. Voices
of the Black Theatre, p. 72

Wortis, Irving. "Review: Five Plays by Ed Bullins." Library Journal sciv (July 1969): 2635

Xeroxed Abstracts: Stage I

CRITICISMS OF INDIVIDUAL PLAYS:

Black Love Fable
 Miller, Jeanne-Marie A. "Images of Black Women in
 Plays by Black Playwrights." CLA Journal 20 (June
 1977): 503

Clara's Old Man
 Benston, Kimberly W. "'Cities in Bezique': Adrienne
 Kennedy's Expressionistic Vision." CLA Journal 20
 (December 1976): 235

 Brooks, Mary Ellen. "Reactionary Trends in Recent Black
 Drama." Literature and Ideology (Montreal). no. 10
 (1970): 46

 Current Biography 38 (May 1977): 16

 Dace and Dace. The Student Theatre: Modern Theatre
 and Drama, p. 57

 Hay, Samuel A. "African-American Drama, 1950-1960."
 Negro History Bulletin 36 (January 1973): 7

 Keller, Joseph. "Black Writing and the White Critic."
 Negro American Literature Forum 3 (Winter 1970): 108

 Miller, Jeanne-Marie A. "Images of Black Women in
 Plays by Black Playwrights." CLA Journal 20 (June
 1977): 502

 Oliver, Edith. "Report from 137th Street." In Theatre
 5: The American Theatre, 1971-1972, pp. 132-133

 Smitherman, Geneva. "Everybody Wants to Know Why I
 Sing the Blues." Black World 23 (April 1974): 8, 9

 Tener, Robert L. "Pandora's Box: A Study of Ed Bullins'
 Dramas." CLA Journal 19 (June 1976): 537+

 True, Warren R. "Ed Bullins, Anton Chekov, and the
 'Drama Mood'." CLA Journal 20 (June 1977): 525, 531

The Corner
 Benston, Kimberly W. "'Cities in Bezique': Adrienne
 Kennedy's Expressionistic Vision." CLA Journal 20
 (December 1976): 235

 Current Biography 38 (May 1977): 17

 Oliver, Edith. "Report from 137th Street." In Theatre 5:
 The American Theatre, 1971-1972, p. 133

 Smitherman, Geneva. "Everybody Wants to Know Why I

Sing the Blues." Black World 23 (April 1974): 5, 6
True, Warren R. "Ed Bullins, Anton Chekov, and the
'Drama Mood'." CLA Journal 20 (June 1977): 526, 529
Death List
Eckstein, George. "The New Black Theater." Dissent
20 (Winter 1973): 111
The Duplex
Current Biography 28 (May 1977): 17
Dace and Dace. The Theatre Student: Modern Theatre
and Drama, p. 57
Eddy, Bill. "4 Directors on Criticism." Drama Review
18 (September 1974): 24, 26-27
Evans, Don. "The Theatre of Confrontation: Ed Bullins,
Up Against the Wall." Black World 23 (April 1974):
14-18
Gant, Lisbeth. "The New Lafayette Theatre." Drama
Review 16 (December 1972): 51-52
Hay, Samuel A. "African-American Drama, 1950-1970."
Negro History Bulletin 36 (January 1973): 7
Mendelson and Bryfonski, eds. Contemporary Literary
Criticism vol. 7, p. 36
Miller, Jeanne-Marie A. "Images of Black Women in
Plays by Black Playwrights." CLA Journal 20 (June
1977): 503
Oliver, Edith. "Report from 137th Street." In Theatre
5: The American Theatre, 1971-1972, p. 133
Simon. Uneasy Stages, pp. 359, 376-378
Smitherman, Geneva. "Everybody Wants to Know Why I
Sing the Blues." Black World 23 (April 1974): 5, 6, 10
Stasio, Marilyn. "Off-Broadway." In Theatre 5: The
American Theatre, 1971-1972, pp. 38, 41
Tener, Robert L. "Pandora's Box: A Study of Ed Bullins'
Dramas." CLA Journal 19 (June 1976): 533-44
True, Warren R. "Ed Bullins, Anton Chekov, and the
'Drama Mood'." CLA Journal 20 (June 1977): passim
The Electronic Nigger
Clurman, Harold. "Je Seme Partout." In Theatre 1:
The American Theatre, 1967-1968, p. 59
Current Biography 38 (May 1977): 16
Dace and Dace. The Student Theatre: Modern Theatre
and Drama, p. 57
Harris, Jessica B. "The New Lafayette: 'Nothing Lasts
Forever'." Black Creation 4 (Summer 1973): 8, 9
Haslam, Gerald W. "Two Traditions in Afro-American
Literature." Research Studies 37 (September 1969): 187
Oliver, Edith. "Report from 137th Street." In Theatre
5: The American Theatre, 1971-1972, pp. 132-133
Smitherman, Geneva. "Everybody Wants to Know Why I
Sing the Blues." Black World 23 (April 1974): 10
Tedesco, John L. "The White Image as Second 'Persona'
in Black Drama, 1955-1970." Ph.D. Dissertation, Uni-
versity of Iowa, 1974

The Fabulous Miss Marie
  Brukenfeld, Dick. "Off-Off-Broadway." In Theatre 4:
    The American Theatre, 1970-1971, pp. 48-49
  Current Biography 38 (May 1977): 17
  Gant, Lisbeth. "The New Lafayette Theatre." Drama
    Review 16 (December 1972): 52
  Mendelson and Bryfonski, eds. Contemporary Literary
    Criticism. vol. 7, p. 36
  Miller, Jeanne-Marie A. "Images of Black Women in
    Plays by Black Playwrights." CLA Journal 20 (June
    1977): 503
  True, Warren R. "Ed Bullins, Anton Chekov and the
    'Drama Mood'." CLA Journal 20 (June 1977): passim
  Weales, Gerald. "Birthday Mutterings." Modern Theatre
    and Drama 19 (December 1976): 420-21
The Gentleman Caller
  Current Biography 38 (May 1977): 16
  Dace and Dace. The Student Theatre: Modern Theatre
    and Drama, pp. 57-58
  Miller, Jeanne-Marie A. "Images of Black Women in
    Plays by Black Playwrights." CLA Journal 20 (June
    1977): 503
Goin' a Buffalo
  Brooks, Mary Ellen. "Reactionary Trends in Recent
    Black Drama." Literature and Ideology (Montreal).
    no. 10 (1970): 45-46
  Brukenfeld, Dick. "Off-Off Broadway: Profile Rising."
    In Theatre 5: The American Theatre, 1971-1972, pp.
    52, 54, 55-56
  Current Biography 38 (May 1977): 17
  Dace and Dace. The Student Theatre: Modern Theatre
    and Drama, p. 57
  Hay, Samuel A. "African-American Drama, 1950-1970."
    Negro History Bulletin 36 (January 1973): 7
  Mendelson and Bryfonski, eds. Contemporary Literary
    Criticism. vol. 7, p. 36
  Miller, Jeanne-Marie A. "Images of Black Women in
    Plays by Black Playwrights." CLA Journal 20 (June
    1977): 503
  Oliver, Edith. "Report from 137th Street." In Theatre
    5: The American Theatre, 1971-1972, p. 133
  Smitherman, Geneva. "Everybody Wants to Know Why I
    Sing the Blues." Black World 23 (April 1974): 6, 8, 9
  Tener, Robert L. "Pandora's Box: A Study of Ed Bullins'
    Dramas." CLA Journal 19 (June 1976): 538-9+
  True, Warren R. "Ed Bullins, Anton Chekov, and the
    'Drama Mood'." CLA Journal 20 (June 1977): 525, 532
House Party
  Current Biography 38 (May 1977): 17
  Evans, Don. "The Theatre of Confrontation: Ed Bullins,
    Up Against the Wall." Black World 23 (April 1974):
    14-18

Greer, Edw. G. "Broadway--On and Off." Drama 112
(Spring 1974): 54
Mendelson and Bryfonski, eds. Contemporary Literary
Criticism. vol. 7, p. 36
How Do You Do
Current Biography 38 (May 1977): 16
Smitherman, Geneva. "Everybody Wants to Know Why I
Sing the Blues." Black World 23 (April 1974): 8
The Hungered One
Jackson, Kennell Jr. "Notes on the Works of Ed Bullins
and 'The Hungered One'." CLA Journal 18 (December
1974): 297
I Am Lucy Terry
Current Biography 38 (May 1977): 18
In New England Winter
"Black Theatre: A Bid for Cultural Identity." Black
Enterprise 2 (September 1971): 32, 34
Current Biography 38 (May 1977): 17
Dace and Dace. The Student Theatre: Modern Theatre
and Drama, p. 57
Eckstein, George. "The New Black Theater." Dissent
20 (Winter 1973): 113
Hay, Samuel A. "African-American Drama, 1950-1970."
Negro History Bulletin 36 (January 1973): 7
Miller, Jeanne-Marie A. "Images of Black Women in
Plays by Black Playwrights." CLA Journal 20 (June
1977): 503
Oliver, Edith. "Report from 137th Street." In Theatre
5: The American Theatre, 1971-1972, p. 133
Smitherman, Geneva. "Everybody Wants to Know Why I
Sing the Blues." Black World 23 (April 1974): 5, 6,
8-10
Tener, Robert L. "Pandora's Box: A Study of Ed Bullins'
Dramas." CLA Journal 19 (June 1976): 534-35
True, Warren R. "Ed Bullins, Anton Chekov, and the
'Drama Mood'." CLA Journal 20 (June 1977): 527, 528,
532
In the Wine Time
Current Biography 38 (May 1977): 17
Dace and Dace. The Student Theatre: Modern Theatre
and Drama, p. 57
Harris, Jessica B. "The New Lafayette: 'Nothing Lasts
Forever'." Black Creation 4 (Summer 1973): 8, 9
Hay, Samuel A. "African-American Drama, 1950-1970."
Negro History Bulletin 36 (January 1973): 7
Keyssar-Franke, Helen. "Strategies in Black Drama."
Ph.D. Dissertation, University of Iowa, 1974
Lahr, John. "The Deli: Off Broadway and Off, '68-69."
In Theatre 2: The American Theatre, 1968-1969, p. 49
Marvin X. "The Black Ritual Theatre: An Interview with
Robert Macbeth." Black Theatre no. 3 (1969): 23-24
Miller, Jeanne-Marie A. "Images of Black Women in

Plays by Black Playwrights." CLA Journal 20 (June 1977): 503

Oliver, Edith. "Report from 137th Street." In Theatre 5: The American Theatre, 1971-1972, pp. 129-30, 133

Patterson, Lindsay. "New Home, New Troupe, New Play: 'In the Wine Time' on Off-Broadway Theatre." Negro History Bulletin 32 (April 1969): 18-19

Smitherman, Geneva. "Everybody Wants to Know Why I Sing the Blues." Black World 23 (April 1974): 5, 6, 9, 11

Tener, Robert L. "Pandora's Box: A Study of Ed Bullins' Dramas." CLA Journal 19 (June 1976): 533-44

True, Warren R. "Ed Bullins, Anton Chekov, and the 'Drama Mood'." CLA Journal 20 (June 1977): 527

Jo Anne!
Current Biography 38 (May 1977): 18

The Mystery of Phillis Wheatley
Mendelson and Bryfonski, eds. Contemporary Literary Criticism. vol. 7, p. 37

The Pig Pen
Brukenfeld, Dick. "Off-Off-Broadway." In Theatre 4: The American Theatre, 1970-1971, pp. 48-49
Current Biography 38 (May 1977): 17
Oliver, Edith. "Report from 137th Street." In Theatre 5: The American Theatre, 1971-1972, p. 133
Tener, Robert L. "Pandora's Box: A Study of Ed Bullins' Dramas." CLA Journal 19 (June 1976): 535-36, 539

The Psychic Pretenders
Garnett, Bernard. "Black Drama Finds New Audience." Race Relations Reporter 3 (7 February 1972): 5
Oliver, Edith. "Report from 137th Street." In Theatre 5: The American Theatre, 1971-1972, p. 131

The Rally
Jackson, Kennell, Jr. "Notes on the Works of Ed Bullins' the 'Hungered One'." CLA Journal 18 (December 1974): 296

A Son Come Home
Current Biography 38 (May 1977): 16
Dace and Dace. The Student Theatre: Modern Theatre and Drama, p. 57
Hay, Samuel A. "African-American Drama, 1950-1970." Negro History Bulletin 36 (January 1973): 7
Oliver, Edith. "Report from 137th Street." In Theatre 5: The American Theatre, 1971-1972, pp. 132-33
Smitherman, Geneva. "Everybody Wants to Know Why I Sing the Blues." Black World 23 (April 1974): 10
Tener, Robert L. "Pandora's Box: A Study of Ed Bullins' Dramas." CLA Journal 19 (June 1976): 533-44

Street Sounds
Brukenfeld, Dick. "Off-Off-Broadway." In Theatre 4: The American Theatre, 1970-1971, p. 40

The Taking of Miss Janie
Blackman, Brandon R. IV. "Black Hope of Broadway."

Sepia 24 (December 1975): 63, passim

Current Biography 38 (May 1977): 17

Eckstein, George. "Softened Voices in the Black Theater."
Dissent 23 (Summer 1976): 308

Guernsey. The Best Plays of 1974-1975, pp. 27, 28, 39,
365

Mackay, Barbara. "Studies in Black and White." Saturday Review 2 (12 July 1975): 52

Mendelson and Bryfonski, eds. Contemporary Literary
Criticism. vol. 7, p. 37

Weales, Gerald. "Birthday Mutterings." Modern Theatre
and Drama 19 (December 1976): 420-21

CRITICISMS OF FILM SCRIPTS:

The Night of the Beast

Tener, Robert L. "Pandora's Box: A Study of Ed Bullins'
Dramas." CLA Journal 19 (June 1976): 536+

CRITICISMS OF COLLECTIONS:

Black Quartet

Blum and Willis, eds. A Pictorial History of the American Theatre: 1860-1976, p. 401

Salaam, Kalamu ya. "Making the Image Real." The
Black Collegian. 7 (May-April 1977): 56

The New Lafayette Theatre Presents

Current Biography 38 (May 1977): 18

McElroy, Hilda Njoki. "Books Noted." Black World 24
(April 1975): 51-52, 80-83

The Theme Is Blackness: The Corner and Other Plays

Booklist 69 (15 April 1973): 787

Buck, Richard M. Library Journal 98 (15 January 1973):
180-81

Choice 10 (May 1973): 452

REVIEWS OF INDIVIDUAL PLAYS:

Absurdities in Black

Gilbert, Ruth, ed. 'In and Around Town: Off and Off-Off
Broadway." New York 10 (15 August 1977): 19; (22
August 1977): 16; (29 August 1977): 14

Rich, Alan. "Off and Off-Off Broadway." New York 10
(15 August 1977): 19

Clara's Old Man

Clurman, Harold. "Theatre." Nation 206 (25 March
1968): 420-21

Kroll, Jack. "Black Mood." Newsweek 71 (18 March
1968): 110

Daddy

Fox, Terry Curtis. "The Con Man in the Minor." Village
Voice 22 (20 June 1977): 71-72

Gilbert, Ruth, ed. 'In and Around Town: Off and Off-
Off Broadway." New York 10 (20 June 1977): 20

Oliver, Edith. "Off-Broadway." New Yorker 53 (20
June 1977): 89

Death List

Kupa, Kushauri. "Closeups: The New York Scene--Black

Theatre in New York, 1970-1971." Black Theatre no.
6 (1971): 42

The Duplex
    Clurman, Harold. "Theatre." Nation 214 (27 March
        1972): 412
    Kroll, Jack. "In Black America." Newsweek 79 (20
        March 1972): 98-99
    Oliver, Edith. "The Theatre: Off Broadway." New
        Yorker 48 (18 March 1972): 85
    Orman, Roscoe. "The New Lafayette Theatre." Black
        Theatre no. 5 (1971): 13
    Perrier, Paulette. "Review: the Black Magicians."
        Black Theatre no. 5 (1971): 51-52

The Electronic Nigger
    Clurman, Harold. "Theatre." Nation 206 (25 March
        1968): 420-21
    "'The Electronic Nigger'." Cue (23 March 1968)
    Kroll, Jack. "Black Mood." Newsweek 71 (18 March
        1968): 110
    Oliver, Edith. "Three Cheers: 'The Electronic Nigger'
        and Others." New Yorker 44 (9 March 1968): 133-34
    Rendle, A. "'Electronic Nigger' and Other Plays: Re-
        view." Drama 157 (Winter 1970): 70

The Fabulous Miss Marie
    "'The Fabulous Miss Marie' Opens at the Locust."
        Philadelphia (Pa.) Tribune, 22 March 1975, in News-
        bank--Performing Arts. March-April 1975, 29: A 3
    Oliver, Edith. "Off Broadway: An Evening with Bullins
        & Co." New Yorker 47 (20 March 1971): 94-95

The Gentleman Caller
    Barnes, Clive. "Off-Broadway and Off-Off 1969-70." In
        Theatre 3: The American Theatre, 1969-1970, pp. 72, il

Goin' a Buffalo
    Oliver, Edith. "Off-Broadway: A Hard Night's Sleep."
        New Yorker 48 (4 March 1972): 83

Home Boy
    Oliver, Edith. "The Theatre: Off-Broadway." New
        Yorker 52 (11 October 1976): 81

House Party
    Greer, Edward G. "Broadway--On and Off." Drama
        112 (Spring 1974): 54
    Willis' Theatre World. vol. 30, 1973-1974, p. 97

I Am Lucy Terry
    Oliver, Edith. "The Theatre: Off-Broadway." New
        Yorker 52 (23 February 1976): 82, 84

In New England Winter
    Oliver, Edith. "'In New England Winter'." New Yorker
        46 (6 February 1971): 72
    Stasio, Marilynn. "Review: 'In New England Winter'."
        Cue (6 February 1971): 8

In the Wine Time
    Oliver, Edith. "Off-Broadway: Superior Vintage." New

Yorker 52 (10 May 1976): 104-105

Peterson, Maurice. "Rising Stars." Essence 7 (December 1976): 86

Jo Anne!

Oliver, Edith. "The Theatre: Off-Broadway." New Yorker 52 (25 October 1976): 62+

The Pig Pen

Clurman, Harold. "Theatre." Nation 210 (1 June 1970): 668-669

Oliver, Edith. "Off Broadway: Rejoice." New Yorker 46 (30 May 1970): 72-73

A Son Come Home

Clurman, Harold. "Theatre." Nation 206 (25 March 1968): 420-21

Gilbert, Ruth, ed. "In and Around Town: Off and Off-Off Broadway--Triple Bill." New York 10 18 (July 1977): 18; (25 July 1977): 16; (1 August 1977): 16

"Goings On About Town: 'A Son Come Home', 'On Being Hit', and 'Gettin' It All Together'." New Yorker 53 (25 July 1977): 2

Kroll, Jack. "Black Mood." Newsweek 71 (18 March 1968): 110

The Taking of Miss Janie

Blum and Willis, eds. A Pictorial History of the American Theatre: 1860-1976, pp. 425, 427

Clurman, Harold. "Theatre." The Nation 220 (5 April 1976): 414

Hewes, Henry. "Theatre: Brief Chronicles." Saturday Review 2 (17 May 1975): 52

Hughes, Catharine. "White on Black." America 132 (31 May 1975): 427

Kalem, T. E. "Requiem for the '60s." Time 105 (19 May 1975): 80

Kaufmann, Stanley. "Now and Also Then." New Republic 172 (7 June 1975): 20

Mancini, Joseph. "Bullins' 'Miss Janie' Brings Cliches to Life." New York Post, 14 March 1975, in Newsbank--Performing Arts. March-April 1975, 29: A 4

"New Breed Theatre Producer." The Afro-American (Baltimore, Md.), 12-16 April 1977, p. 11

The New York Theatre Critics' Reviews--1975 36 (2 June 1975): 243-247; containing: Barnes, Clive, "The Stage: 'Miss Janie'" (New York Times, 5 May 1975). Watt, Douglas, "Miss Janie Is a Stunner" ([N.Y.] Daily News 5 May 1975). Gottfried, Martin, "A Radical Idea" (New York Post, 5 May 1975). Wilson, Edwin, "The Theatre: The Topsy Turvy Sixties" (The Wall Street Journal, 9 May 1975). Beaufort, John, "Protest Drama at Lincoln Center" (Christian Science Monitor, 9 May 1975). Sharp, Christopher, "The Taking of Miss Janie" (Women's Wear Daily, 5 May 1975). Kalem, T. E., "Requiem for the 60's" (Time, 19 May 1975)

Oliver, Edith. "Off-Broadway: Fugue for Three Room-
mates." New Yorker 51 (24 March 1975): 61-63

Peterson, Maurice. "On the Aisle." Essence 6 (July
1975): 19

_____. "On the Aisle: Spotlight on Dianne Oyama
Dixon." Essence 6 (November 1975): 39

Simon, John. "Don't Let's Be Beastly to the Nuns."
New York Magazine 9 (19 May 1975): 93

Watt, Douglas. "'Miss Janie' Is a Stunner." (N.Y.)
Daily News, 6 May 1975, in Newsbank--Performing
Arts. May-June 1975, 39: G 9

Willis' Theatre World. vol. 31, 1974-1975, p. 126

REVIEWS OF COLLECTIONS OF BULLINS:

Four Dynamite Plays

Booklist 68 (15 April 1972): 696

Choice 9 (March 1972): 73

Current Biography 38 (May 1977): 18

The New Lafayette Theatre Presents

Abramson, Doris. "'The New Lafayette Theatre Presents...'" [review] Quarterly Journal of Speech 62
(April 1976): 210-11

Book World 24 (April 1975): 51

Booklist 70 (15 March 1974): 769-70

Buck, Richard. Library Journal 99 (1 May 1974): 1322

Choice 11 (May 1974): 436

Publisher's Weekly 204 (17 December 1973): 39

The Theme Is Blackness: The Corner and Other Plays

Buck, Richard L. Library Journal 98 (15 January 1973):
180-81

Choice 10 (May 1973): 452

AWARDS:

The Taking of Miss Janie

New York Drama Critics' Circle Award as Best American
Play of the Year, 1975

Obie Award for Distinguished Playwrighting, 1974-1975

BURDINE, W. B., JR.

PLAYS:

A Night Class at Harlem U.

BURGIE, IRVING (Lord Burgess)

MUSICALS:

[with Loften Mitchell] A Ballad for Bimshire, 1963

CRITICISMS OF INDIVIDUAL MUSICALS:

A Ballad for Bimshire

Hartnoll. The Oxford Companion to the Theatre, p. 681

†BURRILL, MARY

PLAYS:

They That Sit in Darkness

CRITICISMS OF INDIVIDUAL PLAYS:

They That Sit in Darkness

Molette, Barbara. "Black Women Playwrights: They
Speak: Who Listens?" Black World 25 (April 1976):
31

BURROUGHS, CHARLES
PLAYS:
Black Man of Fantasy
CRITICISMS OF BURROUGHS:
"The Words of Regina M. Andrews." In Mitchell. Voices
of the Black Theatre, p. 70

BURROWS, VINIE
PLAYS:
Dark Fire, a one woman show

BUSH, ROY
PLAYS:
Two Daughters
REVIEWS OF INDIVIDUAL PLAYS:
Two Daughters
Willis' Theatre World. vol. 31, 1974-1975, p. 91; play
bill

†BUTCHER, JAMES W., JR.
PLAYS:
Milk and Honey
The Seer
CRITICISMS OF BUTCHER:
Sandle. The Negro in the American Educational Theatre,
p. 19
CRITICISMS OF INDIVIDUAL PLAYS:
The Seer
Sandle. The Negro in the American Educational Theatre,
p. 19, 127

BUTLER, E.
PLAYS:
The Smile and Wonder Cycle
REVIEWS OF INDIVIDUAL PLAYS:
The Smile and Wonder Cycle
Durrah, James W. "'The Smile and Wonder Cycle': Pro-
duction and Audience Suffer." (N.Y.) Amsterdam News:
Arts and Entertainment, 14 May 1976 D-7

BUTLER, TOMMY
MUSICALS:
Selma
REVIEWS OF INDIVIDUAL MUSICALS:
Selma
"'Selma' Folds." The Afro-American (Baltimore, Md.),
8-12 March 1977, p. 11
Steverson, William. "Musical About Civil Rights Has

Heart-Stopping Scenes." (Memphis, Tenn.) Commercial
Appeal, 4 April 1977, in Newsbank--Performing Arts.
March-April 1977, 23: F 8

CAESAR, ADOLPH
PLAYS:
The Square Root of Soul
REVIEWS OF INDIVIDUAL PLAYS:
The Square Root of Soul
"Caesar at De Lys." (N.Y.) Amsterdam News: Arts and
Entertainment, 2 July 1977, D-11
Gilbert, Ruth. "In and Around Town: Off and Off-Off
Broadway." New York 10 (20 June 1977): 20; (27 June
1977): 19; (4 July 1977): 16; (25 July 1977): 16
Oliver, Edith. "The Theatre: Off-Broadway." New
Yorker 53 (27 June 1977): 54
Taylor, Cassandra. "'Square Root of Soul'." (N.Y.)
Amsterdam News: Arts and Entertainment, 16 July
1977, D-7
Walker, Jesse H. "And Now a Word..." The Afro-Ameri-
can (Baltimore, Md.), 19-23 July 1977, p. 11

†CAIN, BROTHER
PLAYS:
Epitaph to a Coagulated Trinity, 1970
CRITICISMS OF INDIVIDUAL PLAYS:
Epitaph to a Coagulated Trinity
Simmons, Bill. "The Last Poets." Black Theatre 2
(1969): 32-33
REVIEWS OF INDIVIDUAL PLAYS:
Epitaph to a Coagulated Trinity
Simmons, Bill. "Reviews." Black Theatre no. 2 (1969):
32-33

†CALDWELL, BEN (Bakr, El Toure, Askia Muhammed Abu)
PLAYS:
Family Portrait; or, My Son the Black Militant
The First Militant Preacher. Newark, N.J.: Jihad, 1967
The Interview
The Job
Mission Accomplished
Prayer Meeting; or, The First Militant Minister
Riot Sale
Run Around
Top Secret
CRITICISMS OF CALDWELL:
Hall, Frederick Douglass, Jr. "The Black Theatre in New
York from 1960-1969." Ed.D. Columbia University 1973,
Part III
Houghton. The Exploding Stage, p. 201
Ladwig, Ronald V. "The Black Black Comedy of Ben Cald-
well." Players Magazine 51 (February/March 1976): 88-91

Robinson, Le Roy. "Black Theatre: A Need for the Seventies." Soul Illustrated 2 (February 1970): 57

CRITICISMS OF INDIVIDUAL PLAYS:

The Family Portrait; or, My Son the Black Militant

Hay, Samuel A. "African-American Drama, 1950-1970." Negro History Bulletin 36 (January 1973): 8

Potter, Vilma R. "New Politics, New Mothers." CLA Journal 16 (December 1972): 247-255

The First Militant Preacher

Hay, Samuel A. "African-American Drama, 1950-1970." Negro History Bulletin 36 (January 1973): 8

Keller, Joseph. "Black Writing and the White Critic." Negro American Literature Forum 3 (Winter 1970): 107

Ladwig, Ronald V. "The Black Black Comedy of Ben Caldwell." Players Magazine 51 (February/March 1976): 91

Meserve, Walter J. "Black Drama." In Robbins. American Literary Scholarship--1970, p. 344

The Interview

Ladwig, Ronald V. "The Black Black Comedy of Ben Caldwell." Players Magazine 51 February/March 1976): 90

The Job

Ladwig, Ronald V. "The Black Black Comedy of Ben Caldwell." Players Magazine 51 (February/March 1976): 90

Mission Accomplished

Keller, Joseph. "Black Writing and the White Critic." Negro American Literature Forum 3 (Winter 1970): 107

Ladwig, Ronald V. "The Black Black Comedy of Ben Caldwell." Players Magazine 51 (February/March 1976): 90

Prayer Meeting; or, The First Militant Minister

Dance, Darrell. "Contemporary Militant Black Humor." Negro American Literature Forum 8 (Summer 1974): 220

Riot Sale

Ladwig, Ronald V. "The Black Black Comedy of Ben Caldwell." Players Magazine 51 (February/March 1976): 88-90

Top Secret

Keller, Joseph. "Black Writing and the White Critic." Negro American Literature Forum 3 (Winter 1970): 107

Ladwig, Ronald V. "The Black Black Comedy of Ben Caldwell." Players Magazine 51 (February/March 1976): 90-91

CRITICISMS OF COLLECTIONS:

Black Quartet: Four New Black Plays. N.Y.: New American Library, 1970

Salaam, Kalamu ya. "Making the Image Real." The Black Collegian 7 (March-April 1977): 56

REVIEWS OF INDIVIDUAL PLAYS:

Run Around
  Kupa, Kushauri. "Closeup: The New York Scene--Black
    Theatre in New York, 1970-1971." Black Theatre no.
    6 (1972): 46
  Perrier, Paulette. "Review: The Black Magicians."
    Black Theatre no. 5 (1971): 51

CAMPBELL, DICK
  CRITICISMS OF CAMPBELL:
    "A Voice: Dick Campbell." In Mitchell. Voices of the
    Black Theatre, pp. 85-89

†CAMPBELL, HERBERT
  PLAYS:
    Middle Class Blacks
  REVIEWS OF INDIVIDUAL PLAYS:
    Middle Class Blacks
      Gant, Liz. "'Middle Class! Black?' at the Bed-Stuy
        Theatre." Black Theatre no. 5 (1971): 52

CARRILL, REPE
  PLAYS:
    Shango De Ima

†CARROLL, VINNETTE (b. March 11, 1922)
  PLAYS:
    Beyond the Blues
    But Never Jam Today, 1969 (based on Lewis' Alice in
      Wonderland)
    Jubilation, 1964
    Love Power
  MUSICALS:
    [with Micki Grant] Croesus and the Witch
    [with Micki Grant] Don't Bother Me I Can't Cope
    [with Micki Grant] I'm Laughin' But I Ain't Tickled
    [with Micki Grant] Step Lively, Boy, 1972 (based on a play
      by Irvin Shaw)
    Trumpets of the Lord, (adapted from J. W. Johnson's God's
      Trombones)
    [with Micki Grant] The Ups and Downs of Theophilus Mait-
      land, 1975
    [with Micki Grant and Alex Bradford] Your Arms Too Short
      to Box with God (conceived from the Book of Matthew)
  CRITICISMS OF CARROLL:
    George, Nelson. "Ms. Carroll Brings Black Richness to
      the Stage." (N.Y.) Amsterdam News: Arts and Enter-
      tainment, 5 March 1977, D-9
    Parker. Who's Who in the Theatre. 15th ed., p. 614
    Peterson, Maurice. "On the Aisle: Spotlight on Vinnette
      Carroll." Essence 7 (March 1977): 8
    Riley, Clayton. "Black Theatre." In Theatre 5: The
      American Theatre, 1971-1972, p. 65

"The Victim's Revenge: Broadway Reviews the Critics."
   More 7 (July/August 1977): 30
Walker, Jesse H.   "And Now a Word...."   The Afro-Ameri-
   can (Baltimore, Md.), 19-23 July 1977, p. 11
Xeroxed Abstracts: Stage I
CRITICISMS OF INDIVIDUAL MUSICALS:
Croesus and the Witch
   Riley, Clayton.   "Black Theatre."   In Theatre 5:   The
      American Theatre, 1971-1972, p. 61
Don't Bother Me I Can't Cope
   Blum and Willis, eds.   A Pictorial History of the Ameri-
      can Theatre: 1860-1976, pp. 414, 416
   Brukenfeld, Dick.   "Off-Off Broadway: Profile Rising."
      In Theatre 5:   The American Theatre, 1971-1972,
      pp. 52, 56
   Engel.   The Critics, pp. 27-28
   Harris, Leonard.   "Broadway."   In Theatre 5:   The Ameri-
      can Theatre, 1971-1972, pp. 29-30
   Peterson, Maurice.   "Rising Stars."   Essence 7 (Decem-
      ber 1976): 89
   Ribowsky, Mark.   "'Father' of the Black Theater Boom."
      Sepia 25 (November 1976): 72
   Sullivan, Dan.   "Theatre West."   In Theatre 5:   The
      American Theatre, 1971-1972, p. 88
REVIEWS OF INDIVIDUAL PLAYS:
But Never Jam Today
   Parker.   Who's Who in The Theatre, 15th ed., p. 614
REVIEWS OF INDIVIDUAL MUSICALS:
Don't Bother Me I Can't Cope
   Beutel, Paul.   "Talented Cast Transforms 'Don't Bother
      Me' Into a Hit."   (Austin, Tex.) American Statesman,
      24 November 1975, in Newsbank--Performing Arts.
      November-December 1975, 83: A 11
   Blum and Willis, eds.   A Pictorial History of the Ameri-
      can Theatre: 1860-1976, pp. 414, 416
   DeVine, Laurence.   "A Four Year Run and Still Coping."
      Detroit (Mich.) Free Press, 19 June 1975, in News-
      bank--Performing Arts.   May-June 1975, 38: D 4
   Gorney, Carole.   "Black Revue Excites Popejoy Hall
      Crowd."   Albuquerque (N.M.) Journal, 20 November
      1975, in Newsbank--Performing Arts.   November-
      December 1975, 83: A 10
   Hughes, Catharine.   "Three New Musicals."   America
      135 (27 November 1976): 373
      _____ .   "Two Black Plays."   America 135 (27 Novem-
      ber 1976): 373
   Mackay, Barbara.   "Black Musical 'Cope' Lights Up
      Stage."   Denver (Colo.) Post, 15 April 1977, in News-
      bank--Performing Arts.   March-April 1977, 23: G 7
   Michelson, Herb.   "'Heavy' Stuff, Without Any Weight."
      Sacramento (Calif.) Bee, 19 June 1976, in Newsbank--
      Performing Arts.   May-June 1976, 40: E 3

Miller, Jeanne. "'Can't Cope'--Soft, Biting." San Francisco (Calif.) Examiner, 16 June 1976, in Newsbank--
Performing Arts. May-June 1976, 40: E 2

Mootz, William. "'Don't Bother Me' Is Black, Bold, and
Brilliant." (Louisville, Ken.) Courier-Journal, 8
October 1975, in Newsbank--Performing Arts. Septem-
ber-October 1975, 66: G 14

Murray, James P. "Blacks Invade Broadway in a Big
Way ... With Soul Cheers, and Society Bows." St.
Louis (Mo.) Argus, 17 April 1975, in Newsbank--Per-
forming Arts. March-April 1975, 28: D 9

Parker. Who's Who in The Theatre, 15th ed., p. 614

Ryan, Barbara Haddad. "'Can't Cope' Belies Title--With
Pride, Wit." (Denver, Colo.) Rocky Mountain News,
16 April 1977, in Newsbank--Performing Arts. March-
April 1977, 23: G 8

Trescott, Jacqueline. "Robert Guillame: The Leading
Guy." Washington (D.C.) Post, 6 May 1976, in News-
bank--Performing Arts. May-June 1976, 40: D 5-6

Watt, Douglas. "Poems Slow Songfest." (N.Y.) Daily
News, 19 May 1976, in Newsbank--Performing Arts.
May-June 1976, 40: E G

Willis' Theatre World. vol. 30, 1973-1974, p. 148, 196,
205

I'm Laughin' But I Ain't Tickled
  Clurman, Harold. "Theatre." Nation 222 (5 June 1976):
  701-02

  Hughes, Catharine. "Theatre." America 134 (12 June
  1976): 519

Trumpets of the Lord
  Parker. Who's Who in The Theatre, 15th ed., p. 614

The Ups and Downs of Theophilus Maitland
  Hughes, Catharine. "Three New Musicals." America 135
  (27 November 1976): 373

  _____. "Two Black Plays." America 135 (27 November
  1976): 373

  Mackay, Barbara. "Off-Beat Off-Broadway Musicals."
  Saturday Review 2 (22 March 1975): 40

  Peterson, Maurice. "On the Aisle." Essence 6 (May
  1975): 12

Your Arms Too Short to Box with God
  Adams, Zy Ace. "Music is the Message." (N.Y.) Amsterdam News: Arts and Entertainment, 1 January
  1977, D-10

  "Amen! ... Yes ... Lord! 'Box' Hot Time at Old Ford's."
  Afro-American (Baltimore, Md.), 14 February 1976, in
  Newsbank--Performing Arts. January-February 1975,
  11: G 13

  Berkvist, Robert. "New Face: Hector Jaime Mercalo:
  The Ailey Disciple Who Portrays Judas." New York
  Times, 7 October 1977, C 3

  "Blackstone Musical Puts Fun Into Old-Time Religion."

Chicago (Ill.) Sun Times, 10 April 1976, in Newsbank--
Performing Arts. March-April 1976, 27: G 6

Blum and Willis, eds. A Pictorial History of the American Theatre: 1860-1976, pp. 429, 430

Clurman, Harold. "Theatre." Nation 224 (15 January
1977): 61

Davis, Curt. "Welcome 'Arms'." Encore 6 (17 January
1977): 36

Dreyfuss, Joel. "Marvelous Music and Dancing, But the
Plot's No Revelation." Washington (D.C.) Post, 6
November 1975, in Newsbank--Performing Arts. No-
vember-December 1975, 83: A 5

Facts On File. 1976, pp. 12-22: 1014 F 3

Forbes, Cheryl. "Black 'Box' Is Best." Christianity Today 20 (30 January 1976): 16-17

George, Nelson. "Ms. Carroll Brings Black Richness to
the Stage." (N.Y.) Amsterdam News: Arts and Entertainment, 5 March 1977, D - 9

Gilbert, Ruth, ed. "In and Around Town: On Broadway."
New York 10 (2 May 1977): 20; (6 June 1977): 20; (20
June 1977): 20; (27 June 1977): 16; (4 July 1977): 14;
(11 July 1977): 20; (18 July 1977): 15; (25 July 1977):
16; (1 August 1977): 15; (8 August 1977): 16; (15 August
1977): 16; (22 August 1977): 15; (29 August 1977): 14;
(19 September 1977): 19; (26 September 1977): 16; (3
October 1977): 19

Gill, Brendan. "The Theatre--Having a Good Time."
New Yorker 52 (3 January 1977): 60

"Gospel Truth." Newsweek 89 (19 January 1977): 66

Hughes, Catharine. "Broadway Round-Up." America 136
(22 January 1977): 60

Kalem, T. E. "Oh, When the Saints...." Time 109 (24
January 1977): 55

New York Theatre Critics' Reviews--1976. 37 (31 Decem-
ber 1976): 52-56; containing: Barnes, Clive, "Stage:
'Your Arms Too Short ...'" (New York Times, 23 De-
cember 1976). Gottfried, Martin, "'Arms' Short of
Good Theater" (New York Post, 23 December 1976).
Watt, Douglas, "A Show for All Seasons" ([N.Y.] Daily
News, 23 December 1976). Wilson, Edwin, "Your Arms
Too Short to Box with God" (Wall Street Journal, 23
December 1976). Sharp, Christopher, "Your Arms Too
Short to Box with God" (Women's Wear Daily 23 Decem-
ber 1976). Beaufort, John, "Gospel Music" (The Chris-
tian Science Monitor, 27 December 1976). Kroll, Jack,
"Gospel Truth" (Newsweek, 10 January 1977). Lape,
Bob, "Your Arms ..." (WABC-TV 6 January 1977).
Probst, Leonard, NBC 22 December 1976

Philp, Richard. "Revivals." Dance Magazine 51 (May
1977): 36-40

Richards, David. "A Musical in Touch with the Spirit."
Washington (D.C.) Star News, 5 November 1975, in

Newsbank--Performing Arts. November-December
1976, 83: A 6
Roberts, Susan O. "Tony Winner Delores Hall Thanks
God for Success." (N.Y.) Amsterdam News: Arts
and Entertainment, 9 July 1977, D-2
Robinson, Major. "Invisible Stars Twinkle." (N.Y.)
Amsterdam News: Arts and Entertainment, 25 June
1977, D-15
Tapley, Mel. "Trazana, Dolores, and Diana Win Tonys."
(N.Y.) Amsterdam News: Arts and Entertainment, 11
June 1977, D-2
"Welcome to the Great Black Way." Time 108 (1 Novem-
ber 1976): 75
Willis' Theatre World. vol. 32, 1975-1976, p. 205
Winer, Linda. "The Boom in Black Theatre: Growing
Profits ... and Growing Pains." Chicago Tribune:
Arts & Fun, 30 May 1976, 6:2
"'Your Arms Are [sic] Too Short to Box With God'."
Milwaukee (Wis.) Journal, 24 December 1976, 2:2
AWARDS:
Emmy for conceiving Beyond the Blues
Ford Foundation Grant for Directors, 1960-61
Obie Award, for role in Moon On a Rainbow Shawl, 1961

CARSON, ROBERT (Sonny) (Mwina Imiri Abubadika)
FILM SCRIPTS:
The Education of Sonny Carson, based on the autobiography
of Sonny Carson, now Mwina Imiri Abubadika
CRITICISMS OF INDIVIDUAL FILM SCRIPTS:
The Education of Sonny Carson
"The Education of Sonny Carson." Ebony 29 (August
1974): 157-59
Peterson, Maurice. "Movies: Movies that Hit Home
and Strike Out." Essence 5 (November 1974): 19
Wander, Brandon. "Black Dreams: The Fantasy and
Ritual of Black Films." Film Quarterly 29 (Fall 1975):
9-10
REVIEWS OF INDIVIDUAL FILM SCRIPTS:
The Education of Sonny Carson
"Black Man's Burden." Time 104 (16 September 1974): 6+
Cooper, Arthur. "Education in Blood." Newsweek 84
(12 August 1974): 74
"'The Education of Sonny Carson'." Ebony 29 (August
1974): 157-159
"Movies." New Times 3 (8 August 1974): 62-63
Peterson, Maurice. "On the Aisle." Essence 5 (November
1974): 19
"Playboy After Hours--Movies." Playboy 21 (October 1974):
26

CARTER, BEN
MUSICALS:
[with Saundra McClain and David Martin] Bitter Trails

†CARTER, STEVE
  PLAYS:
    Eden
    Terraces
  CRITICISMS OF CARTER:
    Xeroxed Abstracts: Stage II
  REVIEWS OF INDIVIDUAL PLAYS:
    Eden
      Clurman, Harold. "Theatre." Nation 222 (27 March
        1976): 381-82
      Guernsey. The Best Plays of 1975-1976, pp. 23, 382
      Lewis, Barbara. "Actress Ethel Ayler." (N.Y.) Amster-
        dam News: Arts and Entertainment, 17 July 1976,
        D - 2
      New York Theatre Critics' Reviews--1976 37 (5 May 1976):
        278-280; containing: Watt, Douglas, "Black on Black
        in '27 N.Y." (N.Y.] Daily News, 4 March 1974).
        Gussow, Mel, "Negro Ensemble Stages 'Eden', a Black
        'Hester' Street?" (New York Times, 4 March 1976).
        Gottfried, Martin, "Romeo and Juliet in 'Eden'" (New
        York Post, 4 March 1976). Beaufort, John, "'Eden'"
        (The Christian Science Monitor, 11 March 1976)
      O'Haire, Patricia. "One Man's Family History." (N.Y.)
        Daily News, 9 April 1976, in Newsbank--Performing
        Arts. March-April 1976, 30: 1 C
      Raidy, Wm. A. "'Eden': Riveting Theater." Long Is-
        land (N.Y.) Press, 4 March 1976, in Newsbank--Per-
        forming Arts. March-April 1976, 30: C 2
      Willis' Theatre World. vol. 32, 1975-1976, p. 124
    Terraces
      Oliver, Edith. "Off-Broadway: Three to Get Ready."
        New Yorker 50 (22 April 1974): 103-104
      Willis' Theatre World. vol. 30, 1973-1974, p. 118

CAUSLEY, ED
  PLAYS
    The Paisley Convertible

†CHARLES, MARTE EVANS (Marti Charles)
  PLAYS:
    Jamimma
    Job Security
  CRITICISMS OF INDIVIDUAL PLAYS:
    Jamimma
      Harris, Jessica B. "The New Lafayette: 'Nothing Lasts
        Forever'." Black Creation 4 (Summer 1973): 9
      Oliver, Edith. "Report from 137th Street." In Theatre
        5: The American Theatre, 1971-1972, p. 133
  REVIEWS OF INDIVIDUAL PLAYS:
    Job Security
      Kupa, Kushauri. "Closeup: The New York Scene--
        Black Theatre in New York, 1970-1971." Black

Theatre no. 6 (1972): 42-43, 50
Perrier, Paulette. "Review: The Black Magicians."
Black Theatre no. 5 (1971): 52

CHARLES, the Rev. NORMAN
PLAYS:
Infirmity Is Running
REVIEWS OF INDIVIDUAL PLAYS:
Infirmity Is Running
Hazziezah. "'Infirmity Is Running': Uneven Black Family
Love." (N.Y.) Amsterdam News: Arts and Entertain-
ment, 30 October 1976, D - 8

CHAUNCEY, ANTHONY
FILM SCRIPTS:
[with Laurence (Larry) Swan and Aunt Alice Swan] Mini-Marvin
REVIEWS OF INDIVIDUAL FILM SCRIPTS:
Mini-Marvin
Tapley, Mel. "Chet French's Problem: Second Baseman
or Movie Star?" (N.Y.) Amsterdam News: Arts and
Entertainment, 18 December 1976, D - 2
_____. "Did 'Bugsy Malone' Rip-Off 'Mini-Marvin'?"
(N.Y.) Amsterdam News: Arts and Entertainment, 18
December 1976, D - 13

CHAUNCEY, HARRELL CORDELL see SALIM

†CHILDRESS, ALICE
PLAYS:
Florence
Gold Through the Trees, children's play
Just a Little Simple
Let's Hear It for the Queen (one act) N.Y.: Coward,
McCann, & Geoghegan, 1976
Martin Luther King at Montgomery, Alabama
Mojo
String
Trouble in Mind
Wedding Band. N.Y.: Samuel French, Inc., 1972
When the Rattlesnake Sounds: A Play About Harriet Tubman.
N.Y.: Coward, McCann, & Geoghegan, 1975
Wine in the Wilderness. N.Y.: Dramatists Play Service,
Inc., 1969
PLAYS PUBLISHED IN ANTHOLOGIES:
Wedding Band in Moore. The New Women's Theatre
Wine in the Wilderness, in Sullivan and Hatch. Plays by and
About Women
TELEVISION SCRIPTS:
A Hero Ain't Nothin' but a Sandwich (adapted from the novel)
CRITICISMS OF CHILDRESS:
David. Black Joy, p. 199
Miller, Jeanne-Marie A. "Images of Black Women in Plays

by Black Playwrights. " CLA Journal 20 (June 1977): 494-
95, 507
Robinson, Le Roy. "Black Theatre: A Need for the Seven-
ties. " Soul Illustrated 2 (February 1970): 57
Xeroxed Abstracts: Stage I
CRITICISMS OF INDIVIDUAL PLAYS:
Florence
Miller, Jeanne-Marie A. "Images of Black Women in
Plays by Black Playwrights. " CLA Journal 20 (June
1977): 495
Gold Through the Trees
Moore. The New Women's Theatre, pp. xixx, 257
Just a Little Simple
Hartnoll. The Oxford Companion to the Theatre, p. 680
Mojo
Bailey, Peter. "Annual Round-Up: Black Theatre in
America--New York. " Black World 21 (April 1972): 36
String
Current Biography 37 (September 1976): 29
Trouble in Mind
Evans, Donald T. "Bring It All Back Home. " Black
World 20 (February 1971): 41-45
_____. "Playwrights of the Fifties: Bringing It All
Back Home. " Black World 20 (February 1971): 44
Hartnoll. The Oxford Companion to the Theatre, p. 680
Hay, Samuel A. "African-American Drama, 1950-1970. "
Negro History Bulletin 36 (January 1973): 6
Miller, Jeanne-Marie A. "Images of Black Women in
Plays by Black Playwrights. " CLA Journal 20 (June
1977): 495-96
Tedesco, John L. "The White Image as Second 'Persona'
in Black Drama, 1955-1970. " Ph.D. Dissertation, Uni-
versity of Iowa, 1974
Wedding Band
Geisinger. Plays, Players, & Playwrights, p. 733
Miller, Jeanne-Marie A. "Images of Black Women in
Plays by Black Playwrights. " CLA Journal 20 (June
1977): 497-98
Molette, Barbara. "Black Women Playwrights: They
Speak: Who Listens?" Black World 25 (April 1976):
32-33
Moore. The New Women's Theatre, pp. xxxiii
Taylor, Clarke. "In the Soul of Theatre. " Essence 5
(April 1975): 48
Wine in the Wilderness
Anderson, Mary Louise. "Black Matriarchy: Portrayals
of Women in Three Plays. " Negro American Literature
Forum 10 (Fall 1976): 93
Hatch, James. "Speak to Me in Those Old Words, You
Know, Those La-La Words, Those Tung-Tung Sounds. "
Yale/Theatre 8 (Fall 1976): 33
Miller, Jeanne-Marie A. "Images of Black Women in

Plays by Black Playwrights." CLA Journal 20 (June 1977): 496-97
REVIEWS OF INDIVIDUAL PLAYS:
Mojo
  Kupa, Kushauri. "Closeup: The New York Scene--Black Theatre in New York, 1970-1971." Black Theatre no. 6 (1972): 39
String
  Oliver, Edith. "Theatre: Off Broadway." New Yorker 45 (12 April 1969): 131
Trouble in Mind
  Evans, Donald T. "Bring It All Back Home." Black World 20 (February 1971): 41-45
Wedding Band
  Blum and Willis, eds. A Pictorial History of the American Theatre: 1860-1976, p. 415
  Chernin, Donna. "Karamu 'Wedding Band' has Vivid Memories." (Cleveland, O.) Plain Dealer, 26 May 1975, in Newsbank--Performing Arts. May-June 1975, 39: G 10
  Clurman, Harold. "Theatre." Nation 215 (13 November 1972): 475-476
  Kauffmann, Stanley. "Stanley Kauffmann on Theatre." The New Republic 167 (25 November 1972): 22, 36
  Thomas, Barbara. "'Wedding Band' Brimming with Emotion." Atlanta (Ga.) Journal, 22 August 1975, in Newsbank--Performing Arts. July-August 1975, 53: D 11
Wine in the Wilderness
  Kupa, Kushauri. "Closeup: The New York Scene--Black Theatre in New York, 1970-1971." Black Theatre no. 6 (1972): 39
REVIEWS OF INDIVIDUAL TELEVISION SCRIPTS:
A Hero Ain't Nothin' but a Sandwich
  Harris, Robert R. "The Hollywood Connection." Bookviews 1 (November 1977): 30-31

†CHILDRESS, ALVIN
  CRITICISMS BY CHILDRESS:
  "What Ever Happened to ... the 'Amos 'n Andy' Cast?" Ebony 28 (July 1973): 138

†CLARK, CHINA
  PLAYS:
  In Sorrow's Room

†CLAY, BURIEL, II
  PLAYS:
  Liberty Call
  Rawhead and Bloody Bones
  PLAYS PUBLISHED IN ANTHOLOGIES:
  Rawhead and Bloody Bones (scene), in Reed. Yardbird Reader, vol. 5

REVIEWS OF INDIVIDUAL PLAYS:
Liberty Call
  Guernsey. The Best Plays of 1974-1975, p. 377
  Oliver, Edith. "The Theatre: Off-Broadway." New
    Yorker 51 (12 May 1975): 109
  Watt, Douglas. "It's Lively But Crude." (N.Y.) Daily
    News, 1 May 1975, in Newsbank--Performing Arts.
    May-June 1975, 40: G 12
  Willis' Theatre World. vol. 31, 1974-1975, p. 118

CLEVELAND, CHARLES
  PLAYS:
  [with James de Jongh] Hail, Hail the Gangs

†CLIMMONS, ARTIE
  PLAYS:
  My Troubled Soul, 1969
  REVIEWS OF INDIVIDUAL PLAYS:
  My Troubled Soul
    Miller, Adam David. "California Report from the San
      Francisco Bay Area, 1970-71." Black Theatre no. 6
      (1972): 7-8

†COLE, BOB (Robert)
  MUSICALS:
  Black Patti's Troubadours
  [with J. Rosamond Johnson] Red Moon
  [with J. Rosamond Johnson] The Shoofly Regiment
  A Trip to Coontown, 1898
  CRITICISMS OF COLE:
  Mitchell. Voices of the Black Theatre, p. 24
  CRITICISMS OF INDIVIDUAL MUSICALS:
  Black Patti's Troubadours
    Hartnoll. The Oxford Companion to the Theatre, p. 674
  Red Moon
    Edmonds, Randolph. "The Blacks in The American
      Theatre, 1700-1969." The Pan-African Journal 7
      (Winter 1974): 315
    Mitchell. Voices of the Black Theatre, p. 24
    Shafer, Yvonne. "Black Actors in the Nineteenth Century
      American Theatre." CLA Journal 20 (March 1977):
      400
  The Shoofly Regiment
    Edmonds, Randolph. "The Blacks in the American
      Theatre, 1700-1969." The Pan-African Journal 7
      (Winter 1974): 314
    Mitchell. Voices of the Black Theatre, p. 24
  A Trip to Coontown
    Hartnoll. The Oxford Companion to the Theatre, p. 674
    Edmonds, Randolph. "The Blacks in the American
      Theatre, 1700-1969." The Pan-African Journal 7 (Win-
      ter 1974): 314

Lemons, J. Stanley. "Black Stereotypes as Reflected in Popular Culture, 1880-1920." American Quarterly 29 (Spring 1977): 114-115

Shafer, Yvonne. "Black Actors in the Nineteenth Century American Theatre." CLA Journal 20 (March 1977): 400

COLE, TOM

PLAYS:
Medal of Honor Rag
CRITICISMS OF INDIVIDUAL PLAYS:
Medal of Honor Rag
Simonds, P. Munoz. "'Medal of Honor Rag'." Educational Theatre Journal 28 (October 1976): 412-413
REVIEWS OF INDIVIDUAL PLAYS:
Medal of Honor Rag
"Cleavon Little Has Got to be 'Gooood'." New York Post, 3 January 1977, in Newsbank--Performing Arts. January-February 1977, 5: G 1
Cole, Richard L. "Poignant, Polished 'Medal'." Washington (D.C.) Post, 27 January 1976, in Newsbank-- Performing Arts. January-February 1976, 13: C 11
Guernsey. The Best Plays of 1975-1976, pp. 24, 87-88, 382
Hewes, Henry. "To 'Disneyland' and Back." Saturday Review 3 (17 April 1976): 48-49
"New Breed Theatre Producer." The Afro-American (Baltimore, Md.), 12-16, April 1977, p. 11
New York Theatre Critics Reviews--1976. 37 (5 May 1976): 271-274; containing: Barnes, Clive, "'Medal of Honor Rag' Relieves Trauma of Vietnam" (The New York Times, 29 March 1976). Gottfried, Martin, "Profile of a Hero" (New York Post, 29 March 1976). Watt, Douglas, "Taut Duel of Wits" ([N.Y.] Daily News, 29 March 1976). Kalem, T. E., "Living with Defeat" (Time, 12 April 1976). Beaufort, John, (The Christian Science Monitor, 6 April 1976). Kissel, Howard, "Medal of Honor Rag" (Women's Wear Daily, 29 March 1976). Wilson, Edwin, "The Personal Anguish of Vietnam" (The Wall Street Journal, 31 March 1976). Probst, Leonard, "Medal of Honor Rag" (NBC, 29 March 1976)
Oliver, Edith. "Theatre--Off Broadway: Hero." The New Yorker 52 (12 April 1976): 101-102
Richards, Davis. "'The Medal of Honor's' Psychological Burden." Washington (D.C.) Star, 26 January 1976, in Newsbank--Performing Arts. January-February 1976, 13: C 12
Willis' Theatre World. vol. 32, 1975-1976, pp. 84, 204

COLE, ZAIDA
PLAYS:
Scenes of Love and Freedom

†COLES, EROSTINE
   PLAYS:
     Festus de Fus, ms. only
     Mimi La Crox, ms. only
   CRITICISMS OF INDIVIDUAL PLAYS:
     Mimi La Crox
       Sandle.   The Negro in The American Educational Theatre,
          p. 49

†COLLIE, KELSEY
   PLAYS:
     Randy Dandy's Circus, also filmed for television
   TELEVISION SCRIPTS:
     Randy Dandy's Circus (based on the play)

†CONWAY, MEL
   PLAYS:
     Best of Them All

COOK, S. N.
   PLAYS:
     Out in the Streets: A Temperance Play. N.Y.: American
       Temperance Publishing House, n.d.

†COOK, WILL MARION (1869-1944)
   MUSICALS:
     [with Paul L. Dunbar] Clorindy--or, The Origin of the Cake-
       Walk, 1898
     [with Paul L. Dunbar] Jes Lak White Folks
   CRITICISMS OF COOK:
     Mitchell. Voices of the Black Theatre, pp. 23, 24
   CRITICISMS OF INDIVIDUAL MUSICALS:
     Clorindy--or, The Origin of the Cake-Walk
       Edmonds, Randolph. "The Blacks in the American
          Theatre, 1700-1969." The Pan-African Journal 7
          (Winter 1974): 314
     Jes Lak White Folks
       Edmonds, Randolph. "The Blacks in the American
          Theatre, 1700-1969. The Pan-African Journal 7 (Win-
          ter 1974): 314

†COOPER, TED
   PLAYS:
     Good Night, Mary Beck

†COTTER, JOSEPH S. SR.
   PLAYS:
     Caleb, The Degenerate
   CRITICISMS OF COTTER:
     Jackson. The Waiting Years, p. 201
   CRITICISMS OF INDIVIDUAL PLAYS:
     Caleb, The Degenerate

Davis, Arthur P. From the Dark Tower, p. 11
Edmonds, Randolph. "The Blacks in the American
    Theatre, 1700-1969." The Pan-African Journal 7
    (Winter 1974): 302
Hartnoll. The Oxford Companion to the Theatre, p. 674
Shockley, Ann Allen. "Joseph S. Cotter, Sr. Biographi-
    cal Sketch of a Black Louisville Bard." CLA Journal
    18 (March 1975): 338-9

COUSIN, LINDA
    PLAYS:
    The Divorcing
    Karma

CRAWFORD, ROBERT
    PLAYS:
    The Brass Medallion
    CRITICISMS OF INDIVIDUAL PLAYS:
    The Brass Medallion
        Miller, Jeanne-Marie A. "Annual Round-up: Black
            Theater in America--Washington, D.C." Black World
            25 (April 1976): 83

†CULLEN, COUNTEE
    MUSICALS:
    [with Arna Bontemps] The Saint Louis Woman, 1946, musical
        adaptation of God Sends Sunday, 1931. Revised for Federal
        Theatre Project by Langston Hughes
    CRITICISMS OF INDIVIDUAL MUSICALS:
    The Saint Louis Woman
        Davis, Arthur P. From the Dark Tower, p. 75, 87
        Edmonds, Randolph. "The Blacks in the American
            Theatre, 1700-1969." The Pan-African Journal 7 (Win-
            ter 1974): 314
    REVIEWS OF INDIVIDUAL MUSICALS:
    The Saint Louis Woman
        "Pearl Bailey." In Parker. Who's Who in The Theatre,
            15th ed., p. 491

D.C. BLACK REPERTORY COMPANY
    PLAYS:
    Brown Sterling, (adaptation of Sterling Brown's works by
        D.C. Black Repertory Company)

DAFORA, ASADATA
    MUSICALS:
    Kykunkor: Or Witch Woman, 1934

DANIELS, RON
    PLAYS:
    Swing Low Sweet Steamboat
    REVIEWS OF INDIVIDUAL PLAYS:

Swing Low Sweet Steamboat
  Richards, Davis. "Rambling Rather than Swinging."
  Washington (D.C.) Star News, 14 November 1975, in
  Newsbank--Performing Arts. November-December
  1975, 84: F 5

†DAVIS, AL
  PLAYS:
  Black Sunlight
  Man, I Really Am, 1969
  REVIEWS OF INDIVIDUAL PLAYS:
  Black Sunlight
    Oliver, Edith. "The Theatre: Off Broadway." New
      Yorker 50 (1 April 1974): 52
    Willis' Theatre World. vol. 30, 1973-1974, p. 118

DAVIS, BUSTER
  PLAYS:
  Doctor Jazz
  REVIEWS OF INDIVIDUAL PLAYS:
  Doctor Jazz
    Giddins, Gary. "Doctored Jazz." New York Magazine
      8 (10 March 1975): 69
    Guernsey. The Best Plays of 1974-1975, pp. 345-46
    The New York Theatre Critics' Reviews--1975. 36 (17
      April 1975): 294-96; containing: Barnes, Clive, "'Doctor
      Jazz' Opens at Winter Garden" (New York Times, 20
      March 1975). Watt, Douglas, "'Dr. Jazz' Flat, Lola
      Sparkles" ([N.Y.] Daily News, 20 March 1975). Gott-
      fried, Martin, "Poor 'Doctor Jazz'" (New York Post,
      20 March 1975). Sharp, Christopher, "Doctor Jazz"
      (Women's Wear Daily, 21 March 1975). Probst,
      Leonard, "Doctor Jazz" (NBC-TV, 19 March 1975)
    Willis Theatre World. vol. 3, 1974-1975, p. 49

†DAVIS, OSSIE
  PLAYS:
  Alice in Wonder
  Curtain Call Mr. Aldridge, Sir
  Last Dance for Sybil
  Montgomery Footprints, 1956
  Purlie Victorious
  PLAYS PUBLISHED IN ANTHOLOGIES:
  Purlie Victorious, in Allison, et al., Masterpieces of the
      Drama, 3rd ed.; Elkind, 32 Scenes for Acting Practice
      (2 scenes)
  MUSICALS:
  Purlie
  FILM SCRIPTS:
  Cotton Comes to Harlem
  [with Al Freeman] Countdown at Kusini
  TELEVISION SCRIPTS:

School Teacher, 1963 (for East Side/West Side)
CRITICISMS BY DAVIS:
"The English Language Is My Enemy." Negro History Bulletin 30 (April 1967): 18
"Flight from Broadway." Negro Digest 15 (April 1966): 14-19
"The Power of Black Movies." Freedomways 14 (Third Quarter 1974): 230-232
CRITICISMS OF DAVIS:
Chernin, Donna. "Ruby Dee with Ossie Davis Is Poetry in Motion." (Cleveland, O.) Plain Dealer, 29 October 1975, in Newsbank--Performing Arts. September-October 1975, 71-B 13
Cook and Henderson. The Militant Black Writer, p. 80, 84
Hall, Frederick Douglass. "The Black Theatre in New York. From 1960-1969." Ed.D. Columbia University, 1973, Part II
Mitchell, Louis D. "Ossie Davis." In Vinson. Contemporary Dramatists, pp. 192-193
Parker. Who's Who in The Theatre, 15th ed., p. 699
Peterson, Maurice. "Being About Ossie Davis." Essence 3 (February 1973): 20
Robbins. American Literary Scholarship: 1972, p. 381
Robinson, Le Roy. "Black Theatre: A Need for the Seventies." Soul Illustrated 2 (February 1970): 57
"Soul Stirrin' Theatre: 'Purlie'." Soul Illustrated 2 (October 1972): 15
Taubman. The Making of the American Theatre, p. 20
Taylor, Clarke. "Fortune Smiles on Broadway's Gypsies." Essence 7 (August 1976): 78
CRITICISMS OF INDIVIDUAL PLAYS:
Alice in Wonder
  Hartnoll. The Oxford Companion to the Theatre, p. 680
  Parker. Who's Who in The Theatre, 15th ed., p. 699
Curtain Call Mr. Aldridge, Sir
  Parker. Who's Who in The Theatre, 15th ed., p. 699
Last Dance for Sybil
  Parker. Who's Who in The Theatre, 15th ed., p. 699
Purlie Victorious
  "Black Theater in Transition, Playwright (Milner) Says." In Nykoruk. Authors in the News. vol. 1, p. 349
  Edmonds, Randolph. "The Blacks in the American Theatre, 1700-1969." The Pan-African Journal 7 (Winter 1974): 306
  Engel. The Critics, pp. 28, 247, 296
  Garland, Phyl. "The Prize Winners." Ebony 25 (July 1970): 29, 32, 34
  Gibbs, Vernon. "Melba Moore in Touch with the Good Things." Essence 6 (November 1976): 42
  Hartnoll. The Oxford Companion to the Theatre, p. 680
  Hay, Samuel A. "African-American Drama, 1950-1970." Negro History Bulletin 36 (January 1973): 6

Keller, Joseph. "Black Writing and the White Critic."
Negro American Literature Forum 3 (Winter 1970): 107
Littlejohn. Black on White, p. 72
Oliver, Edith. "Report from 137th Street." In Theatre
5: The American Theatre, 1971-1972, p. 132
Taubman. The Making of the American Theatre, p. 335
CRITICISMS OF INDIVIDUAL MUSICALS:
Purlie
"Black Theatre: A Bid for Cultural Identity." Black
Enterprise 2 (September 1971): 30
Geisinger. Plays, Players, & Playwrights, p. 742
McGraw-Hill Encyclopedia of World Drama. vol. 3,
p. 285
Murphy, Frederick D. "Melba Moore's Mystical, Magical
Music." Encore 6 (7 February 1977): 32-33
Taylor, Clarke. "In the Soul of Theatre." Essence 5
(April 1975): 48
Tedesco, John L. "The White Image as Second 'Persona'
in Black Drama, 1955-1970." Ph.D. Dissertation, Uni-
versity of Iowa, 1974
CRITICISMS OF INDIVIDUAL FILM SCRIPTS:
Cotton Comes to Harlem
"Ossie Davis Quits 'Cotton' Sequel; Mark Warren Takes
Over." Jet (3 February 1972): 60
Countdown at Kusini
Peterson, Maurice. "On the Aisle: Part II: Deltas Go
Hollywood." Essence 6 (May 1975): 30, 32, 77
CRITICISMS OF INDIVIDUAL TELEVISION SCRIPTS:
School Teacher
Parker. Who's Who in The Theatre, 15th ed., p. 699
REVIEWS OF INDIVIDUAL PLAYS:
Purlie Victorious
Chernin, Donna. "Ruby Dee with Ossie Davis Is Poetry
in Motion." (Cleveland, O.) Plain Dealer, 29 October
1975, in Newsbank--Performing Arts. September-
October 1975, 71-B 13
Davis, Curt. "Isabel Is a Belly Laugh." Encore 6 (6
June 1977): 32
Peterson, Maurice. "Rising Stars." Essence 7 (Decem-
ber 1976): 86
Taubman, Howard. The Making of the American Theatre,
p. 335
_____. "Ossie Davis Stars in His Play at Cort--
'Purlie Victorious'." In Beckerman and Siegman. On
Stage: Selected Theatre Reviews from the New York
Times 1920-1970, pp. 433-35
REVIEWS OF INDIVIDUAL MUSICALS:
Purlie
Dagnal, Cynthia. "Melba Moore's Cinderelle Life."
Chicago (Ill.) Tribune, 17 February 1977, in Newsbank--
Performing Arts. January-February 1977, 6: B 2,
B 3

Davis, Curt. "Ken Page Is Doing Nicely--Nicely, Thanks."
Encore 6 (7 February 1977): 35
Erdman, Richard. "'Purlie' Mostly Fun at Bonfils'
Theatre." (Denver, Colo.) Rocky Mountain News, 10
January 1976, in Newsbank--Performing Arts. January-
February 1976, 11: E 8
Hurst, John V. "'Purlie': Prolonged But Pleasant."
Sacramento (Calif.) Bee, 30 May 1976, in Newsbank--
Performing Arts. May-June 1976, 40: B 13
Los Angeles Magazine 20 (August 1975): 142+
Mills, James. "Bonfils' Satire 'Purlie' No Pearl with
Its Dated Material." Denver (Colo.) Post, 9 January
1976, in Newsbank--Performing Arts. January-February
1976, 11: E 7
Neville, John. "Theater 3 'Purlie' Is a Joy." Dallas
(Tex.) Morning News, 19 April 1975, in Newsbank--
Performing Arts. March-April 1975, 26: G 8
"'Purlie': Spirited Good Fun." Washington (D.C.) Post,
5 June 1975, in Newsbank--Performing Arts. May-
June 1975, 38: F 10
Russell, Candice. "Patti Jo Returns in 'Purlie' Role;
'Won't Let Up'." Miami (Fla.) Herald, 6 April 1975,
in Newsbank--Performing Arts. March-April 1975,
27: A 9, 10
"Soul Stirrin' Theatre: 'Purlie'." Soul Illustrated 2
(October 1972): 14-15
REVIEWS OF INDIVIDUAL FILM SCRIPTS:
Cotton Comes to Harlem
Farber, Stephen. "Cotton Comes to Harlem." Hudson
Review 23 (Winter 1970-1971): 692-696
Countdown at Kusini
Baird, Keith E. "A Movie Review: 'Countdown at
Kusini'." Freedomways 16 (Fourth Quarter, 1976):
251-52
Ms. 4 (June 1976): 45
Peterson, Maurice. "On the Aisle." Essence 7 (July
1976): 7
Purlie (Film Version)
Peterson, Maurice. "Movies: Willie Dynamite, Blazing
Saddles and Others." Essence 5 (May 1974): 16
AWARDS:
Bonin. Major Themes in Prize-Winning American Drama,
p. 176
Emmy Award, for Role in Teacher, Teacher, 1969
Frederick Douglass Award of the New York Urban League

†DAVIDSON, NORBERT R. JR. (b. 1940)
PLAYS:
Contraband, 1974
El Hajj Malik: The Dramatic Life and Death of Malcolm X
CRITICISMS OF DAVIDSON:
Garnett, Bernard. "Black Drama Finds New Audience."

Race Relations Reporter 3 (7 February 1972): 5
Xeroxed Abstracts: Stage II
CRITICISMS OF INDIVIDUAL PLAYS:
Contraband
    Taylor, Clarke. "In the Soul of Theatre." Essence 5
        (April 1975): 49
El Hajj Malik
    Brukenfeld, Dick. "Off-Off-Broadway." In Theatre 4:
        The American Theatre, 1970-1971, p. 48
        _____. "Off-Off Broadway: Profile Rising." In
        Theatre 5: The American Theatre, 1971-1972, p. 56
    Hay, Samuel A. "African-American Drama, 1950-1970."
        Negro History Bulletin 36 (January 1973): 8
    Hughes, Catharine. "Of Harlem and Verona." America
        125 (18 December 1971): 534-35
    Riley, Clayton. "Black Theatre." In Theatre 5: The
        American Theatre, 1971-1972, p. 62
    Simon. Uneasy Stages, pp. 358, 362
REVIEWS OF INDIVIDUAL PLAYS:
Contraband
    Cuthbert, David. "Dashiki, 'Contraband'." (New Orleans,
        La.) Times-Picayune, 2 February 1975, in Newsbank--
        Performing Arts. January-February 1975, 13: D 12
El Hajj Malik
    Argetsinger, Gerald S. "Theatre in Review." Educational
        Theatre Journal 26 (October 1974): 399-400
    Clurman, Harold. "Theatre." Nation 213 (20 December
        1971): 669-70
    Dodds, Richard. "Dashiki '76 Finale." (New Orleans,
        La.) Times-Picayune, 8 January 1977, in Newsbank--
        Performing Arts. January-February 1977, 11: E 11
    Garnett, Richard. "Black Drama Finds New Audience."
        Race Relations Reporter 3 (7 February 1972): 4-6
    Hughes, Catharine. "Off Harlem and Verona." America
        125 (18 December 1971): 534
    Kupa, Kushauri. "Closeup: The New York Scene--Black
        Theatre in New York, 1970-1971." Black Theatre
        no. 6 (1972): pp. 38-39
    Oliver, Edith. "Off Broadway: Joan of Washington
        Square." New Yorker 47 (11 December 1971): 102
    Smith, Marian. "Black Theater Week Reviews Basic Aim:
        Reflect Community." Chicago (Ill.) Sun-Times, 23
        May 1976, in Newsbank--Performing Arts. May-June
        1976, 41: G 6

DEAN, PEYTON
    MUSICALS:
        [with Dorothy Silver] Hamlet Jones (based on an original
           play Ham by Langston Hughes and retitled from Little
           Ham)
    REVIEWS OF INDIVIDUAL MUSICALS:
    Hamlet Jones

"Hamlet Jones." (Cleveland, O.) Call and Post, 27 September 1975, in Newsbank--Performing Arts. September-October 1975, 66: D 11

†DEAN, PHILLIP HAYES
  PLAYS:
    American Night Cry: A Trilogy
    Every Night When the Sun Goes Down
    Freeman
    Minstrel Boy (one act)
    The Owl Killer
    Paul Robeson
    Relationships
    The Sty of the Blind Pig
    Thunder in the Index
  TELEVISION SCRIPTS:
    Freeman (based on play)
  CRITICISMS OF DEAN:
    Ogunbiyi, Yemi. "New Black Playwrights in America, 1960-1975." Ph.D. Dissertation, New York University, 1976, Chap. 5
  CRITICISMS OF INDIVIDUAL PLAYS:
    Freeman
      Eckstein, George. "Softened Voices in the Black Theater." Dissent 23 (Summer 1976): 307
      Simon. Uneasy Stages, pp. 428, 451-452
    The Owl Killer
      Taylor, Clarke. "In the Soul of Theatre." Essence 5 (April 1975): 71
    The Sty of the Blind Pig
      Current Biography 37 (September 1976): 30
      Geisinger. Plays, Players, & Playwrights, p. 239
      Simon. Uneasy Stages, pp. 358, 361
      Stasio, Marilyn. "Off-Broadway." In Theatre 5: The American Theatre, 1971-1972, pp. 38-39, 41
      Weales, Gerald. "Birthday Mutterings." Modern Theatre and Drama 19 (December 1976): 420-21
  REVIEWS OF INDIVIDUAL PLAYS:
    American Night Cry: A Trilogy
      Willis' Theatre World. vol. 30, 1973-1974, p. 96
    Every Night When the Sun Goes Down
      Clurman, Harold. "Theatre." Nation 222 (6 March 1976): 282-3
      Gottfried, Martin. "Play's Problem: Too Many Ideas." New York Post, 16 February 1976, in Newsbank--Performing Arts. January-February 1976, 13: D 2
      New York Theatre Critics' Reviews--1976. 37 (1 March 1976), 338-340; containing: Barnes, Clive, "The Stage: 'Every Night'" (New York Times, 16 February 1976). Watt, Douglas, "Symbol Banging" ([N.Y.] Daily News, 16 February 1976). Gottfried, Martin, "Play's Problem: Too Many Ideas" (New York Post, 16 February

1976). Sharp, Christopher, "Every Night When the Sun Goes Down" (Women's Wear Daily, 17 February 1976). Beaufort, John, Christian Science Monitor, 23 February 1976

Oliver, Edith. "Theatre: Off Broadway." New Yorker 52 (1 March 1976): 77-79

Willis' Theatre World. vol. 32, 1975-1976, p. 97

Freeman

Davis, Curt. "Bill Cobbs: The Death of a Salesman, The Birth of an Artist." Encore 6 (17 January 1977): 33-34

Kroll, Jack. "Hopes, Dreams, Fantasies." Newsweek 81 (19 February 1973): 75

Oliver, Edith. "The Theatre: Off Broadway." New Yorker 48 (10 February 1973): 75

The Sty of the Blind Pig

Blum and Willis, eds. A Pictorial History of the American Theatre: 1860-1976, p. 410

Clurman, Harold. "Theatre." Nation 213 (20 December 1971): 668

Crowther, Hal. "Triumphant 'Sty' a Fresh Start." Buffalo (N.Y.) Evening News, 25 March 1975, in Newsbank--Performing Arts. March-April 1977, 25: A 13

Cuthbert, David. "Dashiki 'Blind Pig' Eerie, Effective." (New Orleans, La.) Times-Picayune, 16 July 1975, in Newsbank--Performing Arts. July-August 1975, 55: D - 1

Kalem, T. E. "Consecration." Time 98 (6 December 1971): 81

Kroll, Jack. "Between Negro and Black." Newsweek 78 (6 December 1971): 121-22

Oliver, Edith. "Off Broadway." New Yorker 47 (4 December 1971): 131

Steele, Mike. "'Sty of the Blind Pig' Presented by Mixed Blood Theatre Company." Minneapolis (Mn.) Tribune, 5 April 1977, in Newsbank--Performing Arts. March-April 1977, 25: A 12

REVIEWS OF INDIVIDUAL TELEVISION SCRIPTS:

Freeman

O'Connor, John J. "TV: Venturesome 'Visions'." New York Times, 6 October 1977, C:26

†DE ANDA, PETER

PLAYS:

Sweetbread

DEE, RUBY (b. October 27, 1923)

TELEVISION SCRIPTS:

Tomorrow Is Ours (CBS), children's telescript

CRITICISMS ON DEE:

Atkinson and Hirschfeld. The Lively Years 1920-1973, p. 261

Chernon, Donna. "Ruby Dee with Ossie Davis Is Poetry in
Motion." (Cleveland, O.) Plain Dealer, 29 October 1975,
in Newsbank--Performing Arts. September-October 1975,
71 - B 13
Parker. Who's Who in The Theatre, 15th ed., pp. 701-02
Simon. Uneasy Stages, pp. 263-64

DE JOUGH, JAMES
    PLAYS:
      [with Charles Cleveland] Hail, Hail The Gangs

DENNIS, DORIS L.
    PLAYS:
      Outcast
    CRITICISMS OF INDIVIDUAL PLAYS:
      Outcast
        Sandle. The Negro in the American Educational Theatre,
          p. 156

†DENT, THOMAS C. (Kush)
    CRITICISMS BY DENT:
      "Black Theater in the South: Report and Reflections."
        Freedomways 14 (Third Quarter 1974): 247-54

DE VEAUX, ALEX
    TELEVISION SCRIPTS:
      Circles
      The Tapestry
    CRITICISMS OF DE VEAUX:
      Moore, Honor. "Theater Will Never be the Same." Ms. 6
        (December 1977): 38

DEVORE, JESSE
    TELEVISION SCRIPTS:
      [with Jo Jackson] Movin' On Up, (Series)

DE WINAT, HAL
    PLAYS:
      Raisin' Hell in the Son, 1962

†DICKERSON, GLENDA
    MUSICALS:
      Jesus Christ, Lawd Today
      [with Mike Malone] Owen's Song: A Tribute to Owen Dodson
    CRITICISMS OF DICKERSON:
      "Sara Webster Fabio Presents a Tribute to 'Owen's Song'."
        Black World 24 (July 1975): 77-96
    CRITICISMS OF INDIVIDUAL MUSICALS:
      Jesus Christ, Lawd Today
        "Black Theatre: A Bid for Cultural Identity." Black
          Enterprise 2 (September 1971): 33, 34
      Owen's Song

Fabio, Sarah Webster. "A Tribute to 'Owen's Song'."
Black World 24 (April 1975): 76-87
Miller, Jeanne-Marie A. "Annual Roundup: Black Theater
in America--Washington, D.C." Black World 24 (April
1975): 37
REVIEWS OF INDIVIDUAL MUSICALS:
Jesus Christ, Lawd Today
"'Jesus Christ, Lawd Today'." Washington (D.C.) Star,
11 June 1976, in Newsbank--Performing Arts. May-
June 1976, 40: B 3
Trescott, Jacqueline. "A Revival of 'Jesus Christ--Lawd
Today'." Washington (D.C.) Post, 12 June 1976, in
Newsbank--Performing Arts. May-June 1976, 40: B 4

†DODSON, OWEN (b. November 28, 1914)
PLAYS:
The Amistad
Divine Comedy
The Garden of Time, 1939
MUSICALS:
[with Jack Landron] Bayou Legend
[with Mark Fax] Till Victory Is Won, an opera
CRITICISM OF DODSON:
Fabio, Sarah Webster. "A Tribute to 'Owen's Song'." Black
World 24 (July 1975): 76-87
Houghton. Advance from Broadway, p. 102
Sandle. The Negro in the American Educational Theatre, p.
19
"Sara Fabio Webster Presents: A Tribute to 'Owen's Song'."
Black World 24 (July 1975): X 87
Xeroxed Abstracts: Stage I, no. 1, no. 2, no. 3
CRITICISMS OF INDIVIDUAL PLAYS:
The Amistad
Hartnoll. The Oxford Companion to the Theatre, p. 679
Sandle. The Negro in the American Educational Theatre,
p. 43, 45
Divine Comedy
Hartnoll. The Oxford Companion to the Theatre, p. 679
Hatch, James. "Speak to Me in Those Old Words, You
Know, Those La-La Words, Those Tung-Tung Sounds."
Yale/Theatre 8 (Fall 1976): 33
Sandle. The Negro in the American Educational Theatre,
p. 19
The Garden of Time
Hartnoll. The Oxford Companion to the Theatre, p. 679
Sandle. The Negro in the American Educational Theatre,
p. 19
REVIEWS OF INDIVIDUAL MUSICALS:
Bayou Legend
Willis' Theatre World. vol. 31, 1974-1975, p. 91
Till Victory Is Won
"Opera Named from Medgar Evans Words Praised." Jet
(21 May 1970): 54-55

DORR, DONALD
    MUSICALS:
        [with Ulysses Kay] Jubilee (musical adaptation of Margaret
            Walker's novel)
    REVIEWS OF MUSICALS:
        "Opera--South's 'Jubilee' Played Before Sell-Out Audience."
            The Afro-American (Baltimore, Md.), 30 November-4 De-
            cember 1976, p. 6

†DU BOIS, SHIRLEY GRAHAM (Shirley Lola Graham) (b. November
    11, 1907-1977)
    PLAYS:
        Little Black Sambo and The Swing Mikado (created by the
            Negro Unit of the Chicago Federal Theatre while she was
            supervisor)
    MUSICALS:
        Tom Tom (first written as a musical then later as an opera)
    CRITICISMS OF DU BOIS:
        Edelin, Ramona. "Shirley Graham Du Bois." First World
            1 (May/June 1977): 36-38
        Houghton. Advance from Broadway, p. 102
        Peterson, Bernard L. Jr. "Shirley Graham Du Bois: Com-
            poser and Playwright." Crisis 84 (May 1977): 177-79
            [biography of Shirley G. Du Bois and a listing of her
            plays: Dust to Earth, I Gotta Home, It's Morning, Track
            Thirteen, Elijah's Ravens; and musical: Tom Tom]
        "Shirley Graham Du Bois 1907-1977: Biographer, Playwright-
            Composer, Stage Director." The Afro-American: Afro
            Magazine (Baltimore, Md.), 12-16 April 1977, p. 14
    CRITICISMS OF INDIVIDUAL MUSICALS:
        Tom Tom
            Hatch, James. "Speak to Me in Those Old Words, You
                Know, Those La-La Words, Those Tung-Tung Sounds."
                Yale/Theatre 8 (Fall 1976): 27
            "The Words of Regina M. Andrews." In Mitchell. Voices
                of the Black Theatre, p. 72

†DU BOIS, W. E. B. (February 23, 1868-August 27, 1963)
    PLAYS:
        Haiti
        The Star of Ethiopia
    COLLECTIONS:
        An ABC of Color: Selections from over a Half Century of
            the Writing of W. E. B. Du Bois. Berlin: Seven Seas,
            1963; Bell Press, 1964
    CRITICISMS BY DU BOIS:
        "Du Bois' Review of 'Nigger Heaven'." In Davis and Peplow.
            The New Negro Renaissance, pp. 193-194
    CRITICISMS OF DU BOIS:
        Chrisman, Robert. "Shirley Graham Du Bois Dies in China."
            Black Scholar 8 (May 1977): 12
        Contee, Clarence G. "A Crucial Friendship Begins; Du Bois
            and Nkrumah: 1935-1945." Crisis 78 (August 1971):

181-185
Green, Dan S. "Resurrection of the Writing of an American
Scholar." Crisis 79 (November 1972): 311-13
Hatch, James. "Speak to Me in Those Old Words, You
Know, Those La-La Words, Those Tung-Tung Sounds."
Yale/Theatre 8 (Fall 1976): 28
Henderson, Lenneal J., Jr. "W. E. B. Du Bois: Black
Scholar and Prophet." Black Scholar 1 (January-February
1970): 48-57
Nesbitt, Geo. "W. E. B. Du Bois: An Apostle of Black-
ness." Crisis 79 (June-July 1972): 194-97
Rampersad, Arnold. The Art and Imagination of W. E. B.
Du Bois. Cambridge, Mass.: Harvard University Press,
1977
Shipley, W. Maurice. "Reaching Back to Glory: Compara-
tive Sketches in the 'Dreams' of W. B. Yeats and W. E. B.
Du Bois." Crisis 83 (January 1976): 195-201
Turner, Darwin T. "Afro-American Literary Critics."
Black World 19 (July 1970): 54
————. "W. E. B. Du Bois and the Theory of a Black Aes-
thetic." Studies in Literary Imagination 8 (Fall 1974):
1-21
"The Words of Regina M. Andrews." In Mitchell. Voices
of the Black Theatre, pp. 68-71, 73, 78-80
CRITICISMS OF INDIVIDUAL PLAYS:
Haiti
    Edmonds, Randolph. "The Blacks in the American
    Theatre, 1700-1969." The Pan-African Journal 7
    (Winter 1974): 311
    Goldstein. The Political Stage, pp. 254, 261
The Star of Ethiopia
    Hartnoll. The Oxford Companion to the Theatre, p. 678
    Hatch, James. "Speak to Me in Those Old Words, You
    Know, Those La-La Words, Those Tung-Tung Sounds
    (Some African Influences on the Afro American Theatre)."
    Yale/Theatre 8 (Fall 1976): 26
    Turner, Darwin. "W. E. B. Du Bois and the Theory of a
    Black Aesthetic." Studies in Literary Imagination 7
    (Fall 1974): 6

†DUMAS, AARON
    PLAYS:
    Encounter: 3 Acts in a Restaurant, 1969
    Hobis

†DUNBAR, ALICE
    CRITICISMS OF DUNBAR:
    Jackson. The Waiting Years, p. 201

†DUNBAR, PAUL LAURENCE (June 27, 1872-February 9, 1906)
    MUSICALS:
    [with Will Marion Cook] Clorindy--or, The Origin of the

Cake-Walk, 1898
[with Will Marion Cook] Jes Lak White Folks, 1900
CRITICISMS OF DUNBAR:
  Edmonds, Randolph. "The Blacks in the American Theatre,
    1700-1969." The Pan-African Journal 7 (Winter 1974):
    302
  Mitchell. Voices of the Black Theatre, pp. 23-24
  Pawley, Thomas D. "Dunbar as Playwright." Black World
    26 (April 1975): 70-79 [11 works are discussed or listed
    in this article]
CRITICISMS OF INDIVIDUAL MUSICALS:
  Clorindy--The Origin of the Cake-Walk
    Edmonds, Randolph. "The Blacks in the American Theatre,
      1700-1969." The Pan-African Journal 7 (Winter 1974):
      314
  In Dahomey
    Hatch, James. "Speak to Me in Those Old Words, You
      Know, Those La-La Words, Those Tung-Tung Sounds."
      Yale/Theatre 8 (Fall 1976): 26
  Jes Lak White Folks
    Edmonds, Randolph. "The Blacks in the American Theatre,
      1700-1969." The Pan-African Journal 7 (Winter 1974):
      314

DUNCAN, JOHN, JR.
  PLAYS:
    A Crimson Fountain for Harlingscourt. N.Y.: Ashley Books
      Inc., 1976

†DUNCAN, THELMA
  CRITICISMS OF INDIVIDUAL MUSICALS:
    Death Dance
      Hatch, James. "Speak to Me in Those Old Words, You
        Know, Those La-La Words, Those Tung-Tung Sounds."
        Yale/Theatre 8 (Fall 1976): 27

DUNDEE, CALVA
  PLAYS:
    Running Through Paradise

DURHAM, ALICE MARIE
  PLAYS:
    Golden Gloves
  CRITICISMS OF INDIVIDUAL PLAYS:
    Golden Gloves
      Sandle. The Negro in the American Educational Theatre,
        pp. 87, 97

†DURRAH, JAMES W.
  MUSICALS:
    [with Victor Willis and Donna Brown] How Do You Spell
      Watergait?

DYSON, DIERDRA
PLAYS:
Black Ritual--A Definition
CRITICISMS BY DYSON:
"Annual Round-up: Black Theater in America--Chicago. "
Black World 25 (April 1976): 71-74

†EASTON, WILLIAM E.
PLAYS:
Christophe: A Tragedy in Praise of Imperial Haiti. Los
Angeles: Grafton, 1911
Dessalines. Galveston, Tex. J. W. Burson--Company
Pub., 1893
CRITICISMS OF EASTON:
Fehrenbach, Robert J. "William Edgar Easton's Dessalines:
A Nineteenth Century Drama of Black Pride." CLA
Journal 19 (September 1975): 75-89
CRITICISMS OF INDIVIDUAL PLAYS:
Christophe
Fehrenbach, Robert J. "William Edgar Easton's Dessa-
lines: A Nineteenth Century Drama of Black Pride."
CLA Journal 19 (September 1975): 77
Dessalines
Fehrenbach, Robert J. "William Edgar Easton's Dessa-
lines: A Nineteenth Century Drama of Black Pride."
CLA Journal 19 (September 1975): 75-89
Hatch, James. "Speak to Me in Those Old Words, You
Know, Those La-La Words, Those Tung-Tung Sounds. "
Yale/Theatre 8 (Fall 1976): 26

EBONY TALENT
MUSICALS:
Second Coming Last Chance, (collective effort by students of
Ebony Talent)

EDMONDS, IRENE
PLAYS:
The Lost Gem, a children's play
CRITICISMS OF INDIVIDUAL PLAYS:
The Lost Gem
Sandle. The Negro in the American Educational Theatre,
p. 71

†EDMONDS, RANDOLPH
PLAYS:
Breeders
Earth and Stars
Gangsters Over Harlem
In the Land of Cotton
Nat Turner. N.Y.: Baker, 1934; 1962
Prometheus and the Atom
Shades and Shadows
Yellow Death

PLAYS PUBLISHED IN ANTHOLOGIES:
    Nat Turner, in Davis and Peplow. The New Negro Renais-
        sance
CRITICISMS BY EDMONDS:
    "The Blacks in the American Theatre, 1700-1969." The Pan-
        African Journal 7 (Winter 1974): 297-322
CRITICISMS OF EDMONDS:
    Houghton. Advance from Broadway, pp. 157-162
    Sandle. The Negro in the American Educational Theatre,
        pp. 32-34, 40, 42, 44; passim
    Xeroxed Abstracts: Stage II
CRITICISMS OF INDIVIDUAL PLAYS:
    Breeders
        Sandle. The Negro in the American Educational Theatre,
            p. 47
    Earth and Stars
        Sandle. The Negro in the American Educational Theatre,
            p. 69
    Gangsters Over Harlem
        Sandle. The Negro in the American Educational Theatre,
            pp. 69, 85, 110
    In the Land of Cotton
        Hartnoll. The Oxford Companion to the Theatre, p. 678
        Houghton. Advance from Broadway, p. 159
    Nat Turner
        Sandle. The Negro in the American Educational Theatre,
            pp. 62, 69
    Prometheus and the Atom
        Sandle. The Negro in the American Educational Theatre,
            p. 69
    Shades and Shadows
        Sandle. The Negro in the American Educational Theatre,
            p. 107
    Yellow Death
        Sandle. The Negro in the American Educational Theatre,
            p. 39
CRITICISMS OF COLLECTIONS:
    Six Plays for a Negro Theatre. Boston: Baker, 1934
        Davis, Arthur P. From the Dark Tower, p. 12
        Hartnoll. The Oxford Companion to the Theatre, p. 678
        Sandle. The Negro in the American Educational Theatre,
            pp. 18-19

†EL MUHAJIR see JACKSON, M. E.; MARVIN X

†ELDER, LONNE, III
    PLAYS:
        Ceremonies in Dark Old Men
        Charades
    FILM SCRIPTS:
        Part 2, Sounder
    TELEVISION SCRIPTS:
        Camera 3, series

CRITICISMS BY ELDER:
"Comment." Black Creation 4 (Summer 1973): 48
CRITICISMS OF ELDER:
Atkinson and Hirschfeld. The Lively Years 1920-1973, p. 261
Brooks, Mary Ellen. "Reactionary Trends in Recent Black
Drama." Literature and Ideology (Montreal). 10 (1970):
46-48
Duckett, Alfred. "The Birth of a Screenwriter" (Wesley).
Sepia 26 (January 1977): 63
Eckstein, George. "Softened Voices in the Black Theater."
Dissent 23 (Summer 1976): 307
Hall, Frederick Douglass. "The Black Theatre in New York
from 1960-1969." Ed.D. Columbia University 1973,
Part II
Horton and Edwards. Backgrounds of American Literary
Thought. 3rd. ed., p. 588
Parker. Who's Who in The Theatre, 15th ed., p. 747
Taubman. The Making of the American Theatre, p. 261
Turner, Darwin T. "Lonnie Elder III." In Vinson. Con-
temporary Dramatists, pp. 233-34
Wilson, John M. "Making It As a Screenwriter." 1978
Writer's Yearbook no. 49 (Annual--1978): 18
Woodress. American Literary Scholarship: 1973, p. 380
CRITICISMS OF INDIVIDUAL PLAYS:
Ceremonies in Dark Old Men
Ballet, Arthur. "The Theatre of Middle America." In
Theatre 4: The American Theatre, 1970-1971, p. 79
Benston, Kimberly W. "'Cities in Bezique': Adrienne
Kennedy's Expressionistic Vision." CLA Journal 20
(December 1976): 241
"Black Theater Workshop at OU." (Oklahoma City, Okla.)
Black Dispatch, 1 April 1976, in Newsbank--Performing
Arts. March-April 1976, 31: F 14
Brooks, Mary Ellen. "Reactionary Trends in Recent
Black Drama." Literature and Ideology (Montreal).
no. 10 (1970): 47
Current Biography 38 (1977): 417, 419
Engel. The Critics, p. 265
Fenderson, Lewis H. "The New Breed of Black Writers
and Their Jaundiced View of Tradition." CLA Journal
15 (September 1971): 23
Geisinger. Plays, Players, & Playwrights, p. 239
Hay, Samuel A. "African-American Drama, 1950-1970."
Negro History Bulletin 36 (January 1973): 7
Hill, Edward Steven. "A Thematic Study of Selected
Plays Produced by the Negro Ensemble Company."
Ph.D. Dissertation, Bowling Green State University,
1975
Houghton. The Exploding Stage, pp. 202, 237
Lee, Dorothy. "Three Black Plays: Alienation and Paths
to Recovery." Modern Theatre and Drama 19 (Decem-
ber 1976): 397-404

Peterson, Maurice. "On the Aisle." Essence 5 (January 1975): 25

Potter, Vilma R. "New Politics, New Mothers." CLA Journal 16 (December 1972): 247-255

Ribowski, Mark. "'Father' of the Black Theater Boom." Sepia 25 (November 1976): 69, 70

Simon. Uneasy Stages, pp. 181, 187-88

Zeisler, Peter. "The East Coast." In Theatre 4: The American Theatre, 1970-1971, p. 62

Charades

Hill, Edward Steven. "A Thematic Study of the Selected Plays Produced by the Negro Ensemble Company." Ph.D. Dissertation, Dowling Green State University, 1975

REVIEWS OF INDIVIDUAL PLAYS:

Ceremonies in Dark Old Men

Barnes, Clive. "Ceremonies in Dark Old Men at the St. Marks." In Beckerman and Siegman. On Stage: Selected Theatre Reviews from the New York Times, 1920-1970, pp. 522-24

Batdorf, Emerson. "Black Play Has Ring of Truth." (Ceremonies in Dark Old Men) Cleveland (O.) Plain Dealer, 20 February 1975, in Newsbank--Performing Arts. January-February 1975, 13: E 1

"Black Theater Workshop at O.U." (Oklahoma City, Okla.) Black Dispatch, 1 April 1976, in Newsbank--Performing Arts. March-April 1976, 31: F 14

Blum and Willis, eds. A Pictorial History of the American Theatre: 1860-1976, p. 402

"Ceremonies in Dark Old Men." (N.Y.) Amsterdam News: Arts and Entertainment, May 14, 1977, D-2

"'Ceremonies' of Laughter with Something Missing." (Chicago, Ill.) Sun-Times, 28 February 1975, in Newsbank--Performing Arts. January-February 1975, 29: C 5

Parker. Who's Who in The Theatre, 15th ed., p. 747

Willis' Theatre World. vol. 31, 1974-1975, p. 216

REVIEWS OF FILM SCRIPTS:

Part 2, Sounder

Maslin, Janet. "Home on the Porch." Newsweek 88 (8 November 1976): 107-08

Roman, Margaret. "Films: 'Part 2, Sounder'." Senior Scholastic 109 (16 December 1976): 23

Thingvall, Joel. "Simple Story of 'Sounder'." Twin Cities Courier (Minneapolis/St. Paul, Mn.) 9 December 1976, p. 2

AWARDS:

Ceremonies in Dark Old Men

Bonin. Major Themes in Prize-Winning American Drama, p. 178

ELIOT, MARGE
FILM SCRIPTS:

You Can't Go Home Again
CRITICISMS OF ELIOT:
Peterson, Maurice. "On the Aisle: Focus on Marge Eliot."
Essence 6 (May 1975): 12

†EMERUWA, L. W.
CRITICISMS BY EMERUWA:
"Annual Roundup: Black Theater in America--Cleveland."
Black World 25 (April 1976): 62-70

†ERROL, JOHN
REVIEWS OF INDIVIDUAL PLAYS:
Moon On a Rainbow Shawl
Parker. Who's Who in The Theatre, 15th ed., p. 1005

†EVANS, DON
PLAYS:
Change of Mind
Matters of Choice
Orrin
Showdown
Sugar Mouth Sam Don't Dance No More (one act)
CRITICISMS OF INDIVIDUAL PLAYS:
Matters of Choice
Taylor, Clarke. "In the Soul of Theatre." Essence 5
(April 1975): 48
Sugar Mouth Sam Don't Dance No More
Woodress. American Literary Scholarship: 1973, pp.
380-381
REVIEWS OF INDIVIDUAL PLAYS:
Matters of Choice
Batdorff, Emerson. "Karamu's 'Choice' is Fresh, Funny
Play." (Cleveland, O.) Plain Dealer, 1 February 1975,
in Newsbank--Performing Arts. January-February 1975,
13: E 1
Van Atta, Jean. "'Matters of Choice', A Timely Drama
at Karamu." Call and Post, (Cincinnati, O.) 8 February
1975, in Newsbank--Performing Arts. January-February
1975, 13: E 6
Woolten, Dick. "Karamu Serves Up Tense Comedy."
Cleveland (O.) Press, 31 January 1975, in Newsbank--
Performing Arts. January-February 1975, 13: E 7
Orrin
Guernsey. The Best Plays of 1974-1975, p. 377
Sugar Mouth Sam Don't Dance No More
Guernsey. The Best Plays of 1974-1975, p. 377
"Kuumba Dancers Perform in Plaza." Chicago Daily De-
fender, 3 August 1977, p. 23
"Two Afro-American Plays Featured at Kuumba." Chicago
Daily Defender, 14 July 1977, p. 18

EVANS, MIKE
    TELEVISION SCRIPTS:
    [with Eric Monte] Good Times
    CRITICISMS OF INDIVIDUAL TELEVISION SCRIPTS:
    Good Times
        Collier, Eugenia. "'Black' Shows for White Viewers."
            Freedomways 14 (Third Quarter 1974): 212-216
        Robinson, Louis. "Bad Times on the 'Good Times' Set."
            Ebony 30 (September 1975): 33-42
    REVIEWS OF INDIVIDUAL TELEVISION SCRIPTS:
    Good Times
        Lucas, Bob. "A 'Salt Pork, and Collard Greens' TV
            Show." Ebony 29 (June 1974): 50-53

EVANS, ZISHAW
    PLAYS:
    Zetta
    REVIEWS OF INDIVIDUAL PLAYS:
    Zetta
        Taki. "'Zetta'--Alive or Dead (or who cares?)." (Chi-
            cago, Ill.) Courier, 6 September 1975, in Newsbank--
            Performing Arts. September-October 1975, 66: G 11,
            12

†FABIO, SARAH WEBSTER
    CRITICISMS BY FABIO:
    "A Tribute to 'Owen's Song'." Black World 24 (July 1975):
        76-87

†FANN, AL
    PLAYS:
    King Heroin
    CRITICISMS OF INDIVIDUAL PLAYS:
    Brukenfeld, Dick. "Off-Off-Broadway." In Theatre 4: The
        American Theatre, 1970-1971, p. 51
    "'King Heroin': Harlem Play on the Destructive Effects of
        Dope Addiction in the Black Community." Ebony 26 (June
        1971): 56-58

†FANN, ERNIE
    PLAYS:
    A Fair and Impartial Verdict
    The First Tuesday in November

FAX, MARK
    MUSICALS:
    [with Owen Dodson] Till Victory Is Won, an opera
    REVIEWS OF INDIVIDUAL MUSICALS:
    "Opera Named from Medgar Evans Words Praised." Jet
        (21 May 1970): 54-55

†FELTON, H. S.
　　PLAYS:
　　　College Blunders, 1931
　　　The Diamond Necklace, 1931

†FERDINAND, VAL　see　SALAAM, KALAMU YA

†FISHER, RUDOLPH
　　PLAYS:
　　　The Conjure Man Dies (based on the novel)
　　CRITICISMS OF INDIVIDUAL PLAYS:
　　　The Conjure Man Dies
　　　　Edmonds, Randolph. "The Blacks in the American
　　　　　Theatre, 1700-1969." The Pan-African Journal 7
　　　　　(Winter 1974): 311
　　　　Goldstein. The Political Stage, p. 259
　　　　Hartnoll. The Oxford Companion to the Theatre, p. 677
　　　　Schmuhl, Robert. "Treating the Harlem Human Condi-
　　　　　tion." Negro History Bulletin 37 (January 1974): 196-97

FORBES, JOHN
　　TELEVISION SCRIPTS:
　　　[with Illunga Adell] Stone and Steel

FORDE, JOHN
　　PLAYS:
　　　The Passing Cloud

FORSYTHE, JOHN
　　PLAYS:
　　　Defiant Island

†FOSTER, ALEX
　　PLAYS:
　　　Community Kitchen
　　REVIEWS OF INDIVIDUAL PLAYS:
　　　Community Kitchen
　　　　Grimes, Nikki. "'Community Kitchen': A Showcase."
　　　　　(N.Y.) Amsterdam News: Arts and Entertainment, 20
　　　　　November 1976, D-8

FOSTER, GREG
　　PLAYS:
　　　Freeze
　　　Mainline Blues
　　REVIEWS OF INDIVIDUAL PLAYS:
　　　Freeze
　　　　Smith, Marian. "Black Theater Week Renews Basic Aim:
　　　　　Reflect Community." Chicago (Ill.) Sun-Times, 23
　　　　　May 1976, in Newsbank--Performing Arts. May-June
　　　　　1976, 41: G 6
　　　　Winer, Linda. "Local Curtains Going Up for 10 Black

Troupes." Chicago Tribune: Arts & Fun, 30 May
1976, 6: 3
Mainline Blues
Smith, Marian. "Black Theatre Week Renews Basic Aim:
Reflect Community." Chicago (Ill.) Sun-Times, 23
May 1976, in Newsbank--Performing Arts. May-June
1976. 41: G 6
Winer, Linda. "Local Curtain Going Up for 10 Black
Troupes." Chicago Tribune: Arts & Fun, 30 May
1976, 6: 3

FOX, WILLIAM PRICE
MUSICALS:
Southern Fried
REVIEWS OF INDIVIDUAL MUSICALS:
Green, Jean G. "T. S. Young to Direct Play." The Afro-
American (Baltimore, Md.), 22-26 March 1977, p. 15

†FRANKLIN, J. E.
PLAYS:
Black Girl. N.Y.: Dramatists Play Service, 1971
[with Micki Grant] The Prodigal Sister
FILM SCRIPTS:
Black Girl (based on play)
CRITICISMS BY FRANKLIN:
Black Girl: From Genesis to Revelation. Washington, D.C.:
Howard University Press, 1976
CRITICISMS OF INDIVIDUAL PLAYS:
Black Girl
"Black Theatre: A Bid for Cultural Identity." Black
Enterprise 2 (September 1971): 33
Brukenfeld, Dick. "Off-Off-Broadway." In Theatre 4:
The American Theatre, 1970-1971, p. 51
Clurman, Harold. "Theatre and Films." Nation 213 (1
November 1971): 445
Lamb, Margaret. "Feminist Criticism." Drama Review
18 (September 1974): 49
Miller, Jeanne-Marie A. "Images of Black Women in
Plays by Black Playwrights." CLA Journal 20 (June
1977): 500-01
"New Breed Producer." The Afro-American (Baltimore,
Md.), 12-16 April 1977, p. 11
Parks, Carole A. "Perspectives: J. E. Franklin, Play-
wright." Black World 21 (April 1972): 49-50
Peterson, Maurice. "Rising Stars." Essence 7 (Decem-
ber 1976): 82
Salaam, Kalamu ya. "Making the Image Real." The
Black Collegian 7 (March-April 1977): 54, 57
The Prodigal Sister
Bailey, Peter. "Annual Round-Up: Black Theatre in
America--New York." Black World 24 (April 1975):
22-23

Engel. The Critics, pp. 27-29
Guernsey. The Best Plays of 1974-1975, pp. 31, 369-70
CRITICISMS OF INDIVIDUAL FILM SCRIPTS:
Black Girl
   Sloan, Margaret. "Film: Keeping the Black Woman in
      Her Place." Ms. 2 (January 1974): 31
REVIEWS OF INDIVIDUAL PLAYS:
Black Girl
   Blum and Willis, eds. A Pictorial History of the Ameri-
      can Theatre: 1860-1976, p. 410
   Garnett, Richard. "Black Drama Finds New Audience."
      Race Relations Reporter 3 (7 February 1972): 4-6
   Kroll, Jack. "Caught in the Web." Newsweek 77 (28
      June 1971): 85
   Kupa, Kushauri. "Closeup: The New York Scene--Black
      Theatre in New York, 1970-1971." Black Theatre no.
      6 (1972): 48-50
   Oliver, Edith. "Off Broadway." New Yorker 47 (26 June
      1971): 76
   Peterson, Maurice. "Being About Ossie Davis." Essence
      3 (February 1973): 20
The Prodigal Sister
   Brukenfeld, Dick. "The Unfortunate Sag." Village Voice
      19 (18 July 1974): 57
   Gill, Brendon. "Off Broadway: The Second Time Around."
      New Yorker 50 (9 December 1974): 69-70
   Simon, John. "Mad, Bad, Sad, and Glad." New York
      Magazine 7 (16 December 1974): 96
   Willis' Theatre World. vol. 31, 1974-1975, p. 75

†FULLER, CHARLES
   PLAYS:
      The Brownsville Raid
      In My Many Names and Days
      In the Deepest Part of Sleep
      The Layout
      The Rise
      The Sunflower Majorette, 1971
   CRITICISMS OF INDIVIDUAL PLAYS:
      In My Many Names and Days
         Riley, Clayton. "Black Theatre." In Theatre 5: The
            American Theatre, 1971-1972, p. 65
      In the Deepest Part of Sleep
         Current Biography 37 (September 1976): 30
         Hay, Samuel A. "African-American Drama, 1950-1970."
            Negro History Bulletin 36 (January 1973): 8
         Willis' Theatre World. vol. 31, 1974-1975, p. 117
      The Layout
         Taylor, Clarke. "In the Soul of Theatre." Essence 5
            (April 1975): 49
   REVIEWS OF INDIVIDUAL PLAYS:
      Brownsville Raid

Clurman, Harold. "Theatre." Nation 223 (25 December 1976): 701-2

Davis, Curt. "Bill Cobbs: The Death of a Salesman, the Birth of an Artist." Encore 6 (17 January 1977): 33-34
_____. "Sound Taps for 'Brownsville Raid'." Encore 6 (3 January 1977): 33-34

Grimes, Nikki. "The Brownsville Raid Saunters into Town." (N.Y.) Amsterdam News: Arts and Entertainment, 1 January 1977, D-7

Kalem, T. E. "Blind Injustice." Time 108 (20 December 1976): 58

New York Theatre Critics' Reviews--1976 37 (31 December 1976): 76-79; containing: Barnes, Clive, "Stage: 'The Brownsville Raid'" (New York Times, 6 December 1976). Watt, Douglas, "An Honorable 'Raid'" ([N.Y.] Daily News, 6 December 1976). Gottfried, Martin, "A Powerful Play in 'Brownsville'" (New York Post, 6 December 1976). Sharp, Christopher, "The Brownsville Raid" (Women's Wear Daily, 6 December 1976). Beaufort, John, "The Brownsville Raid" (Christian Science Monitor, 10 December 1976). Kalem, T. E., "Blind Injustice" (Time, 20 December 1976)

Oliver, Edith. "The Theatre: Off-Broadway." New Yorker 52 (20 December 1976): 84

Peterson, Maurice. "On the Aisle." Essence 7 (March 1977): 8

In the Deepest Part of Sleep

Brukenfeld, Dick. "A Fresh Look at Black Manhood." Village Voice 19 (13 June 1974): 81

Guernsey. The Best Plays of 1974-1975, p. 353

Oliver, Edith. "The Theatre: Off-Broadway." New Yorker 50 (17 June 1974): 84

†FURMAN, ROGER
PLAYS:
The Long Black Block
MUSICALS:
[with Del Robinson] Fat Tuesday
CRITICISMS OF FURMAN:
Xeroxed Abstracts: Stage II
CRITICISMS OF INDIVIDUAL PLAYS:
The Long Black Block
Riley, Clayton. "Black Theatre." In Theatre 5: The American Theatre, 1971-1972, p. 61
REVIEWS OF INDIVIDUAL PLAYS:
The Long Black Block
Davis, Curt. "'The Long Black Block' Alternate Side-of-the-Street Goodness." Encore 6 (18 April 1977): 40
REVIEWS OF INDIVIDUAL MUSICALS:
Fat Tuesday
Bailey, Peter. "Annual Round-up: Black Theater in America--New York." Black World 25 (April 1976): 55-56

†GAINES, J. E. (Sonny Jim)
  PLAYS:
    Don't Let It Go to Your Head, 1970
    Heaven and Hell's Agreement
    Sometimes a Hard Head Makes a Soft Behind, 1972
  CRITICISMS OF INDIVIDUAL PLAYS:
    Don't Let It Go to Your Head
      Eddy, Bill. "4 Directors on Criticism." Drama Review
        18 (September 1974): 24-25
      Harris, Jessica B. "The New Lafayette: 'Nothing Lasts
        Forever'." Black Creation 4 (Summer 1973): 9
      Oliver, Edith. "Report from 137th Street." In Theatre
        5: The American Theatre, 1971-1972, p. 133
    Sometimes a Hard Head Makes a Soft Behind
      Harris, Jessica B. "The New Lafayette: 'Nothing Lasts
        Forever'." Black Creation 4 (Summer 1973): 9
      Oliver, Edith. "Report from 137th Street." In Theatre
        5: The American Theatre, 1971-1972, p. 133
  REVIEWS OF INDIVIDUAL PLAYS:
    Don't Let It Go to Your Head
      Eddy, Bill. "4 Directors on Criticism." The Drama
        Review 18 (September 1974): 25
      Oliver, Edith. "Report from 137th Street." In Theatre
        5: The American Theatre, 1971-1972, p. 133
    Heaven and Hell's Agreement
      Oliver, Edith. "Off Broadway: Three to Get Ready."
        New Yorker 50 (22 April 1974): 103-04
      Willis' Theatre World. vol. 30, 1973-1974, p. 118

†GARRETT, JIMMY
  PLAYS:
    We Own the Night
  CRITICISMS OF GARRETT:
    Robinson, Le Roy. "Black Theatre: A Need for the Seven-
      ties." Soul Illustrated 2 (February 1970): 57
    Taylor, Willene Pulliam. "The Reversal of the Tainted
      Blood Theme in the Works of Writers of the Black Revo-
      lutionary Theatre." Negro American Literature Forum
      10 (Fall 1976): 84-90, 91
  CRITICISMS OF INDIVIDUAL PLAYS:
    We Own the Night
      Billingsley, Ronald G. "The Burden of the Hero in
        Modern Afro-American Fiction." Black World 25
        (December 1975): 72
      Brown, Lloyd W. "The Cultural Revolution in Black
        Theatre." Negro American Literature Forum 8 (Spring
        1974): 163-164
      Hay, Samuel A. "African-American Drama, 1950-1970."
        Negro History Bulletin 36 (January 1973): 8
      Houghton. The Exploding Stage, pp. 201-202
      Keller, Joseph. "Black Writing and the White Critic."
        Negro American Literature Forum 3 (Winter 1970): 107

Meserve, Walter J. "Black Drama." In Robbins. American Literary Scholarship--1970, p. 344

Miller, Jeanne-Marie A. "Images of Black Women in Plays by Black Playwrights." CLA Journal 20 (June 1977): 505

Potter, Vilma R. "New Politics, New Mothers." CLA Journal 16 (December 1972): 247-255

Taylor, Willene Pulliam. "The Reversal of the Tainted Blood Theme in the Works of Writers of the Black Revolutionary Theatre." Negro American Literature Forum 10 (Fall 1976): 89-90, 91

Willis, Robert. "Anger and Contemporary Black Theatre." Negro American Literature Forum 8 (Summer 1974): 215

GAY, CEDRIC
    MUSICALS:
    Survival
    REVIEWS OF INDIVIDUAL MUSICALS:
    Survival
        "Gay's 'Survival' Staged at Kenwood High." Chicago Daily Defender, 22 June 1977, p. 24
        "Jean Pace Checks Out Gay's 'Survival' at AAP." Chicago Daily Defender, 9 June 1977, p. 17

GAYE, IRWIN
    MUSICALS:
    The Spirit of Christmas

GELBER, JACK
    PLAYS:
    Rehearsal
    REVIEWS OF INDIVIDUAL PLAYS:
    Rehearsal
        Austin, William. "Controlled Chaos Dramatized." (N.Y.) Amsterdam News: Arts and Entertainment, 13 November 1976, D-9

GERIMA, HAILE
    PLAYS:
    Bush Mama
    FILM SCRIPTS:
    Bush Mama (from the play)
    CRITICISMS OF INDIVIDUAL FILM SCRIPTS:
    Bush Mama
        "Haile Gerima Discusses 'Bush Mama'." Tricontinental Film Center: 1977-78, p. 44
        "Independence Day." Tricontinental Film Center: 1977-78, p. 45
        Tricontinental Film Center: 1977-78 Catalog. Berkeley, Ca.: Tricontinental Film Center, 1977, p. 44
    REVIEWS OF INDIVIDUAL PLAYS:

Bush Mama
"Ethiopian Directs." (N.Y.) Amsterdam News: Arts and
Entertainment, 13 November 1976, D-15

GILLIAM, TED
PLAYS:
What You Say?; or, How Christopher Columbus Discovered
Ray Charles, 1970 (based on Flip Wilson's "Columbus"
story)

GIOFFRE, MARISSA
PLAYS:
Bread and Roses
REVIEWS OF INDIVIDUAL PLAYS:
Bread and Roses
"Riverside Has 'Bread and Roses'." (N.Y.) Amsterdam
News: Arts and Entertainment, 27 November 1976,
D-4

GOOD, JACK
MUSICALS:
Santa Fe Satan (musical interpretation of Othello)

†GORDONE, CHARLES
PLAYS:
Gordone Is a Mutha
The Last Chord
No Place to be Somebody
PLAYS PUBLISHED IN ANTHOLOGIES:
No Place for Tea, in Ritter, Masterpieces of the Theatre.
CRITICISMS OF GORDONE:
"Author of Play with Jet in Role Wins Pulitzer." Jet (21
May 1970): 59
Bonin, Jane F. Prize-Winning American Drama: A Bib-
liography and Descriptive Guide. Metuchen, N.J.: Scare-
crow Press, 1973, pp. 197-198
Clayborne, Jon L. "Modern Black Drama and the Gay
Image." College English 36 (November 1974): 383
Garland, P. "The Prize Winner: C. Gordonne, M. Moore,
and C. Little." Ebony 25 (July 1970): 29-32
Geisinger. Plays, Players, & Playwrights, p. 620
Hall, Frederick Douglass. "The Black Theatre in New
York from 1960-1969." Ed.D. Columbia University,
1973, Part II
Hughes, Catharine. "Bicentennial Reflections." America
135 (24 July 1976): 32
Kerr, Walter. "Not Since Edward Albee." In Weiss.
Drama in the Modern World, pp. 606-608
CRITICISMS OF INDIVIDUAL PLAYS:
Gordone Is a Mutha
Garland, Phyl. "The Prize-Winners." Ebony 25 (July
1970): 37

The Last Chord
  Wilkins, Patricia. "Reflections on One Black Experience."
    (N.Y.) Amsterdam News: Arts and Entertainment, 28
    August 1976, D-14
No Place to be Somebody
  Atkinson and Hirschfeld. The Lively Years 1920-1973,
    pp. 286-89
  "Black Theatre: A Bid for Cultural Identity." Black
    Enterprise 2 (September 1971): 30-31
  Bonin, Jane F. Major Themes in Prize-Winning Ameri-
    can Drama, pp. 52, 54-55, 74-76, 178
    _____. Prize-Winning American Drama: A Bibliog-
    raphy and Descriptive Guide. Metuchen, N.J.: Scare-
    crow Press, 1973, pp. 196-197
  Cameron and Hoffman. A Guide to Theatre Study, p. 205
  Dace and Dace. The Theatre Student: Modern Theatre
    and Drama, p. 55
  Fenderson, Lewis H. "The New Breed of Black Writers
    and Their Jaundiced View of Tradition." CLA Journal
    15 (September 1971): 23
  Garland, Phyl. "The Prize Winners." Ebony 25 (July
    1970): 30, 37
  Geisinger. Plays, Players, & Playwrights, pp. 620-621
  Gussow, Mel. "Theatre East." In Theatre 5: The
    American Theatre, 1971-1972, pp. 72, 73
  Hatch, James. "Speak to Me in Those Old Words, You
    Know, Those La-La Words, Those Tung-Tung Sounds."
    Yale/Theatre 8 (Fall 1976): 33
  Hay, Samuel A. "African-American Drama, 1950-1970."
    Negro History Bulletin 36 (January 1973): 7
  Hirsch, Foster. "No Place to be Somebody." In Vinson.
    Contemporary Dramatists, pp. 299-300
  Houghton. The Exploding Stage, p. 202
  Lee, Dorothy. "Three Black Plays: Alienation and Paths
    to Recovery." Modern Theatre and Drama 19 (Decem-
    ber 1976): 397-404
  Simon. Uneasy Stages, pp. 200, 203-05
  Taylor, Clarke. "In the Soul of Theatre." Essence 5
    (April 1975): 48
REVIEWS OF INDIVIDUAL PLAYS:
  No Place to be Somebody
    Cuthbert, David. "Violent 'Comedy' at Dashiki." (New
      Orleans, La.) Times-Picayune, 18 September 1975, in
      Newsbank--Performing Arts. September-October 1975,
      69: C 4
    Gottfried, M. "The New Ethnic Theater." New York
      Post, 4 October 1975, in Newsbank--Performing Arts.
      September-October 1975, 68: B 4
    Hewes, Henry. "Black Hopes." Saturday Review 53
      (14 February 1970): 30
    Thomas, Barbara. "Opening Night Troubled." Atlanta
      (Ga.) Journal, 28 October 1975, in Newsbank--Per-
      forming Arts. September-October 1975, 69: C 3

Trescott, Jacqueline. "Robert Guillame: The Leading
Guy." Washington (D.C.) Post, 6 May 1976, in News-
bank--Performing Arts. May-June 1976, 40: D 5-6
Willis' Theatre World. vol. 30, 1973-1974, pp. 214, 217

†GOSS, CLAY
PLAYS:
Home Cookin': Five Plays. Washington, D.C.: Howard
University Press, 1974. (Andrew, Home Cookin', Mars:
Monument to the Last Black Eunuch, on Being Hit, and
Our Sides)
Three Dishes: On Being Hit, Home Cookin', and Spaces in
Time
CRITICISMS OF GOSS:
Stasio, Marilyn. "Off-Broadway." In Theatre 5: The
American Theatre, 1971-1972, p. 33
CRITICISMS OF INDIVIDUAL PLAYS:
Andrew
Oliver, Edith. "Report from 137th Street." In Theatre
5: The American Theatre, 1971-1972, p. 133
Home Cookin'
Bates, Delores A. "A Comment on Culture." Freedom-
ways 14 (First Quarter 1974): 55-56
On Being Hit
Bates, Delores A. "A Comment on Culture." Freedom-
ways 14 (First Quarter 1974): 55
Spaces in Time
Bates, Delores A. "A Comment on Culture." Freedom-
ways 14 (First Quarter 1974): 56
REVIEWS OF INDIVIDUAL PLAYS:
Mars
Smith, Marian. "Black Theater Week Renews Basic Aim:
Reflect Community." Chicago (Ill.) Sun-Times, 23
May 1976, in Newsbank--Performing Arts. May-June
1976, 41: G 6
On Being Hit
Gilbert, Ruth, ed. "In and Around Town: Off and Off-
Off Broadway--Triple Bill." New York 10 (18 July
1977): 18; (25 July 1977): 16; (1 August 1977): 16
"Goings On About Town: 'A Son Come Home', 'On Being
Hit', and 'Gettin' It All Together'." New Yorker 53
(25 July 1977): 2

GOUGHIS, R. A.
PLAYS:
The Tenement

†GRAHAM, ARTHUR
PLAYS:
The Nationals: a Black Happening in Three Acts. San
Diego: Black Book Productions, 1968

†GRANT, MICKI (Mrs. Roy McCutcheon)
   PLAYS:
     An Evening of Black Folktales
     [with J. E. Franklin] The Prodigal Sister
   MUSICALS:
     [with Vinnette Carroll] Croesus and the Witch
     [with Vinnette Carroll] Don't Bother Me I Can't Cope
     [with Vinnette Carroll] I'm Laughin' But I Ain't Tickled
     [with Vinnette Carroll] Step Lively, Boy, 1972 (based on a
       play by Irvin Shaw)
     [with Vinnette Carroll] The Ups and Downs of Theophilus
       Maitland, 1975
     [with Vinnette Carroll] Your Arms Too Short to Box with God
   CRITICISMS BY GRANT:
     Guernsey. Playwrights, Lyricists, Composers, on Theater,
       pp. 137-38
   CRITICISMS OF INDIVIDUAL PLAYS:
     The Prodigal Sister
       Bailey, Peter. "Annual Round-up: Black Theater in
         America--New York." Black World 24 (April 1975):
         22-23
       Engel. The Critics, pp. 27-29
       Guernsey. The Best Plays of 1974-1975, pp. 31, 369-70
   CRITICISMS OF INDIVIDUAL MUSICALS:
     Croesus and the Witch
       Riley, Clayton. "Black Theatre." In Theatre 5: The
         American Theatre, 1971-1972, p. 61
     Don't Bother Me I Can't Cope
       Blum and Willis, eds. A Pictorial History of the Ameri-
         can Theatre: 1860-1976, pp. 414, 416
       Brukenfeld, Dick. "Off-Off Broadway: Profile Rising."
         In Theatre 5: The American Theatre, 1971-1972, pp.
         52, 56
       Engel. The Critics, pp. 27-28
       Harris, Leonard. "Broadway." In Theatre 5: The
         American Theatre, 1971-1972, pp. 29-30
       Ribowsky, Mark. "'Father' of the Black Theatre Boom."
         Sepia 25 (November 1976): 72
       Sullivan, Dan. "Theatre West." In Theatre 5: The
         American Theatre, 1971-1972, p. 88
   REVIEWS OF INDIVIDUAL PLAYS:
     The Prodigal Sister
       Brukenfeld, Dick. "The Unfortunate Sag." Village Voice
         19 (18 July 1974): 57
       Gill, Brendon. "Off-Broadway: The Second Time Around."
         New Yorker 50 (9 December 1974): 69-70
       Simon, John. "Mad, Bad, Sad, and Glad." New York
         Magazine 7 (16 December 1974): 96
       Willis' Theatre World. vol. 31, 1974-1975, p. 75
   REVIEWS OF INDIVIDUAL MUSICALS:
     Don't Bother Me I Can't Cope
       Beutel, Paul. "Talented Cast Transforms 'Don't Bother

Me' Into a Hit." (Austin, Tex.) American Statesman,
24 November 1975, in Newsbank--Performing Arts.
November-December 1975, 83: A 11

Blum and Willis, eds. A Pictorial History of the American Theatre: 1860-1976, pp. 414, 416

DeVine, Laurence. "'I Can't Cope' Keeps Coping with a
Rhythmic Message." Detroit (Mich.) Free Press, 5
June 1975, in Newsbank--Performing Arts. May-June
1975, 38: D 5

Gorney, Carole. "Black Revue Excites Popejoy Hall
Crowd." Albuquerque (N.M.) Journal, 20 November
1975, in Newsbank--Performing Arts. November-
December 1975, 83: H 10

Hughes, Catharine. "Three New Musicals." America
135 (27 November 1976): 373

_____. "Two Black Plays." America 135 (27 November 1976): 373

Mackay, Barbara. "Black Musical 'Cope' Lights Up
Stage." Denver (Colo.) Post, 15 April 1977, in News-
bank--Performing Arts. March-April 1977, 23: G 7

Michelson, Herb. "'Heavy' Stuff, Without Any Weight'."
Sacramento (Calif.) Bee, 19 June 1976, in Newsbank--
Performing Arts. May-June 1976, 40: E 3

Miller, Jeanne. "'Can't Cope'--Soft, Biting." San
Francisco (Calif.) Examiner, 16 June 1976, in News-
bank--Performing Arts. May-June 1976, 40: E 2

Mootz, William. "'Don't Bother Me' Is Black, Bold,
and Brilliant." (Louisville, Ken.) Courier-Journal,
8 October 1975, in Newsbank--Performing Arts. September-October 1975, 66: G 14

Murray, James P. "Blacks Invade Broadway in a Big
Way ... With Soul Cheers and Society Bows." St.
Louis (Mo.) Argus, 17 April 1975, in Newsbank--Per-
forming Arts. March-April 1975, 28: D 9

_____. "Broadway Show Is ... On the Road With."
(N.Y.) Amsterdam News: Arts and Entertainment, 20
August 1975, in Newsbank--Performing Arts. July-
August 1975, 71: D 9

Parker. Who's Who in The Theatre, 15th ed., p. 614

Ryan, Barbara Haddad. "'I Can't Cope' Belies Title--
with Pride, Wit." (Denver, Colo.) Rocky Mountain
News, 16 April 1977, in Newsbank--Performing Arts.
March-April 1977, 23: G 8

Trescott, Jacqueline. "Robert Guillame: The Leading
Guy." Washington (D.C.) Post, 6 May 1976, in News-
bank--Performing Arts. May-June 1976, 40: D 5-6

Watt, Douglas. "Poems Slow Songfest." (N.Y.) Daily
News, 19 May 1976, in Newsbank--Performing Arts.
May-June 1976, 40: E G

Willis' Theatre World. vol. 32, 1975-1976, p. 162

Winer, Linda. "The Boom in Black Theatre: Growing
Profits ... and Growing Pains." Chicago Tribune:

Arts & Fun, 30 May 1976, 6:3
I'm Laughin' But I Ain't Tickled
   Clurman, Harold. "Theatre." Nation 222 (5 June 1976):
     701-02
   Hughes, Catharine. "Theatre." America 134 (12 June
     1976): 519
The Ups and Downs of Theophilus Maitland
   Hughes, Catharine. "Three New Musicals." America
     135 (27 November 1976): 373
         . "Two Black Plays." America 135 (27 Novem-
     ber 1976): 373
   Mackay, Barbara. "Off-Beat Off-Broadway Musicals."
     Saturday Review 2 (22 March 1975): 40
   Peterson, Maurice. "On the Aisle." Essence 6 (May
     1975): 12
Your Arms Too Short to Box with God
   Adams, Zy Ace. "Music Is the Message." (N.Y.)
     Amsterdam News: Arts and Entertainment. 1 January
     1977, D-10
   "Amen! ... Yes ... Lord! 'Box' Hot Time at Old Ford's."
     Afro-American (Baltimore, Md.) 14 February 1976, in
     Newsbank--Performing Arts. January-February 1975,
     11: G 13
   Berkvist, Robert. "Now Face: Hector Jaime Mercado:
     The Ailey Disciple Who Portrays Judas." New York
     Times, 7 October 1977, C 3
   "Blackstone Musical Puts Fun Into Old-Time Religion."
     Chicago (Ill.) Sun Times, 10 April 1976, in Newsbank--
     Performing Arts. March-April 1976, 27: G 6
   Blum and Willis, eds. A Pictorial History of the Ameri-
     can Theatre: 1860-1976, pp. 429, 430
   Clurman, Harold. "Theatre." Nation 224 (15 January
     1977): 61
   Davis, Curt. "Welcome 'Arms'." Encore 6 (17 January
     1977): 36
   Dreyfuss, Joel. "Marvelous Music and Dancing, But the
     Plot's No Revelation." Washington (D.C.) Post, 6
     November 1975, in Newsbank--Performing Arts. No-
     vember-December 1975, 83: A 5
   Facts on File. 1976, pp. 12-22; 1014 F 3
   Forbes, Cheryl. "Black 'Box' Is Best." Christianity
     Today 20 (30 January 1976): 16-17
   Gilbert, Ruth, ed. "In and Around Town: On Broadway."
     New York 10 (2 May 1977): 20; (6 June 1977): 20;
     (20 June 1977): 20; (27 June 1977): 16; (4 July 1977):
     14; (11 July 1977): 20; (18 July 1977): 15; (25 July
     1977): 16; (1 August 1977): 15; (8 August 1977): 16;
     (15 August 1977): 16; (22 August 1977): 15; (29 August
     1977): 14; (19 September 1977): 19; (26 September 1977):
     16; (3 October 1977): 19
   Gill, Brendan. "The Theatre--Having a Good Time." New
     Yorker 52 (3 January 1977): 60

"Gospel Truth." Newsweek 89 (10 January 1977): 66

Hughes, Catharine. "Broadway Round-Up." America 136 (22 January 1977): 60

Kalem, T. E. "Oh, When the Saints...." Time 109 (24 January 1977): 55

New York Theatre Critics' Reviews--1976 37 (31 December 1976): 52-56; containing: Barnes, Clive, "Stage: 'Your Arms Too Short ... '" (New York Times, 23 December 1976). Gottfried, Martin, "'Arms' Short of Good Theater" (New York Post, 23 December 1976). Watt, Douglas, "A Show for all Seasons" ([N.Y.] Daily News, 23 December 1976). Wilson, Edwin, "Your Arms Too Short to Box with God" (Wall Street Journal, 23 December 1976). Sharp, Christopher, "Your Arms Too Short to Box with God" (Women's Wear Daily, 23 December 1976). Beaufort, John, "Gospel Music" (The Christian Science Monitor, 27 December 1976). Kroll, Jack, "Gospel Truth" (Newsweek, 10 January 1977). Lape, Bob, "Your Arms ..." (WABC-TV 6 January 1977). Probst, Leonard, NBC, 22 December 1976

Philip, Richard. "Revivals." Dance Magazine 51 (May 1977): 36-40

Richards, David. "A Musical in Touch With the Spirit." Washington (D.C.) Star News, 5 November 1975, in Newsbank--Performing Arts. November-December 1976, 83: A 6

Roberts, Susan O. "Tony Winner Delores Hall Thanks God for Success." (N.Y.) Amsterdam News: Arts and Entertainment, 9 July 1977, D-2

Robinson, Major. "Invisible Stars Twinkle." (N.Y.) Amsterdam News: Arts and Entertainment, 25 June 1977, D-15

Tapley, Mel. "Trazana, Dolores, and Diana Win Tonys." (N.Y.) Amsterdam News: Arts and Entertainment, 11 June 1977, D-2

"Welcome to the Great Black Way." Time 108 (1 November 1976): 75

Willis' Theatre World. vol. 32, 1975-1976, p. 205

Winer, Linda. "The Boom in Black Theatre: Growing Profits ... and Growing Pains." Chicago Tribune: Arts & Fun, 30 May 1976, 6:2

"'Your Arms Are [sic] Too Short to Box with God'." Milwaukee (Wis.) Journal, 24 December 1976, 2:2

GRAY, C.
PLAYS:
Family Name

GREAVES, WM.
FILM SCRIPTS:
[with Woody Robinson] The Marijuana Affair

GREEN, PAUL
  PLAYS:
    [with Richard Wright] Native Son (based on the novel by
      Wright
  PLAYS PUBLISHED IN ANTHOLOGIES:
    Native Son, in Richards. America On Stage
  FILM SCRIPTS:
    [with Richard Wright] Native Son
  CRITICISMS OF GREEN:
    Richards. America On Stage. pp. 785-788
  CRITICISMS OF INDIVIDUAL PLAYS:
    Native Son
      Frenz, ed. American Playwrights on Drama, p. 76
      Gagey. Revolution in American Drama, p. 157
      Geisinger. Plays, Players, & Playwrights, p. 556
      Goldstein. The Political Stage, pp. 298-299
      Hartnoll. The Oxford Companion to the Theatre, pp.
        677-78
      Houghton. Advance from Broadway, p. 103
      O'Hara and Bros. Invitation to the Theatre, p. 48
      Sandle. The Negro in the American Educational Theatre,
        pp. 21-23
  CRITICISMS OF INDIVIDUAL FILM SCRIPTS:
    Native Son
      Edmonds, Randolph. "The Blacks in the American
        Theatre, 1700-1969." The Pan-African Journal 7
        (Winter 1974): 299, 304
      Pyros, John. "Richard Wright: A Black Novelists' Ex-
        perience on Film." Negro American Literature Forum
        9 (Summer 1975): 53-54
  AWARDS:
    Bonin. Major Themes in Prize-Winning American Drama,
      p. 171

GREENE, CHARLES
  PLAYS:
    [with Gus Narin] The Legend of Toby Kingdom
  FILM SCRIPTS:
    [with Charles Nero and Gus Narin] The Legend of Toby King-
      dom (adapted from the play)
  CRITICISMS OF INDIVIDUAL FILM SCRIPTS:
    The Legend of Toby Kingdom
      Pantovic, Stan. "The Making of a Black Movie." Sepia
        22 (December 1973): 54-62

GREENFIELD, JOSH
  PLAYS:
    I Have a Dream (adaptation of "I Have a Dream" by Robert
      Greenwald)
  REVIEWS OF INDIVIDUAL PLAYS:
    I Have a Dream
      Blum and Willis, eds. A Pictorial History of the

American Theatre: 1860-1976, pp. 429, 430
Facts on File, 1976, 9-30, 1014 E 3
Gill, Brendan. "The Theatre: Open for Business." New
Yorker 52 (4 October 1976): 75
Gottfried, M. "Profile of a Hero." New York Post, 29
March 1976, in Newsbank--Performing Arts. March-
April 1976, 30: C 9
Hughes, Catharine. "Theatre: Two Black Plays."
America 135 (9 October 1976): 214
Kalem, T. E. "A Kind in Darkness." Time 108 (4
October 1976): 100
New York Theatre Critics' Reviews--1976 37 (27 Septem-
ber 1976): 186: 190; containing; Watt, Douglas, "Blurry
'Dream', with Songs" ([N.Y.] Daily News, 21 September
1976). Barnes, Clive, "'I Have a Dream' Plays Tribute
on Stage to Martin Luther King" (New York Times, 21
September 1976). Gottfried, Martin, "Some Dreams
Don't Come True" (New York Post, 21 September 1976).
Wilson, Edwin, "The Black Experience" (The Wall
Street Journal, 21 September 1976). Beaufort, John,
"Martin Luther King on Stage" (The Christian Science
Monitor, 23 September 1976). Sharp, Christopher, "I
Have a Dream" (Women's Wear Daily, 21 September
1976). Kalem, T. E., "A King in Darkness" (Time, 4
October 1976). Sanders, Kevin, "I Have a Dream"
(WABC-TV, 20 September 1976).
Pyatt, Richard I. "Will Moses Gunn Shoot Down Father
Time?" Encore 6 (3 January 1977): 29
Winer, Linda. "The Boom in Black Theatre: Growing
Profits ... and Growing Pains." Chicago Tribune:
Arts & Fun, 30 May 1976, 6:2
_____. "Looking at the 60's with Different Eyes."
Chicago Tribune: Arts & Fun, 2 May 1977, sec. 6,
p. 5

GREENLEE, SAM
PLAYS:
The Spook Who Sat by the Door (based on the novel)
REVIEWS OF INDIVIDUAL PLAYS:
The Spook Who Sat by the Door
Crist, Judith. "Sink or Swim in Watergate: The Year's
Ten Best and Worst." New York Magazine 7 (14
January 1974): 75

GREENRIDGE, GERTRUDE
PLAYS:
Ma Lou's Daughters
CRITICISMS OF INDIVIDUAL PLAYS:
Ma Lou's Daughters
Peterson, Maurice. "On the Aisle: Theatre." Essence
6 (July 1975): 19

GREENWALD, ROBERT
  PLAYS:
    I Have a Dream
  CRITICISMS OF INDIVIDUAL PLAYS:
    I Have a Dream
      Bell, Roseanne Pope. "'For Colored Girls Who Have
        Considered Suicide/When the Rainbow Is Enuf." The
        Black Collegian 7 (May-June 1977): 48
  REVIEWS OF INDIVIDUAL PLAYS:
    I Have a Dream
      "Billy Dee Williams as King Opens on Broadway." (N.Y.)
        Amsterdam News: Arts and Entertainment, 7 August
        1976, D-4
      "Billy Dee Williams Opens in 'Dream'." (N.Y.) Amster-
        dam News: Arts and Entertainment, 18 September
        1976, D-18
      Hughes, Catherine. "Two Black Plays." America 135
        (9 October 1976): 214
      Smith, Alexis. "'I Have a Dream'; A Powerful Emotion
        Filled Drama." (N.Y.) Amsterdam News: Arts and
        Entertainment, 25 September 1976, D-9

†GREENWOOD, FRANK J.
  PLAYS:
    The Cotton Curtain
  CRITICISMS OF INDIVIDUAL PLAYS:
    The Cotton Curtain
      Sandle. The Negro in the American Educational Theatre,
        p. 87

GREER, BONNIE
  PLAYS:
    1919

†GRIFFIN, OSCAR
  PLAYS:
    Miss Ann Is Still Alive (M.A.I.S.A.)
  REVIEWS OF INDIVIDUAL PLAYS:
    Miss Ann Is Still Alive
      Smith, Marian. "Black Theater Week Renews Basic Aim:
        Reflect Community." Chicago (Ill.) Sun-Times, 23
        May 1976, in Newsbank--Performing Arts. May-June
        1976, 41: G 6
      Winer, Linda. "The Boom in Black Theatre: Growing
        Profits ... and Growing Pains." Chicago Tribune:
        Arts & Fun, 30 May 1976, 6:3
      _____ . "Local Curtain Going Up for 10 Black Stage
        Troupes." Chicago Tribune: Arts & Fun, 30 May
        1976, 6:3
†GRIMKÉ, ANGELINE
  PLAYS:
    Rachel

CRITICISMS OF INDIVIDUAL PLAYS:
Rachel
    Davis. From the Dark Tower, pp. 11, 58
    Edmonds, Randolph. "The Blacks in the American
        Theatre, 1700-1969." The Pan-African Journal 7
        (Winter 1974): 302
    Hartnoll. The Oxford Companion to the Theatre, p. 678
    Miller, Jeanne-Marie A. "Images of Black Women in
        Plays by Black Playwrights." CLA Journal 20 (June
        1977): 494
    Molette, Barbara. "Black Women Playwrights: They
        Speak: Who Listens?" Black World 25 (April 1976):
        30
    Stevenson, Robert Louis. "The Image of the White Man
        as Projected in the Published Plays of Black Ameri-
        cans, 1847-1973." Ph.D. Dissertation, Indiana Uni-
        versity, 1976

†GUNN, BILL (William Harrison) (b. 1934)
  PLAYS:
    Black Picture Show. Berkeley, Calif.: Reed, Cannon &
        Johnson, 1976
    Marcus in the High Grass, 1960
  CRITICISMS OF GUNN:
    "Bill Gunn's Play a 'Mental Trip', No 'Sounder' or 'Jane
        Pittman'." In Nykoruk. Authors in the News. vol. 1,
        p. 206
  CRITICISMS OF INDIVIDUAL PLAYS:
    Black Picture Show
        Bailey, Peter. "Annual Round-up: Black Theater in
          America--New York." Black World 24 (April 1975):
          20-21
  REVIEWS OF INDIVIDUAL PLAYS:
    Black Picture Show
        "Black Fury at Lincoln Center." New York Post, 7
          January 1975, in Newsbank--Performing Arts. January-
          February 1975; 13: G 8
        Blum and Willis, eds. A Pictorial History of the Ameri-
          can Theatre: 1860-1976
        Brukenfeld, Dick. "Black Picture Show." Village Voice
          20 (3 February 1975): 85
        Clurman, Harold. "Theatre." Nation 220 (25 January
          1975): 94
        Delaunoy, Didier. "Black Picture Show." Encore 4 (17
          March 1975): 4
        Gill, Brendan. "The Theatre: Writing About Writing."
          The New Yorker 51 (20 January 1975): 61-62
        Gottfried, Martin. "The New Ethnic Theater." New
          York Post, 4 October 1975, in Newsbank--Performing
          Arts. September-October 1975, 68: B 4
        Greer, Edward G. "On and Off Broadway, Spring 1975."
          Drama 117 (Summer 1975): 34

Guernsey. The Best Plays of 1974-1975, p. 325
Kalem, T. E. "The Blame Game." Time 105 (20 January
   1975): 76
Kauffmann, Stanley. "Stanley Kauffmann on Theatre."
   The New Republic 172 (8 February 1975): 22, 34
Kroll, Jack. "Black and White Picture." Newsweek 85
   (20 January 1975): 83
Murray, James P. "Blacks Invade Broadway in a Big
   Way ... With Soul Cheers, and Society Bows." St.
   Louis (Mo.) Argus, 17 April 1975, in Newsbank--Per-
   forming Arts. March-April 1975, 28: D 9
New York Theatre Critics' Reviews--1975 36 (13 January
   1975): 386-389; containing: Barnes, Clive, "'Black
   Picture Show' a Tale of Corruption" (New York Times,
   7 January 1975). Watt, Douglas, "'Black Picture Show'
   Rates No Stars" ([N.Y.] Daily News, 7 January 1975).
   Gottfried, Martin, "Black Fury at Lincoln Center"
   (New York Post, 7 January 1975). Ettore, Barbara,
   "Black Picture Show" (Women's Wear Daily, 8 January
   1975). Kalem, T. E., "The Black Game" (Time, 20
   January 1975). Kroll, Jack, "Black and White Picture"
   (Newsweek, 20 January 1975). Sanders, Kevin, WABC-
   TV 6 January 1975
Peterson, Maurice. "On the Aisle." Essence 6 (May
   1975): 12
Simon, John. "Black Picture Show." New York 8 (27
   January 1975): 51
   _____. "Music of the Squares." New York Magazine
   8 (27 January 1975): 51
Willis' Theatre World. vol. 31, 1974-1975, p. 123
AWARDS:
   Black Picture Show
      AUDELCO Award: Best Playwright, Best Play

HÁCKET, HARLEY
   PLAYS:
      On Toby Time
   REVIEWS OF INDIVIDUAL PLAYS:
      On Toby Time
         Davis, Curt. "The Second Time Around for Maurice
         Hines May be Twice as Good." Encore 6 (21 March
         1977): 31-32
         _____. "Set Your Watch 'On Toby Time'." Encore
         6 (21 March 1977): 30-31

†HAIRSTON, WILLIAM
   PLAYS
      Walk in Darkness
   CRITICISMS OF INDIVIDUAL PLAYS:
      Walk in Darkness
         Hartnoll. The Oxford Companion to the Theatre, p.
         681

HALEY, ALEX
  TELEVISION SCRIPTS:
    Roots (based on the novel)
  CRITICISMS OF HALEY:
    Davis, Curtis. "People in the News." Encore 6 (20 June
      1977): 49
    "Haley Receives Spingarn." Minneapolis (Mn.) Spokesman,
      23 June 1977, p. 7
    "Haley Receives Spingarn." Twin Cities Courier (Minneapo-
      lis/St. Paul, Mn.), 2 June 1977, p. 5
    Hicks, James. "Alex Haley Still Modest Despite Fame and
      Fortune." (N.Y.) Amsterdam News: New Horizons, 5
      February 1977, D-9
    Morgan, Geri. "Haley Wins Harlemites in Speech on Roots."
      (N.Y.) Amsterdam News: New Horizons, 5 February
      1977, D-9
    "Roots Gets 37 Emmy Award Nominations." St. Louis Post
      Dispatch, 4 August 1977, p. 16C
  CRITICISMS OF TELEVISION SCRIPTS:
    Roots
      Blake, Richard A. "Humanity Against Itself." America
        136 (15 January 1977): 34-35
      Staples, Robert. "'Roots': Melodrama of the Black Ex-
        perience." Black Scholar 8 (May 1977): 37
      Stone, Chuck. "Roots: An Electronic Orgy in White
        Guilt." Black Scholar 8 (May 1977): 39-41
      Taylor, Clyde. "'Roots': A Modern Minstrel Show."
        Black Scholar 8 (May 1977): 37-38
      Waters, H. F. and V. E. Smith. "One Man's Family:
        Filming 12 Part Serialization of Alex Haley's 'Roots'."
        Newsweek 87 (21 June 1976): 73
  REVIEWS OF INDIVIDUAL TELEVISION SCRIPTS:
    Roots
      Davis, Curt. "The Inner Voice of Louis Gossett."
        Encore 6 (6 June 1977): 28, 31
      "Emmy Show Stars 'Roots'." Milwaukee (Wis.) Journal,
        13 September 1977, 2:3
      Pyatt, Richard I. "Will Moses Gunn Shoot Down Father
        Time?" Encore 6 (3 January 1977): 29-30
      Rojas, Don. "Roots Captivates Millions of T.V. Viewers."
        (N.Y.) Amsterdam News: New Horizons, 5 February
        1977, D-8
  AWARDS:
    37 Emmy Awards
    Spingarn Medal

HALL, H.
  PLAYS:
    Best Intentions
    Try Again

HANDY, W. C.

CRITICISMS OF HANDY:
Birmingham. Certain People, p. 191

HANLEY, WILLIAM (b. October 31, 1931)
PLAYS:
Conversations in the Dark, 1963
Flesh and Blood, 1968
Mrs. Dally Has a Lover, one act, 1962; changed to Mrs.
Dally, 1965
Show Dance on the Killing Ground, 1964
Slow Dance on the Killing Ground (Danse Lente sur un Champ
de Bataille; adapted by Eric Kahane; mise en scene by
Jean Tosso)
Today Is Independence Day
Whisper into My Good Ear, one act, 1962
FILM SCRIPTS:
The Gypsy Moths, 1969
CRITICISMS OF HANLEY:
Parker. Who's Who in The Theater, 15th ed., pp. 884-85
Smiley. Playwrighting: The Structure of Action, pp. 66,
101, 178, 244
CRITICISMS OF INDIVIDUAL PLAYS:
Slow Dance on the Killing Ground
Ballet, Arthur. "The Theatre of Middle America." In
Theatre 4: The American Theatre, 1970-1971, p. 74
Falb. American Drama in Paris, 1945-1970, pp. 160,
168
Simon. Uneasy Stages, p. 66
Smiley. Playwrighting: The Structure of Action, pp. 66,
101, 178
REVIEWS OF INDIVIDUAL PLAYS:
Slow Dance on the Killing Ground
"B.A./W. Scores with 'Dance'." Seattle (Wash.) Times,
17 January 1977, in Newsbank--Performing Arts.
January-February 1977, 11: G 13
Jackson, Judy. "'Slow Dance' Role a Dream for 'Line'."
Boston (Mass.) Globe, 7 April 1976, in Newsbank--
Performing Arts. March-April 1976, 32: F 3
Kelly, Kevin. "'Slow Dance' Comes Back with Sharpened
Edges." Boston (Mass.) Globe, 9 April 1976, in
Newsbank--Performing Arts. March-April 1976, 30:
F 9
"Length of Run of American Plays in Paris." In Lewis W.
Falb. American Drama in Paris: 1945-1970, p. 168
"Slow Dance on a Killing Ground." (Boston, Mass.) Bay
State Banner, 22 April 1976, in Newsbank--Performing
Arts. March-April 1976, 30: F 8
AWARDS:
Mrs. Dally Has a Lover; Whisper into My Good Ear
Vernon Rice Award

†HANSBERRY, LORRAINE (May, 1930-January 16, 1954)
PLAYS:

The Drinking Gourd
Les Blancs (completed by Robert Nemiroff and Charlotte Zaltz-
  berg)
Les Blancs: The Last Collected Plays of Lorraine Hansberry.
  Edited by Robert Nemiroff. N.Y.: Random House, 1972
A Raisin in the Sun. N.Y.: Random House, 1961; N.Y.:
  New American Library, 1961; N.Y.: Samuel French,
  1961
The Sign in Sidney Brustein's Window. N.Y.: Random House,
  1965; N.Y.: Samuel French, 1965
To Be Young, Gifted, and Black. Englewood Cliffs, N.J.:
  Prentice-Hall, 1969; N.Y.: Samuel French, 1971
What Use Are Flowers?
PLAYS PUBLISHED IN ANTHOLOGIES:
  The Drinking Gourd, in Fanell, et al. Upstage/Downstage:
    A Theatre Festival
  A Raisin in the Sun, in Altenbernd, Exploring Literature;
    Barranger and Dodson, eds., Generations: An Introduc-
    tion to Drama; Cassady, An Introduction to Theatre and
    Drama; Cerf, Four Contemporary American Plays; Elkind,
    Twenty-Eight Scenes for Acting Practice; Griffith and
    Mersand, Eight American Ethnic Plays; Groves, Plays on
    a Human Theme; Oliver and Sills, Contemporary Black
    Drama; Schneider, Walker, and Childs, The Range of
    Literature: Drama; White and Whiting, Playreader's
    Repertory Drama on Stage
  What Use Are Flowers? in Works In Progress, No. 5
MUSICALS:
  Raisin
CRITICISMS BY HANSBERRY:
  "Lorraine Hansberry: The Black Experience in the Creation
    of Drama." Films for the Humanities (16mm, 35 min.,
    or Video cassette) FFH 128
  "The Negro in the American Theatre." In Horst Frenz, ed.
    American Playwrights on Drama, pp. 160-167 [first pub-
    lished as "Me Tink Me Hear Sounds in de Night" Theatre
    Arts 44 (October 1960)]
CRITICISMS OF HANSBERRY:
  Benston. Baraka: The Renegade and the Mask, p. 227
  Bigsby. Confrontation and Commitment, p. xix, passim
  Bonin, Jane F. Major Themes in Prize-Winning American
    Drama, pp. 52, 122, 141
  _____. Prize-Winning American Drama: A Bibliographi-
    cal and Descriptive Guide. Metuchen, N.J.: Scarecrow
    Press, 1973, p. 152
  Brooks, Mary Ellen. "Reactionary Trends in Recent Black
    Drama." Literature and Ideology (Montreal). no. 10
    (1970): 46-48
  Brown. Soviet Attitudes Toward American Writing, p. 177
  Dace and Dace. The Theatre Student: Modern Theatre and
    Drama, pp. 55-56
  Davis, Arthur P. From the Dark Tower, pp. 203-207

Fletcher, Leah. "Black Theatre Alive and Struggling Hard."
(Boston, Mass.) Bay State Banner, 20 March 1975, in
Newsbank--Performing Arts. March-April 1975, 28: G 1
Freedman. American Drama in Social Context, p. 86
Hatch, James. "Speak to Me in Those Old Words, You
Know, Those La-La Words, Those Tung-Tung Sounds."
Yale/Theatre 8 (Fall 1976): 27
Hobson. International Theatre Annual: No. 4, pp. 54, 64-70
Horton and Edwards. Backgrounds of American Literary
Thought, 3rd ed., p. 588
Houghton. The Exploding Stage, p. 202
Lewis, Theophilus. "Social Protest in 'A Raisin in the Sun'."
Catholic World 190 (October 1959): 31-35
"Lorraine Hansberry: The Black Experience in the Creation
of Drama." Films for the Humanities (16mm, 35 min.,
or Video cassette) FFH 128
McGraw-Hill Encyclopedia of World Drama. vol. 2, p. 286
Marowitz, Milne and Hale. The Encore Reader, p. 175
Melchinger, Siegfried. The Concise Encyclopedia of Modern
Drama. N.Y.: Horizon, 1964, p. 287
Miller, Jeanne-Marie A. "Images of Black Women in Plays
by Black Playwrights." CLA Journal 20 (June 1977): 498
Nellhouse, Arlynn. "Robert Nemiroff and Lorraine Hans-
berry." In Nykoruk. Authors in the News. vol. 2.
Detroit: Gale Research, 1976, p. 211
"New ACTF Award." Theatre News 8 (May 1976): 9
Ross and Ross. The Player and A Profile of an Art, p. 108
Sandle. The Negro in the American Educational Theatre,
pp. 23-24
Schneider, Walker, and Childs. The Range of Literature,
3rd ed., pp. 1022-1023
Steele, Mike. "Mixed Blood Theater Opens with 'To Be
Young, Gifted, Black'." The Minneapolis (Mn.) Tribune,
9 July 1977, p. 78
Weales, G. "Losing the Playwright." Commonweal 90
(5 September 1969): 542-43
Zastrow, Sylvia V. Horning. "Structure of Selected Plays
by American Women Playwrights." Dissertation, Ph.D.
Northwestern University, 1975
CRITICISMS OF INDIVIDUAL PLAYS:
The Drinking Gourd
Miller, Jeanne-Marie A. "Images of Black Women in
Plays by Black Playwrights." CLA Journal 20 (June
1977): 499-500
Molette, Barbara. "Black Women Playwrights: They
Speak: Who Listens?" Black World 25 (April 1976):
32
Le Blancs
Dace and Dace. The Theatre Student: Modern Theatre
and Drama, p. 56
Davis, Curt. "Earle Hyman Is Running the Other Race."
Encore 6 (4 April 1977): 35

Hatch, James. 'Speak to Me of Those Old Words, You Know, Those La-La Words, Those Tung-Tung Sounds (Some African Influences on the Afro-American Theatre)." Yale/Theatre 8 (Fall 1976): 28

Simon. Uneasy Stages, pp. 290, 296

Raisin in the Sun

Adams, George R. "Black Militant Drama." American Imago 28 (Summer 1971): 109, 110-11, passim

Anderson, Mary Louise. "Black Matriarchy: Portrayals of Women in Three Plays." Negro American Literature Forum 10 (Fall 1976): 93-94

Atkinson and Hirschfeld. The Lively Years 1920-1973, pp. 258-61

"B: Literature; Theater." In Green, Bernard. The Timetables of History. N.Y.: Simon and Schuster, 1975

Benston, Kimberly W. Baraka: The Renegade and the Mask, p. 227

_____. "'Cities in Bezique': Adrienne Kennedy's Expressionistic Vision." CLA Journal 20 (December 1976): 237

Bigsby. Confrontation and Commitment, pp. 122, 156-61, 168, 172

"Black Theatre in Transition, Playwright (Milner) Says." In Nykoruk. Authors in the News. vol. 1, p. 349

"Black Theater Workshop at OU." (Oklahoma City, Okla.) Black Dispatch, 1 April 1976, in Newsbank--Performing Arts. March-April 1976, 31: F 14

Blum and Willis, eds. A Pictorial History of the American Theatre: 1860-1976, pp. 367, 389

Bonin, Jane F. Major Themes in Prize-Winning American Drama, pp. 51, 52-53, 54, 122-123, 141

_____. Prize-Winning American Drama: A Bibliographical and Descriptive Guide. Metuchen, N.J.: Scarecrow Press, 1973, pp. 150-151

Brooks, Mary Ellen. "Reactionary Trends in Recent Black Drama." Literature and Ideology (Montreal). no. 10 (1970): 47

Brown. Soviet Attitudes Toward American Writing, p. 189

Brown, Lloyd W. "Lorraine Hansberry as Ironist: A Reappraisal of 'A Raisin in the Sun'." Journal of Black Studies 4 (March 1974): 237-47

Cameron and Hoffman. A Guide to Theatre Study, p. 203

Dance and Dace. The Theatre Student: Modern Theatre and Drama, pp. 55-56

Davis. From the Dark Tower, pp. 204-206

Durdin, Glenda. "The Theme of Black Matriarchy in 'A Raisin in the Sun'." In Lester. Writing Research Papers, pp. 74-92; passim, 36-74

Edmonds, Randolph. "The Blacks in the American Theatre, 1700-1969." The Pan-African Journal 7 (Winter 1974): 305-306

Engel. The Critics, pp. 68, 127-128, 254-255
Enser. Filmed Books and Plays, p. 323, A (P) Col.
  1960 Metheun
Falb. American Drama in Paris, 1945-1970, pp. 120,
  156, 167
Freedman, Morris. American Drama in Social Context.
  Carbondale: Southern Illinois University Press, 1971.
Geisinger. Plays, Players, & Playwrights, p. 605
Giddings, Paula. "'Raisin' Revisited." Encore 4 (7-14
  July 1975): 28-31
Gill, Glenda. "Techniques of Teaching Lorraine Hans-
  berry: Liberation from Boredom." Negro American
  Literature Forum 8 (Summer 1974), 226-228
Gray, Bill. "Black Theatre in Transition, Playwright
  (Milner) Says." In Nykoruk. Authors in the News.
  vol. 1. Detroit: Gale Research, 1976, p. 348
Hartnoll. The Oxford Companion to the Theatre, p. 680
Hay, Samuel A. "African-American Drama, 1950-1970."
  Negro History Bulletin 36 (January 1973): 7
Hobson. International Theatre Annual: No. 4, pp. 19,
  54, 62, 64-70
Keller, Joseph. "Black Writing and the White Critic."
  Negro American Literature Forum 3 (Winter 1970): 109
Keyssar-Franke, Helen. "Strategies in Black Drama."
  Ph.D. Dissertation, University of Iowa, 1974
Killens, John O. "Hollywood in Black and White." In
  Banks and Burke, eds. Black Americans: Images in
  Conflict, pp. 31-34
Lamb, Margaret. "Feminist Criticism." Drama Review
  18 (September 1974): 46
Lanfe. Anatomy of a Hit, pp. 297-302, 337
Lewis, Theophilus. "Social Protest in 'A Raisin in the
  Sun'." Catholic World 190 (October 1959): 31-35
Littlejohn. Black on White, p. 69, 70-71
Miller, Jeanne-Marie A. "Images of Black Women in
  Plays by Black Playwrights." CLA Journal 20 (June
  1977): 498-99
Molette, Barbara. "Black Women Playwrights: They
  Speak: Who Listens?" Black World 25 (April 1976):
  31-32
Moore. The New Women's Theatre, p. xxxi
Ness, David E. "Lorraine Hansberry's Les Blancs: The
  Victory of the Man Who Must." Freedomways 13
  (Fourth Quarter 1973): 294-306
Oliver, Edith. "Report from 137th Street." In Theatre
  5: The American Theatre, 1971-1972, p. 131
Ribowsky, Mark. "'Father' of the Black Theatre Boom."
  Sepia 25 (November 1976): 69
Ross and Ross. The Player and a Profile of an Art,
  pp. 108, 110
Sandle. The Negro in the American Educational Theatre,
  pp. 17, 23-24, 126

Schneider, Walker, and Childs. The Range of Literature:
Drama, pp. 1022-1023, 1115-1116, 1117-1118

Steele, Mike. "Mixed Blood Theatre Opens with 'To Be
Young, Gifted, Black'." The Minneapolis (Mn.) Tribune
9 July 1977, p. 7B

Taubman. The Making of the American Theatre, p. 299

Tedesco, John L. "The White Image as Second 'Persona'
in Black Drama, 1955-1970." Ph.D. Dissertation,
University of Iowa, 1974

Tyman, Kenneth. Curtains: Selections from the Drama
Criticism and Related Writings, pp. 306-09

Weales, Gerald. "Losing the Playwright." Catholic
World 90 (5 September 1969): 542-543

Weathers, Diane. "Fantasy in Black Theatre: A Kind of
New Freedom." Encore 4 (21 April 1975): 32

White and Whiting. Playreader's Repertory, pp. 681-84,
758-59

Willis, Robert. "Anger and Contemporary Black Theatre."
Negro American Literature Forum 8 (Summer 1974):
213-215

The Sign in Sidney Brustein's Window
Bigsby. Confrontation and Commitment, pp. 54, 122-23,
138, 154, 156, 162-73

Dace and Dace. The Theatre Student: Modern Theatre
and Drama, p. 56

Davis, Arthur P. From the Dark Tower, pp. 206-207

Edmonds, Randolph. "The Blacks in the American
Theatre, 1700-1969." The Pan-African Journal 7
(Winter 1974): 305

Harris, Leonard. "Broadway." In Theatre 5: The
American Theatre, 1971-1972, p. 29

Hartnoll. The Oxford Companion to the Theatre, p. 681

Littlejohn. Black on White, pp. 71-72

Proffer. Soviet Criticism of American Literature in the
Sixties, pp. xxx

Schneider, Walker, and Childs. The Range of Literature:
Drama, p. 115

Simon. Uneasy Stages, p. 66

Thurston, Chuck. "There's a Message Here in All the
Talk." Detroit (Mich.) Free Press, 28 April 1976, in
Newsbank--Performing Arts. March-April 1976, 30:
F 10

Zeisler, Peter. "The East Coast." In Theatre 4: The
American Theatre, 1970-1971, p. 66, 67

To Be Young, Gifted and Black
Dace and Dace. The Theatre Student: Modern Theatre
and Drama, p. 56

Davis. From the Dark Tower, p. 207

Lahr, John. "The Deli: Off Broadway, and Off, 68-69."
In Theatre 2: The American Theatre, 1968-1969, p.
50.

Parker. Who's Who in The Theatre, 15th ed., p. 872

CRITICISMS OF INDIVIDUAL MUSICALS:
Raisin
  Bailey, Peter. "Raisin: Lorraine Hansberry's Award-
    Winning Play Becomes Musical Hit on Broadway."
    Ebony 29 (May 1974): 74-80
  Bates, Delores A. "A Comment on Culture." Freedom-
    ways 14 (First Quarter 1974): 54-55
  "Black Theatre: A Bid for Cultural Identity." Black
    Enterprise 2 (September 1971): 31
  Engle. The Critics, pp. 67-68, 74, 190, 254
  Geisinger. Plays, Players, & Playwrights, p. 740, il.,
    742
  "Lorraine Hansberry's Play Returns a Smash Musical:
    'Raisin'." Sepia 23 (April 1974): 32-39
REVIEWS OF INDIVIDUAL PLAYS:
Les Blancs
  Clurman, Harold. "Theatre." Nation 211 (7 December
    1970): 606
  _____. "Theatre" (Les Blancs). Nation 211 (30
    November 1970): 572-73
  Gill, Brendan. "The Theatre: Things Go Wrong." New
    Yorker 46 (21 November 1970): 104
  "James Earl Jones in 'Exorcist II': The Heretic." The
    Afro-American: Afro Magazine (Baltimore, Md.) 31
    May-4 June 1977, p. 13
  Kroll, Jack. "Between Two Worlds." Newsweek 76 (30
    November 1970): 98
  Ness, David E. "Review: 'Les Blancs?'" Freedomways
    12 (Third Quarter 1972): 245-48
  Parker. Who's Who in The Theatre, 15th ed., p. 1005
Raisin in the Sun
  Atkinson, Brooks. "Raisin in the Sun." In Beckerman
    and Siegman. On Stage: Selected Theatre Reviews
    from the New York Times, 1920-1970, pp. 402-03
  Clurman, Harold. "Theatre." Nation 211 (7 December
    1970): 606
  Davis, Curt. "The Inner Voice of Louis Gossett."
    Encore 6 (6 June 1977): 30
  Gottfried, Martin. "The New Ethnic Theater." New
    York Post, 4 October 1975, in Newsbank--Performing
    Arts. September-October 1975, 68: B 4
  "Hansberry Drama Premieres at Park." Chicago Daily
    Defender, 5 July 1977, p. 21
  "Length of Run of American Plays in Paris." In Lewis
    W. Falb. American Drama in Paris: 1945-1970,
    p. 167
  Michelson, Herb. "'Heavy Stuff, Without Any Weight'."
    Sacramento (Calif.) Bee, 19 June 1976, in Newsbank--
    Performing Arts. May-June 1976, 40: E 3
  Murray, James P. "Broadway Show Is ... On the Road
    With...." (N.Y.) Amsterdam News: Arts and Enter-
    tainment, 20 August 1975, in Newsbank--Performing

Arts. July-August 1975, 71: D 9

Parker. Who's Who in The Theatre, 15th ed., pp. 702, 747

Peterson, Maurice. "Movies: Movies That Hit Home and Strike Out" (Hansberry). Essence 5 (November 1974): 19

Trescott, Jacqueline. "Robert Guillame: The Leading Guy." Washington (D.C.) Post, 6 May 1976, in Newsbank--Performing Arts. May-June 1976. 40: D 5-6

Willis' Theatre World. vol. 31, 1974-1975, p. 203

Winer, Linda. "The Boom in Black Theatre: Growing Profits ... and Growing Pains." Chicago Tribune: Arts & Fun. 30 May 1976, 6:3

The Sign in Sidney Brustein's Window

Blum and Willis, eds. A Pictorial History of the American Theatre: 1860-1976, pp. 383, 385, 414

To Be Young, Gifted, and Black

Blum and Willis, eds. A Pictorial History of the American Theatre: 1860-1976, pp. 401, 403

"Mixed Blood Theatre Co. Opens Summer Session." Minneapolis (Mn.) Spokesman, 30 June 1977, p. 6

Oliver, Edith. "Theatre." New Yorker 54 (11 January 1969): 58

Steele, Mike. "Mixed Blood Theater Opens with 'To Be Young, Gifted, Black'." The Minneapolis (Mn.) Tribune, 9 July 1977, p. 7B

Willis' Theatre World. vol. 31, 1974-1975, p. 200

REVIEWS OF INDIVIDUAL MUSICALS:

Raisin

Bailey, Peter. "'Raisin': Lorraine Hansberry's Award Winning Play Becomes Musical Hit on Broadway." Ebony 29 (May 1974): 74-76, 78, 80

Blum and Willis, eds. A Pictorial History of the American Theatre: 1860-1976, pp. 415, 416, 418

Calloway, Earl. "'Raisin' Explodes with Cool Intensity." Chicago Daily Defender, 30 March 1976, in Newsbank--Performing Arts. March-April 1976, 27: E 13

"Claudia McNeil Won Fame the Hard Way." The Afro-American: Afro Magazine (Baltimore, Md.), 15-19 March 1977, p. 1

Fowler, Giles M. "Theater in Mid-America." Kansas City (Mo.) Star, 9 February 1977, in Newsbank--Performing Arts. January-February 1977, 10: A 4

Greer, Edward G. "Broadway--On and Off." Drama 112 (Spring 1974): 60-61

Kane, George. "Brilliant Cast of 'Raisin' Makes It a Musical of Joy." (Denver, Colo.) Rocky Mountain News, 19 March 1976, in Newsbank--Performing Arts. March-April 1976, 27: E 10

Loynd, Ray. "'Raisin' Opens at the Shubert." Los Angeles (Calif.) Herald Examiner, 23 January 1976, in Newsbank--Performing Arts. January-February 1976, 11: E 9

Michelson, Herb. "'Raisin' Has Problems--Songs, Stage."
Sacramento (Calif.) Bee, 6 March 1976, in Newsbank--
Performing Arts. March-April 1976, 27: E 9
Mills, James. "'Raisin' Can't Match Plays' Old Wrinkles."
Denver (Colo.) Post, 18 March 1976, in Newsbank--
Performing Arts. March-April 1976, 27: E 11
Murray, James P. "Blacks Invade Broadway in a Big
Way ... With Soul Cheers, and Society Bows." St.
Louis (Mo.) Argus, 17 April 1975, in Newsbank--Per-
forming Arts. March-April 1975, 28: D 8, 9, 10
"'Raisin' Is Exciting Theatre Experience." Seattle (Wash.)
Times, 23 March 1977, in Newsbank--Performing Arts.
March-April 1977, 23: F 7
Russell, Candice. "Local Talent Abounds in 'Raisin'."
Miami (Fla.) Herald, 5 April 1976, in Newsbank--Per-
forming Arts. March-April 1976, 27: E 12
Silva, Candelaria. "'Raisin': Capitalizing on an Over-
played Theme." (Boston, Mass.) Bay State Banner, 1
January 1976, in Newsbank--Performing Arts. January-
February 1976, 11: E 10
Thom, Rose Anne. "The Gypsy Camp." Dance Magazine
49 (April 1975): 89-91
Willis' Theatre World. vol. 30, 1973-1974, pp. 14-15
_____. vol. 31, 1974-1975, p. 58
Winer, Linda. "The Boom in Black Theatre: Growing
Profits ... and Growing Pains." Chicago Tribune:
Arts & Fun, 30 May 1976, 6:2
MEDIA RESOURCES:
Film: "Lorraine Hansberry: The Black Experience in the
Creation of Drama." 35 min., 16mm color, FFH 128 (1976)
Film Strip: "Life of Lorraine Hansberry" (Learning Arts,
Wichita, Ka. 67201)
AWARDS:
ACTF, 1976
"An American Library Association 'Select Film for Young
Adults, 1976'"
Tony Award, 1974, for Raisin, best musical

HARDY, SHIRLEY
PLAYS:
Where Is the Pride, What Is the Joy

HARPER, KEN see also BROWN, W. F.; SMALLS, C.
MUSICALS:
Wiz
CRITICISMS OF HARPER:
Peterson, Maurice. "The Wiz's Wizzes: Ken Harper and
Geoffrey Holder." Essence 6 (September 1975): 54-55,
83-84, 87
REVIEW OF INDIVIDUAL MUSICALS:
Wiz
Peterson, Maurice. "The Wiz's Wizzes: Ken Harper

and Geoffrey Holder." Essence 6 (September 1975): 54-55, 83-84, 87

†HARRIS, BILL
PLAYS:
Warn the Wicked
REVIEWS OF INDIVIDUAL PLAYS:
Warn the Wicked
Calloway, Earl. "X-Bag Showcases Drama with Moving Pathos." Chicago Daily Defender, 8 January 1975, in Newsbank--Performing Arts. January-February 1975, 13: G 14

HARRIS, CLARENCE
PLAYS:
The Trip
PLAYS PUBLISHED IN ANTHOLOGIES:
The Trip, in Knight. Black Voices from Prison

†HARRIS, HELEN WEBB
PLAYS:
Genifrede
PLAYS PUBLISHED IN ANTHOLOGIES:
Genifrede, in Richardson and Miller. Negro History in Thirteen Plays

†HARRIS, NEIL (b. February 20, 1936)
PLAYS:
Cop and Blow
Players Inn
So Nice They Named It Twice
[with Miguel Pinero] Straight from the Ghetto
CRITICISMS OF HARRIS:
Stasio, Marilyn. "Off-Broadway." In Theatre 5: The American Theatre, 1971-1972, p. 33
CRITICISMS OF INDIVIDUAL PLAYS:
Cop and Blow
Oliver, Edith. "Report from 137th Street." In Theatre 5: The American Theatre, 1971-1972, p. 133
Players Inn
Oliver, Edith. "Report from 137th Street." In Theatre 5: The American Theatre, 1971-1972, p. 133
REVIEWS OF INDIVIDUAL PLAYS:
Cop and Blow
Clurman, Harold. "Theatre." Nation 214 (17 April 1972): 508-509
Kalem, T. E. "Black on Black--'Black Visions'." Time 99 (1 May 1972): 53
Oliver, Edith. "Off Broadway--'Black Visions'." New Yorker 48 (8 April 1972): 97-100
Players Inn
Clurman, Harold. "Theatre." Nation 214 (17 April 1972): 508-509

Kalem, T. E. "Black on Black--'Black Visions'." <u>Time</u> 99 (1 May 1972): 53

Oliver, Edith. "Off Broadway--'Black Visions'." <u>New Yorker</u> 48 (8 April 1972): 97-100

So Nice They Named It Twice
Oliver, Edith. "Off Broadway: Life on the Edge." <u>New Yorker</u> 52 (7 June 1976): 79-80

Straight from the Ghetto
"Street Theatre: A Way of Life." <u>(N.Y.) Amsterdam News: Arts and Entertainment</u>, 11 September 1976, D-11

†HARRISON, PAUL CARTER (b. 1936)
PLAYS:
Doctor Jazz
The Great MacDaddy, 1972
CRITICISMS OF HARRISON:
Hatch, James. "Speak to Me in Those Old Words, You Know, Those La-La Words, Those Tung-Tung Sounds." Yale/Theatre 8 (Fall 1976): 29, 31, 32

Ogunbiyi, Yemi. "New Black Playwrights in America, 1960-1975." Ph.D. Dissertation, New York University, 1976, Chp. 3

CRITICISMS OF INDIVIDUAL PLAYS:
The Great MacDaddy
Bailey, Peter. "Annual Round-up: Black Theatre in America--New York." Black World 24 (April 1975): 19-20

Current Biography 37 (September 1976): 30
Engel. The Critics, pp. 30, 32, 85-86
Hatch, James. "Speak to Me in Those Old Words, You Know, Those La-La Words, Those Tung-Tung Sounds (Some African Influences on the Afro American Theatre)." Yale/Theatre 8 (Fall 1976): 30-31

REVIEWS OF INDIVIDUAL PLAYS:
Doctor Jazz
Giddins, Gary. "Doctored Jazz." <u>New York Magazine</u> 8 (10 March 1975): 69

Guernsey. The Best Plays of 1974-1975, pp. 345-46
Willis' Theatre World. vol. 3, 1974-1975, p. 49

The Great MacDaddy
Blum and Willis, eds. A Pictorial History of the American Theatre: 1860-1976, pp. 422, 423

Davis, Curt. "No Great Good in 'MacDaddy'." <u>Encore</u> 6 (23 May 1977): 40

Gilbert, Ruth, ed. "In and Around Town: Off and Off-Off Broadway." <u>New York</u> 10 (6 June 1977): 20; (2 May 1977): 20

Gottfried, Martin. "This 'MacDaddy' Is Not So Great." New York Post, 14 April 1977, in Newsbank--Performing Arts. March-April 1977, 23: D 10

Morrow, Lance. "Black People's Time." <u>Time</u> 103 (25 February 1974): 69

Novick, Julius. "Old Legend, New Version." Village
  Voice 19 (21 February 1974): 55
Oliver, Edith. "Off Broadway: O Bold New Prospero!"
  New Yorker 50 (25 February 1974): 83-85
Rich, Alan. "Theatre: A Coal Barge Named Desire."
  New Yorker 10 (2 May 1977): 69
Wadud, Ali. "'Great MacDaddy'." (N.Y.) Amsterdam
  News: Arts and Entertainment, 7 May 1977, D-1
Watt, Douglas. "A Black Odyssey." (N.Y.) Daily News,
  15 April 1977, in Newsbank--Performing Arts. March-
  April 1977, 23: D 9
Willis' Theatre World. vol. 30, 1973-1974, p. 117

HASSEN, UMAR BEN
  PLAYS:
  Aid to Dependent Children

†HATCH, JAMES V. [as non-black collaborator]
  PLAYS:
  [with C. B. Jackson] Fly Blackbirds
  CRITICISMS BY HATCH:
  "Theodore Ward: Black American Playwright." Freedom-
    ways 15 (First Quarter, 1975): 37-41
  CRITICISMS OF INDIVIDUAL PLAYS:
  The Blackbird
    Hartnoll. The Oxford Companion to the Theatre, p. 680

†HAYDEN, ROBERT
  PLAYS:
  The History of Punchinello
  CRITICISMS OF INDIVIDUAL PLAYS:
  Sandle. The Negro in the American Educational Theatre,
    p. 150

HENDRICKS, JON
  MUSICALS:
  Evolution of the Blues
  REVIEWS OF INDIVIDUAL MUSICALS:
  Evolution of the Blues
    Eichelbaum, Stanley. "Onward with the 'Blues'." San
      Francisco (Calif.) Examiner, 16 September 1975, in
      Newsbank--Performing Arts. September-October 1975,
      67: A 3
    Elwood, Philip. "The Evolution of 'Evolution'." San
      Francisco (Calif.) Examiner, 17 June 1975, in News-
      bank--Performing Arts. May-June 1975, 38: G 12
    Michelson, Herb. "'Heavy' Stuff, Without Any Weight."
      Sacramento (Calif.) Bee, 19 June 1976, in Newsbank--
      Performing Arts. May-June 1976, 40: E 3

HENSHAW, JAMES ENE
  PLAYS:
  Jewels of the Shrine

HIGHTOWER, ROBERT
    PLAYS:
       The Train Ride
       The Wait

†HILL, ABRAM (b. 1911)
    PLAYS:
       On Striver's Row
       Walk Hard, Walk Tall (an adaptation of Len Zenberg's novel)
    CRITICISMS OF HILL:
       Birmingham. Certain People, p. 189
       Mitchell. Voices of the Black Theatre, pp. 113-116
    CRITICISMS OF INDIVIDUAL PLAYS:
       On Striver's Row
          Bailey, Peter. "Annual Round-up: Black Theater in
            America--New York." Black World 24 (April 1975):
            23-24
          Hartnoll. The Oxford Companion to the Theatre, p. 678
          "The Words of Dick Campbell." In Mitchell. Voices of
            the Black Theatre, p. 102-103
          "Words of Regina M. Andrews." In Mitchell. Voices of
            the Black Theatre, pp. 74, 101
       Walk Hard, Walk Tall
          Edmonds, Randolph. "The Blacks in the American
            Theatre, 1700-1969." The Pan-African Journal 7
            (Winter 1974): 304
          Hartnoll. The Oxford Companion to the Theatre, p. 678
          "Words of Regina M. Andrews." In Mitchell. Voices of
            the Black Theatre, p. 74

HILL, ARMENTER
    PLAYS:
       Forever My Earth, 1976

†HILL, ERROL (b. August 5, 1921)
    PLAYS:
       Broken Melody. Caribbean Plays Edition. Port-of-Spain:
          University of the West Indies, 1966
       Dance Bongo. In Caribbean Literature: An Anthology. Ed.
          Gabriel R. Coulthard. London: University of London
          Press, 1966
       Square Peg. Caribbean Plays Edition. Kingston: University
          of the West Indies, 1953
    PLAYS PUBLISHED IN ANTHOLOGIES:
       Dance Bongo, in Coulthard. Caribbean Literature
    CRITICISMS BY HILL:
       The Trinidad Carnival: Mandate for a National Theatre.
          Austin: University of Texas Press, 1972

HILL, F.
    PLAYS:
       Betrayal

†HILL, MARS (b. November 18, 1927)
    PLAYS:
        Malice in Wonderland
        Man in the Family
    REVIEWS OF INDIVIDUAL PLAYS:
        Man in the Family
            Kelly, Martin P. "'Man in the Family' a Play About
                Black Society." (Albany, N.Y.) Times-Union, 18
                April 1977, in Newsbank--Performing Arts. March-
                April 1977, 25: D 2

HINES, JOHN
    PLAYS:
        The Boyhood Adventures of Frederick Douglass: A Play.
            N.Y.: New Dimensions, 1968
        The Celebration: A Play. N.Y.: New Dimensions, 1968
        The Genius of Benjamin Banneker: A Play. N.Y.: New
            Dimensions, 1968
        In Memory of Jerry. N.Y.: New Dimensions, 1970
        The Outsider. N.Y.: New Dimensions, 1970

†HOLIFIELD, HAROLD
    PLAYS:
        Cow in the Apartment
        J. Toth
    CRITICISMS OF INDIVIDUAL PLAYS:
        Cow in the Apartment
            Hartnoll. The Oxford Companion to the Theatre, p. 680
        J. Toth
            Hartnoll. The Oxford Companion to the Theatre, p. 680

HOLT, STEVEN
    PLAYS:
        Where the Onus Falls

HOLT, WILL
    MUSICALS:
        [with Linda Hopkins] Me and Bessie
        [with George Abbott and Richard Adler] Music Is (musical
            adaptation of Twelfth Night)
    CRITICISMS OF INDIVIDUAL MUSICALS:
        Me and Bessie
            Bell, Roseanne Pope. "'For Colored Girls Who Have
                Considered Suicide/When the Rainbow Is Enuf'." The
                Black Collegian 7 (May-June 1977): 48
            Weals, Gerald. "Birthday Mutterings." Modern Theatre
                and Drama 19 (December 1976): 420-21
    REVIEWS OF INDIVIDUAL MUSICALS:
        Me and Bessie
            Aaron, Jules. "Theatre in Review." Educational Theatre
                Journal 27 (March 1975): 129-130
            Balliet, Whitney. "Jazz: New York Notes." New

Yorker 51 (10 November 1975): 151-152

Blum and Willis, eds. A Pictorial History of the American Theatre: 1860-1976, pp. 424, 426

Downs, Joan. "Upbeat Blues." Time 106 (3 November 1975): 66

Guernsey. The Best Plays of 1975-1976, p. 329

Hughes, Catharine. "Broadway Roundup." America 133 (6 December 1975): 409

_____ . "Three New Musicals." America 135 (27 November 1976): 373

_____ . "Two Black Plays." America 135 (27 November 1976): 373

McMorrow, Tom. "Broadway Expects a Championship Season." (N.Y.) Daily News, 7 September 1975, in Newsbank--Performing Arts. January-February 1975, 68: C 14-D 1

New York Theatre Critics' Reviews--1975 36 (20 October 1975): 184-187; containing: Watt, Douglas, "Linda Sings Bessie Smith" [N.Y.] Daily News, 23 October 1975). Barnes, Clive, "'Me and Bessie' is All Heart and Soul" (New York Times 23 October 1975). Gottfried, Martin, "Linda 'and Bessie' Are Special" (New York Post, 23 October 1975). Wilson, Edwin, "Me and Bessie" (The Wall Street Journal, 28 October 1975). "Broadway Stages Life of Legendary Singer" (The Christian Science Monitor, 30 October 1975). Ettore, Barbara, "Me and Bessie" (Women's Wear Daily, 23 October 1975). Sanders, Kevin, "Me and Bessie" (WABC-TV, 26 October 1975). Downs, Joan, "Up Beat Blues" (Time, 3 November 1975)

Peterson, Maurice. "On the Aisle: Spotlight on Betty Allen." Essence 6 (February 1976): 31

Raidy, Williams A. "Linda Hopkins." (Newark, N.J.) Star Ledger, 23 November 1975, in Newsbank--Performing Arts. November-December 1975, 83: B 1

Rich, Alan. "Singers Sweet, Singer Sour." New York Magazine 8 (10 November 1975): 84

Sweet, Jeff. "'Like a Goddess ... on that Stage'." (Long Island N.Y.) Newsday, 26 October 1975, in Newsbank--Performing Arts. September-October 1975, 66: E 6, 7

Walker, Jesse H. "And Now a Word...." The Afro-American (Baltimore Md.), 19-23 July 1977, p. 11

"Welcome to the Great Black Way." Time 108 (1 November 1976): 75

Music Is

Farrow, Charles. "'Music Is' Witty and Colorful Adaptation of 'Twelfth Night'." Afro-American (Baltimore, Md.), 30 November-4 December 1976, p. 11

MEDIA RESOURCES:

Me and Bessie

Soundtrack by Columbia Records

†HOPKINS, LINDA
  MUSICALS:
    [with Will Holt] Me and Bessie
  CRITICISMS OF HOPKINS:
    Cosford, Bill. "The Blues Are Gospel to 'Bessie' Star."
      Miami (Fla.) Herald, 10 February 1977, in Newsbank--
      Performing Arts. January-February 1977, 2: D 6
           . "Linda as 'Bessie' Sends Shivers Down the
      Spine." Miami (Fla.) Herald, 3 February 1977, in
      Newsbank--Performing Arts. January-February 1977,
      10: B 11
    Peterson, Maurice. "On the Aisle: Spotlight on Linda Hop-
      kins." Essence 7 (June 1976): 45
    Stein, Shifra. "Actress Brings Back Bessie and the Blues."
      Kansas City (Mo.) Star, 21 April 1977, in Newsbank--
      Performing Arts. March-April 1977, 23: G 9, 10
    Sweet, Jeff. "'Like a Goddess ... on that Stage'." (Long
      Island, N.Y.) Newsday, 26 October 1975, in Newsbank--
      Performing Arts. September-October 1975, 66: E 6, 7
  CRITICISMS OF INDIVIDUAL MUSICALS:
    Me and Bessie
      Bell, Roseanne Pope. "'For Colored Girls Who Have
        Considered Suicide /When the Rainbow is Enuf'." The
        Black Collegian 7 (May-June 1977): 48
      Weales, Gerald. "Birthday Mutterings." Modern Theatre
        and Drama 19 (December 1976): 420-21
  REVIEWS OF INDIVIDUAL MUSICALS:
    Me and Bessie
      Aaron, Jules. "Theatre in Review." Educational Theatre
        Journal, 27 (March 1975): 129-30
      Balliet, Whitney. "Jazz: New York Notes." New
        Yorker 51 (10 November 1975): 151-152
      Blum and Willis, eds. A Pictorial History of the Ameri-
        can Theatre: 1860-1976, pp. 424, 426
      Downs, Joan. "Upbeat Blues." Time 106 (3 November
        1975): 66
      Guernsey. The Best Plays of 1975-1976, p. 329
      Hughes, Catharine. "Broadway Roundup." America 133
        (6 December 1975): 409
           . "Three New Musicals." America 135 (27
      November 1976): 373
           . "Two Black Plays." America 135 (27 Novem-
      ber 1976): 373
    McMorrow, Tom. "Broadway Expects a Championship
      Season." (N.Y.) Daily News, 7 September 1975, in
      Newsbank--Performing Arts. January-February 1975,
      68: C 14-D 1
    New York Theatre Critics' Reviews--1975 36 (20 October
      1975): 184-87; containing: Watt, Douglas, "Linda Sings
      Bessie Smith" ([N.Y.] Daily News, 23 October 1975).
      Barnes, Clive, "'Me and Bessie' Is All Heart and Soul"
      (New York Times, 23 October 1975). Gottfried, Martin,

"Linda 'and Bessie' Are Special" (New York Post, 23
October 1975). Wilson, Edwin, "Me and Bessie" (The
Wall Street Journal, 28 October 1975). "Broadway
Stages Life of Legendary Singer" (The Christian Science
Monitor, 30 October 1975). Ettorre, Barbara, "Me
and Bessie" (Women's Wear Daily, 23 October 1975).
Sanders, Kevin, "Me and Bessie" (WABC-TV, 26
October 1975). Downs, Joan, "Up Beat Blues" (Time,
3 November 1975)
Peterson, Maurice. "On the Aisle." Essence 6 (February
1976): 31
Raidy, Williams A. "Linda Hopkins." (Newark, N.J.)
Star Ledger, 23 November 1975, in Newsbank--Per-
forming Arts. November-December 1975, 83: B 1
Rich, Alan. "Singers Sweet, Singer Sour." New York
Magazine 8 (10 November 1975): 84
Sweet, Jeff. "'Like a Goddess ... on that Stage'."
(Long Island, N.Y.) Newsday, 26 October 1975, in
Newsbank--Performing Arts. September-October 1975,
66: E 6, 7
Walker, Jessie H. "And Now a Word...." The Afro-
American (Baltimore, Md.), 19-23 July 1977, p. 11
"Welcome to the Great Black Way." Time 108 (1 Novem-
ber 1976): 75
MEDIA RESOURCES:
Me and Bessie
Soundtrack by Columbia Records

†HOPKINS, PAULINE ELIZABETH (1859-August 13, 1930)
CRITICISMS OF HOPKINS:
Shockley, Ann Allen. "Pauline Elizabeth Hopkins: A Biographical Excursion into Obscurity." Phylon 33 (Spring
1972): 22-26

HOWARD, VILMA
PLAYS:
The Tam
CRITICISMS OF INDIVIDUAL PLAYS:
The Tam
Sandle. The Negro in the American Educational Theatre,
pp. 87, 157

HUDSON, FRED
PLAYS:
If We Must Die

HUDSON, WADE
PLAYS:
Sam Carter Belongs Here

HUFFMAN, EUGENE H.
PLAYS:

Hoo-dooed, 1932? (later retitled The Victory)
The Imposter in the Red Mausoleum
The Lost Chord
St. Peter Is Out
Unto Us a Child Is Born

HUGHES, ALLISON
  CRITICISMS OF HUGHES:
  Walsh, Elizabeth and Diane Bowers. "WPA Federal Theatre
    Project." Theatre World 8 (April 1976): 2

†HUGHES, LANGSTON
  PLAYS:

Angelo Herndon Jones	Mule Bone
The Barrier	Scottsboro Limited
Don't You Want to be Free?	Simply Heavenly
The Emperor of Haiti	Soul Gone Home
The Gold Piece	The Sun Do Move
Jericho-Jimcrow	[with Jobe Huntley] Tam-
Little Ham	bourines to Glory (based
Mulatto	on a novel)

  PLAYS PUBLISHED IN ANTHOLOGIES:
  Don't You Want to be Free?, in Davis and Peplow. The
    New Negro Renaissance
  Soul Gone Home, in Heston, The Man in the Dramatic Mode,
    vol. V; in Swortzell, All the World's a Stage
  MUSICALS:
  [with C. Bernard Jackson] Langston Hughes Said
  [with Kurt Weill] Street Scene
  [with Jobe Huntley] Tambourines to Glory
  CRITICISMS OF HUGHES:
  Cohn. Dialogue in American Drama, pp. 183-86
  Davis, Arthur P. From the Dark Tower, pp. 61-62; 66-69
  Goldstein. The Political Stage, pp. 162-168
  "Hatch--Billops Archives Interviews with Playwrights."
    Negro American Literature Forum 10 (Summer 1976):
    64-65
  Houghton. Advance from Broadway, p. 102
  "Hughes at Columbia." New Yorker 43 (30 December 1967):
    21-23
  Lemons, J. Stanley. "Black Stereotypes as Reflected in
    Popular Culture, 1880-1920." American Quarterly 29
    (Spring 1977): 107
  McGraw-Hill Encyclopedia of World Drama. vol. 2, pp.
    373-374
  Proffer. Soviet Criticism of American Literature in the
    Sixties, p. 59
  Smythe, Mabel M., ed. The Black American Reference
    Book. rev. ed. Englewood Cliffs, N.J.: Prentice-Hall,
    1976, Part I, p. 22
  CRITICISMS OF INDIVIDUAL PLAYS:

Angelo Herndon Jones
  Goldstein. The Political Stage, pp. 162-163, 165
The Barrier
  McGraw-Hill Encyclopedia of World Drama. vol. 2,
    p. 374
Black Nativity
  Falb. American Drama in Paris, 1945-1970, p. 158
Don't You Want to Be Free?
  Davis, Arthur P. From the Dark Tower, pp. 65, 67
  Edmonds, Randolph. "The Blacks in the American
    Theatre, 1700-1969." The Pan-African Journal, 7
    (Winter 1974): 305, 309
  Goldstein. The Political Stage, pp. 165, 167
  Houghton. Advance from Broadway, p. 159
  Stevenson, Robert Louis. "The Image of the White Man
    As Projected in the Published Plays of Black Ameri-
    cans, 1847-1973." Ph.D. Dissertation, Indiana Uni-
    versity, 1975
  "The Words of Regina M. Andrews." In Mitchell. Voices
    of the Black Theatre, p. 74
Emperor of Haiti
  Goldstein. The Political Stage, p. 166
  Keysaar-Franke, Helen. "Strategies in Black Drama."
    Ph.D. Dissertation, University of Iowa, 1974
The Gold Piece
  Davis, Arthur P. From the Dark Tower, pp. 67+
  Sandle. The Negro in the American Educational Theatre,
    p. 152
Jericho-Jimcrow
  Hartnoll. The Oxford Companion to the Theatre, p. 681
Little Ham
  Cohn. Dialogue in American Drama, pp. 183, 185
  Davis, Arthur P. From the Dark Tower, pp. 68-69
  Goldstein. The Political Stage, p. 166
  Taylor, Clarke. "In the Soul of Theatre." Essence 5
    (April 1975): 48
Mulatto
  Abramson, Doris. "The Great White Way: Critics and
    the First Plack Playwrights on Broadway." Educa-
    tional Theatre Journal 28 (March 1976): 52-53
  Cohn. Dialogue in American Drama, pp. 183-85
  Davis, Arthur P. From the Dark Tower, pp. 68-69
  Edmonds, Randolph. "The Blacks in the American
    Theatre, 1700-1969." The Pan-African Journal 7
    (Winter 1974): 305
  Gagey. Revolution in American Drama, p. 157
  Goldstein. The Political Stage, pp. 165, 166
  McGraw-Hill Encyclopedia of World Drama. vol. 2, pp.
    373-374
  Nasimento, Abdias Do. "The Negro Theater in Brazil."
    In Mezu, ed. Modern Black Literature, p. 172
  Potter, Vilma R. "New Politics, New Mothers." CLA

Journal 16 (December 1972): 247-255
Mule Bone
    Hatch, James. "Speak to Me in Those Old Words, You
       Know, Those La-La Words, Those Tung-Tung Sounds
       (Some African Influences on the Afro-American Theatre)."
       Yale/Theatre 8 (Fall 1976): 33
Scottsboro Limited
    Goldstein. The Political Stage, p. 165, 168
Simply Heavenly
    Davis, Arthur P. From the Dark Tower, p. 69
    Edmonds, Randolph. "The Blacks in the American Theatre,
       1700-1969." The Pan-African Journal 7 (Winter 1974):
       305
    Hartnoll. The Oxford Companion to the Theatre, p. 680
    Sandle. The Negro in the American Educational Theatre,
       pp. 127, 139, il
Soul Gone Home
    Cohn. Dialogue in American Drama, p. 185
    Davis, Arthur P. From the Dark Tower, p. 69
    Goldstein. The Political Stage, pp. 166-167
    McGraw-Hill Encyclopedia of World Drama. vol. 2,
       p. 374
    Potter, Vilma R. "New Politics, New Mothers." CLA
       Journal 16 (December 1972): 247-255
    Sandle. The Negro in the American Educational Theatre,
       p. 152
The Sun Do Move
    McGraw-Hill Encyclopedia of World Drama. vol. 2, p. 374
Tambourines to Glory
    Davis, Arthur P. From the Dark Tower, pp. 65, 69
    Edmonds, Randolph. "The Blacks in the American Theatre,
       1700-1969." The Pan-African Journal 7 (Winter 1974):
       305
    Hartnoll. The Oxford Companion to the Theatre, p. 681
    Hay, Samuel A. "African-American Drama, 1950-1960."
       Negro History Bulletin 36 (January 1973): 7
    Miller, Barter R. "'A Mere Poem': 'Daybreak in Ala-
       bama', A Resolution of Langston Hughes's Theme of
       Music and Art." Obsidian 2 (Summer 1976): 33
CRITICISMS OF INDIVIDUAL MUSICALS:
    Black Nativity
       Wilmer, Valerie. "The Sound in Europe." Soul Illustrated
        2 (October 1969): 32
    Langston Hughes Said
       Willis' Theatre World. vol. 31, 1974-1975, p. 204
    Street Scene
       Atkinson and Hirschfeld. The Lively Years 1920-1973,
        p. 74
REVIEWS OF INDIVIDUAL PLAYS:
    Black Nativity
       Blum and Willis, eds. A Pictorial History of the Ameri-
       can Theatre: 1860-1976, p. 373

Mulatto
    Atkinson, Brooks. "Mulatto." In Beckerman and Siegman.
    On Stage: Selected Theatre Reviews from the New York
    Stage, 1920-1970, pp. 168-169
Simply Heavenly
    "Claudia McNeil Won Fame the Hard Way." The Afro-
    American: Afro Magazine (Baltimore, Md.), 15-19
    March 1977, p. 1
Tambourines to Glory
    Jennings, Robert. "MSU's 'Glory' Is Refreshing." (Mem-
    phis, Tenn.) Commercial Appeal, 12 April 1975, in
    Newsbank--Performing Arts. March-April 1975, 29:
    F 10
REVIEWS OF INDIVIDUAL MUSICALS:
Tambourines to Glory
    Jennings, Robert. "MSU's 'Glory' Is Refreshing."
    (Memphis, Tenn.) Commercial Appeal, 12 April 1975,
    in Newsbank--Performing Arts. March-April 1975, 29:
    F 10
BIBLIOGRAPHIES OF HUGHES:
    Dickinson, Donald C. "A Bio-Bibliography of Langston
    Hughes, 1902-1967, 2nd ed. Hamden, Conn.: Shoe String
    Press, 1972

†HULT, RUBY
    PLAYS:
    The Saga of George W. Bush
    PLAYS PUBLISHED IN PERIODICALS:
    The Saga of George W. Bush. In Black World 11 (September
      1962): 88-96

†HUNTER, EDDIE (b. February 4, 1888)
    PLAYS:
    The Gentleman Burglar
    How Come?
    Leave Home, sketch
    The Railway Porter
    Subway Sal
    What Happens When the Husbands Leave Home
    CRITICISMS BY HUNTER:
    "The Words of Eddie Hunter." In Mitchell. Voices of the
    Black Theatre, pp. 35-57

HUNTLEY, JOBE
    MUSICALS:
    [with Langston Hughes] Tambourines to Glory
    REVIEWS OF INDIVIDUAL MUSICALS:
    Tambourines to Glory
      Jennings, Robert. "MSU's 'Glory' Is Refreshing."
      (Memphis, Tenn.) Commercial Appeal, 12 April 1975,
      in Newsbank--Performing Arts. March-April 1975,
      29: F 10

†HURSTON, ZORA NEALE (January 7, 1903-January 28, 1960)
PLAYS:
[with Langston Hughes] Mule Bone: A Comedy of Negro Life
in Three Acts, 1931
[with Dorothy Waring] Polk County, 1944
Stephen Kelen-d'Oxylion Presents Polk County, a Comedy
of Negro Life on a Sawmill Camp, With Authentic Negro
Music, in Three Acts. N.Y.: 1944 [in The Library of
Congress]
Sermon in the Valley, 1931
CRITICISMS OF HURSTON:
Benston. Baraka: The Renegade and the Mask, pp. 262-63
Houghton. Advance from Broadway, p. 102
CRITICISMS OF INDIVIDUAL PLAYS:
Mule Bone
Hatch, James. "Speak to Me of Those Old Words, You
Know, Those La-La Words, Those Tung-Tung Sounds
(Some African Influences on the Afro American Theatre.)"
Yale/Theatre 8 (Fall 1976): 33

†IMAN, KASISI YUSEF
PLAYS:
Yesterday, Today and Tomorrow

IRVINE, WELDON
MUSICALS:
Young, Gifted and Broke
REVIEWS OF INDIVIDUAL MUSICALS:
Young, Gifted and Broke
Gilbert, Ruth. "In and Around Town--Review: Young,
Gifted and Broke." New York 10 (8 August 1977): 16
Wadud, Ali. "'Young, Gifted and Broke' Rich in Music."
(N.Y.) Amsterdam News: Arts and Entertainment, 11
June 1977, D-7

ISHAM, JOHN W.
MUSICALS:
The Octoroons, 1895
Oriental America, 1895
CRITICISMS OF INDIVIDUAL MUSICALS:
The Octoroons
Edmonds, Randolph. "The Blacks in the American Theatre,
1700-1969." The Pan-African Journal 7 (Winter 1974):
314
Oriental America
Edmonds, Randolph. "The Blacks in the American Theatre,
1700-1969." The Pan-African Journal 7 (Winter 1974):
314

IYAUN, IFA
PLAYS:
Drinkwater

JACK, SAM
    MUSICALS:
        Creole Show, 1890
    CRITICISMS OF INDIVIDUAL MUSICALS:
        Creole Show
            Edmonds, Randolph. "The Blacks in the American
                Theatre, 1700-1969." The Pan-African Journal 7
                (Winter 1974): 314

†JACKMAN, MARVIN see MARVIN X

†JACKSON, C. BERNARD
    PLAYS:
        B/C
        Departure
        [with James V. Hatch] Fly Blackbirds
        The Second Earthquake
        Sweet Nutcracker
    MUSICALS:
        [with Langston Hughes] Langston Hughes Said
        Maggie the Mouse Meets the Dirty Rat Fink
    CRITICISMS OF INDIVIDUAL PLAYS:
        Fly Blackbirds
            Hartnoll. The Oxford Companion to the Theatre, p. 680
    REVIEWS OF INDIVIDUAL PLAYS:
        Departure
            Willis' Theatre World. vol. 31, 1974-1975, p. 204
        Langston Hughes Said
            Willis' Theatre World. vol. 31, 1974-1975, p. 204
        The Second Earthquake
            Willis' Theatre World. vol. 31, 1974-1975, p. 204
        Sweet Nutcracker
            Willis' Theatre World. vol. 31, 1974-1975, p. 204

†JACKSON, ELAINE
    PLAYS:
        Cockfight
        Toe Jam, 1975
    CRITICISMS OF JACKSON:
        Moore, Honor. "Theater Will Never Be the Same." Ms. 6
            (December 1977): 38
    REVIEWS OF INDIVIDUAL PLAYS:
        Cockfight
            Eder, Richard. "New Elaine Jackson Play Takes Old
                Drama Route." New York Times (17 October 1977):
                L 39
        Toe Jam
            Moore, Honor. "Theater Will Never Be the Same." Ms.
            6 (December 1977): 38

JACKSON, JAMES THOMAS
    PLAYS:

Bye, Bye Black Sheep
CRITICISMS BY JACKSON:
"Ned Bobkoff and Me." Writer's Digest 57 (February 1977):
16-18, 20-22
CRITICISMS OF JACKSON:
Bobkoff, Ned. "James Thomas Jackson and Me." Writer's
Digest 57 (February 1977): 19

†JACKSON, JOSEPHINE (Jo)
PLAYS:
[with Joseph Walker] The Believers, 1968
Harlem Heyday
Journey into Blackness
TELEVISION SCRIPTS:
[with Jesse Devore] Movin' On Up (Series)
REVIEWS OF INDIVIDUAL PLAYS:
The Believers
Oliver, Edith. "Off Broadway: Revue by Voices, Inc.:
'The Believers'." New Yorker 44 (May 1968): 75
Sayre, N. "New York's Black Theatre." New Statesman
76 (25 October 1968): 556

JACKSON, the Rev. SPENCER
PLAYS:
Slyster

†JEANNETTE, GERTRUDE
PLAYS:
Bolt from the Blue
This Way Forward
CRITICISMS OF INDIVIDUAL PLAYS:
Bolt from the Blue
Hartnoll. The Oxford Companion to the Theatre, p. 680
This Way Forward
Hartnoll. The Oxford Companion to the Theatre, p. 680

JEFFERSON, ANETTA G.
MUSICALS:
Drown the Wind

JEREMY, JOHN
FILM SCRIPTS:
Jazz Is Our Religion

JOHN, ERROL
PLAYS:
Moon on a Rainbow Shawl
CRITICISMS OF INDIVIDUAL PLAYS:
Moon on a Rainbow Shawl
Hobson. International Theatre Annual, No. 4, p. 32
REVIEWS OF INDIVIDUAL PLAYS:
Moon on a Rainbow Shawl

Davis, Curt. "Earle Hyman Is Running the Other Race."
Encore 6 (4 April 1977): 35
"James Earl Jones in 'Exorcist II: The Heretic'." The
Afro-American: Afro Magazine (Baltimore, Md.), 31
May 4-June 1977, p. 13
Marvin X. "Reviews." Black Theatre no. 1 (1968): 30-31

JOHNSON, FELTON
PLAYS:
The Cabaret Girl, 1925

†JOHNSON, GEORGIA DOUGLAS (September 10, 1886-1966)
PLAYS:
Plumes
PLAYS PUBLISHED IN ANTHOLOGIES:
Plumes, in Davis and Peplow. The New Negro Renaissance
PLAYS PUBLISHED IN PERIODICALS:
Plumes, in Opportunity 5 (May 1925): 200-01, 217-18

†JOHNSON, HALL (March 12, 1888-1970)
PLAYS:
[with Em Jo Basshe] Earth
[with Em Jo Basshe] Hoboken Blues; [or] The Black Rip Van
Winkle
MUSICALS:
Run, Little Chillun
CRITICISMS OF INDIVIDUAL PLAYS:
Earth
Hartnoll. The Oxford Companion to the Theatre, p. 675
Hoboken Blues
Hartnoll. The Oxford Companion to the Theatre, p. 675
CRITICISMS OF INDIVIDUAL MUSICALS:
Run, Little Chillun
Abramson, Doris. "The Great White Way: Critics and
the First Black Playwrights on Broadway." Educational
Theatre Journal 28 (March 1976): 51-52
Edmonds, Randolph. "The Blacks in the American Theatre,
1700-1969." The Pan-African Journal 7 (Winter 1974):
3-4, 314
Gagey. Revolution in American Drama, p. 157
Hartnoll. The Oxford Companion to the Theatre, pp. 676,
677
Hatch, James. "Speak to Me in Those Old Words, You
Know, Those La-La Words, Those Tung-Tung Sounds."
Yale/Theatre 8 (Fall 1976): 33

†JOHNSON, HERMAN
PLAYS:
No Where to Run, No Where to Hide
REVIEWS OF INDIVIDUAL PLAYS:
No Where to Run, No Where to Hide
Oliver, Edith. "Off Broadway: Three to Get Ready."

New Yorker 50 (22 April 1974): 103-04
Willis' Theatre World. vol. 30, 1973-1974, p. 118

†JOHNSON, J. ROSAMOND
    MUSICALS:
        [with Bob Cole] Red Moon
        [with Bob Cole] The Shoofly Regiment
    CRITICISMS OF INDIVIDUAL MUSICALS:
        Red Moon
            Edmonds, Randolph. "The Blacks in the American
                Theatre, 1700-1969." The Pan-African Journal 7
                (Winter 1974): 314
            Mitchell. Voices of the Black Theatre, p. 24
            Shafer, Yvonne. "Black Actors in the Nineteenth Century
                American Theatre." CLA Journal 20 (March 1977):
                400
        The Shoofly Regiment
            Edmonds, Randolph. "The Blacks in the American
                Theatre, 1700-1969." The Pan-African Journal 7
                (Winter 1974): 314
            Mitchell. Voices of the Black Theatre, p. 24

JOHNSON, VEL
    PLAYS:
        Section D
    CRITICISMS OF INDIVIDUAL PLAYS:
        Section D
            Bailey, Peter. "Annual Roundup: Black Theater in
                America--New York." Black World 25 (April 1976):
                55

JONES, Prof. ARNOLD [and class, Ramapo College African/Ameri-
    can Arts Workshop]
    MUSICALS:
        Cinderella Everafter
    REVIEWS OF INDIVIDUAL MUSICALS:
        Cinderella Everafter
            "'Cinderella Everafter'." (N.Y.) Amsterdam News: Arts
                and Entertainment, 7 May 1977, D-5
            Tapley, Mel. "New College Musical Captivates, Charms
                Audience." (N.Y.) Amsterdam News: Arts and Enter-
                tainment, 2 July 1977, D-11

JONES, GAYLE
    PLAYS:
        The Ancestor--A Street Play
    PLAYS PUBLISHED IN ANTHOLOGIES:
        The Ancestor--A Street Play, in Reed. Yardbird Reader,
            vol. 5

†JONES, LE ROI see BARAKA, IMAMU AMIRI

JONES, SILAS
  PLAYS:
    The Afrindi Aspect
    Waiting for Mongo
  REVIEWS OF INDIVIDUAL PLAYS:
    Waiting for Mongo
      Guernsey. The Best Plays of 1974-1975, p. 378
      Leogrande, Ernest. "'Waiting for Mongo' Arrives."
        (N.Y.) Daily News, 20 May 1975, in Newsbank--Per-
        forming Arts. May-June 1975, 40: E 3
      Mackay, Barbara. "Studies in Black and White." Satur-
        day Review 2 (12 July 1975): 52
      Willis' Theatre World. vol. 31, 1974-1975, p. 118
  AWARDS:
    The Afrindi Aspect won the ARTACT Playwrights' Competition

†JONES, WALTER
  PLAYS:
    Jazznite
    Mae's House
    Nigger Nightmare
  REVIEWS OF INDIVIDUALS PLAYS:
    Jazznite
      Kupa, Kushauri. "Closeup: The New York Scene--Black
        Theatre in New York, 1970-1971." Black Theatre
        no. 6 (1972): 45-46
    Nigger Nightmare
      Kupa, Kushauri. "Closeup: The New York Scene--Black
        Theatre in New York, 1970-1971." Black Theatre
        no. 6 (1972): 46

†JOPLIN, SCOTT
  MUSICALS:
    Treemonisha
  CRITICISMS OF JOPLIN:
    Bovosco, Carole. "Discovering Foremothers." Ms. 6
      (September 1977): 59
    Milner, Arthur. "Live from the Library." American Li-
      braries 8 (February 1977): 75-76
  CRITICISMS OF INDIVIDUAL MUSICALS:
    Treemonisha
      Current, Gloster B. "Scott Joplin." Crisis 82 (June-
        July 1975): 220-221
      Kovner, Bruce. "Ragtime Revival." Commentary 61
        (March 1976): 57-60
  REVIEWS OF INDIVIDUAL MUSICALS:
    Treemonisha
      Ardoin, John. "'Treemonisha' Has a Primitive Charm."
        Dallas (Tex.) Morning News, 27 May 1975, in News-
        bank--Performing Arts. May-June 1975, 39: A 11
      Bender, William. "Scott Joplin: From Rags to Opera."
        Time 106 (15 September 1976):'85-86

Blum and Willis, eds. A Pictorial History of the American Theatre: 1860-1976, pp. 424, 426
Farrow, Charles. "Scott Joplin's 'Treemonisha' a Real Musical Jewel." Afro-American (Baltimore, Md.), 16-20 September 1975, in Newsbank--Performing Arts. September-October 1975, 67: D-1
Gardiner, R. H. "Joplin's Only Opera Has Its Points." (Baltimore, Md.) Sun, 8 September 1975, in Newsbank--Performing Arts. September-October 1975, 67: C 14
Giffin, Glenn. "Joplin Entrancing with 'Treemonisha'." Denver (Colo.) Press, 3 October 1975, in Newsbank--Performing Arts. September-October 1975, 67: C 10
Jones, Robert. "'Treemonisha' Return of a Lost Opera." (N.Y.) Daily News, 28 September 1975, in Newsbank--Performing Arts. September-October 1975, 67: C 3, 4, 5
Lowery, Raymond. "Old-Fashioned in Some Ways, 'Treemonisha' Has Good Music." (Raleigh, N.C.) News and Observor 2 May 1976, in Newsbank--Performing Arts. May-June 1976, 41: B 4
McLellan, Joseph. "Something Splendid, Something New, A Dazzling Magical Opera." Washington (D.C.) Post, 7 September 1975, in Newsbank--Performing Arts. September-October 1975, 67: C 12, 13
McMorrow, Tom. "Broadway Expects a Championship Season." (N.Y.) Daily News, 7 September 1975, in Newsbank--Performing Arts. September-October 1975, 68: D 1
McNally, Owen. "Improvising 'Treemonisha'." Hartford (Conn.) Courant, 25 April 1976, in Newsbank--Performing Arts. March-April 1976, 22: G 7
Malitz, Joan. "Joplin Opera Super Entertainment." (Cleveland, O.) Call and Post, 29 October 1975, in Newsbank--Performing Arts. September-October 1975, 67: C 9
Margrave, Wendell. "'Treemonisha': A Crowd Pleaser." Washington (D.C.) Star News, 5 September 1975, in Newsbank--Performing Arts. September-October 1975, 67: C 11
Micklin, Bob. "'Treemonisha' ... Makes a Disappointment." (Long Island, N.Y.) Newsday, 22 October 1975, n.p.
New York Theatre Critics' Reviews--1975 36 (20 October 1975): 189-193; containing: Henahan, D., "'Treemonisha': A Legend Arrives" (New York Times, 22 October 1975). Gottfried, Martin, "Joplin Tried, But Treemonisha Fails as Good Theater" (New York Post, 22 October 1975). Watt, Douglas, "An Endearing 'Treemonisha'" (N.Y.) Daily News, 22 October 1975). Wilson, Edwin. "Scott Joplin's Final Vindication" (Wall Street Journal, 23 October 1975). Beaufort, John, "Scott Joplin's Rag Opera" (Christian Science Monitor, 22 October 1975).

Kissel, Howard, "Treemonisha" (Women's Wear Daily, 21 October 1975). Probst, Leonard, NBC, 21 October 1975. Sanders, Kevin, WABC-TV, 21 October 1975
Peterson, Maurice. "On the Aisle: Focus on Avon Long." Essence 6 (January 1976): 28
Rockwell, John. "Scott Joplin's 'Treemonisha'." Rolling Stone 202 (18 December 1975): 110
Thayer, C.G. "Scott Joplin's 'Treemonisha'." The Ohio Review 18 (Winter 1977): 112-114
Wallach, Allan. "'Treemonisha' Naivete ..." (Long Island N.Y.) Newsday, 22 October 1975, in Newsbank--Performing Arts. September-October 1975, 67: C 6
MEDIA RESOURCES:
Treemonisha
The Houston Grand Opera, Gunther Schuller, Conductor. 2 records. The Deutsche Grammophon Co.
REVIEWS OF INDIVIDUAL MEDIA:
Treemonisha
Willis, Thomas. "Musical Mergers Miss the Vinyl Mark." Chicago Tribune: Arts & Fun, 4 April 1977, pp. 6-7

†JULIEN, MAX
FILM SCRIPTS:
Cleopatra Jones
The Mack
Naked as a Jailbird
Thomasine and Bushrod
CRITICISMS OF INDIVIDUAL FILM SCRIPTS:
Cleopatra Jones
Lucas, Bob. "Super-tall Super Sleuth in 'Cleopatra Jones'." Sepia 22 (September 1973): 38-45
Thomasine and Bushrod
Haynes, Howard. "Off-Screen Lovers Finally United in Movie." Sepia 23 (April 1974): 40-44
REVIEWS OF INDIVIDUAL FILM SCRIPTS:
Cleopatra Jones
Peterson, Maurice. "Today's Film: For Reel or Reality." Essence 5 (July 1974): 25
The Mack
Peterson, Maurice. "Today's Film: For Reel or Reality." Essence 5 (July 1974): 25
Naked as a Jailbird
"Naked as a Jailbird." The Afro-American (Baltimore, Md.), 26-30, July 1977, p. 7
Thomasine and Bushrod
Cocks, Jay. "Quick Cuts." Time 103 (6 May 1974): 91
Peterson, Maurice. "Today's Films: For Reel or Reality." Essence 5 (July 1974): 25
"Playboy After Hours: Movies." Playboy 21 (July 1974): 35
"Still Another." New Yorker 50 (22 April 1974): 32-33

KABAKA, LAWRENCE
  PLAYS:
    Home Grown War

KAY, ULYSSES
  MUSICALS:
    [with Donald Dorr] Jubilee (musical adaptation of Margaret
      Walker's novel)
  REVIEWS OF INDIVIDUAL MUSICALS:
    Jubilee
      "Opera--South's 'Jubilee' Played Before Sell-Out Audi-
        ence." The Afro-American (Baltimore, Md.), 30
        November-4 December 1976, p. 6

KAYDEN, MILDRED
  MUSICALS:
    [with Ed Bullins] Absurdities in Black
    [with Ed Bullins] Storyville
  REVIEWS OF INDIVIDUAL MUSICALS:
    Gilbert, Ruth, ed. "In and Around Town: Off and Off-Off
      Broadway." New York 10 (22 August 1977): 16; (29
      August 1977): 14

†KENNEDY, ADRIENNE (b. September 13, 1931)
  PLAYS:
    A Beast Story, 1966
    Cities in Bezique: Two One Act Plays. N.Y. Samuel
      French, 1970; includes A Beast Story and The Owl
      Answers
    Funny House of a Negro
    A Lesson in Dead Language
    The Owl Answers
    A Rat's Mass
    Sun
  PLAYS PUBLISHED IN ANTHOLOGIES:
    A Lesson in Dead Language, in Parone. Collision Course
    The Owl Answers, in Ashley, Mirrors for Man; in Hoff-
      man, New American Plays, vol. 2
    A Rat's Mass, in Poland and Mailman, The Off Off Broadway
      Book; in Smith, More Plays from Off-Off Broadway
    Sun, in Owens. Spontaneous Combustion
  PLAYS PUBLISHED IN PERIODICALS:
    Sun, in Scripts 1 (November 1971): 51
  CRITICISMS OF KENNEDY:
    Grossman, Samuel L. "Trends in the Avant-Garde Theatre
      of the United States During the 1960s." Ph.D. Disserta-
      tion, University of Minnesota, 1974
    Miller, Jeanne-Marie A. "Images of Black Women in Plays
      by Black American Playwrights." CLA Journal 20 (June
      1977): 505-06
    Ogunbiyi, Yemi. "New Black Playwrights in America, 1960-
      1975." Ph.D. Dissertation, New York University, 1976,
      Chp. 4

Poland and Mailman. The Off Off Broadway Book, pp. 533-34
Smith. More Plays From Off-Off Broadway, p. 345
Tener, Robert L. "Theatre of Identity: Adrienne Kennedy's Portrait of the Black Women." Studies in Black Literature 6 (Summer 1975): 1-5
Turner, Darwin T. "Adrienne Kennedy." In Vinson. Contemporary Dramatists, pp. 436-37
CRITICISMS OF INDIVIDUAL PLAYS:
A Beast Story
    Benston, Kimberly W. "'Cities in Bezique': Adrienne Kennedy's Expressionistic Vision." CLA Journal 20 (December 1976): 236-237, 241
Cities in Bezique
    Benston, Kimberly W. "'Cities in Bezique': Adrienne Kennedy's Expressionistic Vision." CLA Journal 20 (December 1976): 235-244
    Blum and Willis, eds. A Pictorial History of the American Theatre: 1860-1976, p. 402
    Clurman, Harold. "New Playwrights: Boys and Girls on the Burning Deck." In Theatre 4: The American Theatre, 1970-1971, p. 171
    Houghton. The Exploding Stage, pp. 198, 238
    Parker. Who's Who in The Theatre, 15th ed., p. 872
    Simon. Uneasy Stages, pp. 181, 185-87
Funny House of a Negro
    Benston, Kimberly W. "'Cities in Bezique': Adrienne Kennedy's Expressionistic Vision." CLA Journal 20 (December 1976): 236
    Brown, Lorraine. "'For the Characters Are Myself': Adrienne Kennedy's 'Funnyhouse of a Negro'." Negro American Literature Forum 9 (Fall 1975): 86-88
    Hartnoll. The Oxford Companion to the Theatre, p. 681
    Hatch, James. "Speak to Me in Those Old Words, You Know, Those La-La Words, Those Tung-Tung Sounds." Yale/Theatre 8 (Fall 1976): 33
    Hay, Samuel A. "African-American Drama, 1950-1970." Negro History Bulletin 36 (January 1973): 7
    Miller, Jeanne-Marie A. "Images of Black Women in Plays by Black Playwrights." CLA Journal 20 (June 1977): 506
    Taubman. The Making of the American Theatre, p. 334
The Owl Answers
    Benston, Kimberly W. "'Cities in Bezique': Adrienne Kennedy's Expressionistic Vision." CLA Journal 20 (December 1976): 237-238, 240-241
    Miller, Jeanne-Marie A. "Images of Black Women in Plays by Black Playwrights." CLA Journal 20 (June 1977): 506
    Parker. Who's Who in The Theatre, 15th ed., p. 872
    Simon. Uneasy Stages, pp. 185-86
    Tener, Robert L. "Theatre of Identity: Adrienne Kennedy's Portrait of the Black Woman." Studies in

Black Literature 6 (Summer 1975): 1-5
Sun
Benston, Kimberly W. "'Cities in Bezique': Adrienne
Kennedy's Expressionistic Vision." CLA Journal 20
(December 1976): 236
REVIEWS OF INDIVIDUAL PLAYS:
Funnyhouse of a Negro
Clurman, Harold. "Theatre." Nation 198 (10 February
1964): 154

†KILLENS, JOHN OLIVER (b. 1916)
MUSICALS:
[with Richard Wesley and Woodie King] Cotillion
CRITICISMS BY KILLENS:
"The Image of Black Folk in American Literature." Black
Scholar 6 (June 1975): 45-52
CRITICISMS OF INDIVIDUAL MUSICALS:
Cotillion
Bailey, Peter. "Woodie King Jr.: Renaissance Man of
Black Theatre." Black World 24 (April 1975): 5, 9-10
REVIEWS OF INDIVIDUAL MUSICALS:
Cotillion
"Cleavon Little Has Got to be 'Gooood'." New York Post,
3 January 1977, in Newsbank--Performing Arts. Janu-
ary-February 1977, 5: G 1

†KILPATRICK, LINCOLN
PLAYS:
[with Loretta Leverse] Deep Are the Roots
CRITICISMS OF INDIVIDUAL PLAYS:
Deep Are the Roots
Hartnoll. The Oxford Companion to the Theatre, p. 678

†KING, WOODIE (b. July 27, 1937)
MUSICALS:
[with Richard Wesley and John Killens] Cotillion
FILM SCRIPTS:
Harlem Transfer (from the short story by Evon Walker)
The Long Night (based on the novel by Julian Mayfield)
CRITICISMS BY KING:
"Directing 'Winesellers'." Black World 25 (April 1976):
20-26
CRITICISMS OF KING:
Bailey, Peter. "Woodie King Jr.: Renaissance Man of Black
Theatre." Black World 24 (April 1975): 4-10
"Black Theatre: A Bid for Cultural Identity." Black Enter-
prise 2 (September 1971): 33
Fuller, Hoyt W. "Black World Interviews Woody King Jr."
Black World 24 (April 1975): 12-17
"New Breed Theatre Producer." The Afro-American (Balti-
more Md.), 12-16 April 1977, p. 11
Patterson, Lindsay. "Black Theatre: The Search Goes On."

Freedomways (Third Quarter 1974): 242-46

Peterson, Maurice. "On the Road with the Winesellers."
Essence 6 (November 1975): 66-67, 84, 102, 106

Salaam, Kalamu ya. "Making the Image Real." The Black
Collegian 7 (March-April 1977): 56-57

"Stage, Screen and Black Hegemony: Black World Interviews
Woodie King, Jr." Black World 26 (April 1975): 12-17

Xeroxed Abstracts: Stage I; Stage II

CRITICISMS OF INDIVIDUAL MUSICALS:
Cotillion
Bailey, Peter. "Woodie King, Jr.: Renaissance Man
of Black Theater." Black World 24 (April 1975): 5,
9-10

CRITICISMS OF INDIVIDUAL FILM SCRIPTS:
The Long Night
Fuller, Hoyt W. "Black World Interviews Woodie King
Jr.: Stage, Screen, and Black Hegemony." Black
World 24 (April 1975): 15-16
Peterson, Maurice. "On the Aisle." Essence 7 (July
1976): 7

CRITICISMS OF COLLECTIONS:
A Black Quartet
Salaam, Kalamu ya. "Making the Image Real." The
Black Collegian 7 (March-April 1977): 54

REVIEWS OF INDIVIDUAL MUSICALS:
Cotillion
"Cleavon Little Has Got to be 'Gooood'." New York
Post, 3 January 1977, in Newsbank--Performing Arts.
January-February 1977, 5: G 1

KINOY, ERNEST
FILM SCRIPTS:
Leadbelly
REVIEWS OF INDIVIDUAL FILM SCRIPTS:
Leadbelly
Ames, Katrine. "Black Legend." Newsweek 87 (19 April
1976): 95-96
Cocks, Jay. "'Leadbelly'." Time 107 (24 May 1976):
76, 78
Crist, Judith. "Astaire, Kelly and MGM." Saturday Re-
view 3 (29 May 1976): 48
Reed, Rex. "Vogue-Rated Tip-Offs: What to See, Read,
Listen to, and Watch For." Vogue 166 (January 1976):
33
Roman, Margaret. "Films." Senior Scholastic 108 (23
March 1976): 38

†LAMB, A. C.
PLAYS:
Beebee (drama of Negro Lady Doctor), 1940
Millsboro Memorial
Shades of Cotton Lips

CRITICISMS OF INDIVIDUAL PLAYS:
  Millsboro Memorial
    Sandle. The Negro in the American Educational Theatre,
      p. 19
  Shades of Cotton Lips
    Edmonds, Randolph. "The Black in the American Theatre,
      1700-1969." The Pan-African Journal 7 (Winter 1974):
      309-310

LAMB, MYRNA
  PLAYS:
    Crab Quadrille, 1977
  REVIEWS OF INDIVIDUAL PLAYS:
    Crab Quadrille
      "'Crab-Quadrille' a Social Satire." (N.Y.) Amsterdam
      News: Arts and Entertainment, 25 December 1976,
      D-16

LANDRON, J.
  MUSICALS:
    [with Owen Dodson] Bayou Legend (based on play by same
      title)
  REVIEWS OF INDIVIDUAL MUSICALS:
    Bayou Legend
      Willis' Theatre World. vol. 31, 1974-1975, p. 91

LAPIDO, DURO
  PLAYS:
    Oba Koso

LASDUN, GARY
  PLAYS:
    As Long as You're Happy, Barbara

LEAF, PAUL
  FILM SCRIPTS:
    Spookwaffe

LEE, JIM
  PLAYS:
    The Shoeshine Parlor
  REVIEWS OF INDIVIDUAL PLAYS:
    The Shoeshine Parlor
      Sverdlik, Alan. "Queen's Drama about Worn Soles and
        Souls." (N.Y.) Amsterdam News: Arts and Entertain-
        ment, 31 July 1976, D-11

†LEE, LESLIE
  PLAYS:
    As I Lay Dying A Victim of Spring
    Between Now and Then
    The First Breeze of Summer

The War Party
MUSICALS:
Shadows
TELEVISION SCRIPTS:
Almos' A Man (based on a story by Richard Wright)
CRITICISMS OF LEE:
Dubois, John. "Family Finally Accepts His Decision."
    (Philadelphia, Pa.) Evening Bulletin, 2 March 1975, in
    Newsbank--Performing Arts. March-April 1975, 30:
    B 13
CRITICISMS OF INDIVIDUAL PLAYS:
Between Now and Then
    Weales, Gerald. "Birthday Mutterings." Modern Theatre
        and Drama 19 (December 1976): 420-21
The First Breeze of Summer
    Eckstein, George. "Softened Voices in The Black Theater."
        Dissent 23 (Summer 1976): 207-08
    Engel. The Critics, pp. 216-217
    Guernsey. The Best Plays of 1974-1975, pp. 31, 377
        . The Best Plays of 1975-1976, p. 319
    Mackay, Barbara. "Studies in Black and White." Satur-
        day Review 2 (12 July 1975): 52
    Ribowsky, Mark. "'Father' of the Black Theater Boom."
        Sepia 25 (November 1976): 69, 70
    Salaam, Kalamu ya. "Making the Image Real." The
        Black Collegian 7 (March-April 1977): 57
    Weales, Gerald. "Birthday Mutterings." Modern Theatre
        and Drama 19 (December 1976): 420-41
REVIEWS OF INDIVIDUAL PLAYS:
The First Breeze of Summer
    "Black Actor Becomes U of M Summa Cum Laude Gradu-
        ate." Minneapolis (Mn.) Spokesman, 2 June 1977, p. 1
    Blum and Willis, eds. A Pictorial History of the Ameri-
        can Theatre: 1860-1976, pp. 425, 427
    "Claudia McNeil Won Fame the Hard Way." The Afro-
        American: Afro-Magazine (Baltimore, Md.), 15-19
        March 1977, p. 1
    Clurman, Harold. "Theatre." Nation 220 (22 March
        1975): 348-350
    Dodds, Richard. "A Welcome 'First Breeze'." (New
        Orleans, La.) Times-Picayune, 19 April 1977, in
        Newsbank--Performing Arts. March-April 1977, 25:
        E 1
    Gardner, R. H. "Play Still Needs Work." (Baltimore,
        Md.) Sun, 17 March 1977, in Newsbank--Performing
        Arts. March-April 1977, 25: E 2
    Haun, Harry. "Everyone's 'Breeze'." (N.Y.) Daily News,
        15 July 1975, in Newsbank--Performing Arts. July-
        August 1975, 54: A 5
    Murray, James P. "Broadway Show Is ... On the Road
        with...." (N.Y.) Amsterdam News: Arts and Entertain-
        ment, 20 August 1975, in Newsbank--Performing Arts.

July-August 1975, 71: D 9

"New Breed Theatre Producer." The Afro-American (Baltimore, Md.), 12-16 April 1977, p. 11

New York Theatre Critics' Reviews--1975 36 (16 June 1975): 228-231; containing: Barnes, Clive, "Theater: 'First Breeze of Summer'" (New York Times, 3 March 1975). Watt, Douglas, "To a Matriarch with Love" ([N.Y.] Daily News, 4 March 1975). Gottfried, Martin, "Negro Company Premiers" (New York Post, 3 March 1975). Wilson, Edwin, "Family Life in a Black Household" (Wall Street Journal, 13 June 1975). Sharp, Christopher, "The First Breeze of Summer" (Women's Wear Daily, 12 June 1975). Beaufort, John, "The First Breeze of Summer" (Christian Science Monitor, 10 March 1970)

Oliver, Edith. "Off Broadway: At Home with the Edwardses." New Yorker 51 (17 March 1975): 74-95

Peters, Ida. "'First Breeze of Summer' Unlocks Family--Leslie Lee ... the Playwright." The Afro-American (Baltimore, Md.), 22-26 March 1977, p. 11

Peterson, Maurice. "On the Aisle." Essence 6 (June 1975): 9

_____. "On the Aisle: Spotlight on Leslie Lee." Essence 6 (October 1975): 9

Pyatt, Richard I. "Will Moses Gunn Shoot Down Father Time?" Encore 6 (3 January 1977): 29-30

Simon, John. "A Dull House." New York Magazine 8 (24 March 1975): 79

Willis' Theatre World. vol. 31, 1974-1975, p. 117

_____. vol. 32, 1975-1976, p. 10

The War Party

Willis' Theatre World. vol. 30, 1973-1974, p. 120

AWARDS:

First Breeze

Obie Award--Best Play 1974-1975

Tony Award--Best Play 1976

LE NOIRE, ROSETTA (b. August 8, 1911)

PLAYS:

[with Clyde Williams] Come Laugh and Cry with Langston Hughes (based on Hughes' Shakespeare in Harlem)

MUSICALS:

Bubbling Brown Sugar (a musical revue based on a book by Loften Mitchell and a concept by Rosetta Le Noire)

CRITICISMS OF LE NOIRE:

Xeroxed Abstracts: Stage I

CRITICISMS OF INDIVIDUAL MUSICALS:

Bubbling Brown Sugar

Bell, Roseanne Pope. "'For Colored Girls Who Have Considered Suicide/When the Rainbow Is Enuf'." The Black Collegian 7 (May-June 1977): 48

Bontemps, Alex. "'Bubbling Brown Sugar'." Ebony 31

(February 1976): 124-31
"'Bubbling Brown Sugar'." Ebony 31 (February 1976):
124-26, 128-31
Guernsey. The Best Plays of 1975-1976, pp. 344-45
Osborne, Gwendolyn, E. "Report from Aisle C: 'Bubbling
Brown Sugar'." Crisis 84 (January 1977): 34
Pacheco, Patrick. "'Bubbling Brown Sugar'." After Dark
9 (May 1976): 58-63
Taylor, Clarke. "Fortune Smiles on Broadway's Gypsies."
Essence 7 (August 1976): 79
Weales, Gerald. "Birthday Mutterings." Modern Theatre
and Drama 19 (December 1976): 420-21
REVIEWS OF INDIVIDUAL PLAYS:
Come Laugh and Cry with Langston Hughes
   "Come Laugh and Cry with Langston Hughes." (N.Y.)
   Amsterdam News: New Horizons, 5 February 1977,
   D-10
REVIEWS OF INDIVIDUAL MUSICALS:
Bubbling Brown Sugar
   Blum and Willis, eds. A Pictorial History of the Ameri-
   can Theatre: 1860-1976, p. 429
   Bontemps, Alex. "'Bubbling Brown Sugar': A Musical
   About Harlem Tells the History of Black Entertain-
   ment." Ebony 31 (February 1976): 124-26, 128-31
   "'Brown Sugar' Is Sweeter for the Eyes and the Ears."
   (Newark, N.J.) Star-Ledger, 14 March 1976, in News-
   bank--Performing Arts. March-April 1976, 28: A 12
   "'Brown Sugar's' Sparkling Return." Washington (D.C.)
   Post, 22 January 1976, in Newsbank--Performing Arts.
   January-February 1976, 12: A 11
   "Bubbling Brown Sugar." The Afro-American (Baltimore,
   Md.) 17-21 May 1977, p. 15
   "'Bubbling Brown Sugar' has 3 Matinees." (N.Y.) Amster-
   dam News: Arts and Entertainment, 6 August 1977,
   D-11
   Calloway, Earl. "'Sugar' Bubbles with Style." Chicago
   Daily Defender, 8 October 1975, in Newsbank--Per-
   forming Arts. September-October 1975, 66: G 13
   Clurman, Harold. "Theatre." Nation 222 (27 March
   1976): 381-82
   Davis, Curt. "Set Your Watch on 'Toby Time'." Encore
   6 (7 March 1977): 36-37
   Durrah, James W. "How Sweet It Is: 'Bubbling Brown
   Sugar'." (N.Y.) Amsterdam News: Arts and Entertain-
   ment, 25 June 1977, D 11
   Evans, Donald. "Bring It All Back Home." Black World
   20 (February 1971): 41-45
   Facts On File. 1976, 3-2, 1014 B-3
   Feingold, Michael. "'Bubbling Brown Sugar'." Village
   Voice 21 (15 March 1976): 139
   George, Nelson. "'Brown Sugar' A Great Actor." (N.Y.)
   Amsterdam News: Arts and Entertainment, 9 April 1977,
   D-2

Gilbert, Ruth, ed. "In and Around Town: On Broadway."
New York 10 (2 May 1977): 19 through 10 (3 October
1977): 19

Gill, Brendan. "The Theatre: The Good Old Days."
New Yorker 52 (15 March 1976): 51

Goddard, Bob. "'Brown Sugar' Swings at American
Theatre." St. Louis (Mo.) Globe Democrat, 5 January
1977, in Newsbank--Performing Arts. January-February
1977, 10: B 10

Gottfried, Martin. "How Sweet It Is." New York Post,
3 March 1976, in Newsbank--Performing Arts. March-
April 1976, 28: A 13

"Harlem, U.S.A." (N.Y.) Amsterdam News: New Horizons, 5 February 1977, D-16

Hodenfield, Jan. "Vivian Reed: All of a Sudden She
Bubbled to Star-dom." New York Post, 12 March
1976, in Newsbank--Performing Arts. March-April
1976, 28: B 9

Hughes, Catharine. "Three New Musicals." America
135 (27 November 1976): 373

_____. "Two Black Plays." America 135 (27 Novem-
ber 1976): 373

Kalem, T. E. "Doing the Harlem Hop." Time 107 (22
March 1976): 79

Mackay, Barbara. "Dancer Washington Takes 'Brooklyn
Act' Nationwide" (Bubbling Brown Sugar). Denver
(Colo.) Post, 15 April 1977, in Newsbank--Performing
Arts. March-April 1977, 23: G 7

"New Bubbling Brown Sugar." The Afro-American (Baltimore, Md.), 26-30 April 1977, p. 11

New York Theatre Critics' Reviews--1976 37 (23 February
1976): 352-356; containing: Watt, Douglas, "Take the
'A' Train, Quick!" ([N.Y.] Daily News, 3 March 1976).
Barnes, Clive, "'Bubbling Brown Sugar' Boils at ANTA"
(New York Times, 3 March 1976). Gottfried, Martin,
"'Sugar' How Sweet It Is!" (New York Post, 3 March
1976). Kissel, Howard, "'Bubbling Brown Sugar' at
the ANTA" (Women's Wear Daily, 3 March 1976).
Wilson, Edwin, "When Swing was King in Harlem"
(Wall Street Journal, 3 March 1976). Beaufort, John,
"Bubbling Brown Sugar" (Christian Science Monitor, 11
March 1976). Kalem, T. E., "Doing the Harlem Hop"
(Time, 22 March 1976). Probst, Leonard, "Bubbling
Brown Sugar" (NBC 2 March 1976). Sanders, Kevin,
"Bubbling Brown Sugar" (WABC-TV 2 March 1976)

O'Haire, Patricia. "White Lightning in Harlem." (N.Y.)
Daily News, 11 March 1976, in Newsbank--Performing
Arts. March-April 1976, 28: B 8

Osborne, Gwendolyn E. "Report from Aisle C: 'Bubbling
Brown Sugar'." Crisis 84 (January 1977): 34

Peters, Ida. "King of Ragtime" (Eubie Blake). The Afro-
American (Baltimore, Md.), 12-16 July 1977, p. 11

_____. "Welcome Home Avon Long." The Afro-American (Baltimore, Md.), 28 June-2 July 1977, p. 11

Peterson, Maurice. "On the Aisle: 'Bubbling Brown Sugar'." Essence 6 (January 1976): 28

_____. "On the Aisle: Focus on Avon Long." Essence 6 (January 1976): 28

_____. "On the Aisle." Essence 7 (August 1976): 125

Philip, Richard. "'Bubbling Brown Sugar'." Dance Magazine 50 (June 1976): 45-46

Pollack, Joe. "'Bubbling Brown Sugar' Opens at American." St. Louis (Mo.) Post-Dispatch, 5 January 1977, in Newsbank--Performing Arts. January-February 1977, 10: B 8

Raidy, Wm. A. "'Bubbling Brown Sugar' Pure Joy." Long Island (N.Y.) Press, 3 March 1976, in Newsbank--Performing Arts. March-April 1976, 28: B 2

Rich, Alan. "'Bubbling Brown Sugar'." New York 9 (22 March 1976): 64-66

Richards, David. "'Brown Sugar' Is Sweeter." Washington (D.C.) Star, 21 January 1976, in Newsbank--Performing Arts. January-February 1976, 12: A 10

Robinson, Major. "Invisible Stars Twinkle." (N.Y.) Amsterdam News: Arts and Entertainment, 25 June 1977, D-15

Ryan, Barbara Haddad. "'Bubbling Brown Sugar' A Sassy Musical." (Denver, Colo.) Rocky Mountain News, in Newsbank--Performing Arts. January-February 1977, 10: B 14

Sonclick, Laurence. "The Boston Theatre Season." New Boston Review 2 (Winter Issue: January 1977): 23

Smith, Agnes R. "'Bubbling Brown Sugar' Hits Town." (Chicago, Ill.) Courier, 11 October 1975, in Newsbank--Performing Arts. September-October 1975, 66: C 2

"Stanley Ramsey Featured in 'Bubbling Brown Sugar'." The Afro-American (Baltimore, Md.), 7-11 December 1976, p. 11

"'Sugar' in Star's Hometown." The Afro-American (Baltimore, Md.), 14-18 June 1977, p. 11

"Summer Schedule." (N.Y.) Amsterdam News: Arts and Entertainment, 23 July 1977, D-14

Sverdlik, Alan. "Joe Attles at 73 Living a Little of His Part Each Day." (N.Y.) Amsterdam News: Arts and Entertainment, 2 October 1976, D-12

Walker, Jesse H. "And Now a Word...." The Afro-American (Baltimore, Md.), 19-23 July 1977, p. 11

Watt, Douglas. "A Bubbling Song for Every Light on Broadway." (N.Y.) Daily News, 14 March 1976, in Newsbank--Performing Arts. March-April 1976, 28: A 14: B 1

Weales, Gerald. "Birthday Mutterings." Modern Theatre and Drama 19 (December 1976): 419, 420

"Welcome to the Great Black Way." Time 108 (1

November 1976): 75
Willis' Theatre World. vol. 31, 1974-1975, p. 91
Winer, Linda. "The Boom in Black Theatre: Growing
Profits ... and Growing Pains." Chicago Tribune:
Arts & Fun, 30 May 1976, 6:2

LERNER, EDWIN H.
PLAYS:
Tea

†LEVERSE, LORETTA
PLAYS:
[with Lincoln Kilpatrick] Deep Are the Roots
CRITICISMS OF INDIVIDUAL PLAYS:
Deep Are the Roots
Hartnoll. The Oxford Companion to the Theatre, p. 678

LIGHTS, FREDERICK
PLAYS:
All Over Nuthin'
REVIEWS OF INDIVIDUAL PLAYS:
All Over Nuthin'
Willis' Theatre World. vol. 31, 1974-1975, p. 91

LORD, IRIS
MUSICALS:
Death--Life--Patience

†LYLE, K. CURTIS
PLAYS:
Da Minstrel Show, 1969

LYLES, AUBREY
MUSICALS:
[with Flournoy Miller] Keep Shufflin', 1928
[with Flournoy Miller] Running Wild, 1923
[with Eubie Blake, Flournoy Miller and Noble Sissle]
Shuffle Along, 1921; 1933
CRITICISMS OF INDIVIDUAL MUSICALS:
Shuffle Along
"Black Theatre: A Bid for Cultural Identity." Black
Enterprise 2 (September 1971): 31
Current, Gloster B. "Noble Sissle." Crisis 83 (March
1976): 86-87
Gagey. Revolution in American Drama, p. 253
Jackson. The Waiting Years, p. 171
Kimball and Bolcom. Reminiscing with Sissle and Blake,
passim
McGraw-Hill Encyclopedia of World Drama. vol. 3,
p. 288
Mitchell. Voices of the Black Theatre, p. 30
Turner, Darwin. "W. E. B. Du Bois and the Theory of

a Black Aesthetic." Studies in Literary Imagination 7
(Fall 1974): 3, 5
REVIEWS OF INDIVIDUAL MUSICALS:
Shuffle Along
Blum and Willis, eds. A Pictorial History of the Ameri-
can Theatre: 1860-1976, pp. 188, 338
Lewis, Barbara. "Metropolitan Museum Highlights Black
Theatre." (N.Y.) Amsterdam News: Arts and Enter-
tainment, 19 February 1977, D-8
Peterson, Maurice. "On the Aisle: Focus on Avon Long."
Essence 6 (January 1976): 28

†MACBETH, ROBERT
PLAYS:
A Black Ritual
PLAYS PUBLISHED IN PERIODICALS:
A Black Ritual in Black Theatre no. 2 (1969): 8-9
CRITICISMS OF MACBETH:
Harris, Jessica B. "The New Lafayette: 'Nothing Lasts
Forever'." Black Creation 4 (Summer 1973): 10
Hatch, James. "Speak to Me in Those Old Words, You
Know, Those La-La Words, Those Tung-Tung Sounds."
Yale/Theatre 8 (Fall 1976): 29
Lewis, Barbara. "New Lafayette Founder Makes Good Come-
back Bid." (N.Y.) Amsterdam News: Arts and Entertain-
ment, 28 May 1977, D-2
Marvin X. "The Black Ritual Theatre: An Interview with
Robert Macbeth." Black Theatre no. 4 (1969): 20-24
Oliver, Edith. "Report from 137th Street." In Theatre 5:
The American Theatre, 1971-1972, pp. 129, 130, 131
Robinson, Le Roy. "Black Theatre: A Need for the
Seventies." Soul Illustrated 2 (February 1970): 57
CRITICISMS OF INDIVIDUAL PLAYS:
A Black Ritual
Mason, Clifford. "The Electronic Nigger Meets the Gold
Dust Twins." Black Theatre no. 1 (October 1968): 24
Oliver, Edith. "Report from 137th Street." In Theatre 5:
The American Theatre, 1971-1972, pp. 129, 130, 131

McCLAIN, SAUNDRA
MUSICALS:
[with Davis Martin and Ben Carter] Bitter Trails

McCOMAS, ANNETTE
PLAYS:
Are You Still in Your Cabin Uncle Tom? (based on the novel
Uncle Tom's Cabin by Harriet Beecher Stowe)
REVIEWS OF INDIVIDUAL PLAYS:
Are You Still in Your Cabin Uncle Tom?
Eichelbaum, Stanley. "Uncle Tom's Cabin' Open for
Inspection." San Francisco (Calif.) Examiner, 24
February 1976, in Newsbank--Performing Arts.
January-February 1976, 14: G 9

McDOWELL, MELODY
PLAYS:
The Conscience

McGRAW, PATRICIA WASHINGTON
PLAYS:
Profile of Four Black Women
REVIEWS OF INDIVIDUAL PLAYS:
Profile of Four Black Women
"Profile of Four Black Women Renewing Experience."
(Little Rock) Arkansas Gazette, 22 March 1976, in
Newsbank--Performing Arts. March-April 1976, 29:
D 11, 12

†McGRIFF, MILTON
PLAYS:
Nigger Killers, 1971

†McIVER, R.
PLAYS:
God Is a (Guess What?)
CRITICISMS OF INDIVIDUAL PLAYS:
God Is a (Guess What?)
Current Biography 38 (1977): 419
REVIEWS OF INDIVIDUAL PLAYS:
God Is a (Guess What?)
Lewis, Theophilus. "'God Is a (Guess What?)'" America
120 (11 January 1969): 50
"Off-Broadway: Play V Players." Time 92 (27 December
1968): 47
Oliver, Edith. "The Comic View: Performance of R.
McIver's 'God Is a (Guess What?)' by Negro Ensemble
Company." New Yorker 44 (28 December 1968): 50-51

McKEE, JOHN
PLAYS:
Livin' Is a Hard Way to Die
REVIEWS OF INDIVIDUAL PLAYS:
Livin' Is a Hard Way to Die
Morris, Al. "'Livin' Is a Hard Way to Die'." (N.Y.)
Amsterdam News: Arts and Entertainment, 16 July
1977, D-5

†MACKEY, WILLIAM WELLINGTON
PLAYS:
Behold! Cometh the Vanderkellans. N.Y.: Azaziel Books,
1967
Family Meeting. N.Y.: Dramatists Play Service, 1973
Saga
CRITICISMS OF MACKEY:
"Bicentennial Assignment." Black World 24 (April 1975): 49
CRITICISMS OF INDIVIDUAL PLAYS:

Behold! Cometh the Vanderkellans
> Barnes, Clive. "Off-Broadway." In Theatre 4: The
> American Theatre, 1970-1971, pp. 32, 33

Family Meeting
> Benston, Kimberly W. "'Cities in Bezique': Adrienne
> Kennedy's Expressionistic Vision." CLA Journal 20
> (December 1976): 241

Saga
> "Bicentennial Assignment." Black World 24 (April 1975):
> 49

REVIEWS OF INDIVIDUAL PLAYS:
Behold! Cometh the Vanderkellans
> Kupa, Kushauri. "Closeup: The New York Scene--Black
> Theatre in New York, 1970-1971." Black Theatre no.
> 6 (1972): 44-45

MADDEN, WILL ANTHONY
PLAYS:
Two and One. New York: Exposition, 1961

†MADDOX, GLORIA D.
PLAYS:
Rare Cut Glass
CRITICISMS OF INDIVIDUAL PLAYS:
Rare Cut Glass
> Sandle. The Negro in the American Educational Theatre,
> p. 66

MALONE, MIKE
MUSICALS:
[with Glenda Dickerson] Owen's Song
CRITICISMS OF INDIVIDUAL MUSICALS:
Owen's Song
> Fabio, Sarah Webster. "A Tribute to Owen's Song."
> Black World 24 (April 1975): 76-87
> Miller, Jeanne-Marie A. "Annual Round-up: Black
> Theater in America--Washington, D.C." Black World
> 24 (April 1975): 37

MANN, CHARLES
PLAYS:
[with Barbara and Carlton Molette, III] Doctor B. S. Black
REVIEWS OF INDIVIDUAL PLAYS:
Doctor B. S. Black
> Albright, William. "Theater: 'Doctor B. S. Black'."
> Houston (Tex.) Post, 29 April 1976, in Newsbank--
> Performing Arts. May-June 1976, 40: A 9

MANNAN, LAILA see SANCHEZ, SONIA

MARTIN, DAVID
MUSICALS:
[with Saundra McClain and Ben Carter] Bitter Trails

†MARVIN X (aka M. E. Jackman; El Muhajir)
PLAYS:
The Black Bird
Flowers for the Trashman
Take Care of Business
CRITICISMS BY MARVIN X:
"The Black Ritual Theatre: An Interview with Robert Mac-
beth." Black Theatre no. 3 (1969): 20-24
"Everything's Cool: An Interview with Le Roi Jones."
Black Theatre no. 1 (1968): 16-23
"Manifesto: The Black Educational Theatre of San Francisco."
Black Theatre no. 6 (1972): 30-35
"Review: Moon on a Rainbow Shawl." Black Theatre no. 1
(1968): 30-31
CRITICISMS OF MARVIN X:
Winer, Linda. "Local Curtain Going Up for 10 Black Stage
Troupes." Chicago Tribune: Arts & Fun, 30 May 1976,
6:3
CRITICISMS OF INDIVIDUAL PLAYS:
The Black Bird
Hay, Samuel A. "African-American Drama, 1950-1970."
Negro History Bulletin 36 (January 1973): 8
Take Care of Business
Meserve, Walter J. "Black Drama." In Robbins.
American Literary Scholarship--1970, p. 344
REVIEWS OF INDIVIDUAL PLAYS:
Flowers for the Trashman
"Kuumba Dancers Perform in Plaza." Chicago Daily De-
fender, 3 August 1977, p. 23
"Two Afro-American Plays Featured at Kuumba." Chicago
Daily Defender, 14 July 1977, p. 18

MASON, CHARLES
MUSICALS:
[with Ron Milner] Season's Reasons
CRITICISMS OF INDIVIDUAL MUSICALS:
Season's Reasons
Smitherman, Geneva. "'We Are the Music': Ron Milner,
People's Playwright." Black World 25 (April 1976):
4-19
REVIEWS OF INDIVIDUAL MUSICALS:
Season's Reasons
Gilbert, Ruth, ed. "In and Around Town: Off and Off-
Off Broadway." New York 10 (11 July 1977): 20; 10
(18 July 1977): 18; 10 (25 July 1977): 16
Novick, Julius. "A Man for All Reasons." Village Voice
22 (1 August 1977): 63
Vincent, Charlie. "His Theater Is of Blacks, for Blacks."
Detroit (Mich.) Free Press, 17 October 1975, in
Newsbank--Performing Arts. September-October 1975,
68: B 6

†MASON, CLIFFORD (b. March 5, 1932)
   PLAYS:
      Midnight Special
      Sister Sadie
   REVIEWS OF INDIVIDUAL PLAYS:
      Midnight Special
         Coe, Richard L. "Midnight Special." Washington (D.C.)
           Post, 5 March 1976, in Newsbank--Performing Arts.
           March-April 1976, 31: D 11
         Richards, David. "'Midnight Special' A Slice of Grimy
           Life in Harlem." Washington (D.C.) Star, 4 March
           1976, in Newsbank--Performing Arts. March-April
           1976, 31: D 10
      Sister Sadie
         Willis' Theatre World. vol. 32, 1975-1976, p. 126

MASON, JUDI ANN
   PLAYS:
      Livin' Fat
      A Star Ain't Nothin' But a Hole in Heaven
   CRITICISMS OF INDIVIDUAL PLAYS:
      Livin' Fat
         Current Biography 37 (September 1976): 30
   REVIEWS OF INDIVIDUAL PLAYS:
      Livin' Fat
         Oliver, Edith. "The Theatre: Off-Broadway." New
           Yorker 52 (14 June 1976): 77-78
         Willis' Theatre World. vol. 32, 1975-1976, p. 125

†MATHEUS, JOHN FREDERICK (b. September 10, 1887)
   PLAYS:
      'Cruiter
      Guitar
   MUSICALS:
      [with Clarence Cameron White] Ouanga, an opera
   CRITICISMS OF INDIVIDUAL PLAYS:
      'Cruiter
         Thompson, Larry. "The Black Image in Early American
           Drama." Black World 24 (April 1975): 69
   CRITICISMS OF INDIVIDUAL MUSICALS:
      Ouanga
         Hatch, James. "Speak to Me in Those Old Words, You
           Know, Those La-La Words, Those Tung-Tung Sounds."
           Yale/Theatre 8 (Fall 1976): 27

MAXWELL, MARINA
   PLAYS:
      Play Mas
   CRITICISM OF MAXWELL:
      Perrier, Paulette. "The Yard Theatre: Jamaica." Black
        Theatre no. 5 (1971): 9-10

CRITICISMS OF INDIVIDUAL PLAYS:
 Play Mas
  Perrier, Paulette. "The Yard Theatre: Jamaica." Black
   Theatre no. 5 (1971): 9-10

†MAYFIELD, JULIAN (b. June 6, 1928)
 PLAYS:
 The Other Foot, one act, 1950
 A World Full of Men, one act, 1952
 FILM SCRIPTS:
 The Long Night (based on the novel)
 CRITICISMS OF MAYFIELD:
  Davis, Arthur P. From the Dark Tower, p. 199
 CRITICISMS OF INDIVIDUAL PLAYS:
 The Other Foot
  Hartnoll. The Oxford Companion to the Theatre, p. 680
 A World Full of Men
  Hartnoll. The Oxford Companion to the Theatre, p. 680
 CRITICISMS OF INDIVIDUAL FILM SCRIPTS:
 The Long Night
  Salaam, Kalamu ya. "Making the Image Real." The
   Black Collegian 7 (March-April 1977): 57
 REVIEWS OF INDIVIDUAL FILM SCRIPTS:
 The Long Night
  Peterson, Maurice. "On the Aisle." Essence 7 (July
   1976): 7

†MEYER, ANNIE N.
 PLAYS:
 Black Souls
 CRITICISMS OF INDIVIDUAL PLAYS:
 Black Souls
  Hartnoll. The Oxford Companion to the Theatre, p. 676

MICHEAUX, OSCAR
 FILM SCRIPTS:
 Hallelujah
 CRITICISMS OF MICHEAUX:
  Cripps. Slow Fade to Black, passim
 CRITICISMS OF INDIVIDUAL FILM SCRIPTS:
 Hallelujah
  "The Words of Dick Campbell." In Mitchell. Voices of
   the Black Theatre, p. 104

†MILLER, FLOURNOY
 MUSICALS:
  [with Eubie Blake, Andy Razaf and Noble Sissle] The Blackbirds, 1929
  [with Aubrey Lyles] Keep Shufflin', 1928
  [with Eubie Blake, Andy Razaf and Noble Sissle] O, Sing A
   New Song
  [with Eubie Blake, Aubrey Lyles and Noble Sissle] Shuffle
   Along, 1921; 1933

CRITICISMS OF INDIVIDUAL MUSICALS:
The Blackbirds
Hatch, James. "Speak to Me in Those Old Words, You
Know, Those La-La Words, Those Tung-Tung Sounds."
Yale/Theatre 8 (Fall 1976): 27
Shuffle Along
"Black Theatre: A Bid for Cultural Identity." Black
Enterprise 2 (September 1971): 31
Current, Gloster B. "Noble Sissle." Crisis 83 (March
1976): 87
Gagey. Revolution in American Drama, p. 253
Jackson. The Waiting Years, p. 171
Kimball and Bolcom. Reminiscing with Sissle and Blake,
passim
McGraw-Hill Encyclopedia of World Drama, vol. 3,
p. 288
Mitchell. Voices of the Black Theatre, p. 30
Turner, Darwin. "W. E. B. Du Bois and the Theory of
a Black Aesthetic." Studies in Literary Imagination
7 (Fall 1974): 3, 5
REVIEWS OF INDIVIDUAL MUSICALS:
Shuffle Along
Blum and Willis, eds. A Pictorial History of the Ameri-
can Theatre: 1860-1976, pp. 188, 338
Lewis, Barbara. "Metropolitan Museum Highlights Black
Theatre." (N.Y.) Amsterdam News: Arts and Enter-
tainment, 19 February 1977, D-8
Peterson, Maurice. "On the Aisle: Focus on Avon Long."
Essence 6 (January 1976): 28

†MILLER, MAY
PLAYS:
Graven Images
Ridin' the Goat
CRITICISMS OF MILLER:
"Hatch-Billops Archives Interviews with Playwrights." Negro
American Literature Forum 10 (Summer 1976): 65
Sandle. The Negro in the American Theatre, p. 17, 18
Xeroxed Abstracts: Stage I
CRITICISMS OF INDIVIDUAL PLAYS:
Graven Images
Molette, Barbara. "Black Women Playwrights: They
Speak: Who Listens?" Black World 25 (April 1976):
30-31
Ridin' the Goat
F. H. K. "Carolina Negro Theatre: In Retrospect."
The Carolina Play Book 8 (June 1935): 45-46

†MILNER, RON
PLAYS:
Circus
The Greatest Gift, a children's play

How's the World Treating You?
Life Agony
(M) Ego and the Green Ball of Freedom, 1972
The Monster
These Three
The Warning--A Theme for Linda
What the Winesellers Buy. N.Y.: Samuel French, 1974
Who's Got His Own
MUSICALS:
[with Charles Mason] Season's Reasons (Just a Natural
    Change)
CRITICISMS OF MILNER:
"Black Theater in Transition, Playwright Says." In Nykoruk.
    Authors in the News. vol. 1, p. 349
Cameron and Hoffman. A Guide to Theatre Study, p. 204
Dance, Darrell. "Contemporary Militant Black Humor."
    Negro American Literature Forum 8 (Summer 1974): 218
Daughtry, Willia A. "A Quarter Century in the Fine Arts,
    1950-1974." The Negro Educational Review 27 (January
    1976): 27
De Ramus, Betty. "A Man Who Captures Detroit ... and
    Life." In Nykoruk. Authors in the News, vol. 1. De-
    troit: Gale Research, 1976, p. 348
Geisinger. Plays, Players, & Playwrights, p. 742
Gilder, Rosamond. "Theatre As People: Book Report."
    In Theatre 4: The American Theatre, 1970-1971, p. 187
Gray, Bill. "Black Theatre in Transition, Playwright Says."
    In Nykoruk. Authors in the News. vol. 1. Detroit:
    Gale Research, 1976, p. 348
Houghton. The Exploding Stage, p. 201
Lahr, John. "The Deli: Off Broadway and Off, 68-69." In
    Theatre 2: The American Theatre, 1968-1969, p. 50
Richards, David. "Ron Milner's Upbeat View of the Ghetto."
    In Nykoruk. Authors in the News. vol. 1. Detroit:
    Gale Research, 1976, p. 349
Robinson, Le Roy. "Black Theatre: A Need for the Seven-
    ties." Soul Illustrated 2 (February 1970): 57
Saddler, Jeanne E. "On the Aisle: Ron Milner--The People's
    Playwright." Essence 5 (November 1974): 20
Salaam, Kalamu ya. "Making the Image Real." Black Col-
    legian 7 (March-April 1977): 54
Smitherman, Geneva. "'We Are the Music': Ron Milner,
    People's Playwright." Black World 25 (April 1976): 4-19
Turner, Darwin T. "Ron Milner." In Vinson. Contemporary
    Dramatists, pp. 547-48
CRITICISMS OF INDIVIDUAL PLAYS:
The Warning--A Theme for Linda
    De Ramus, Betty. "A Man Who Captures Detroit ... And
        Life." In Nykoruk. Authors in the News. vol. 1.
        Detroit: Gale Research, 1976, p. 348
    Junker, H. "No Miracles: Black Quartet." Newsweek
        74 (11 August 1969): 82

Miller, Jeanne-Marie A. "Images of Black Women in
Plays by Black Playwrights." CLA Journal 20 (June
1977): 502-503
Smitherman, Geneva. "'We Are the Music': Ron Milner,
People's Playwright." Black World 25 (April 1976): 11

What the Winesellers Buy

Davis, Curt. "Bill Cobbs: The Death of a Salesman,
The Birth of an Artist." Encore 6 (17 January 1977):
33-34
De Ramus, Betty. "A Man Who Captures Detroit ... and
Life." In Nykoruk. Authors in the News. vol. 1.
Detroit: Gale Research, 1976, p. 348
Engel. The Critics, pp. 4, 30, 32, 85-86
Geisinger. Plays, Players, & Playwrights, pp. 732, il.;
n. 733
King, Woodie, Jr. "Directing 'Winesellers'." Black
World 25 (April 1976): 20-26
Nicholas, Xavier and Addison Gayle, Jr. "Two Views
of ... 'Winesellers'...." Black World 25 (April 1976):
95-97
Peterson, Maurice. "On the Aisle: Theater and Films."
Essence 5 (September 1974): 24
_____. "On the Road with 'The Winesellers'." Essence
6 (November 1975): 66-67, 84, 102, 106
Richards, David. "Ron Milner's Upbeat View of the
Ghetto." In Nykoruk. Authors in the News. vol. 1.
Detroit: Gale Research, 1976, p. 349
Saddler, Jeanne E. "On the Aisle: Ron Milner--The
People's Playwright." Essence 5 (November 1974): 20
Smitherman, Geneva. "'We Are the Music': Ron Milner,
People's Playwright." Black World 25 (April 1976):
11-14
Weales, Gerald. "Birthday Mutterings." Modern Theatre
and Drama 19 (December 1976): 420-21

Who's Got His Own

Benston, Kimberly W. "'Cities in Bezique': Adrienne
Kennedy's Expressionistic Vision." CLA Journal 20
(December 1976): 241
Bermel. Contradictory Characters, p. 250 n
De Ramus, Betty. "A Man Who Captures Detroit ... And
Life." In Nykoruk. Authors in the News. vol. 1.
Detroit: Gale Research, 1976, p. 348
Evans, Donald. "'Who's Got His Own' at Cheyney." Black
World 19 (April 1970): 43-48, 97-98
Harris, Jessica B. "The New Lafayette: 'Nothing Lasts
Forever'." Black Creation 4 (Summer 1973): 8, 9
Hay, Samuel A. "African-American Drama, 1950-1970."
Negro History Bulletin 36 (January 1973): 7
Marvin X. "The Black Ritual Theatre: An Interview with
Robert Macbeth." Black Theatre no. 3 (1969): 23-24
Miller, Jeanne-Marie A. "Images of Black Women in
Plays by Black Playwrights." CLA Journal 20 (June
1977): 501-02

Saddler, Jeanne E. "On the Aisle: Ron Milner--The People's Playwright." Essence 5 (November 1974): 20

Weales, Gerald. "Birthday Mutterings." Modern Theatre and Drama 19 (December 1976): 420-21

Willis, Robert. "Anger and Contemporary Black Theatre." Negro American Literature Forum 8 (Summer 1974): 215

CRITICISM OF INDIVIDUAL MUSICALS:

Season's Reasons

Smitherman, Geneva. "'We Are the Music': Ron Milner, People's Playwright." Black World 25 (April 1976): 4-19

CRITICISMS OF COLLECTIONS:

Black Quartet

Salaam, Kalamu ya. "Making the Image Real." The Black Collegian 7 (March-April 1977): 56

REVIEWS OF INDIVIDUAL PLAYS:

What the Winesellers Buy

Asante sana. "'What the Wine Sellers Buy'." (Chicago, Ill.) Courier, 22 March 1975, in Newsbank--Performing Arts. March-April 1975, 30: D 12, 13, 14

Bellamy, Peter. "Allen Stages Black Melodrama." (Cleveland, O.) Plain Dealer, 3 July 1975, in Newsbank--Performing Arts. July-August 1975, 54: B 4

Blum and Willis, eds. A Pictorial History of the American Theatre: 1860-1976, p. 422

Clurman, Harold. "Theatre." Nation 218 (9 March 1974): 315

Dyson, Diedra Soyini. "Annual Round-up: Black Theater in America--Chicago." Black World 25 (April 1976): 73

Emeruwa, Leatrice W. "Annual Round-up: Black Theater in America--Cleveland." Black World 25 (April 1976): 69-70

Gill, Brendan. "The Theatre: Armageddon." New Yorker 50 (25 February 1976): 83

Hughes, Catharine. "New York." Plays and Players 21 (April 1974): 52-53

_____. "Other Cities." America 130 (9 March 1974): 175

Kauffmann, Stanley. "Stanley Kauffmann on Theatre." New Republic 170 (9 March 1974): 24-33

Morrow, Lance. "Ghetto Chayefsky." Time 103 (25 February 1974): 69

"New Breed Theatre Producer." The Afro-American (Baltimore, Md.), 12-16 April 1977, p. 11

Peterson, Maurice. "On the Aisle: Theatre and Film." Essence 5 (September 1974): 24

_____. "On the Road with 'The Winesellers'." Essence 6 (November 1975): 66-67, 84+

_____. "Rising Stars." Essence 7 (December 1976): 52, 86

Sainer, Arthur. "Making It All the Way." Village Voice
19 (28 February 1974): 58
Simon, John. "New Soap, Old Bubbles." New York
Magazine 7 (4 March 1974): 62
Willis, John. Theatre World: 1973-1974 Season. vol.
30, pp. 123, 199
Winer, Linda. "The Boom in Black Theatre: Growing
Profits ... and Growing Pains." Chicago Tribune:
Arts & Fun, 30 May 1976, 6: 2-3
REVIEWS OF INDIVIDUAL MUSICALS:
Season's Reasons
Gilbert, Ruth, ed. "In and Around Town: Off and Off-Off
Broadway." New York 10 (11 July 1977): 20; (18 July
1977): 18; (25 July 1977): 16
Novick, Julius. "A Man for All Reasons." Village Voice
22 (1 August 1977): 63
Thurston, Chuck. "For Black and White: A Change."
Detroit (Mich.) Free Press, 1 January 1977, in News-
bank--Performing Arts. January-February 1977, 12:
E 1
Vincent, Charlie. "His Theater Is of Blacks, for Blacks."
Detroit (Mich.) Free Press, 17 October 1975, in News-
bank--Performing Arts. September-October 1975, 68:
B 6

†MITCHELL, LOFTEN
PLAYS:
The Bancroft Dynasty
The Cellar
Cocktails
Crossroads
Harlem
The Land Beyond the River
Star of the Morning
Tell Pharaoh
MUSICALS:
[with Irving Burgie] Ballad for Bimshire, 1963; revised 1964
Bubbling Brown Sugar (a musical revue based on a book by
Loften Mitchell and a concept by Rosetta Le Noire)
FILM SCRIPTS:
Integration Row, 1959
Young Man of Williamsburg, 1955
TELEVISION SCRIPTS:
Tell Pharaoh, 1963 (based on the play)
RADIO SCRIPTS:
Tribute to C. C. Spaulding, 1952
BOOK:
Voices of the Black Theatre. Clifton, N.J.: White, 1975
CRITICISMS BY MITCHELL:
"Black Theatre: Then and Now." (N.Y.) Amsterdam News:
Black Academy of Arts and Letters Supplement, 18 Septem-
ber 1971, pp. D 11-12

"Negro in the American Theatre." In Hartnoll. The Oxford
  Companion to the Theatre. 3rd ed. London: Oxford Uni-
  versity Press, 1967, pp. 679-81
CRITICISMS OF MITCHELL:
  Bermel. Contradictory Characters, p. 248 n
  Cameron and Hoffman. A Guide to Theatre Study, p. 203
  Gilder, Rosamond. "Theatre As People: Book Report."
    In Theatre 4: The American Theatre, 1970-1971, p. 187
  "I Work Here to Please You." In Gayle. The Black
    Aesthetic, pp. 275-87
  Robinson, Le Roy. "Black Theatre: A Need for the Seven-
    ties." Soul Illustrated 2 (February 1970): 57
  Turner, Darwin T. "Loften Mitchell." In Vinson. Con-
    temporary Dramatists, pp. 549-550
  Xeroxed Abstracts: Stage II, no. 1, no. 2
CRITICISMS OF INDIVIDUAL PLAYS:
  The Bancroft Dynasty
    Hartnoll. The Oxford Companion to the Theatre, p. 680
  The Cellar
    Hartnoll. The Oxford Companion to the Theatre, p. 680
  Cocktails
    Mitchell. Voices of the Black Theatre, p. 64
  Crossroads
    Mitchell. Voices of the Black Theatre, p. 64
  Harlem Homecoming
    Mitchell, Loften. Voices of the Black Theatre, pp. 2-3
  The Land Beyond the River
    Edmonds, Randolph. "The Blacks in the American
      Theatre, 1700-1969." The Pan-African Journal 7
      (Winter 1974): 306
    Evans, Donald T. "Bring It All Back Home." Black
      World 20 (February 1971): 41-45
    _____. "Playwrights of the Fifties: Bringing It All
      Back Home." Black World 20 (February 1971): 44
    Hartnoll. The Oxford Companion to the Theatre, p. 680
    Hay, Samuel A. "African-American Drama, 1950-1970."
      Negro History Bulletin 36 (January 1973): 5
    Tedesco, John L. "The White Image as Second 'Persona'
      in Black Drama, 1955-1970." Ph.D. Dissertation, Uni-
      versity of Iowa, 1974
  Star of the Morning
    Edmonds, Randolph. "The Blacks in the American
      Theatre, 1700-1969." The Pan-African Journal 7
      (Winter 1974): 306
  Tell Pharaoh
    Edmonds, Randolph. "The Blacks in the American
      Theatre, 1700-1969." The Pan-African Journal 7
      (Winter 1974): 306
CRITICISMS OF INDIVIDUAL MUSICALS:
  Ballad for Bimshire
    Edmonds, Randolph. "The Blacks in the American Theatre,
      1700-1969." The Pan-African Journal 7 (Winter 1974): 306

Hartnoll. The Oxford Companion to the Theatre, p. 681

Bubbling Brown Sugar

Bell, Roseanne Pope. "'For Colored Girls Who Have Considered Suicide/When the Rainbow Is Enuf." The Black Collegian 7 (May-June 1977): 48

Bontemps, Alex. "'Bubbling Brown Sugar'." Ebony 31 (February 1976): 124-26, 128-31

Guernsey. The Best Plays of 1975-1976, pp. 344-45

Osborne, Gwendolyn E. "Report from Aisle C: 'Bubbling Brown Sugar'." Crisis 84 (January 1977): 34

Pacheco, Patrick. "'Bubbling Brown Sugar'." After Dark 9 (May 1976): 58-63

Taylor, Clarke. "Fortune Smiles on Broadway's Gypsies." Essence 7 (August 1976): 79

Weales, Gerald. "Birthday Mutterings." Modern Theatre and Drama 19 (December 1976): 420-21

REVIEWS OF INDIVIDUAL MUSICALS:

Bubbling Brown Sugar

Blum and Willis, eds. A Pictorial History of the American Theatre: 1860-1976, p. 429

Bontemps, Alex. "'Bubbling Brown Sugar': A Musical About Harlem Tells the History of Black Entertainment." Ebony 31 (February 1976): 124-26; 128-31

"'Brown Sugar' Is Sweeter for the Eyes and the Ears." (Newark, N.J.) Star-Ledger, 14 March 1976, in Newsbank--Performing Arts. March-April 1976, 28: H 12

"'Brown Sugar's' Sparkling Return." Washington (D.C.) Post, 22 January 1976, in Newsbank--Performing Arts. January-February 1976, 12: A 11

"Bubbling Brown Sugar." The Afro-American (Baltimore, Md.), 17-21, May 1977, p. 15

"'Bubbling Brown Sugar' Has 3 Matinees." (N.Y.) Amsterdam News: Arts and Entertainment, 6 August 1977, D-11

Calloway, Earl. "'Sugar' Bubbles With Style." Chicago Daily Defender, 8 October 1975, in Newsbank--Performing Arts. September-October 1975, 66: G 13

Clurman, Harold. "Theatre." Nation 222 (27 March 1976): 381-82

Davis, Curt. "Set Your Watch 'On Toby Time'." Encore 6 (7 March 1977): 36-37

Durrah, James W. "How Sweet It Is: 'Bubbling Brown Sugar'." (N.Y.) Amsterdam News: Arts and Entertainment, 25 June 1977, D-11

Evans, Donald T. "Bring It All Back Home." Black World 20 (February 1971): 41-45

Facts on File. 1976, 3-2, 1014 B-3

Feingold, Michael. "'Bubbling Brown Sugar'." Village Voice 21 (15 March 1976): 139

George, Nelson. "'Brown Sugar' A Great Actor." (N.Y.) Amsterdam News: Arts and Entertainment, 9 April 1977, D-2

Gilbert, Ruth, ed. "In and Around Town: On Broadway."
New York 10 (2 May 1977): through 10 (3 October 1977):
19

Gill, Brendan. "The Theatre: The Good Old Days." New
Yorker 52 (15 March 1976): 51

Goddard, Bob. "'Brown Sugar' Swings at American
Theatre." St. Louis (Mo.) Globe-Democrat, 5 January
1977, in Newsbank--Performing Arts. January-February
1977, 10: B 10

Gottfried, M. "How Sweet It Is." New York Post, 3
March 1976, in Newsbank--Performing Arts. March-
April 1976, 28: H 13

"Harlem, U.S.A." (N.Y.) Amsterdam News: New Horizons, 5 February 1977, D-16

Hodenfield, Jan. "Vivian Reed: All of a Sudden She
Bubbled to Stardom." New York Post, 12 March 1976,
in Newsbank--Performing Arts. March-April 1976,
28: B 9

Hughes, Catharine. "Three New Musicals." America
135 (27 November 1976): 373

_____. "Two Black Plays." America 135 (27 Novem-
ber 1976): 373

Kalem, T. E. "Doing the Harlem Hop." Time 109 (22
March 1976): 79

Mackay, Barbara. "Dancer Washington Takes 'Brooklyn
Act' Nationwide" (Bubbling Brown Sugar). Denver
(Colo.) Post, in Newsbank--Performing Arts.

"New Bubbling Brown Sugar." The Afro-American (Baltimore, Md.), 26-30 April 1977, p. 11

New York Theatre Critics' Reviews--1976 37 (23 February
1976): 352-356; containing: Watt, Douglas, "Take the
'A' Train, Quick!" ([N.Y.] Daily News, 3 March 1976).
Barnes, Clive, "'Bubbling Brown Sugar' Boils at ANTA"
(New York Times, 3 March 1976). Gottfried, Martin,
"'Sugar' How Sweet It Is!" (New York Post, 3 March
1976). Kissel, Howard, "'Bubbling Brown Sugar' at
the ANTA" (Women's Wear Daily, 3 March 1976).
Wilson, Edwin, "When Swing Was King in Harlem"
(Wall Street Journal, 3 March 1976). Beaufort, John,
"Bubbling Brown Sugar" (Christian Science Monitor, 11
March 1976). Kalem, T. E., "Doing the Harlem Hop"
(Time, 22 March 1976). Probst, Leonard, "Bubbling
Brown Sugar" (NBC, 2 March 1976). Sanders, Kevin,
"Bubbling Brown Sugar" (WABC-TV, 2 March 1976)

O'Haire, Patricia. "White Lightning in Harlem." (N.Y.)
Daily News, 11 March 1976, in Newsbank--Performing
Arts. March-April 1976, 28: B 8

Osborne, Gwendolyn E. "Report from Aisle C: 'Bubbling
Brown Sugar'." Crisis 84 (January 1977): 34

Peters, Ida. "King of Ragtime (Eubie Blake)." The Afro-
American (Baltimore, Md.) 12-16 July 1977, p. 11

_____. "Welcome Home Avon Long." The Afro-
American (Baltimore, Md.), 28 June-2 July 1977, p. 11

Peterson, Maurice. "On the Aisle: Focus on Avon Long."
Essence 6 (January 1976): 28
———. "On the Aisle." Essence 7 (August 1976): 125
Philp, Richard. "'Bubbling Brown Sugar'." Dance Maga-
zine 50 (June 1976): 45-46
Pollack, Joe. "'Bubbling Brown Sugar' Opens at Ameri-
can." St. Louis (Mo.) Post-Dispatch, 5 January 1977,
in Newsbank--Performing Arts. January-February 1977,
10: B 8
Raidy, Wm. A. "'Bubbling Brown Sugar' Pure Joy."
Long Island (N.Y.) Press, 3 March 1976, in Newsbank--
Performing Arts. March-April 1976, 28: B 2
Rich, Alan. "'Bubbling Brown Sugar." New York 9 (22
March 1976): 64-66
Richards, David. "'Brown Sugar' Is Sweeter." Washing-
ton (D.C.) Star, 21 January 1976, in Newsbank--Per-
forming Arts. January-February 1976, 12: A 10
Robinson, Major. "Invisible Stars Twinkle." (N.Y.)
Amsterdam News: Arts and Entertainment, 25 June
1977, D-15
Ryan, Barbara Haddad. "'Bubbling Brown Sugar' a Sassy
Musical." (Denver, Colo.) Rocky Mountain News, 20
January 1977, in Newsbank--Performing Arts. January-
February 1977, 10: B 14
Senelick, Laurence. "The Boston Theatre Season." New
Boston Review 2 (Winter Issue: January 1977): 23
Smith, Agnes R. "'Bubbling Brown Sugar' Hits Town."
(Chicago, Ill.) Courier, 11 October 1975 in Newsbank--
Performing Arts. September-October 1975, 66: C 2
"Stanley Ramsey Featured in 'Bubbling Brown Sugar'."
The Afro-American (Baltimore, Md.), 7-11 December
1976, p. 11
"'Sugar' in Star's Hometown." The Afro-American (Balti-
more, Md.), 14-18 June 1977, p. 11
"Summer Schedule." (N.Y.) Amsterdam News: Arts and
Entertainment, 23 July 1977, D-14
Sverdlik, Alan. "Joe Attles at 73 Living a Little of His
Part Each Day." (N.Y.) Amsterdam News: Arts and
Entertainment, 2 October 1976, D-2
Walker, Jesse H. "And Now a Word ..." The Afro-
American (Baltimore, Md.), 19-23 July 1977, p. 11
Watt, Douglas. "A Bubbling Song for Every Light on
Broadway." (N.Y.) Daily News, 14 March 1976, in
Newsbank--Performing Arts. March-April 1976, 28:
A 14; B 1
Weales, Gerald. "Birthday Mutterings." Modern Theatre
and Drama 19 (December 1976): 419, 420
"Welcome to the Great Black Way." Time 108 (1 Novem-
ber 1976): 75
Willis' Theatre World. vol. 31, 1974-1975, p. 91
Winer, Linda. "The Boom in Black Theatre: Growing
Profits .. and Growing Pains." Chicago Tribune:

Arts & Fun, 30 May 1976, 6:2
AWARDS:
Bubbling Brown Sugar
Tony Award--Best Musical 1975-1976 Season

†MOLETTE, BARBARA (b. 1940)
PLAYS:
[with Carlton Molette, III, and Charles Mann] Doctor B. S. Black
[with Carlton Molette, III] Noah's Ark (in progress)
[with Carlton Molette, III] Rosalee Pritchett. N.Y.: Dramatists Play Service, 1973
WORKS BY MOLETTE:
Afro-American Theatre: A Bibliography. N.p., n.p., copyright 1972 by Barbara and Carlton Molette
CRITICISMS BY MOLETTE:
"Black Women Playwrights: They Speak: Who Listens?" Black World 25 (April 1976): 28-34
"The First Afro-American Theater." Black World 19 (April 1970): 4
"Manifesto for a Revolutionary Theatre." Encore 12 (1969): 44
"Our Theatre: Los Angeles." Encore 12 (1969): 55
CRITICISMS OF INDIVIDUAL PLAYS:
Rosalee Pritchett
Quick, Paula N. "Black Theatre." Black Creation 2 (April 1974): 54
REVIEWS OF INDIVIDUAL PLAYS:
Doctor B. S. Black
Albright, William. "Theater: 'Doctor B. S. Black'." Houston (Tex.) Post, 29 April 1976, in Newsbank--Performing Arts. May-June 1976, 40: A 9
Rosalee Pritchett
Kupa, Kushauri. "Closeups: The New York Scene--Black Theatre in New York, 1970-1971." Black Theatre no. 6 (1971): 40

†MOLETTE, CARLTON W., III (b. August 23, 1939)
PLAYS:
[with Barbara Molette and Charles Mann] Doctor B. S. Black
[with Barbara Molette] Noah's Ark (in progress)
[with Barbara Molette] Rosalee Pritchett. N.Y.: Dramatists Play Service, 1973
WORKS BY MOLETTE:
Afro-American Theatre: A Bibliography. N.p., n.p., copyright 1972 by Barbara and Carlton Molette
CRITICISMS OF MOLETTE:
Benston. Baraka: The Renegade and the Mask, pp. 255, 260
Edmonds, Randolph. "The Blacks in the American Theatre, 1700-1969." The Pan-African Journal 7 (Winter 1974): 318
Sandle. The Negro in the American Educational Theatre, p. 127

CRITICISMS OF INDIVIDUAL PLAYS:
  Rosalee Pritchett
    Quick, Paula N. "Black Theatre." Black Creation 2
      (April 1971): 54
REVIEWS OF INDIVIDUAL PLAYS:
  Doctor B. S. Black
    Albright, William. "Theater: 'Doctor B. S. Black'."
      Houston (Tex.) Post, 29 April 1976, in Newsbank--
      Performing Arts. May-June 1976, 40: A 9
  Rosalee Pritchett
    Kupa, Kushauri. "Closeups: The New York Scene--Black
      Theatre in New York, 1970-1971." Black Theatre
      no. 6 (1971): 40

†MONTE, ERIC
  PLAYS:
  This Is Our World
  FILM SCRIPTS:
  Cooley High
  TELEVISION SCRIPTS:
  [with Mike Evans] Good Times
  CRITICISMS OF MONTE:
    Duckett, Alfred. "The Birth of a Screenwriter." Sepia 26
      (January 1977): 63, 65
    Lloyd, Llana. "Hollywood's 'Hottest' New Black Movie Di-
      rector." Sepia 25 (November 1976): 26-34
  CRITICISMS OF INDIVIDUAL FILM SCRIPTS:
  Cooley High
    Duckett, Alfred. "The Birth of a Screenwriter." Sepia
      26 (January 1977): 63, 65
    Lloyd, Llana. "Hollywood's 'Hottest' New Black Movie
      Director." Sepia 25 (November 1976): 26-34
  CRITICISMS OF INDIVIDUAL TELEVISION SCRIPTS:
  Good Times
    Collier, Eugenia. "'Black' Shows for White Viewers."
      Freedomways 14 (Third Quarter 1974): 212-16
    Robinson, Louie. "Bad Times on the 'Good Times' Set."
      Ebony 30 (September 1975): 33-42
  REVIEWS OF INDIVIDUAL PLAYS:
  This Is Our World
    Hassinger, Peter. "Stage." Soul Illustrated 3 (Summer
      1972): 14, 62-63
  REVIEWS OF INDIVIDUAL FILM SCRIPTS:
  Cooley High
    Cocks, Jay. "City Slickers." Time 106 (1 September
      1975): 45
    Peterson, Maurice. "On the Aisle." Essence 6 (October
      1975): 9
    "Playboy After Hours: 'Cooley High'." Playboy 22
      (October 1975): 45
    Roman, Margaret. "Films: 'Cooley High'." Senior
      Scholastic 107 (23 September 1975): 40

REVIEWS OF INDIVIDUAL TELEVISION SCRIPTS:
Good Times
>Lucas, Bob. "A 'Salt Pork and Collard Greens' TV
Show." Ebony 29 (June 1974): 50-53

MOORE, HOWARD
PLAYS:
Don't Call Me Man

MORELL, PETER
PLAYS:
[with J. Augustus Smith] Turpentine, 1936
CRITICISMS OF INDIVIDUAL PLAYS:
Turpentine
>Edmonds, Randolph. "The Blacks in the American
Theatre, 1700-1969." The Pan-African Journal 7
(Winter 1974): 311
Goldstein. The Political Stage, p. 259
Hartnoll. The Oxford Companion to the Theatre, p. 677
Walsh, Elizabeth and Diane Bowers. "WPA Federal
Theatre Project." Theatre News 8 (April 1976): 3, il

MORRIS, GARRETT
PLAYS:
Patchwork
The Secret Place

†MOSES, GILBERT
PLAYS:
Roots
CRITICISMS OF INDIVIDUAL PLAYS:
Roots
>Moses, Gilbert. "Hubert Humphrey Is to Politics...."
In Theatre 2: The American Theatre, 1968-1969,
p. 110

†MOSS, CARLTON
PLAYS:
Prelude to Swing, 1939
CRITICISMS OF INDIVIDUAL PLAYS:
Prelude to Swing
Hartnoll. The Oxford Companion to the Theatre, p. 677

MOSS, GRANT
PLAYS:
Death Come Creeping in the Room
CRITICISMS OF INDIVIDUAL PLAYS:
Death Come Creeping in the Room
>Sandle. The Negro in the American Educational Theatre,
p. 87

MOTOJICHO
MUSICALS:

[with Valerian Smith] Changes
Daybreak Dreams
REVIEWS OF INDIVIDUAL MUSICALS:
Daybreak Dreams
    Papier, Deboran. "'Dreams' a Tribute to Two Poets."
    Washington (D.C.) Star News, 30 September 1975, in
    Newsbank--Performing Arts. September-October 1975,
    66: C 9

†MUSTAPHA, MATURA
PLAYS:
    Black Slaves, White Chains
    Rum an' Coca-Cola
CRITICISMS OF INDIVIDUAL PLAYS:
    Black Slaves, White Chains
        Craig, Randall. "Plays in Performance: Experimental."
        Drama 118 (August 1975): 73
    Rum an' Coca-Cola
        Emerson, Sally. "Rum an' Coca-Cola." Plays and
        Players 24 (January 1977): 32

†MYERS, GAYTHER
PLAYS:
    The God from the Machine, NYPL
    Memphis Aside

NAPIER, LONNIE L.
PLAYS:
    Play Me No Carols
CRITICISMS OF INDIVIDUAL PLAYS:
    Play Me No Carols
        Sandle. The Negro in the American Educational Theatre,
        p. 87

NARIN, GUS
PLAYS:
    [with Charles Green]
    The Legend of Toby Kingdom
FILM SCRIPTS:
    [with Charles Nero and Charles Green] The Legend of Toby
        Kingdom (adapted from the play)
CRITICISMS OF INDIVIDUAL FILM SCRIPTS:
    The Legend of Toby Kingdom
        Pantovic, Stan. "The Making of a Black Movie." Sepia
        22 (December 1973): 54-62

NASH, JOHNNY
FILM SCRIPTS:
    Love Is Not a Game

†NEAL, LARRY
MUSICALS:
    Kansas City Stomp Down

CRITICISMS OF NEAL:
Cameron and Hoffman. A Guide to Theatre Study, p. 203
Gilder, Rosamond. "Theatre as People: Book Report."
    In Theatre 4: The American Theatre, 1970-1971, p. 187
Houghton. The Exploding Stage, pp. 198-199
Turner, Darwin. "W. E. B. Du Bois and the Theory of a Black
    Aesthetic." Studies in Literary Imagination 7 (Fall 1974): 1

NELSON, MARCUS
    PLAYS:
    The Essence of Pathos
    Temperance

NELSON, NATALIE
    PLAYS:
    More Things That Happen to Us. N.Y.: New Dimensions,
        1970
    Things That Happen to Us. N.Y.: New Dimensions, 1970

NEMIROFF, R.
    CRITICISMS OF NEMIROFF:
    Gottfried, Martin. "Broadway." In Theatre 4: The Ameri-
        can Theatre, 1970-1971, p. 22
    Walker, Jesse H. "And Now a Word...." The Afro-Ameri-
        can (baltimore, Md.), 12-16 July 1977, p. 11

NERO, CHARLES
    PLAYS:
    [with Charles Greene] The Legend of Toby Kingdom
    FILM SCRIPTS:
    [with Charles Greene and Gus Narin] The Legend of Toby
        Kingdom (adapted from play)
    CRITICISMS OF INDIVIDUAL FILM SCRIPTS:
    The Legend of Toby Kingdom
        Pantovic, Stan. "The Making of a Black Movie." Sepia
            22 (December 1973): 54-62

NOBLE, GIL
    TELEVISION SCRIPTS:
    The Life and Times of Frederick Douglass
    REVIEWS OF INDIVIDUAL TELEVISION SCRIPTS:
    The Life and Times of Frederick Douglass
        Allen, Zita D. "'The Life and Times of Frederick
            Douglass' An Enlightening Journey." (N.Y.) Amster-
            dam News: Arts and Entertainment, 10 July 1976, D-6

†NORFORD, GEORGE
    PLAYS:
    Joy Exceeding Glory
    CRITICISMS OF INDIVIDUAL PLAYS:
    Joy Exceeding Glory
        "The Words of Dick Campbell." In Mitchell. Voices of
            the Black Theatre, pp. 101, 103, 108

NSABE, NIA
PLAYS:
Mama Don't Know What Love Is
PLAYS PUBLISHED IN ANTHOLOGIES:
Mama Don't Know What Love Is in Sonia Sanchez Writers
Workshop, Three Hundred and Sixty Degrees of Blackness
Comin' At You

OBAYANI, KAMBON
PLAYS:
The Pendulum
PLAYS PUBLISHED IN PERIODICALS:
The Pendulum in Obsidian 1 (Winter 1975): 73-80

†O'NEAL, JOHN
PLAYS:
When the Opportunity Scratches, Itch It
CRITICISMS OF O'NEAL:
Mahoney, John C. "Free Southern Group Performs." Los
Angeles (Calif.) Times, 10 December 1975, in Newsbank--
Performing Arts. November-December 1975, 85: D 6
CRITICISMS OF INDIVIDUAL PLAYS:
When the Opportunity Scratches, Itch It
Taylor, Clarke. "In the Soul of the Theatre." Essence
5 (April 1975): 49

O'NEAL, REGINA
TELEVISION SCRIPTS:
And Then the Harvest; Three Television Plays. Detroit:
Broadside Press, n.d.

O'NEAL, RON
CRITICISMS OF O'NEAL:
Duckett, Alfred. "The Birth of a Screenwriter." Sepia
26 (January 1977): 68
Smith, Agnes R. "Superfly Has Flown Away." (Chicago,
Ill.) Courier 6 September 1975, in Newsbank--Performing
Arts. September-October 1975, 70: B 10, 11
AWARDS:
Clarence Derwent
Drama Desk
Obie Theatre World Awards

OWA
PLAYS:
That All Depends on How the Drop Falls, part of the Soledad
Tetrad

†OWENS, DANIEL
PLAYS:
Arife and Pendabus
Bargainin' Thing
Emily T

CRITICISMS OF INDIVIDUAL PLAYS:
Arife and Pendabus
    Bailey, Peter. "Annual Round-up: Black Theater in
        America--New York." Black World 24 (April 1975): 21
REVIEWS OF INDIVIDUAL PLAYS:
Emily T
    "'Emily T' Opens." (N.Y.) Amsterdam News: Arts and
        Entertainment, 16 October 1976, D-8
    "Lights Up on Black Women." (N.Y.) Amsterdam News:
        Arts and Entertainment, 14 August 1976, D-16

OWOMOYELA, OYEKAN
PLAYS:
The Slave, Master's Thesis, UCLA, 1966

†OYAMO (Charles F. Gordon) (b. 1943)
PLAYS:
The Breakout
Chimpanzee
His First Step
Lovers, 1969
Out of Site
The Thieves, 1970
Willie Bignigga
PLAYS PUBLISHED IN PERIODICALS:
Out of Site in Black Theatre no. 4 (April 1970): 28-31
CRITICISMS OF OYAMO:
    Stasio, Marilyn. "Off-Broadway." In Theatre 5: The
        American Theatre, 1971-1972, p. 33
CRITICISMS OF INDIVIDUAL PLAYS:
The Breakout
    Oliver, Edith. "Report from 137th Street." In Theatre 5:
        The American Theatre, 1971-1972, p. 133
His First Step
    Oliver, Edith. "Report from 137th Street." In Theatre
        5: The American Theatre, 1971-1972, p. 133
REVIEWS OF INDIVIDUAL PLAYS:
The Breakout
    Clurman, Harold. "Theatre." Nation 220 (17 May 1975):
        605
    Oliver, Edith. "Theatre: Off-Broadway." New Yorker
        51 (12 May 1975): 109
Chimpanzee
    Clarke, Sebastian. "Magic/al Delight(s)." Black Theatre
        no. 5 (1971): 54-55
Lovers
    Kupa, Kushauri. "Closeup: The New York Scene--Black
        Theatre in New York, 1970-1971." Black Theatre no.
        6 (1972): 47
    Perrier, Paulette. "Review: The Black Magicians."
        Black Theatre no. 5 (1971): 51

The Thieves
    Kupa, Kushauri. "Closeup: The New York Scene--Black
      Theatre in New York, 1970-1971." Black Theatre no.
      6 (1972): 46
Willie Bignigga
    Clarke, Sebastian. 'Magic/al Delight(s)." Black
      Theatre no. 5 (1971): 54-55

OYEWOLE, ABIODUN
  PLAYS:
    Comments (a Black Man's Response to the Broadway Hit,
      "For Colored Girls Who....")
  REVIEWS OF INDIVIDUAL PLAYS
    Comments
      Mathews, Les. "That's Showbiz...." (N.Y.) Amsterdam
        News: Arts and Entertainment, 7 May 1977, D-11
      Tapley, Mel. "Abiodum Oyewole's 'Comments' Answer to
        'For Colored Girls' Applauded." (N.Y.) Amsterdam
        News: Arts and Entertainment, 14 May 1977, D-15

PALMER, JON PHILLIPS
  PLAYS:
  The Trial of James McNeill Whistler
  MUSICALS:
  The Starting Five
  REVIEWS OF INDIVIDUAL MUSICALS:
  The Starting Five
    "Setting Basketball to Music." San Francisco (Calif.)
      Examiner, 7 September 1975, in Newsbank--Performing
      Arts. September-October 1975, 66: F 14

†PANNELL, LYNN K.
  PLAYS:
  It's A Shame
  REVIEWS OF INDIVIDUAL PLAYS:
  It's A Shame
    Kupa, Kushauri. "Closeup: The New York Scene--Black
      Theatre in New York, 1970-1971." Black Theatre no.
      6 (1972): 47

†PARKS, GORDON
  CRITICISMS OF PARKS:
    Burns, Ben. "The Creative Wizardry of Gordon Parks."
      Sepia 25 (April 1976): 36-40, 44-46
    Myers, Walter Dean. "Gordon Parks: John Henry with a
      Camera." Black Scholar 7 (January-February 1976):
      27-30
    "Parks: Success by Fright." In Nykoruk. Authors in the
      News. vol. 2, p. 215
  AWARDS:
  1972 Spingarn Medal

†PATTERSON, CHARLES (b. October 29, 1941)
    PLAYS:
      Black Ice
      Legacy
    CRITICISMS OF INDIVIDUAL PLAYS:
      Black Ice
        Brown, Lloyd W. "The Cultural Revolution in Black
          Theatre." Negro American Literature Forum 8 (Spring
          1974): 163
      Legacy
        Fenderson, Lewis H. "The New Breed of Black Writers
          and Their Jaundiced View of Tradition." CLA Journal
          15 (September 1971): 23-24

†PAWLEY, THOMAS
    PLAYS:
      Judgment Day
      The Messiah
      Son of Liberty
    CRITICISMS OF PAWLEY:
      Sandle. The Negro in the American Educational Theatre,
        pp. 19-20
      Xeroxed Abstracts: Stage II
    CRITICISMS OF INDIVIDUAL PLAYS:
      Judgment Day
        Sandle. The Negro in the American Educational Theatre,
          p. 20

PAYTON, LEW
    PLAYS:
      Did Adam Sin? Los Angeles: by author, 1937

†PERKINS, EUGENE
    PLAYS:
      Black Fairy, children's play
      Fred
      God Is Black But He's Dead
      The Image Makers
      Our Street
    CRITICISMS OF INDIVIDUAL PLAYS:
      Fred
        Dyson, Dierdra. "Annual Round-up: Black Theater in
          America--Chicago." Black World 24 (April 1975): 30-31
    MEDIA RESOURCES:
      Black Fairy
        Third World Press. Chicago, Ill. $5.00 (Useni Record)

PERKINS, JOHN
    PLAYS:
      The Yellow Pillow

PERRY, FELTON
    PLAYS:

Buy the Bi and By
Or
CRITICISMS OF PERRY:
"Felton Perry Minus All Labels." Los Angeles (Calif.)
Herald Examiner, 29 January 1976, in Newsbank--Per-
forming Arts. January-February 1976, 14: C 2
REVIEWS OF INDIVIDUAL PLAYS:
Buy the Bi and By
Byrne, Bridget. "Laugh Dimension Makes Good 'Buy'."
Los Angeles (Calif.) Herald Examiner, 14 January
1976, in Newsbank--Performing Arts. January-February
1976, 14: C 3

Or
Smith, Marian. "Black Theater Week Renews Basic Aim:
Reflect Community." Chicago (Ill.) Sun-Times, 23
May 1976, in Newsbank--Performing Arts. May-June
1976, 41: G 6

†PERRY, LESLIE D.
PLAYS:
Sis' Goose an' de Fox
PLAYS PUBLISHED IN ANTHOLOGIES:
Sis' Goose an' de Fox in Reed. Yardbird Reader: 4 (1975):
112-122

†PERRY, SHAUNIELLE
PLAYS:
Clinton
MUSICALS:
[with Neal Tate] Music Magic
CRITICISMS OF PERRY:
"Creative Directions." Essence 3 (May 1972): 76
REVIEWS OF INDIVIDUAL MUSICALS:
Music Magic
Austin, William. "New Musical at the Billie Holiday."
(N.Y.) Amsterdam News: Arts and Entertainment,
1 January 1977, D-7
"'Music Magic' Opens at Billie Holiday." (N.Y.) Amster-
dam News: Arts and Entertainment, 20 November
1976, D-9

PETERS, CHARLES
PLAYS:
Fine Print

†PETERSON, LOUIS
PLAYS:
Mrs. Patterson
Take A Giant Step
CRITICISMS OF INDIVIDUAL PLAYS:
Mrs. Patterson
Hartnoll. The Oxford Companion to the Theatre, p. 680

Take A Giant Step
    Davis, Curt. "The Inner Voice of Louis Gosset." Encore
      6 (6 June 1977): 28-30
    Evans, Donald T. "Bring It All Back Home." Black
      World 20 (February 1971): 41-45
          . "Playwrights of the Fifties: Bringing It All
    Back Home." Black World 20 (February 1971): 44
    Hartnoll. The Oxford Companion to the Theatre, p. 680
    Hay, Samuel A. "African-American Drama, 1950-1970."
      Negro History Bulletin 36 (January 1973): 7
REVIEWS OF INDIVIDUAL PLAYS:
Take a Giant Step
    "Beah Richards Combines Poetic Touch with Acting."
      Chicago Daily Defender, 1 August 1977, p. 18
    Parker. Who's Who in The Theatre, 15th ed., p. 702

PINERO, MIGUEL [as non-black collaborator]
  PLAYS:
  [with Neil Harris] Straight from the Ghetto

POWELL, RICHARD
  PLAYS:
  Aaron Asworth. New York: New Dimensions, 1970

PROVIDENCE, WAYNE
  PLAYS:
  Where Are You Black Dream
  PLAYS PUBLISHED IN ANTHOLOGIES:
  Where Are You Black Dream, in Sonia Sanchez Writers
    Workshop. Three Hundred and Sixty Degrees of Black-
    ness Comin' at You

RAFF, WILLIAM JOURDAN
  PLAYS:
  Harlem: A Melodrama of Negro Life in Harlem, 3 acts
    (originally called Black Belt). Manuscript in the James
    Weldon Johnson Collection of Yale University Library
  [with Wallace Thurman] Jeremiah, the Magnificent, 3 acts,
    1930
  CRITICISMS OF INDIVIDUAL PLAYS:
  Harlem
    Abrahson, Doris. "The Great White Way: Critics and
      the First Black Playwrights on Broadway." Educa-
      tional Theatre Journal 28 (March 1976): 49-51
    Edmonds, Randolph. "The Blacks in the American Thea-
      tre, 1700-1969." The Pan-African Journal 7 (Winter
      1974): 3-4
    Hartnoll. The Oxford Companion to the Theatre, p. 675
    "The Words of Dick Campbell." In Mitchell. Voices of
      the Black Theatre, p. 106

†RAHMAN, AISHAH
  PLAYS:

Transcendental Blues
Unfinished Women Cry in No Man's Land While a Bird Dies
   in a Gilded Cage
CRITICISMS OF INDIVIDUAL PLAYS:
Unfinished Women Cry in No Man's Land While a Bird Dies
   in a Gilded Cage
   Moore, Honor. "Theater Will Never Be the Same." Ms.
     6 (December 1977): 37-38
REVIEWS OF INDIVIDUAL PLAYS:
Transcendental Blues
   "Lights Up on Black Women." (N.Y.) Amsterdam News:
     Arts and Entertainment, 14 August 1976, D-16

†RAPHAEL, LENNOX
   PLAYS:
     Che!
   CRITICISMS OF INDIVIDUAL PLAYS:
     Che!
       Geisinger. Plays, Players, & Playwrights, p. 609
       Simon. Uneasy Stages, pp. 200, 201-03

†RAZAF, ANDY (Andreamanentania Paul Razafinkeriefo) (b. 1895)
   MUSICALS:
     [with Eubie Blake, Flournoy Miller and Noble Sissle] The
       Blackbirds, 1929
     Hot Chocolate, 1929
     [with Eubie Blake, Flournoy Miller and Noble Sissle] O, Sing
       A New Song, 1934
   CRITICISMS OF RAZAF:
     Hatch, James. "Speak to Me in Those Old Words, You
       Know, Those La-La Words, Those Tung-Tung Sounds."
       Yale/Theatre 8 (Fall 1976): 27
   CRITICISMS OF INDIVIDUAL MUSICALS:
     Hot Chocolate
       "The Words of Dick Campbell." In Mitchell. Voices of
       the Black Theatre, pp. 104-105

REAGON, BERNICE
   MUSICALS:
     A Day, A Life, A People

†REDMOND, EUGENE
   CRITICISMS BY REDMOND:
     "The Black Scholar Reviews: 'And Still I Rise!' by Maya
       Angelou." Black Scholar 8 (September 1976): 50-51
   CRITICISMS OF REDMOND:
     Rowell, Charles H. "Teaching Black American Literature:
       A Review." Negro American Literature Forum 7 (Spring
       1973): 17

REED, ISHMAEL
   FILM SCRIPTS:

Yellow Back Radio Broke-Down (based on book)
CRITICISMS OF INDIVIDUAL FILM SCRIPTS:
Yellow Back Radio Broke-Down
"Ishmael Reed on Ishmael Reed." Black World 23 (June
1974): 20-34

†RHONE, TREVOR
PLAYS:
Comic Strip
Smile Orange
CRITICISMS OF INDIVIDUAL PLAYS:
Comic Strip
Smith, Ed. "Special Reports: The Performing Arts in
Jamaica--Theatre." Black World 23 (July 1974): 73
Smile Orange
Smith, Ed. "Special Reports: The Performing Arts in
Jamaica--Theatre." Black World 23 (July 1974): 73

RIBMAN, RONALD
PLAYS:
Cold Storage
The Poison Tree
REVIEWS OF INDIVIDUAL PLAYS:
Cold Storage
Gottfried, Martin. "'Cold Storage' Defrosts Into Luke-
warm Theatre." New York Post, 17 April 1977, in
Newsbank--Performing Arts. March-April 1977, 26:
A 12
The Poison Tree
Blum and Willis, eds. A Pictorial History of the Ameri-
can Theatre: 1860-1976, pp. 429, 430
Gottfried, Martin. "'Cold Storage' Defrosts Into Lukewarm
Theatre." New York Post, 17 April 1977, in Newsbank--
Performing Arts. March-April 1977, 26: A 12
. "Ribman Out on a Limb." New York Post, 9
January 1976, in Newsbank--Performing Arts. January-
February 1976, 14: D 7
New York Theatre Critics' Reviews--1976 37 (12 January
1976): 394-97; containing: Watt, Douglas, "Undigested
Prison Thriller" ([N.Y.] Daily News, 9 January 1976).
Barnes, Clive, "'Poison Tree' Portrays Men in Cages"
(New York Times, 9 January 1976). Kissell, Howard,
"The Poison Tree" (Women's Wear Daily, 9 January
1976). Kroll, Jack, "Locking the Door" (Newsweek,
19 January 1976). Gottfried, Martin, "Ribman Out on
a Limb" (New York Post, 9 January 1976). Beaufort,
John, "The Poison Tree" (Christian Science Monitor,
16 January 1976). Probst, Leonard, "The Poison Tree"
(NBC, 8 January 1976). Sanders, Kevin, "The Poison
Tree" (WABC-TV, 8 January 1976)
Pyatt, Richard I. "Will Moses Gunn Shoot Down Father
Time." Encore 6 (3 January 1977): 29-30

Wallach, Allan. "Hate Behind the Bars." (Long Island, N.Y.) Newsday, 9 January 1976, in Newsbank--Performing Arts. January-February 1976, 14: D 8

Watt, Douglas. "An Undigested Prison Thriller." (N.Y.) Daily News, 10 January 1976, in Newsbank--Performing Arts. January-February 1976, 14: D 9

Winer, Linda. "The Boom in Black Theatre: Growing Profits ... and Growing Pains." Chicago Tribune: Arts & Fun, 30 May 1976, 6:2

†RICHARDS, BEAH
    PLAYS:
        A Black Woman Speaks
    CRITICISMS OF RICHARDS:
        "Beah Richards Combines Poetic Touch with Acting." Chicago Daily Defender, 1 August 1977, p. 18
        Brown, Marcia L. "'One Is a Crown'." Soul Illustrated 3 (Winter 1971): 10
    REVIEWS OF INDIVIDUAL PLAYS:
        A Black Woman Speaks
        Willis' Theatre World. vol. 31, 1974-1975, p. 204

RICHARDSON, THOMAS
    PLAYS:
        Place: America (A Theatre Piece). New York: N.A.A.C.P., 1940 (based on the History of the N.A.A.C.P.)

RICHARDSON, VIRGIL
    PLAYS:
        After Hours

†RICHARDSON, WILLIS (b. November 5, 1889)
    PLAYS:
        Attucks, the Martyr
        The Black Horseman
        The Broken Banjo
        [with E. C. Williams] The Chase
        The Chip Woman's Fortune
        The Elder Dumas
        The Flight of the Natives
        The House of Sham
        In Menelik's Court
        The King's Dilemma
        The Man Who Married a Young Wife
        Mortgaged
        Near Calvary
        Peacock's Feathers
    PLAYS PUBLISHED IN ANTHOLOGIES:
        Attucks, the Martyr, in Richardson and Miller. Negro History in Thirteen Plays
        The Black Horseman, in Richardson. Plays and Pageants

from the Life of the Negro

The Elder Dumas, in Richardson and Miller. Negro History in Thirteen Plays

The House of Sham, in Richardson. Plays and Pageants from the Life of the Negro

In Menelik's Court, in Richardson and Miller. Negro History in Thirteen Plays

The King's Dilemma, in Richardson. Plays and Pageants from the Life of the Negro

Mortgaged, in Davis and Peplow. The New Negro Renaissance, pp. 103-117

Near Calvary, in Richardson and Miller. Negro History in Thirteen Plays

CRITICISMS OF RICHARDSON:

Peterson, Bernard L. Jr. "An Evaluation, Willis Richardson: Pioneer Playwright." Black World 24 (April 1975): 40-48, 86-88 [all of Richardson's plays are mentioned or discussed in this article]

Sandle. The Negro in the American Educational Theatre, pp. 17, 18

Xeroxed Abstracts: Stage I

CRITICISMS OF INDIVIDUAL PLAYS:

The Broken Banjo

F. H. K. "Carolina Negro Theatre: In Retrospect." The Carolina Play Book 8 (June 1935): 46

Keyssar-Franke, Helen. "Strategies in Black Drama." Ph.D. Dissertation, University of Iowa, 1974

Sandle. The Negro in the American Educational Theatre, p. 17

Thompson, Larry. "The Black Image in Early American Drama." Black World 24 (April 1975): 68

The Chip Woman's Fortune

Edmonds, Randolph. "The Blacks in the American Theatre, 1700-1969." The Pan-African Journal 7 (Winter 1974): 303

Hartnoll. The Oxford Companion to the Theatre, p. 675

Keyssar-Franke, Helen. "Strategies in Black Drama." Ph.D. Dissertation, University of Iowa, 1974

Turner, Darwin. "W. E. B. Du Bois and the Theory of a Black Aesthetic." Studies in Literary Imagination 7 (Fall 1974): 5

Vacha, J. E. "Black Man on the Great White Way." Journal of Popular Culture 7 (Fall 1973): 293

The Flight of the Natives

Thompson, Larry. "The Black Image in Early American Drama." Black World 24 (April 1975): 68

RILEY, CLAYTON

PLAYS:

Gilbeau

REVIEWS OF INDIVIDUAL PLAYS:

Gilbeau

Peterson, Maurice. "On the Aisle." Essence 6 (April 1976): 8
DRAMA CRITIC: Liberator

ROACH, E.
PLAYS:
Belle Fanto
Letter from Leonora

ROBINSON, BETSY JULIA
PLAYS:
The Shanglers

ROBINSON, DEL
MUSICALS:
[with Roger Furman] Fat Tuesday
CRITICISMS OF INDIVIDUAL MUSICALS:
Fat Tuesday
Bailey, Peter. "Annual Round-up: Black Theater in America--New York." Black World 25 (April 1976): 55-56

†ROBINSON, GARRETT
PLAYS:
Land of Lem
REVIEWS OF INDIVIDUAL PLAYS:
Land of Lem
Bailey, Peter. "Annual Round-Up: Black Theater in America--New York." Black World 21 (April 1972): 36

ROBINSON, WOODY
FILM SCRIPTS:
[with William Greaves] The Marijuana Affair

ROGERS, IRA
PLAYS:
[with Chuck Smith] Tetragrammonon Is
CRITICISMS OF ROGERS:
Mitchell. Voices of the Black Theatre, pp. 23-24

ROLLERI, WILLIAM
PLAYS:
[with Anna Antaramia and Martin Zurla] Night Shift
REVIEWS OF INDIVIDUAL PLAYS:
Night Shift
Grimes, Nikki. "'Night Shift'." (N.Y.) Amsterdam News: Arts and Entertainment, 4 December 1976, D-3

ROSEMOND, HENRI
PLAYS:
Haiti, Our Neighbor. Brooklyn: The Haitian Publishing Company, 1944

†ROSS, JOHN M.
    PLAYS:
      Wonga Doll
    CRITICISMS OF ROSS:
      Sandle. The Negro in the American Educational Theatre,
        pp. 20, 48, passim
    CRITICISMS OF INDIVIDUAL PLAYS:
      Wonga Doll
        Sandle. The Negro in the American Educational Theatre,
          p. 20

†RUSSELL, CHARLIE
    PLAYS:
      Five on the Black Hand Side
    FILM SCRIPTS:
      Five on the Black Hand Side (based on the play)
    CRITICISMS OF INDIVIDUAL PLAYS:
      Five on the Black Hand Side
        "'Five on the Black Hand Side'." Ebony 29 (May 1974):
          96-102
    REVIEWS OF INDIVIDUAL PLAYS:
      Five on the Black Hand Side
        Clurman, Harold. "Theatre." Nation 210 (2 February
          1970): 124
        Hewes, Henry. "Black Hopes." Saturday Review 53 (14
          February 1970): 30

SAGGITTARUS
    PLAYS:
      I Am Ishmael, Son of the Blackamoor. Washington, D.C.:
        Nuclassics and Science Pub., 1975

SAHKOOR, SALAHUDIN
    PLAYS:
      Armageddon
    REVIEWS OF INDIVIDUAL PLAYS:
      Armageddon
        "Community Keynotes." (N.Y.) Amsterdam News: Arts
          and Entertainment, 11 June 1977, D-17

†SALAAM, KALAMU YA (Val Ferdinand)
    PLAYS:
      Black Liberation Army
    CRITICISMS OF INDIVIDUAL PLAYS:
      Black Liberation Army
        Moses, Gilbert. "Hubert Humphrey Is To Politics...."
          In Theatre 2: The American Theatre, 1968-1969, p. 110

SALIM (Chauncey, Harrell Cordell)
    PLAYS:
      We Heard From Martin
    CRITICISMS OF SALIM:

Tapley, Mel. "MLK Players' director Changes his name."
(N.Y.) Amsterdam News: Arts and Entertainment. 28
August 1976, D-9
REVIEWS OF INDIVIDUAL PLAYS:
We Heard From Martin
"MLK Players on RCA." (N.Y.) Amsterdam News: Arts
and Entertainment, 14 May 1977, D-15

†SALIMU (Netti McGray)
PLAYS:
Growin' Into Blackness
PLAYS PUBLISHED IN PERIODICALS:
"Growin' Into Blackness" in Black Theatre no. 2 (1969): 20-22
CRITICISMS OF SALIMU:
Clayborne, Jon L. "Modern Black Drama and the Gay Image."
College English 36 (November 1974): 383
CRITICISMS OF INDIVIDUAL PLAYS:
Growin' Into Blackness
Benston, Kimberly W. "'Cities in Bezique': Adrienne
Kennedy's Expressionistic Vision." CLA Journal 20
(December 1976): 235

†SANCHEZ, SONIA (Mannan, Laila)
PLAYS:
The Bronx Is Next
Sister Son/ji
CRITICISMS OF SANCHEZ:
Cameron and Hoffman. A Guide to Theatre Study, p. 204
Clayborne, Jon L. "Modern Black Drama and the Gay
Image." College English 36 (November 1974): 383
Miller, Jeanne-Marie A. "Images of Black Women in Plays
by Black Playwrights." CLA Journal 20 (June 1977): 505
Taylor, Willene Pulliam. "The Reversal of the Tainted
Blood Theme in the Works of Writers of the Black Revo-
lutionary Theatre." Negro American Literature Forum
10 (Fall 1976): 89, 91
Xeroxed Abstracts: Stage I
CRITICISMS OF INDIVIDUAL PLAYS:
The Bronx Is Next
Taylor, Willene Pulliam. "The Reversal of the Tainted
Blood Theme in the Works of Writers of the Black
Revolutionary Theatre." Negro American Literature
Forum 10 (Fall 1976): 89, 91
Sister Son/ji
Newman, Jill. "The Players the Thing at Clay Steven-
son's Workshop." Encore 6 (21 February 1977): 35
REVIEWS OF INDIVIDUAL PLAYS:
The Bronx Is Next
Kupa, Kushauri. "Closeups: The New York Scene--Black
Theatre in New York, 1970-1971." Black Theatre no.
6 (1971): 42
Sister Son/ji

Clurman, Harold. "Theatre: 'Black Visions,' Four One
Acts." Nation 214 (17 April 1972): 508
———. "Theatre." Nation 214 (17 April 1972): 508-
509
Kalem, T. E. "Black On Black--'Black Visions'." Time
99 (1 May 1972): 53
Oliver, Edith. "The Theatre: Off-Broadway." New
Yorker 48 (8 April 1972): 97-99

SAPIN, LOUIS
PLAYS:
[with Richard Wright] Daddy Goodness
CRITICISMS OF INDIVIDUAL PLAYS:
Daddy Goodness
Current Biography 37 (September 1976): 29
REVIEWS OF INDIVIDUAL PLAYS:
Daddy Goodness
Blum and Willis, eds. A Pictorial History of the Ameri-
can Theatre: 1860-1976, p. 398
Sayre, N. "New York's Black Theatre." New Statesman
76 (25 October 1968): 556

SAUNDERS, BRYON C.
PLAYS:
The Promised Land, a Black Soap Opera

SAUNDERS, FRANK G.
PLAYS:
Balloons in Her Hair
CRITICISMS OF INDIVIDUAL PLAYS:
Balloons in Her Hair
Sandle. The Negro in the American Educational Theatre,
p. 152

†SCOTT, JOHNIE
PLAYS:
Ride a Black Horse
CRITICISMS BY SCOTT:
"The Ceremony of the Land." Arts in Society 10 (Fall-
Winter 1973): 33-39
REVIEWS OF INDIVIDUAL PLAYS:
Ride a Black Horse
Kupa, Kushauri. "Closeup: The New York Scene--Black
Theatre in New York, 1970-1971." Black Theatre no.
6 (1971): 40-42

SEALS, HOWARD E.
PLAYS:
After-'Yuh, Mamma, 1972

†SEBREE, CHARLES
CRITICISMS OF SEBREE:
Xeroxed Abstracts: Stage I

†SEILER, CONRAD
PLAYS:
Sweet Land
CRITICISMS OF SEILER:
Hartnoll. The Oxford Companion to the Theatre, p. 677
CRITICISMS OF INDIVIDUAL PLAYS:
Sweet Land
   Goldstein. The Political Stage, pp. 260-261

SHAFFER, PETER
PLAYS:
Black Comedy, Including White Lies; Two Plays. N.Y.:
   Stein and Day, 1969

SHANGE, NTOZAKE (Paulette Williams)
PLAYS:
For Colored Girls Who Have Considered Suicide/When the
   Rainbow Is Enuf; A Choreopoem. N.Y.: Macmillan, 1977
A Photograph: A Still Life with Shadows/A Photograph: A
   Study of Cruelty
CRITICISMS BY SHANGE:
"Ntozake Shange Interviews Herself." Ms. 6 (December
   1977): 34-35, 70, 72
CRITICISMS OF SHANGE:
Considine, Shaun. "British Theatre Had Its Angry Young
   Men--Off-Broadway Savors Its First Furious Women,
   Ntozake Shange." People 6 (5 July 1976): 68-69
Jarrett, Vernon. "A Vicious Lynching Delights Audience."
   Chicago Tribune, 1 January 1978, 1:19
Latour, Martine. "Ntozake Shange: Driven Poet/Playwright."
   Mademoiselle 82 (September 1976): 182+
Lewis, Barbara. "The Poet." Essence 7 (November 1976):
   86, 119-20
"Ntozake Shange: Interviews." New Yorker 52 (2 August
   1976): 17-19
Winer, Linda. "Black Feminism Sparkles Under a Poetic
   Rainbow." Chicago Tribune: Arts & Fun/Books, 25
   December 1977, pp. 2, 5
CRITICISMS OF INDIVIDUAL PLAYS:
For Colored Girls/When the Rainbow Is Enuf
   Bambara, Toni Cade. "'For Colored Girls'--And White
      Girls Too." Ms. 5 (September 1976): 36, 38
   Bell, Roseanne Pope. "'For Colored Girls Who Have Con-
      sidered Suicide/When the Rainbow Is Enuf'." The
      Black Collegian 7 (May-June 1977): 48-49
   Bond, Jean Carey. "For Colored Girls Who Have Con-
      sidered Suicide." Freedomways 16 (Third Quarter,
      1976): 187-91
   Harris, Jessica. "The Women Who Are the Rainbow."
      Essence 7 (November 1976): 87-89, 102, 104, 120,
      122, 147
   Lewis, Barbara. "For Colored Girls Who Have Con-
      sidered Suicide/When the Rainbow Is Enuf." Essence

7 (November 1976): 86, 119-120

Moore, Honor. The New Women's Theatre, pp. xxxi, xxxii

_____. "Theater Will Never Be the Same." Ms. 6 (December 1977): 38

Ribowsky, Mark. "A Poetess Scores a Hit with 'What's Wrong With Black Men'." Sepia 25 (December 1976): 42-46

Salaam, Kalamu ya. "Making the Image Real." The Black Collegian 7 (March-April 1977): 57

Stone, Laurie. "Act 1 for Women Playwrights." Ms. 6 (August 1977): 38

REVIEWS OF INDIVIDUAL PLAYS:

For Colored Girls/When the Rainbow Is Enuf

Austin, William. "Blacks, 'The Great White Way'." (N.Y.) Amsterdam News: Arts and Entertainment, 9 October 1976, D-11

Blum and Willis, eds. A Pictorial History of the American Theatre: 1860-1976, p. 431

Bond, Jean Carey. "For Colored Girls Who Have Considered Suicide." Freedomways 16 (Third Quarter, 1976): 187-191; reprint from The Easy Guide to Black Art, September 1, 1976

Clurman, Harold. "Theatre." Nation 222 (1 May 1976): 542

Facts on File. 1976, 9-15, 1014 D 3

Guernsey. The Best Plays of 1975-1976, p. 366

Harris, Jessica B. "'For Colored Girls' ... from Ntozake to Broadway." (N.Y.) Amsterdam News: Arts and Entertainment. 9 October 1976, D 10-11

Hughes, Catharine. "Three New Musicals." America 135 (27 November 1976): 373

_____. "Two Black Plays." America 135 (9 October 1976): 214

Kalem, T. E. 'He Done Her Wrong." Time 197 (14 June 1976): 74

Kauffmann, Stanley. "Arts and Lives: Stanley Kauffmann on the Theater: Suite and Sour." New Republic 174 (3 & 10 July 1976): 20-21

Kroll, Jack. "Women's Rites." Newsweek 87 (14 June 1976): 99

Latour, Martine. "Ntozake Shange: Driven Poet/Playwright." Mademoiselle 82 (September 1976): 182+

McGinty, Robin. "'... It's About a Sister Who's Been Hurt a Lot'." The Afro-American (Baltimore, Md.), 5-9 June 1977, p. 11

"New Breed Theatre Producer." The Afro-American (Baltimore, Md.), 12-16 April 1977, p. 11

New York Theatre Critics' Reviews--1976 37 (27 September 1976): 199-202; containing: Watt, Douglas, "Here's to the Ladies Again" [N.Y.] Daily News, 16 September 1976). Wilson, Edwin, "For Colored Girls...." (The

Wall Street Journal, 21 September 1976). Gussow,
Mel, "Stage: 'Colored Girls' on Broadway" (New York
Times, 16 September 1976). Kalem, T. E., "He Done
Her Wrong" (Time, 14 June 1976). Gottfried, Martin,
"Rainbow Over Broadway" (New York Post, 16 Septem-
ber 1976). Kroll, Jack, "Women's Rites" (Newsweek,
14 June 1976). Beaufort, John, "For Colored Girls"
(The Christian Science Monitor, 24 September 1976).
Sanders, Kevin, "For Colored Girls Who ..." (WABC-
TV, 19 September 1976). Probst, Leonard, (NBC-TV,
15 September 1976)

"Ntozake Shange: Interview." New Yorker 52 (2 August
1976): 17-19

Oliver, Edith. "The Theatre: Off-Broadway." New
Yorker 52 (14 June 1976): 77-78

Peterson, Maurice. "On the Aisle." Essence 7 (October
1976): 48

_____. "On the Aisle--Theatre: Ntozake Shange."
Essence 7 (October 1976): 48

Rich, Allan. "For Audiences of Any Color When 'Rex'
Is Not Enuf." New York 9 (14 June 1976): 62

Rogers, Curtis E. "Black Men View 'For Colored Girls':
Good Theatre but Poor Sociological Statement." (N.Y.)
Amsterdam News: Arts and Entertainment, 9 October
1976, D-11

Tapley, Mel. "Trazana, Dolores, and Diana Win Tonys."
(N.Y.) Amsterdam News: Arts and Entertainment, 11
June 1977, D-2

Walker, Jesse H. "And Now a Word...." The Afro-
American (Baltimore, Md.), 19-23 July 1977, p. 11

"Welcome to the Great Black Way." Time 108 (1 November 1976): 72, 74

Wetzsteon, Ross. "A Season for All Seasons." Village
Voice 22 (June 6, 1977): 91, 93. This is a collection
of short reviews of the winners of the Obie awards
and includes a short blurb on: Shange, Ntozake. For
Colored Girls Who Have Considered Suicide/When the
Rainbow Is Enuf

Winer, Linda. "On Broadway ... Profits Earn Top
Billing." Chicago Tribune: Arts & Fun/Books, 23
January 1977, pp. 2-3

_____. "... the State Is Set for a Hit Season." Chicago
Tribune: Arts & Fun, 26 June 1977, sec. 7, pp. 3, 12

SHARKEY, TOM
    PLAYS:
      Together Again
    MUSICALS:
      Cinderella Brown

SHARP, SAUNDRA
    PLAYS:

The Sistuhs
CRITICISMS OF INDIVIDUAL PLAYS:
The Sistuhs
Moore, Honor. "Theater Will Never Be the Same."
Ms. 6 (December 1977): 38
REVIEWS OF INDIVIDUAL PLAYS:
The Sistuhs
"Shaw Players Slate 'The Sistuhs', Here." The Afro-
American (Baltimore, Md.), 8-12 March 1977, p. 6
Smith, Marian. "Black Theater Week Renews Basic Aim:
Reflect Community." Chicago (Ill.) Sun-Times, 23
May 1976, in Newsbank--Performing Arts. May-June
1976, 41: G 6

SHAW, G. TITO
PLAYS:
He's Got a Jones
REVIEWS OF INDIVIDUAL PLAYS:
He's Got a Jones
Willis' Theatre World, vol. 31, 1974-1975, p. 198

†SHEPP, ARCHIE (b. May 24, 1937)
PLAYS:
Junebug Graduates Tonight!, 1967
CRITICISMS OF INDIVIDUAL PLAYS:
Junebug Graduates Tonight!
Parker. Who's Who in The Theatre, 15th ed., p. 872

†SHERMAN, JIMMIE
PLAYS:
A Ballad for Watts
CRITICISMS BY SHERMAN:
"From the Ashes." Antioch Review 27 (Fall 1967): 285-93
CRITICISMS OF INDIVIDUAL PLAYS:
A Ballad for Watts
Sherman, Jimmie. "From the Ashes." Antioch Review
27 (Fall 1967): 285-93

†SHINE, TED
PLAYS:
Come Back After the Fire
Contribution
CRITICISMS OF INDIVIDUAL PLAYS:
Contribution
Bailey, Peter. "Annual Round-Up: Black Theatre in
America--New York." Black World 21 (April 1972): 36
Current Biography 37 (1976)
Klotman. Another Man Gone, p. 96, ff 15
REVIEWS OF INDIVIDUAL PLAYS:
Contribution
Oliver, Edith. "Theatre: Off Broadway." New Yorker
45 (12 April 1969): 131

†SHIPP, J. A.
   CRITICISMS OF SHIPP:
      Mitchell. Voices of the Black Theatre, pp. 23-24
   CRITICISMS OF INDIVIDUAL MUSICALS:
      In Dahomey
         Hatch, James. "Speak to Me in Those Old Words, You
           Know, Those La-La Words, Those Tung-Tung Sounds."
           Yale/Theatre 8 (Fall 1976): 26

SILVER, DOROTHY
   MUSICALS:
      [with Peyton Dean] Hamlet Jones, (based on an original play
         Ham by Langston Hughes, and retitled from Little Ham)
   REVIEWS OF INDIVIDUAL MUSICALS:
      Hamlet Jones
         "Hamlet Jones." (Cleveland, O.) Call and Post, 27 Sep-
           tember 1975, in Newsbank--Performing Arts. Septem-
           ber-October 1975, 66: D 11

†SILVERA, FRANK
   CRITICISMS OF SILVERA:
      Barrow, William. "Man of Many Faces: Frank Silvera."
         Negro Digest 12 (September 1963): 40-43

†SISSLE, NOBLE (b. 1889)
   MUSICALS:
      [with Eubie Blake, Flournoy Miller and Andy Razaf] The
         Blackbirds, 1929
      In Bamville 1924 became The Chocolate Dandies
      [with Eubie Blake] The Chocolate Dandies
      [with Eubie Blake, Flournoy Miller and Andy Razaf] O, Sing
         a New Song, 1934
      [with Eubie Blake, Flournoy Miller and Aubrey Lyles]
         Shuffle Along, 1921; 1933
   CRITICISMS OF SISSLE:
      Birmingham. Certain People, p. 191
      Current, Gloster B. "Noble Sissle." Crisis 83 (March
         1976): 84-87
      Kimball and Bolcom. Reminiscing with Sissle and Blake,
         passim
      Xeroxed Abstracts: Stage I
   CRITICISMS OF INDIVIDUAL MUSICALS:
      The Chocolate Dandies
         Bovosco, Carole. "Discovering Foremothers." Ms. 6
           (September 1977): 59
         Current, Gloster B. "Noble Sissle." Crisis 83 (March
           1976): 87
         Gagey. Revolution in American Drama, p. 253
         Kimball and Bolcom. Reminiscing with Sissle and Blake,
           passim
      Shuffle Along
         "Black Theatre: A Bid for Cultural Identity." Black

Enterprise 2 (September 1971): 31
Current, Gloster B. "Noble Sissle." Crisis 83 (March
1976): 87
Gagey. Revolution in American Drama, p. 253
Jackson. The Waiting Years, p. 171
Kimball and Bolcom. Reminiscing with Sissle and Blake,
passim
McGraw-Hill Encyclopedia of World Drama. vol. 3,
p. 288
Mitchell. Voices of the Black Theatre, pp. 30, 43, 103
Turner, Darwin. "W. E. B. Du Bois and the Theory of a
Black Aesthetic." Studies in Literary Imagination 7
(Fall 1974): 3, 5
REVIEWS OF INDIVIDUAL MUSICALS:
Shuffle Along
Blum and Willis, eds. A Pictorial History of the Ameri-
can Theatre: 1860-1976, pp. 188, 338
Lewis, Barbara. "Metropolitan Museum Highlights Black
Theatre." (N.Y.) Amsterdam News: Arts and Enter-
tainment, 19 February 1977, D-8
Peterson, Maurice. "On the Aisle: Focus on Avon Long."
Essence 6 (January 1976): 28

SMALLS, C.
MUSICALS:
[with W. F. Brown] The Wiz based on The Wonderful Wizard
of Oz by Frank Baum; originally conceived as a TV special
by former disc jockey, Ken Harper
CRITICISMS OF INDIVIDUAL MUSICALS:
The Wiz
Bailey, Peter. "Annual Round-Up: Black Theater in
America--New York." Black World 24 (April 1975): 33
Engle. The Critics, pp. 155, passim
Davis, Curt. "People in the News--'Wiz'." Encore 6
(7 February 1977): 26
Douglas, Carlyle C. "The Whiz behind 'The Wiz'."
Ebony 30 (October 1975): 114-116+
Geisinger. Plays, Players, & Playwrights, pp. 241, il;
742
Martin, Sharon Stockard. "Bring It Down Front: The
Tanning of Oz--Reflections on the Usurpation of a
Myth." Essence 6 (September 1975): 32, 35
Nachman, Gerald. "Who's Afraid of the Broadway Critics?"
More 7 (July 1977): 22
Peterson, Maurice. "Rising Stars." Essence 7 (Decem-
ber 1976): 52, 89
Ribowsky, Mark. "'Father' of the Black Theater Boom."
Sepia 25 (November 1976): 70
Taylor, Clarke. "Fortune Smiles on Broadway's Gypsies."
Essence 7 (August 1976): 78
Weathers, Diane. "Fantasy in Black Theatre: A King of
New Freedom." Encore 4 (21 April 1975): 28, 32-34

Winer, Linda. "... the Stage Is Set for a Hit Season."
   Chicago Tribune: Arts & Fun, 26 June 1977, sec. 6,
   p. 12

REVIEWS OF INDIVIDUAL PLAYS:

The Wiz

   Bellamy, Peter. "'The Wiz' Musical a Whiz of a Show."
      (Cleveland, O.) Plain Dealer 25 May 1975, in News-
      bank--Performing Arts. May-June 1975, 38: G 8
   Blum and Willis, eds. A Pictorial History of the Ameri-
      can Theatre: 1860-1976, pp. 424, 426, 428
   Calloway, Earl. "Kamol as the Wiz Is Electrifying."
      Chicago Daily Defender, 7 June 1977, p. 20
   Clurman, Harold. "Theatre." Nation 220 (25 January
      1975): 94
   Davis, Curt. "It's Happening for Mabel King." Encore
      6 (20 June 1977): 51
      _____. "Ken Page is Doing Nicely--Nicely, Thanks."
      Encore 6 (7 February 1977): 35
      _____. "Welcome 'Arms'." Encore 6 (17 January
      1977): 36
   Drew, Michael F. "Critic's Seem Unkind to Theater in
      Uneven Season." Milwaukee (Wis.) Journal, 26 February
      1976, in Newsbank--Performing Arts. January-February
      1976, 13: A 5
   Flippo, Chet. "Broadway Rocks 'The Wiz' and the Worst."
      Rolling Stone 187 (22 May 1975): 18
   Gilbert, Ruth, ed. "In and Around Town: On Broadway."
      New York 10 (2 May 1977): 20; through 10 (3 October
      1977): 19
   Gill, Brendan. "The Theatre: Tennis with the Net Down."
      New Yorker 50 (13 January 1975): 64
   Harris, Jessica B. "Harper a Show Biz 'Wiz'." (N.Y.)
      Amsterdam News: Arts and Entertainment, 29 March
      1975, in Newsbank--Performing Arts. March-April
      1975, 29: F 2
   Hieronymus, Clara. "'The Wiz' a Wiz Show." (Nash-
      ville) Tennessean, 31 October 1975, in Newsbank--Per-
      forming Arts. September-October 1975, 66: G 4, 5
   Higginson, Vy. "Oh, Yeah." Essence 5 (November
      1974): 12
   Hodgson, Moira. "Warming Up on Broadway." Dance
      Magazine 49 (March 1975): 34+
   Kalem, T. E. "Jumping Jivernacular." Time 105 (20
      January 1975): 76
   Kroll, Jack. "Oz with Soul." Newsweek 85 (20 January
      1975): 82
   Lewis, Barbara. "Mini-Wiz Captivates Riker's Audience."
      (N.Y.) Amsterdam News: Arts and Entertainment, 30
      April 1977, D-5
   "Long Runs." Facts on Files, 1976, 1015 A 3
   McKenzie, Vashti. "The McKenzie Report: 'The Wiz'
      was a WOW ... Won Seven Tonys." Afro-American

(Baltimore, Md.), 22 April 1975, in Newsbank--Performing Arts. March-April 1975, 31: D 12, 13
McMorrow, Tom. "Broadway Expects a Championship Season." (N.Y.) Daily News, 7 September 1975, in Newsbank--Performing Arts. September-October 1975, 68: C 14-D 1
Mancini, Joseph. "A Wiz." New York Post, 26 April 1975, in Newsbank--Performing Arts. March-April 1975, 27: A 4,5
Meade, James. "Big Man Brings Elegance Back." San Diego (Calif.) Union, 26 October 1975, in Newsbank--Performing Arts. September-October 1975, 69: C 12
Murray, James P. "Blacks Invade Broadway in a Big Way ... With Soul Cheers, and Society Bows." St. Louis (Mo.) Argus, 17 April 1975, in Newsbank--Performing Arts. March-April 1975, 28: D 9
New York Theatre Critics' Reviews--1975 36 (13 January 1975): 390-394, containing: Watt, Douglas, "Fine Cast and Splendid Looking in "Wiz"" ([N.Y.] Daily News, 6 January 1975). Barnes, Clive, "Stage: 'The Wiz' of Oz" (New York Times, 6 January 1975). Gottfried, Martin, "Black Wizard of Oz Musical" (New York Post, 6 January 1975). Wilson, Edwin. "Jivey Dudes" (The Wall Street Journal, 9 January 1975). Kissel, Howard, "The Wiz!" (Women's Wear Daily, 6 January 1975). Beaufort, John, "Broadway's Wizard of Oz" (Christian Science Monitor, 10 January 1975). Kalem, T. E., "Jumping Jivernacular" (Time, 20 January 1975). Kroll, Jack, "Oz with Soul" (Newsweek, 20 January 1975). Probst, Leonard, "The Wiz" (NBC, 6 January 1975). "The Wiz" (WABC-TV, 5 January 1975)
Novick, Julius. "In Search of the New Consensus." Saturday Review 3 (3 April 1976): 42
Peterson, Maurice. "On the Aisle." Essence 5 (March 1975): 11
_____. "The Wiz's Wizzes: Ken Harper and Geoffrey Holder." Essence 6 (September 1975): 54-55, 83-84, 87
"Playboy After Hours--Theatre." Playboy 22 (June 1975): 41
Rich, Alan. "Broadway's Senior Musicals--A Tourists' Guide." New York 10 (27 June 1977): 114
Robinson, Major. "Invisible Stars Twinkle." (N.Y.) Amsterdam News: Arts and Entertainment, 25 June 1977, D-15
Simon, John. "Music of the Squares." New York 8 (27 January 1975): 51
Smith, Angela E. "All-Black, All Soulful and Very Together." St. Louis (Mo.) Argus, 17 April 1975, in Newsbank--Performing Arts. March-April 1975, 27: A 6
Tapley, Mel. "Long Island 'Scarecrow' Gets Broadway Break." (N.Y.) Amsterdam News: Arts and Entertain-

ment, 11 September 1976, D-2

Trescott, Jacqueline. "Robert Guillame: The Leading
Guy." Washington (D.C.) Post, 6 May 1976, in News-
bank--Performing Arts. May-June 1976, 40: D 5-6

Walker, Jesse H. "And Now a Word...." The Afro-
American (Baltimore, Md.), 19-23 July 1977, p. 11

Weales, Gerald. "Birthday Mutterings." Modern Theatre
and Drama 19 (December 1976): 420-21

"Welcome to the Great Black Way." Time 108 (1 November 1976): 75

Willis' Theatre World. vol. 31, 1974-1975, p. 35
_____. vol. 32, 1975-1976, p. 64 (playbill)

Winer, Linda. "The Boom in Black Theatre: Growing
Profits ... and Growing Pains." Chicago Tribune:
Arts & Fun, 30 May 1976, 6:2-3
_____. "Here It's Promises, Promises." Chicago
Tribune: Arts & Fun/Books, 23 January 1977, p. 3
_____. "Over the Rainbow, Into the Shubert." Chi-
cago Tribune: Arts & Fun, 7 November 1976, 6:3

MEDIA RESOURCES:
The Wiz
_____ Soundtrack by Atlantic

AWARDS:
Antoinette Perry (Tony) Award 1975 (7 Awards)
Drama Desk Award for a Musical: 1974-1975
1976 Grammy Award. Best Original Cast Album, Shubert
Theatre, Chicago

†SMITH, AUGUSTUS J.
PLAYS:
Louisiana
[with Peter Morell] Turpentine, 1936
CRITICISMS OF INDIVIDUAL PLAYS:
Turpentine
Edmonds, Randolph. "The Blacks in the American
Theatre, 1700-1969." The Pan-African Journal 7
(Winter 1974): 311
Goldstein. The Political Stage, p. 259
Hartnoll. The Oxford Companion to the Theatre, p. 677
Walsh, Elizabeth and Diane Bowers. "WPA Federal
Theatre Project." Theatre News 8 (April 1976): 3, il

SMITH, CHUCK
PLAYS:
[with Ira Rogers] Tetragrammonon Is

SMITH, DONALD
PLAYS:
Harriet Tubman. N.Y.: New Dimensions, 1970

SMYRL, DAVID LANGSTON
PLAYS:

A Slice of Life Caught and Spun
On the Lock-In
REVIEWS OF INDIVIDUAL PLAYS:
On the Lock-In
   David, Curt. "Smyrl Locks Up 'Lock-In'. " Encore 6
     (20 June 1977): 53
   Gottfried, Martin. "'Lock-In' Pleasant Due to Good
     Vibes." New York Post, 28 April 1977, in Newsbank--
     Performing Arts. March-April 1977, 23: F 6
   Lewis, Barbara. "New Lafayette Founder Makes Good
     Comeback Bid. " (N.Y.) Amsterdam News: Arts and
     Entertainment, 28 May 1977, D-2
     _____. "Smyrl and 'On the Goddam Lock-In." (N.Y.)
     Amsterdam News: Arts and Entertainment, 23 October
     1976, D-8
   Martin, Sharon S. "David Langston Smyrl Is Making It
     All Real." Encore 6 (3 January 1977): 36
   New York Theatre Critics' Reviews 38 (5 September 1977):
     225-227; containing: Watt, Douglas, "With This, Even
     Audience Does Time" (N.Y.] Daily News, 28 April
     1977). Gussow, Mel, "Stage: Musical Inmates with
     Dream" (New York Times, 28 April 1977). Ettore,
     Barbara, "'On--'the Lock-In'" [sic] (Women's Wear
     Daily, 28 April 1977). Gottfried, Martin, "'Lock-In'
     Pleasant Due to Good Vibes" (New York Post, 28 April
     1977). Beaufort, John, "'On the Lock-In'" (Christian
     Science Monitor, 28 April 1977). Lape, Bob, "On the
     Lock-In" (WABC-TV, 27 April 1977).
   Oliver, Edith. "The Theatre: Off-Broadway." New
     Yorker 53 (9 May 1977): 59

SNIPES, MARGARET FORD TAYLOR
   PLAYS:
     Folklore Black American Style
     Hotel Happiness
     Sing a Song of Watergate

†SPENCE, EULALIE
   PLAYS:
     Episode
     The Fool's Errand
   PLAYS PUBLISHED IN PERIODICALS:
     Episode in The Archive (April 1928)
   CRITICISMS OF SPENCE:
     Xeroxed Abstracts: Stage II
   CRITICISMS OF INDIVIDUAL PLAYS:
     The Fool's Errand
       "The Words of Regina M. Andrews." In Mitchell. Voices
       of the Black Theatre, p. 72

STARKES, JAISON
   FILM SCRIPTS:

J. D. 's Revenge
REVIEWS OF INDIVIDUAL FILM SCRIPTS:
J. D. 's Revenge
    Smith, Angela E. "'J.D.'--Ghostly Thrillers." (N.Y.)
    Amsterdam News: Arts and Entertainment, 4 September 1976, D-3

STATEN, PAT
  PLAYS:
    Heartland

†STAVIS, B.
  PLAYS:
    Harper's Ferry: A Play About John Brown. A. S. Barnes, 1967

†STEWART, RON
  PLAYS:
    [with Neal Tate] Sambo
  REVIEWS OF INDIVIDUAL PLAYS:
    Sambo
      Clurman, Harold. "Theatre." Nation 210 (2 February 1970): 125
      Hewes, Henry. "Black Hopes." Saturday Review 53 (14 February 1970): 30

STILLS, WILLIAM GRANT
  MUSICALS:
    A Bayou Legend, an Opera

†STOCKARD, SHARON
  PLAYS:
    Boson's Box Truth

†STOKES, HERBERT
  PLAYS:
    The Man Who Trusted the Devil Twice
    The Uncle Toms
  CRITICISMS OF STOKES:
    Houghton. The Exploding Stage, p. 201
    Taylor, Willene Pulliam. "The Reversal of the Tainted Blood Theme in the Works of Writers of the Black Revolutionary Theatre." Negro American Literature Forum 10 (Fall 1976): 89, 90
  CRITICISMS OF INDIVIDUAL PLAYS:
    The Man Who Trusted the Devil Twice
      Clayborne, Jon L. "Modern Black Drama and the Gay Image." College English 36 (November 1974): 382
      Hay, Samuel A. "African-American Drama, 1950-1970." Negro History Bulletin 36 (January 1973): 8
    The Uncle Toms
      Bloom, Arthur W. "The Theatre of Non-Mimetic Propaganda:

Critical Criteria." Xavier University Studies 11 (no. 1):
29-30, 34-35

Taylor, Willene Pulliam. "The Reversal of the Tainted
Blood Theme in the Works of Writers of the Black Revolutionary Theatre." Negro American Literature Forum
10 (Fall 1976): 89, 90

STOKES, JACK
PLAYS:
The Incredible Jungle Journey of Fenda Maria
REVIEWS OF INDIVIDUAL PLAYS:
The Incredible Jungle Journey of Fenda Maria
Smith, Marian. "Black Theater Week Renews Basic Aim:
Reflect Community." Chicago (Ill.) Sun-Times, 23
May 1976, in Newsbank--Performing Arts. May-June
1976, 41: G 6

SWAN, Aunt ALICE
FILM SCRIPTS:
[with Anthony Chauncey and Laurence Swan] Mini-Marvin
REVIEWS OF INDIVIDUAL FILM SCRIPTS:
Mini-Marvin
Tapley, Mel. "Chet French's Problem: Second Baseman
or Movie Star?" (N.Y.) Amsterdam News: Arts and
Entertainment, 18 December 1976, D-2
_____. "Did 'Bugsy Malone' Rip-Off 'Mini Marvin'?"
(N.Y.) Amsterdam News: Arts and Entertainment, 18
December 1976, D-13

SWAN, LAURENCE
FILM SCRIPTS:
[with Anthony Chauncey and Aunt Alice Swan] Mini-Marvin
REVIEWS OF INDIVIDUAL FILM SCRIPTS:
Mini-Marvin
Tapley, Mel. "Chet French's Problem: Second Baseman
or Movie Star?" (N.Y.) Amsterdam News: Arts and
Entertainment, 18 December 1976, D-2
_____. "Did 'Bugsy Malone' Rip-Off 'Mini Marvin'?"
(N.Y.) Amsterdam News: Arts and Entertainment, 18
December 1976, D-13

TANNER, WILLIAM H.
PLAYS:
The Birth of Freedom and the Present Age. Dayton, Ohio:
1919

†TATE, NEAL
PLAYS:
[with Ron Stewart] Sambo
MUSICALS:
[with Shaunielle Perry] Music Magic·
REVIEWS OF INDIVIDUAL PLAYS:

Sambo
  Clurman, Harold. "Theatre." Nation 210 (2 February
    1970): 124
  Hewes, Henry. "Black Hopes." Saturday Review 53 (14
    February 1970): 30
REVIEWS OF INDIVIDUAL MUSICALS:
  Music Magic
    Austin, William. "New Musical at the Billie Holiday."
      (N.Y.) Amsterdam News: Arts and Entertainment, 1
      January 1977, D-7
    "'Music Magic' Opens at Billie Holiday." (N.Y.) Amster-
      dam News: Arts and Entertainment, 20 November 1976,
      D-9

†TAYLOR, JACKIE
  MUSICALS:
  The Other Cinderella, fantasy
  CRITICISMS OF TAYLOR:
    Winer, Linda. "Taylor and Troupe Face Last Act." Chi-
      cago Tribune: Arts & Fun, 11 December 1977, 6:9
  REVIEWS OF INDIVIDUAL MUSICALS:
  The Other Cinderella
    Winer, Linda. "Local Curtain Going Up for 10 Black
      Stage Troupes." Chicago Tribune: Arts & Fun, 30
      May 1976, 6:3

†TAYLOR, MARGARET FORD see SNIPES, MARGARET FORD
  TAYLOR

TEAGUE, TONY
  PLAYS:
  Tuff T

†TEER, BARBARA ANN
  PLAYS:
  Rituals
  Soljourney Into Truth
  CRITICISMS BY TEER:
    "We Are Liberators Not Actors." Essence 7 (March 1971):
      56-59
  CRITICISMS OF TEER:
    "Black Theatre: A Bid for Cultural Identity." Black Enter-
      prise 2 (September 1971): 33-34
    Cook and Henderson. The Militant Black Writer, p. 82
    "Creative Directions." Essence 3 (May 1972): 76
    Davis, Arthur P. From the Dark Tower, p. 228
    Frye, Charles A. "Archetypes and Truth: Spiritual Hier-
      archies--Another Look at the Movement." Black Images
      3 (Autumn 1974): 30-33
    Hatch, James. "Speak to Me in Those Old Words, You
      Know, Those La-La Words, Those Tung-Tung Sounds."
      Yale/Theatre 8 (Fall 1976): 29

Peterson, Maurice. "On the Aisle: Spotlight on Barbara
Ann Teer." Essence 6 (August 1975): 19
Porter, Curtiss E. "This Here Child Is Naked and Free as
a Bird." Black Lines 2 (Spring 1973): 22-31, 34-35
CRITICISMS OF INDIVIDUAL PLAYS:
Rituals
Brukenfeld, Dick. "Off-Off-Broadway." In Theatre 4:
The American Theatre, 1970-1971, p. 51
REVIEWS OF INDIVIDUAL PLAYS:
Soljourney Into Truth
"NBT 'Soljourney' Embarks Aug. 12." (N.Y.) Amsterdam
News: Arts and Entertainment, 14 August 1976, D-14

†TERRILL, VINCENT
PLAYS:
A Trotter Woman
From These Shores ... Crispus Attucks
REVIEWS OF INDIVIDUAL PLAYS:
From These Shores ... Crispus Attucks
Murphy, Ray. "Play Celebrates Crispus Attucks." Boston
(Mass.) Globe, 13 March 1976, in Newsbank--Performing
Arts. March-April 1976, 32: D 8

THEATRE FOR THE FORGOTTEN:
PLAYS:
Dream 76
Collective Writing by young drama students of the Summer
Work Program, given in Theatre for the Forgotten

THOMAS, JOYCE CAROL
MUSICALS:
Look! What a Wonder!
REVIEWS OF INDIVIDUAL MUSICALS:
Look! What a Wonder!
Chrisman, Robert. "The Black Scholar Reviews: 'Look!
What a Wonder!'." Black Scholar 8 (September 1976):
53

THOMAS, PIRI
PLAYS:
Saturday Night

†THOMPSON, ELOISE BIBB
PLAYS:
Africannus, one-act, 1922
Caught, 1925
FILM SCRIPTS:
A Reply to the Clansman, 1915
CRITICISMS OF INDIVIDUAL FILM SCRIPTS:
A Reply to the Clansman
Molette, Barbara. "Black Women Playwrights: They
Speak: Who Listens?" Black World 25 (April 1976):
33-34

THOMPSON, RON S.
    PLAYS:
        Cotton Club Revue
    CRITICISMS OF INDIVIDUAL PLAYS:
        Cotton Club Revue
            Murphy, Gloria Sewell. "Annual Round-up: Black
            Theater in America--San Francisco-Oakland Bay Area."
            Black World 25 (April 1976): 91-92

†THURMAN, WALLACE (1901-1934)
    PLAYS:
        [with William Jourdan Rapp] Harlem· A Melodrama of Negro
            Life in Harlem, 3 acts, 1929. Manuscript in the James
            Weldon Johnson Collection of Yale University Library
        [with William Jourdan Rapp] Jeremiah, the Magnificent, 3
            acts, 1930
    CRITICISMS OF INDIVIDUAL PLAYS:
        Harlem: A Melodrama of Negro Life in Harlem
            Abramson, Doris. "The Great White Way: Critics and
            the First Black Playwrights on Broadway." Educational
            Theatre Journal 28 (March 1976): 49-51
            Edmonds, Randolph. "The Blacks in the American Theatre,
            1700-1969." The Pan-African Journal 7 (Winter 1974):
            304
            Hartnoll. The Oxford Companion to the Theatre, p. 675
            "The Words of Dick Campbell." In Mitchell. Voices of
            the Black Theatre, p. 106

†TOLSON, MELVIN BEAVNORUS
    PLAYS:
        Black No More (adaptation of George Schuyler's novel)
        Fire in the Flint (based on the novel by Walter White)
        The Moses of Beale Street
        Southern Front
    CRITICISMS OF TOLSON:
        Sandle. The Negro in the American Educational Theatre,
            pp. 40, 41, 44; passim
    CRITICISMS OF INDIVIDUAL PLAYS:
        Black No More
            Davis, Arthur P. From the Dark Tower, p. 168
        Fire in the Flint
            Davis, Arthur P. From the Dark Tower, p. 168
        The Moses of Beale Street
            Davis, Arthur P. From the Dark Tower, p. 168
            Sandle. The Negro in the American Educational Theatre,
                p. 19
        Southern Front
            Davis, Arthur P. From the Dark Tower, p. 168
            Sandle. The Negro in the American Educational Theatre,
                p. 19

†TOOMER, JEAN
    PLAYS:

A Drama of the Southwest, 1935
Balo
The Gallonwerps (originally a satirical novel transformed
    into a play for gigantic marionettes)
Kabnis
Natalie Mann
The Sacred Factory
CRITICISMS OF TOOMER:
Davis, Arthur P.   From the Dark Tower, pp. 44-45, 57-58
Griffin, John C.   "Jean Toomer: A Bibliography."   The
    South Carolina Review 7 (April 1975): 61-64
Reilly, John M.   "Jean Toomer: An Annotated Checklist of
    Criticism."   Resources for American Literary Study 4
    (Spring 1974): 27-54
Thompson, Larry E.   "Jean Toomer as Modern Man."
    Renaissance 2 Issue One (1971): 7-10
CRITICISMS OF INDIVIDUAL PLAYS:
A Drama of the Southwest
    Davis, Arthur P.   From the Dark Tower, p. 45
    Turner, Darwin T.   "The Failure of a Playwright."   CLA
        Journal 10 (June 1967): 317-318
Balo
    Davis, Arthur P.   From the Dark Tower, p. 45
    Hatch, James.   "Speak to Me in Those Old Words, You
        Know, Those La-La Words, Those Tung-Tung Sounds."
        Yale/Theatre 8 (Fall 1976): 33
    Turner, Darwin T.   "The Failure of a Playwright."   CLA
        Journal 10 (June 1967): 313, 314
The Gallonwerps
    Davis, Arthur P.   From the Dark Tower, p. 45
    Turner, Darwin T.   "The Failure of a Playwright."   CLA
        Journal 10 (June 1967): 316-317
Kabnis
    Bell, Bernard W.   "Jean Toomer's Cane."   Black World
        23 (September 1974): 4-19, 92-97
    Davis, Arthur P.   From the Dark Tower, pp. 48-49,
        50-51
    Turner, Darwin T.   "The Failure of a Playwright."   CLA
        Journal 10 (June 1967): 312-14, 318
Natalie Mann
    Davis, Arthur P.   From the Dark Tower, p. 45
    Thompson, Larry E.   "Jean Toomer as Modern Man."
        Renaissance 2 Issue One (1971): 8
    Turner, Darwin T.   "The Failure of a Playwright."   CLA
        Journal 10 (June 1967): 309-10, 312-313
The Sacred Factory
    Davis, Arthur P.   From the Dark Tower, p. 45
    Thompson, Larry E.   "Jean Toomer as Modern Man."
        Renaissance 2 Issue One (1971): 8
    Turner, Darwin T.   "The Failure of a Playwright."   CLA
        Journal 10 (June 1967): 314, 316, 318

TRASS, VEL
    PLAYS:
        From Kings and Queens to Who Knows What

TREE, E. WAYNE
    PLAYS:
        Yesterday Continued

TRUESDALE, TOD
    PLAYS:
        Godsong (adaptation of Johnson's 'God's Trombones')
    REVIEWS OF INDIVIDUAL PLAYS:
        Godsong
            Davis, Curt. "'Godsong' Is Godless." Encore 6 (21
                February 1977): 41

TUOTTI, JOSEPH DOLAN
    PLAYS:
        Big Time Buck White

TURNER, BETH
    PLAYS:
        Sing On Ms. Griot

TURPIN, WATERS
    PLAYS:
        Let the Day Perish, 1950's
        St. Michael's Dawn, 1950, for the Ira Aldridge Players,
            Baltimore

†TUTT, HOMER J.
    PLAYS:
        Gospel Train
    CRITICISMS OF INDIVIDUAL PLAYS:
        Gospel Train
            "The Words of Dick Campbell." In Mitchell. Voices of
                the Black Theatre, p. 107

UWEN, NATHAN
    PLAYS:
        Martin Luther King, Jr. N.Y.: New Dimensions, 1970

†VAN PEEBLES, MELVIN (b. August 21, 1932)
    MUSICALS:
        Ain't Supposed to Die a Natural Death. N.Y.: Bantam, 1973
        Don't Play Us Cheap. N.Y.: Bantam, 1973
    FILM SCRIPTS:
        La Permission became a movie: Story of a Three Day Pass
        Sweet Sweetback's Baadasssss Song
        Watermelon Man
    TELEVISION SCRIPTS:
        Just an Old Sweet Song (G.E. Theater)

CRITICISMS OF VAN PEEBLES:
Gray, Bill. "Black Theatre in Transition, Playwright (Milner) Says." In Nykoruk. Authors in the News, vol. 1. Detroit: Gale Research 1976, p. 348

Horton and Edwards. Backgrounds of American Literary Thought. 3rd ed., p. 588

Murray, James P. "Running with Sweetback." Black Creation 3 (Fall 1971): 10-12

Riley, Clayton. "A New Black Magic--And They Weave It Well." New York Times: Arts and Leisure, 7 November 1971, pp. 1, 13

Siskel, Gene. "Van Peebles: A Man Who Keeps on Popping Up." Chicago (Ill.) Tribune, 27 July 1975, in Newsbank--Performing Arts. July-August 1975, 54: G 12, 13

Ward, Francis. "Black Male Images in Films." Freedomways 14 (Third Quarter 1974): 226-27

"Welcome to the Great Black Way." Time 108 (1 November 1976): 75

CRITICISMS OF INDIVIDUAL MUSICALS:

Ain't Supposed to Die a Natural Death
Azenberg, Emmanuel. "An Interview: Producer of Broadway Musicals." Yale/Theatre 4 (Summer 1973): 99-101

Garnett, Bernard. "Black Drama Finds New Audience." Race Relations Reporter 3 (7 February 1972): 4-6

Geisinger. Plays, Players, & Playwrights, p. 742

Hanis, Leonard. "Broadway." In Theatre 5: The American Theatre, 1971-1972, p. 29

Riley, Clayton. "A New Black Magic--And They Weave It Well." New York Times: Arts and Leisure, 7 November 1971, pp. 1, 13

Simon. Uneasy Stages, pp. 400, 401-03

Weathers, Diane. "Fantasy in Black Theatre: A Kind of New Freedom." Encore 4 (21 April 1975): 32

Don't Play Us Cheap
Geisinger. Plays, Players, & Playwrights, p. 742

Harris, Leonard. "Broadway." In Theatre 5: The American Theatre, 1971-1972, p. 29

Riley, Clayton. "A New Black Magic--And They Weave It Well." New York Times: Arts and Leisure, 7 November 1971, pp. 1, 13

Schier, Ernest. "Van Peebles' Musical Has Been Intentions." Philadelphia (Pa.) Evening Bulletin, 16 May 1975, in Newsbank--Performing Arts. May-June 1975, 38: D 6

Simon. Uneasy Stages, pp. 400, 402-03

REVIEWS OF INDIVIDUAL MUSICALS:

Ain't Supposed to Die a Natural Death
Bartley, G. Fitz. "Soul Stirrin' Theatre: 'Ain't Supposed to Die a Natural Death'." Soul Illustrated 3 (Spring 1972): 18, 65

Garnett, Bernard. "Black Drama Finds New Audience." Race Relations Reporter 3 (7 February 1972): 4-6

Peterson, Maurice. "Movies: Willie Dynamite, Blazing

Saddles and Others." Essence 5 (May 1974): 16
_____. "On the Aisle: Focus on Avon Long."
Essence 6 (January 1968): 28
Don't Play Us Cheap
Blum and Willis, eds. A Pictorial History of the Ameri-
can Theatre: 1860-1976, pp. 413, 414
Peterson, Maurice. "On the Aisle: Focus on Avon
Long." Essence 6 (January 1976): 28
Siskel, Gene. "Van Peebles: A Man Who Keeps on Pop-
ping Up." Chicago (Ill.) Tribune, 27 July 1975, in
Newsbank--Performing Arts. July-August 1975, 54:
G 12, 13
CRITICISMS OF INDIVIDUAL FILM SCRIPTS:
Story of a Three Day Pass
Murray, James P. "Running with Sweetback." Black
Creation 3 (Fall 1971): 10
Sweet Sweetback's Baadasssss Song
Jones, Norma R. "Sweetback: The Black Hero and Uni-
versal Myth." CLA Journal 19 (June 1976): 559-65
Murray, James P. "Running with Sweetback." Black
Creation 3 (Fall 1971): 10-12
Riley, Clayton. "A New Black Magic--And They Weave
It Well." New York Times: Arts and Leisure. 7
November 1971, pp. 1, 13
Sloan, Margaret. "Film: Keeping the Black Women in
Her Place." Ms. 2 (January 1974): 30
Wander, Brandon. "Black Dreams: The Fantasy and
Ritual of Black Films." Film Quarterly 29 (Fall 1975):
7-9
Watermelon Man
Murray, James P. "Running with Sweetback." Black
Creation 3 (Fall 1971): 10
REVIEWS OF INDIVIDUAL FILM SCRIPTS:
Sweet Sweetback's Baadasssss Song
Bartley, G. Fitz. "Soul Stirrin' Theater: Ain't Supposed
to Die a Natural Death." Soul Illustrated 3 (Spring
1972): 19
Wander, Brandon. "Black Dreams: The Fantasy and
Ritual of Black Films." Film Quarterly 29 (Fall 1975):
2-11
REVIEWS OF INDIVIDUAL TELEVISION SCRIPTS:
Just An Old Sweet Song
"Beah Richards: Actress, Author and Human Being."
(N.Y.) Amsterdam News: Arts and Entertainment, 31
July 1976, D-6
"Beah Richards Combines Poetic Touch with Acting."
Chicago Daily Defender, 1 August 1977, p. 18
Hazziezah. "Innervisions." (N.Y.) Amsterdam News:
Arts and Entertainment, 16 October 1976, D-17
Salaam, Yusef Abdul. "Van Peeble's Warm and Sensitive
Song." (N.Y.) Amsterdam News: Arts and Entertain-
ment, 2 October 1976, D-17

"Tyson: Lady of Many Roles." Chicago Daily Defender,
21 July 1977, p. 19
AWARDS:
Ain't Supposed to Die a Natural Death
Bonin. Major Themes in Prize-Winning American Drama,
p. 179

VERONA, STEPHEN
FILM SCRIPTS:
Pipe Dreams

†VOTEUR, FERDINAND
PLAYS:
A Right Angle Triangle
The Unfinished Symphony. Boston: Bruce Humphries, n.d.
CRITICISMS OF INDIVIDUAL PLAYS:
A Right Angle Triangle
"The Words of Dick Campbell." In Mitchell. Voices of
the Black Theatre, p. 101

†WALCOTT, DEREK (Caribbean)
PLAYS:
Dream on Monkey Mountain and Other Plays. N.Y.: Farrar,
Straux & Giroux, 1970
Drums and Colours
Henri Christophe. Bridgetown, Barbados: Advocate, 1950
Ione. Kingston: University of the West Indies, 1957
Jourmard. Caribbean Plays Edition. Port-of-Spain: Uni-
versity of the West Indies, 1967
Malcauchon [sic], or Six in the Rain. Caribbean Plays
Edition. Port-of-Spain: University of the West Indies,
1966
The Sea at Daughpin: Caribbean Plays Edition. Kingston:
University of the West Indies, 1958
Ti Jean and His Brothers
The Wedding
Wine of the Country. Caribbean Plays. Kingston: Univer-
sity of the West Indies, 1953
CRITICISMS BY WALCOTT:
"What the Twilight Says: An Overture." In Dream on Monkey
Mountain and Other Plays. N.Y.: Farrar, Straus and
Giroux, 1970, pp. 3-40
CRITICISMS OF WALCOTT:
Brown, Lloyd W. "Dreamers and Slaves: The Ethos of
Revolution in Derek Walcott and Le Roi Jones." Carib-
bean Quarterly 16 (September 1971): 36-44
CRITICISMS OF INDIVIDUAL PLAYS:
Dream on Monkey Mountain
Barnes, Clive. "Off Broadway." In Theatre 4: The
American Theatre, 1970-1971, pp. 34-35
Current Biography 38 (1977): 420
Geisinger. Plays, Players, & Playwrights, p. 239

Hirsch, Samuel. "The O'Neill Experience." In Theatre
5: The American Theatre, 1971-1972, p. 151
Stasio, Marilyn. "Off-Broadway." In Theatre 5: The
American Theatre, 1971-1972, p. 34
Malcochon
Current Biography 38 (1977): 419
REVIEWS OF INDIVIDUAL PLAYS:
Dream on Monkey Mountain
Blum and Willis, eds. A Pictorial History of the Ameri-
can Theatre: 1860-1976, p. 410
Johnson, Malcom L. "HSC Obscures Walcott's 'Dream on
Monkey Mountain'." Hartford (Conn.) Courant, 21
March 1976, in Newsbank--Performing Arts. March-
April 1976, 32: E 1, 2
Kupa, Kushauri. "Closeups: The New York Scene--Black
Theatre in New York, 1970-1971." Black Theatre no.
6 (1971): 40
Willis' Theatre World. vol. 32, 1975-1976, p. 194
Malcochon
Oliver, Edith. "The Theatre: Off Broadway." New
Yorker 45 (12 April 1969): 131
The Wedding
Craig, Randall. "Plays in Performance--Experimental."
Drama 119 (Winter 1975): 79-80

†WALKER, EVAN
CRITICISMS OF WALKER:
Xeroxed Abstracts: Stage II

†WALKER, GEORGE
MUSICALS:
[with Bert Williams] The Ghost of a Coon
CRITICISMS BY WALKER:
"The Negro on the American Stage." Colored American
Magazine 11 (October 1906): 243-48
CRITICISMS OF WALKER:
Mitchell. Voices of the Black Theatre, pp. 23-26, 145, 148,
217
Weathers, Diane. "Fantasy in Black Theatre: A Kind of
New Freedom." Encore 4 (21 April 1975): 32

†WALKER, JOSEPH H. (b. February 23, 1935)
PLAYS:
[with Jo Jackson] The Believers, 1968
The Lion is a Soul Brother
Tribal Harangue
Tribal Harangue Two
Yin Yang
PLAYS PUBLISHED IN ANTHOLOGIES:
Tribal Harangue Two in Richards. Best Short Plays 1971
MUSICALS:
Ododo

The River Niger
FILM SCRIPTS:
The River Niger
CRITICISMS OF WALKER:
 Cooper, Grace C. "Joseph A. Walker: Evolution of a Play-
  wright." New Directions: The Howard University Maga-
  zine 2 (October 1974): 10-13
 Geisinger. Plays, Players, & Playwrights, p. 742
 Peterson, Maurice. "Taking Off with Joseph Walker."
  Essence 4 (April 1974): 54+
 Xeroxed Abstracts: Stage I; Stage II
CRITICISMS OF INDIVIDUAL PLAYS:
 Harangues
  Black Theatre: A Bid for Cultural Identity." Black Enter-
   prise 2 (September 1971): 34
  Cooper, Grace C. "Joseph A. Walker: Evolution of a
   Playwright." New Directions: The Howard University
   Magazine 2 (October 1974): 10-13
 Yin Yang
  Cooper, Grace C. "Joseph A. Walker: Evolution of a
   Playwright." New Directions: The Howard University
   Magazine 2 (October 1974): 10-13
CRITICISMS OF INDIVIDUAL MUSICALS:
 Ododo
  "Black Theatre: A Bid for Cultural Identity." Black
   Enterprise 2 (September 1971): 34
  Cooper, Grace C. "Joseph A. Walker: Evolution of a
   Playwright." New Directions: The Howard University
   Magazine 2 (October 1974): 10-13
  Hill, Edward Steven. "A Thematic Study of Selected
   Plays Produced by the Negro Ensemble Company."
   Ph.D. Dissertation, Bowling Green State University,
   1975
  Kupa, Kushauri. "Closeup: The New York Scene--Black
   Theatre in New York, 1970-1971." Black Theatre no.
   6 (1972): 40
 The River Niger
  Cooper, Grace C. "Joseph A. Walker: Evolution of a
   Playwright." New Directions: The Howard University
   Magazine 2 (October 1974): 10-13
  Current Biography 38 (1977): 420
  Eckstein, George. "Softened Voices in the Black Theater."
   Dissent 23 (Summer 1976): 307
  Engel. The Critics, pp. 6, 30, 32, 85-87, 137
  Geisinger. Plays, Players, & Playwrights, p. 239
  Hatch, James. "Speak to Me in Those Old Words, You
   Know, Those La-La Words, Those Tung-Tung Sounds."
   Yale/Theatre 8 (Fall 1976): 29
  Hill, Edward Steven. "A Thematic Study of Selected Plays
   Produced by the Negro Ensemble Company." Ph.D.
   Dissertation, Bowling Green State University, 1975.
  Lee, Dorothy. "Three Black Plays: Alienation and Paths

to Recovery." Modern Theatre and Drama 19 (December 1976): 397-404

Ribowsky, Mark. "'Father' of the Black Theater Boom." Sepia 25 (November 1976): 69, 70, 72

Simon, John. "Improbable Extremists." New York Magazine 9 (26 April 1976): 72

Taylor, Clarke. "In the Soul of Theatre." Essence 5 (April 1975): 70, 72

Weathers, Diane. "Fantasy in Black Theatre: A Kind of New Freedom." Encore 4 (21 April 1975): 32

REVIEWS OF INDIVIDUAL PLAYS:

The Believers

Oliver, Edith. "Off Broadway: Revue by Voices, Inc.: 'The Believers'." New Yorker 44 (May 1968): 75

Sayre, N. "New York's Black Theatre." New Statesman 76 (25 October 1968): 556

Harangues

Clurman, Harold. "Theatre." Nation 210 (2 February 1970): 124-25

Hewes, Henry. "Black Hopes." Saturday Review 53 (14 February 1970): 30

REVIEWS OF INDIVIDUAL MUSICALS:

The River Niger

Blum and Willis, eds. A Pictorial History of the American Theatre: 1860-1976, pp. 414, 415, 416

Davis, Curt. "The Inner Voice of Louis Gossett." Encore 6 (6 June 1977): 31

————. "People In the News." Encore 6 (20 June 1977): 49

Fisher, Titus. "'River Niger' Is Portrait of Life." Omaha (Neb.) World Herald, 3 March 1975, in Newsbank--Performing Arts. March-April 1975, 31: C 5

George, Nelson. "Is Hollywood Changing Its View of Black Man?" (N.Y.) Amsterdam News: Arts and Entertainment, 2 July 1977, D-9

"James Earl Jones in 'Exorcist II: The Heretic'." The Afro-American: Afro Magazine (Baltimore, Md.), 31 May-4 June 1977, p. 13

Kroll, Jack. "Hopes, Dreams, Fantasies." Newsweek 81 (19 February 1973): 75

Murphy, Ray. "Black Rep. Stages 'River Niger'." Boston (Mass.) Globe, 13 February 1976, in Newsbank--Performing Arts. January-February 1976, 15: A 6

Murray, James P. "Blacks Invade Broadway in a Big Way ... With Soul Cheers and Society Boos." St. Louis (Mo.) Argus, 17 April 1975, in Newsbank--Performing Arts. March-April 1975, 28: D 9

Peterson, Maurice. "On the Aisle: Theater and Film." Essence 5 (September 1974): 24

"'River Niger' at Music Hall Tomorrow Night." (Memphis, Tenn.) Commercial Appeal, 16 March 1975, in Newsbank--Performing Arts. March-April 1975, 31: C 2

"'River Niger' Yields Fine Performances." Birmingham
(Ala.) News, 10 March 1975, in Newsbank--Performing
Arts. March-April 1975, 31: C 3
Taggart, Patrick. "'River Niger' Tribute to Humanity."
(Austin, Tex.) American Statesman, 10 March 1975,
in Newsbank--Performing Arts. March-April 1975,
31: C 6
Thomas, Barbara. "'River Niger' Angry Play on Poverty."
Atlanta (Ga.) Journal, 12 March 1975, in Newsbank--
Performing Arts. March-April 1975, 31: C 4
Trescott, Jacqueline. "Robert Guillame: The Leading
Guy." Washington (D.C.) Post, 6 May 1976, in News-
bank--Performing Arts. May-June 1976, 40: D 5-6
Willis' Theatre World. vol. 30, 1973-1974, p. 173
Winer, Linda. "The Boom in Black Theatre: Growing
Profits ... and Growing Pains." Chicago Tribune:
Arts & Fun. 30 May 1976, 6: 3
REVIEWS OF INDIVIDUAL FILM SCRIPTS:
The River Niger
Peterson, Maurice. "On the Aisle" Essence 7 (June
1976): 45
"Playboy After Hours: Movies." Playboy 23 (June 1976):
34-36
AWARDS:
The River Niger
Bonin. Major Themes in Prize-Winning American Drama,
p. 179
Tony Award 1974, best play

WALKER, SAUNDERS
PLAYS:
Roots in the South
CRITICISMS OF INDIVIDUAL PLAYS:
Roots in the South
Sandle. The Negro in the American Educational Theatre,
p. 150

†WALLACE, RUDY
PLAYS:
The Dark Tower
Moonlight Arms
REVIEWS OF INDIVIDUAL PLAYS:
The Dark Tower
Willis' Theatre World. vol. 31, 1974-1975, p. 118
Moonlight Arms
Guernsey. The Best Plays of 1974-1975, p. 377
Willis' Theatre World. vol. 31, 1974-1975, p. 118

†WARD, DOUGLAS TURNER (b. May 5, 1930)
PLAYS:
Brotherhood
Day of Absence

A Happy Ending
Reckoning
PLAYS PUBLISHED IN ANTHOLOGIES:
Day of Absence, in Corlin & Balf, Twelve American Plays;
in Griffith and Mersand, Eight American Ethnic Plays;
in Raines, Modern Drama and Social Change
CRITICISMS BY WARD:
"Black Answers to White Questions." In Theatre 1: Ameri-
can Theatre, 1967-1968. N.Y.: International Theatre
Institute of the United States, 1969, pp. 68-75
CRITICISMS OF WARD:
Brooks, Mary Ellen. "Reactionary Trends in Recent Black
Drama." Literature and Ideology (Montreal), 10 (1970):
46-48
Current Biography 38 (1977): 417-421
Eckstein, George. "Softened Voices in the Black Theater."
Dissent 23 (Summer 1976): 306-07
Edmonds, Randolph. "The Blacks in the American Theatre,
1700-1969." The Pan-African Journal 7 (Winter 1974):
308, 312
Engel. The Critics, p. 87
"Four Portraits: Douglas Turner Ward." Saturday Review
3 (15 November 1975): 18
Hatch, James V. "Theodore Ward: Black American Play-
wright." Freedomways 15 (First Quarter 1975): 37-41
Houghton. The Exploding Stage, p. 202, 239
Moss, Robert F. "The Arts in Black America." Saturday
Review 3 (15 November 1975): 18
Oliver, Edith. "Report from 137th Street." In Theatre 5:
The American Theatre, 1971-1972, p. 132
Parker. Who's Who in The Theatre, 15th ed., pp. 1423-
1424
Ribowsky, Mark. "'Father' of the Black Theater Boom."
Sepia, 25 (November 1976): 66-78
Robinson, Le Roy. "Black Theatre: A Need for the
Seventies." Soul Illustrated 2 (February 1970): 57
Turner, Darwin T. "Douglas Turner Ward." In Vinson.
Contemporary Dramatists, pp. 788-89
CRITICISMS OF INDIVIDUAL PLAYS:
Brotherhood
Current Biography 38 (1977): 417
Day of Absence
Brooks, Mary Ellen. "Reactionary Trends in Recent
Black Drama." Literature and Ideology (Montreal),
no. 10 (1970): 47-48
Current Biography 38 (1977): 417, 418, 419
Dace and Dace. The Theatre Student: Modern Theatre
and Drama, p. 55
Edmonds, Randolph. "The Blacks in the American
Theatre, 1700-1969." The Pan-African Journal 7
(Winter 1974): 306
Griffith and Mersand, eds. Eight American Ethnic

Plays, pp. 275-277
Hay, Samuel A. "African-American Drama, 1950-1970."
Negro History Bulletin 36 (January 1973): 6
Hill, Edward Steven. "A Thematic Study of Selected Plays
Produced by the Negro Ensemble Company." Ph.D.
Dissertation, Bowling Green State University, 1975
Klotman. Another Man Gone, pp. 90-91, 95, 96, ff. no. 7
Weathers, Diane. "Fantasy in Black Theatre: A Kind of
New Freedom." Encore 4 (21 April 1975): 32
A Happy Ending
Brooks, Mary Ellen. "Reactionary Trends in Recent Black
Drama." Literature and Ideology (Montreal), no. 10
(1970): 47-48
Current Biography 38 (1977): 418
Edmonds, Randolph. "The Blacks in the American Theatre,
1700-1969." The Pan African Journal 7 (Winter 1974):
306
Hay, Samuel A. "African-American Drama, 1950-1970."
Negro History Bulletin 36 (January 1973): 6
Hill, Edward Steven. "A Thematic Study of Selected Plays
Produced by the Negro Ensemble Company." Ph.D.
Dissertation, Bowling Green State University, 1975
Reckoning
Current Biography 38 (1977): 419
REVIEWS OF INDIVIDUAL PLAYS:
Brotherhood
Oliver, Edith. "Off Broadway: Happy Day Is Here Again."
New Yorker 46 (28 March 1970): 84
Parker. Who's Who in The Theatre, 15th ed., p. 1524
Day of Absence
Blum and Willis, eds. A Pictorial History of the Ameri-
can Theatre: 1860-1976, pp. 388, 389, 406
Oliver, Edith. "Off Broadway: Happy Day Is Here Again."
New Yorker 46 (28 March 1970): 84
Parker. Who's Who in The Theatre, 15th ed., pp. 1523-
1524
Smith, Marian. "Black Theater Week Renews Basic Aim:
Reflect Community." Chicago (Ill.) Sun-Times, 23
May 1976, in Newsbank--Performing Arts. May-June
1976, 41: G 6
A Happy Ending
Parker. Who's Who in The Theatre, 15th ed., p. 1523
Peterson, Maurice. "On the Aisle: Spotlight on Dianne
Oyama Dixon." Essence 7 (November 1975): 39
Smith, Marian. "Black Theater Week Renews Basic Aim:
Reflect Community." Chicago (Ill.) Sun-Times, 23
May 1976, in Newsbank--Performing Arts. May-June
1976, 41: G 6
The Reckoning
Parker. Who's Who in The Theatre, 15th ed., p. 1523

†WARD, FRANCIS
PLAYS:

Harriet Tubman
Trumbull Park, 1967 (based on novel by Frank London Brown)
CRITICISMS BY WARD:
"Black Male Images in Film." Freedomways 14 (Third
Quarter 1974): 223-29

†WARD, THEODORE (b. September 15, 1902
PLAYS:
The Big White Fog: A Negro Tragedy, 1937
Candle in the Wind, 1967
Challenge
The Creole
The Daubers
Even the Dead Arise
Falcon of Adowa
Our Lan'
Sick and Tiahd (alternate title: Sick and Tired)
Throw back
MUSICALS:
John de Conqueror, a folk opera
CRITICISMS OF WARD:
Gobbins, Dennis. "The Education of Theodore Ward." New
Masses 28 (October 1947): 10-14
Hatch, James V. "Theodore Ward: Black American Play-
wright." Freedomways 15 (First Quarter 1975): 37-41
Walsh, Elizabeth and Diane Bowers. "WPA Federal Theatre
Project." Theatre News 8 (April 1976): 2
Winer, Linda. "The Boom in Black Theatre: Growing Profits
... and Growing Pains." Chicago Tribune: Arts & Fun,
30 May 1976, 6: 3
CRITICISMS OF INDIVIDUAL PLAYS:
The Big White Fog
Edmonds, Randolph. "The Blacks in the American
Theatre, 1700-1969." The Pan-African Journal 7
(Winter 1974): 309, 311
Goldstein. The Political Stage, p. 255
Hartnoll. The Oxford Companion to the Theatre, p. 677
Hatch, James V. "Theodore Ward: Black American Play-
wright." Freedomways 15 (First Quarter 1975): 38-39
Keyssar-Franke, Helen. "Strategies in Black Drama."
Ph.D. Dissertation, University of Iowa, 1974
Stevenson, Robert Louis. "The Image of the White Man
as Projected in the Published Plays of Black Ameri-
cans, 1847-1973." Ph.D. Dissertation, Indiana Uni-
versity, 1975
The Daubers
Hatch, James V. "Theodore Ward: Black American Play-
wright." Freedomways 15 (First Quarter 1975): 39-40
Falcon of Adowa
Hatch, James. "Speak to Me in Those Old Words, You
Know, Those La-La Words, Those Tung-Tung Sounds."
Yale/Theatre 8 (Fall 1976): 27

Our Lan'
Edmonds, Randolph. "The Blacks in the American
Theatre, 1700-1969." The Pan-African Journal 7
(Winter 1974): 304-305
Hartnoll. The Oxford Companion to the Theatre, p. 679
Hatch, James V. "Theodore Ward: Black American
Playwright." Freedomways 15 (First Quarter 1975):
39+
Jones, John Henry. "Great Themes for Black Plays and
Films." Freedomways 14 (Third Quarter 1974): 262
AWARDS:
John Simon Guggenheim Fellowship

WARD, VAL GRAY
PLAYS:
Trumbull Park, 1967 (based on a novel by Frank London
Brown)
AWARDS:
Paul Robeson, 1976

WARE, ALICE HOLDSLIP
PLAYS:
Like a Flame

WARING, DOROTHY
PLAYS:
[with Nora Zeal Hurston] Polk County, 1944. Stephen
Kelen-d'Oxylion Presents Polk County, a Comedy of Negro
Life on a Sawmill Camp, with Authentic Negro Music, in
Three Acts. N.Y.: 1944 (in The Library of Congress)

WASHINGTON, ERWIN
PLAYS:
Oh, Oh Freedom

†WAY, BRYANT
PLAYS:
Magical Faces

WEAVER, CARL
PLAYS:
Wednesday Afternoon Is Sabbath Day

WEILL, KURT [as non-black collaborator]
MUSICAL:
[with Langston Hughes] Street Scene
CRITICISMS OF INDIVIDUAL MUSICALS:
Street Scene
Atkinson and Hirschfeld. The Lively Years 1920-1973, p. 74

†WESLEY, RICHARD (b. July 11, 1945)
PLAYS:

The Black Terror
Gettin' It Together
Goin' Through the Changes
Knock, Knock--Who's Dat?
The Last Street Play
The Past Is the Past
The Sirens
Strike Heaven in the Face
PLAYS PUBLISHED IN ANTHOLOGIES:
The Past Is the Past, in Richards. The Best Short Plays--
   1975
MUSICALS:
[with John Killens and Woodie King] Cotillion
Let's Do It Again
FILM SCRIPTS:
Heaven Is a Playground (from Rick Telander's book)
Uptown Saturday Night
CRITICISMS OF WESLEY:
Bentley. Theatre of War, pp. 404, 406, 407
Duckett, Alfred. "The Birth of a Screenwriter." Sepia 26
   (January 1977): 62-70
Gant, Lisbeth. "The New Lafayette Theatre--Anatomy of a
   Community Art Institution." Drama Review 16 (December
   1972): 46-55
Geisinger. Plays, Players, & Playwrights, p. 742
Goldsmith, Sheilah. "Richard Wesley." Black Creation 6
   (Annual, 1974-1975): 29-30
Hatch, James. "Speak to Me in Those Old Words, You
   Know, Those La-La Words, Those Tung-Tung Sounds."
   Yale/Theatre 8 (Fall 1976): 29
"Kaleidoscope." Black Creation 6 (Annual, 1974-1975):
   29-30
Lewis, Barbara. "Black Writers Too Conservative According
   to Richard Wesley." (N.Y.) Amsterdam News: Arts and
   Entertainment, 23 July 1977, D-7
Ogunbiyi, Yemi. "New Black Playwrights in America, 1960-
   1975." Ph.D. Dissertation, New York University, 1976
   Chp. 6
Stasio, Marilyn. "Off-Broadway." In Theatre 5: The
   American Theatre, 1971-1972, p. 33
Xeroxed Abstracts: Stage I
CRITICISMS OF INDIVIDUAL PLAYS:
The Black Terror
   Bentley, Eric. "White Plague and Black Terror."
      Theatre of War: Comments on 32 Occasions, pp. 404-
      405
   Coleman, Larry. "Reviews: 'Black Terror'." Black
      Theatre no. 6 (1972): 36-37
   Dace and Dace. The Theatre Student: Modern Theatre
      and Drama, p. 55
   Engel. The Critics, pp. 31, 32
   Garnett, Bernard. "Black Drama Finds New Audience."

Race Relations Reporter 3 (7 February 1972): 5
Harris, Jessica B. "The New Lafayette: 'Nothing Lasts
Forever'." Black Creation 4 (Summer 1973): 9
Oliver, Edith. "Report from 137th Street." In Theatre
5: The American Theatre, 1971-1972, p. 133
Simon. Uneasy Stages, pp. 358, 359-361
Stasio, Marilyn. "Off-Broadway." In Theatre 5: The
American Theatre, 1971-1972, pp. 33, 34
Gettin' It Together
Oliver, Edith. "Report from 137th Street." In Theatre
5: The American Theatre, 1971-1972, p. 133
Goin' Through the Change
Bailey, Peter. "Annual Round-up: Black Theater in
America--New York." Black World 24 (April 1975):
19
Engel. The Critics, pp. 55-56
The Past Is the Past
Bailey, Peter. "Annual Round-up: Black Theater in
America--New York." Black World 24 (April 1975):
19
The Sirens
Bailey, Peter. "Annual Round-up: Black Theater in
America--New York." Black World 24 (April 1975):
19
CRITICISMS OF INDIVIDUAL MUSICALS:
Cotillion
Bailey, Peter. "Woodie King, Jr.: Renaissance Man of
Black Theater." Black World 24 (April 1975): 5, 9-10
Duckett, Alfred. "The Birth of a Screenwriter." Sepia
26 (January 1977): 62+
CRITICISMS OF INDIVIDUAL FILM SCRIPTS:
Uptown Saturday Night
Bogle, Donald. "'Uptown Saturday Night': A Look at Its
Place in Black Film History." Freedomways 14 (Fourth
Quarter 1974): 320-30
Duckett, Alfred. "The Birth of a Screenwriter." Sepia
26 (January 1977): 62-64
Peterson, Maurice. "Movies: They're Just In for Laughs."
Essence 5 (October 1974): 12
REVIEWS OF INDIVIDUAL PLAYS:
Black Terror
Blum and Willis, eds. A Pictorial History of the American
Theatre: 1860-1976, p. 410
Clurman, Harold. "The Theatre." Nation 213 (29 Novem-
ber 1971): 572-73
Garnett, Richard. "Black Drama Finds New Audience."
Race Relations Reporter 3 (7 February 1972): 4-6
Hewes, Henry. "Public Joy and Private Terror."
Saturday Review 55 (8 January 1972): 38
Hughes, Catharine. "Of Harlem and Verona." America
125 (18 December 1971): 534-35
_____. "Theatre--'Black Terror'." America 136

(11 June 1977): 529
Kroll, Jack. "Public Affairs." Newsweek 78 (29 November 1971): 109-110
Newman, Jill. "The Players The Thing at Clay Stevenson's Workshop." Encore 6 (21 February 1977): 39
Oliver, Edith. "Off-Broadway: Twice Hail." New Yorker 47 (20 November 1971): 114-20
Gettin' It Together
    Clurman, Harold. "Theatre." Nation 214 (17 April 1972): 508-509
    Gilbert, Ruth, ed. "In and Around Town: Off-Off Broadway--Triple Bill." New York 10 (18 July 1977): 18
    _____. "In and Around Town: Off- and Off-Off Broadway." New York 10 (25 July 1977): 16
    "Goings On About Town: 'A Son Comes Home', 'On Being Hit', and 'Gettin' It All Together'." New Yorker 53 (25 July 1977): 2
    Kalem, T. E. "Black on Black--'Black Visions'." Time 99 (1 May 1972): 53
    Kupa, Kushauri. "Closeup: The New York Scene--Black Theatre in New York, 1970-1971." Black Theatre no. 6 (1972): 47
    Oliver, Edith. "Off Broadway--'Black Visions'." New Yorker 48 (8 April 1972): 97-100
Goin' Through the Changes
    Doll, Bill. "'Past', 'Changes' Boast Good Scripts at Karamu." (Cleveland, O.) Plain Dealer, 11 October 1975, in Newsbank--Performing Arts. September-October 1975, 31: F 14
    Oliver, Edith. "Theatre: Off Broadway." New Yorker 49 (28 January 1974): 69
    Sainer, Arthur. "Somebody Do Something." Village Voice 19 (25 January 1974): 70, 76
    Willis' Theatre World. vol. 30, 1973-1974, p. 77
Knock, Knock--Who's Dat?
    Kupa, Kushauri. "Closeups: The New York Scene--Black Theatre in New York, 1970-1971." Black Theatre no. 6 (1971): 42
The Last Street Play
    Davis, Curt. "'The Last Street Play' Is First-Rate Wesley." Encore 6 (5 July 1977): 44
    Hughes, Catharine. "Troy Traduced: Newark Revisited." America 136 (11 June 1977): 529
    _____. "Theatre--'The Last Street Play'." America 136 (11 June 1977): 529
    Oliver, Edith. "Off-Broadway: Portrait of the Artist as a Young Husband." New Yorker 53 (30 May 1977): 87
The Past Is the Past
    Davis, Curt. "Bill Cobb: The Death of a Salesman, The Birth of an Artist." Encore 6 (17 January 1977): 33-34
    Doll, Bill. "'Past', 'Changes' Boast Good Scripts at Karamu." (Cleveland, O.) Plain Dealer, 11 October

1975, in Newsbank--Performing Arts. September-
October 1975, 31: F 14

Clurman, Harold. "Theatre." Nation 220 (17 May 1975):
605

Oliver, Edith. "The Theatre: Off Broadway." New
Yorker 49 (28 January 1974): 67

————. "The Theatre: Off-Broadway." New Yorker
51 (12 May 1975): 109

Sainer, Arthur. "Somebody Do Something." Village
Voice 19 (25 January 1974): 70, 76

Willis' Theatre World. vol. 30, 1973-1974, p. 77

The Sirens

Feingold, Michael. "Down to Rock Bottom." Village
Voice 19 (23 May 1974): 89

Oliver, Edith. "Off Broadway: The Newark Story." New
Yorker 50 (27 May 1974): 64

REVIEWS OF INDIVIDUAL MUSICALS:

Cotillion

"Cleavon Little Has Got to be 'Gooood'." New York Post,
3 January 1977, in Newsbank--Performing Arts. January-February 1977, 5: G 1

REVIEWS OF INDIVIDUAL FILM SCRIPTS:

Uptown Saturday Night

Gilliat, Penelope. "The Current Cinema: Brilliant
Bunglers." New Yorker 50 (17 June 1974): 88-91

"Movies." New Times 3 (12 July 1974): 63

Peterson, Maurice. "Movies: They're Just in for Laughs"
(Uptown Saturday Night). Essence 5 (October 1974): 12

"'Uptown Saturday Night': A Comedy Featuring Largest
Black All-Star Cast." Ebony 29 (July 1974): 52-57

Westerbrook, Colin L., Jr. "The Screen." Commonweal
101 (18 October 1974): 65-66

Zimmerman, Paul D. "Black Comedy." Newsweek 83
(24 June 1974): 80, 82

†WHIPPER, LEIGH
CRITICISMS OF LEIGH:
Xeroxed Abstracts: Stage II

WHITE, CLARENCE CAMERON
MUSICALS:
[with J. Matheus] Ouanga, 1920
CRITICISMS OF INDIVIDUAL MUSICALS:
Ouanga
"Speak to Me in Those Old Words, You Know, Those La-
La Words, Those Tung-Tung Sounds." Yale/Theatre 8
(Fall 1976): 27

†WHITE, EDGAR
PLAYS:
The Crucificado
The Defense

La Gente Workers
Lament for Rastafari
Les Femmes Noires
The Life and Times of J. Walter Smintheus, 1970
Seigismundo's Tricycle
The Wonderfull Yeare, 1971 [N.B.: spelling in previous
   volume is incorrect]
PLAYS PUBLISHED IN ANTHOLOGIES:
Seigismundo's Tricycle, in Watkins. Black Review: No. 1
CRITICISMS OF WHITE:
Geisinger. Plays, Players, & Playwrights, p. 742
REVIEWS OF INDIVIDUAL PLAYS:
  The Crucificado
    Black Creation 5 (Fall 1973): 45
  The Defense
    Austin, William. "'The Defense' Dramatizes Survivor's
      Offense." (N.Y.) Amsterdam News: Arts and Enter-
      tainment, 20 November 1976, D-12
    "'Defense' Opens at New Federal." (N.Y.) Amsterdam
      News: Arts and Entertainment, 6 November 1976,
      D-15
    Oliver, Edith. "Off-Broadway." New Yorker 52 (22
      November 1976): 110-111
  Les Femmes Noires
    Feingold, Michael. "It All Adds Up to Zero." Village
      Voice 19 (21 March 1974): 64
    Oliver, Edith. "The Theatre: Off Broadway." New
      Yorker 50 (1 April 1974): 52
    Willis' Theatre World. vol. 30, 1973-1974, p. 127
  The Life and Times of J. Walter Smintheus
    Kupa, Kushauri. "Closeup: The New York Scene--Black
      Theatre in New York, 1970-1971." Black Theatre
      no. 6 (1972): 45

†WHITE, JOSEPH (b. December 2, 1933)
  PLAYS:
    The Hustle, 1970
    The Leader
  REVIEWS OF INDIVIDUAL PLAYS:
    The Hustle
      Kupa, Kushauri. "Black Art at the Kuumba House,
        Newark." Black Theatre no. 5 (1971): 53
    The Leader
      Kupa, Kushauri. "Black Art at the Kuumba House,
        Newark." Black Theatre no. 5 (1971): 53

WHITE, STANLEY
  MUSICALS:
    Beyond Human Understanding
  REVIEWS OF INDIVIDUAL MUSICALS:
    Beyond Human Understanding
      Miller, Jeanne-Marie A. "Annual Round-up: Black

Theater in America--Washington, D.C." Black World
25 (April 1976): 83-84

WILKERSON, DR. MARGARET
PLAYS:
The Funeral

†WILLIAMS, BERT (Egbert Austin) (Bert) (1878-1922)
PLAYS:
[with George Walker] The Ghost of a Coon
CRITICISMS OF WILLIAMS:
Fauset, Jessie. "The Gift of Laughter." In Gayle. Black
Expression, pp. 159-65
Mitchell. Voices of the Black Theatre, pp. 23-24, 25-26,
145, 148
Rowland, Mabel, ed. Bert Williams: Son of Laughter; A
Symposium of Tribute to the Man and His Work. N.Y.:
The English Crafters, 1923
Walker, George W. "The Negro on the American Stage."
Colored American Magazine 11 (October 1906): 243-48
Weathers, Diane. "Fantasy in Black Theatre: A Kind of
New Freedom." Encore 4 (21 April 1975): 32

WILLIAMS, CLYDE
PLAYS:
[with Rosetta Le Noire] Come Laugh and Cry with Langston
Hughes (based on Hughes' Shakespeare in Harlem)
REVIEWS OF INDIVIDUAL PLAYS:
Come Laugh and Cry with Langston Hughes
"'Come Laugh and Cry with Langston Hughes'." (N.Y.)
Amsterdam News: New Horizons, 5 February 1977,
D-10

WILLIAMS, DICK ANTHONY
PLAYS:
A Bit o' Black
MUSICALS:
Black and Beautiful

WILLIAMS, E. C.
PLAYS:
[with Willis Richardson] Chase
Chasm [in N.Y.P.L., 193?]

WILLIAMS, JEFF
FILM SCRIPTS:
Let Go My Black Toe (based on the play, The River Niger)

WILLIAMS, JOHN AJALA
PLAYS:
Ghetto 1999
CRITICISMS OF WILLIAMS:

Xeroxed Abstracts: Stage I; Stage II
REVIEWS OF INDIVIDUAL PLAYS:
    Ghetto 1999
        Grimes, Nikki. "'Ghetto 1999': Long on Message; Short
        on Plot." (N.Y.) Amsterdam News: Arts and Enter-
        tainment, 27 November 1976, D-8

†WILLIAMS, PAULETTE see SHANGE, NTOZAKE

WILLIAMS, SAMM
    PLAYS:
        The Coming
        Do Unto Others
        A Love Play
        Welcome to Black River
    REVIEWS OF INDIVIDUAL PLAYS:
        Welcome to Black River
            Guernsey. The Best Plays of 1974-1975, p. 377
            Willis' Theatre World. vol. 31, 1974-1975, p. 118

WILLIS, VICTOR
    MUSICALS:
        [with James W. Durrah and Donna Brown] How Do You
            Spell Watergait?

WILSON, ANDI
    PLAYS:
        The Black Sheep

†WILSON, FRANK
    PLAYS:
        Brother Mose
        Colored Americans, 1914/24
        Race Pride, 1914/24
        Sugar Cane, 1920
        Walk Together Chillun
    CRITICISMS OF INDIVIDUAL PLAYS:
        Brother Mose
            Abramson, Doris. "The Great White Way: Critics and
            the First Black Playwrights on Broadway." Educa-
            tional Theatre Journal 28 (March 1976): 48-49
            Edmonds, Randolph. "The Blacks in the American
            Theatre, 1700-1969." The Pan-African Journal 7
            (Winter 1974): 311
            Hartnoll. The Oxford Companion to the Theatre, p. 677
        Sugar Cane
            Thompson, Larry. "The Black Image in Early American
            Drama." Black World 24 (April 1975): 68-69
        Walk Together Chillun
            Edmonds, Randolph. "The Blacks in the American
            Theatre, 1700-1969." The Pan-African Journal 7
            (Winter 1974): 311

Goldstein. The Political Party, p. 259
Hartnoll. The Oxford Companion to the Theatre, p. 677

WILSON, MATTIE MOULTRIE
    MUSICALS:
    Charity Suffereth Long

WOLFE, ELTON
    PLAYS:
    Men Wear Mustaches, 1968

†WRIGHT, RICHARD
    PLAYS:
    Almos' A Man
    [with Louis Sapin] Daddy Goodness
    [with Paul Green] Native Son (based on the novel by Wright)
    PLAYS PUBLISHED IN ANTHOLOGIES:
    Native Son in Richards. America on Stage
    FILM SCRIPTS:
    Native Son
    CRITICISMS OF WRIGHT:
    Richards. America On Stage, pp. 785-788
    CRITICISMS OF INDIVIDUAL PLAYS:
        Daddy Goodness
            Current Biography 38 (1977): 419
        Native Son
            Frenz, ed. American Playwrights on Drama, p. 76
            Geisinger. Plays, Players, & Playwrights, p. 556
            Goldstein. The Political Stage, pp. 298-299
            Hartnoll. The Oxford Companion to the Theatre, pp.
                677-678
            Houghton. Advance from Broadway, pp. 103, 297 n
            O'Hara and Bro. Invitation to the Theater, p. 48
            Sandle. The Negro in the American Educational Theatre,
                pp. 21-23
    CRITICISMS OF INDIVIDUAL FILM SCRIPTS:
        Native Son
            Edmonds, Randolph. "The Blacks in the American
                Theatre, 1700-1969." The Pan-African Journal 7
                (Winter 1974): 299, 304
            Pyros, John. "Richard Wright: A Black Novelist's Ex-
                perience on Film." Negro American Literature Forum
                9 (Summer 1975): 53-54
    REVIEWS OF INDIVIDUAL PLAYS:
        Almos' a Man
            Davis, Curt. "People in the News: 'Almos' a Man'."
                Encore 6 (9 May 1977): 30
        Daddy Goodness
            Blum and Willis, eds. A Pictorial History of the Ameri-
                can Theatre: 1860-1976, p. 398
            Sayre, N. "New York's Black Theatre." New Statesman
                76 (25 October 1968): 556

MEDIA RESOURCES:
Life and Times
    Learning Arts, Wichita, Kansas 67201
AWARDS:
Native Son
    Bonin. Major Themes in Prize-Winning American Drama,
        p. 171

†YOUNG, CLARENCE, III
PLAYS:
Perry's Mission
MUSICALS:
Black Love
CRITICISMS OF INDIVIDUAL PLAYS:
Perry's Mission
    Quick, Paula N. "Black Theatre." Black Creation 2
        (April 1971): 54
REVIEWS OF INDIVIDUAL PLAYS:
Perry's Mission
    Kupa, Kushauri. "Closeup: The New York Scene--Black
        Theatre in New York, 1970-1971." Black Theatre no.
        6 (1972): 40

YOUNG, TOMMY SCOTT
PLAYS:
Southern Fried
REVIEWS OF INDIVIDUAL PLAYS:
Southern Fried
    Davis, Curt. "People in the News." Encore 6 (6 June
        1977): 26

ZELLARS, JOHN
PLAYS:
Tribute to Otis Redding, 1971

ZURLA, MARTIN
PLAYS:
[with Anna Antaramia and William Rolleri] Night Shift
REVIEWS OF INDIVIDUAL PLAYS:
Night Shift
    Grimes, Nikke. "'Night Shift'." (N.Y.) Amsterdam
        News: Arts and Entertainment, 4 December 1976,
        D-3

GENERAL BIBLIOGRAPHY

Aaron, Jules. "Theatre in Review." Educational Theatre Journal (March 1975): 129-130.

Abajian, James de T., comp. Blacks and Their Contributions to the American West; A Bibliography and Union List of Library Holdings Through 1970. Boston: G. K. Hall, 1974.

Abdul, Raoul, ed. Famous Black Entertainers of Today. New York: Dodd, 1974.

Abramson, Doris. "The Great White Way: Critics and the First Black Playwrights on Broadway." Educational Theatre Journal 28 (March 1976): 45-55.

Adams, George R. "Black Militant Drama." American Imago 28 (Summer 1971): 109, 110-111, passim.

Adams, Zy Ace. "Music Is the Message" (Your Arms Too Short to Box with God). (N.Y.) Amsterdam News, 1 January 1977, D-10.

Albright, William. "Theater: 'Doctor B. S. Black.'" Houston Post, 29 April 1976; in Newsbank--Performing Arts, May-June 1976, 40:A 9.

Alexander, Francis W. "Stereotyping as a Method of Exploitation in Film." Black Scholar 7 (May 1976): 26-29.

Alkire, Stephen Robert. "The Development and Treatment of the Negro Character as Presented in American Musical Theatre, 1927-1968." Ph.D. Dissertation, Michigan State University, 1972.

Allen, Donald, and Robert Creeley, eds. The New Writing in the USA. New York: Penguin, 1967.

Allen, Zita D. "'The Life and Times of Frederick Douglass,' An Enlightening Journey." (N.Y.) Amsterdam News, 10 July 1976, D-6.

Allison, Alexander W., et al. Masterpieces of the Drama. 3rd ed. New York: Macmillan, 1974.

213

Altenbrand, Lynn. Anthology: An Introduction to Literature. New York: Macmillan, 1977.

_____. Exploring Literature: Fiction, Poetry, Drama, Criticism. New York: Macmillan, 1970.

"Amen! ... Yes ... Lord! 'Box' Hot Time at Old Fords." Afro-American (Baltimore), 14 February 1976; in Newsbank--Performing Arts, January-February 1975, 11:G 13.

Ames, Katrine. "Black Legend." Newsweek 87 (19 April 1976): 95-96.

Amos, John. "Truth and Soul." Soul Illustrated 3 (Spring 1972): 19, 64.

Anderson, Mary Louise. "Black Matriarchy: Portrayals of Women in Three Plays." Negro American Literature Forum 10 (Fall 1976): 93-95.

Anderson, Michael, et al. Crowell's Handbook of Contemporary Drama. New York: Crowell, 1971.

Anderson, Thomas. Crispus Attucks. New York: New Dimensions, 1970.

Anderson, Walt. Bitter Bread! A Dramatic Reading. New York: Seabury Press, 1964.

Arata, Esther S., and Nicholas John Rotoli. Black American Playwrights, 1800 to the Present: A Bibliography. Metuchen, N.J.: Scarecrow Press, 1976.

Ardoin, John. "Scott Joplin." Dallas Morning News, 25 May 1975; in Newsbank--Performing Arts, May-June 1975, 39:A10.

_____. "'Treemonisha' Has a Primitive Charm." Dallas Morning News, 27 May 1975; in Newsbank--Performing Arts, May-June 1975, 39:A 11.

Argetsinger, Gerald S. "Theatre in Review." Educational Theatre Journal 26 (October 1974): 399-400

"Arts and Entertainment for Southern Negroes." New South 17 (September 1962): 10-14.

Asante sano. "'What the Winesellers Buy.'" (Chicago) Courier, 22 March 1975; in Newsbank--Performing Arts, March-April 1975, 30:D12, 13, 14.

Ashley, Leonard R. N., ed. Mirrors for Man: 26 Plays of the World Drama. Cambridge, Mass.: Winthrop, 1974.

Asim. "'Black Journey' A Statement of Truth and Love." (Chicago) Courier, 17 May 1975; in Newsbank--Performing Arts, May-June 1975, 39:E 4, 5.

"At Cannes Film Festival." The Afro-American (Baltimore), 17-21 May 1977, p. 15.

Atkins, Thomas R. "Theater of Possiblities" [Total Action Against Poverty (TAP) Theatre Project in Roanoke]. Kenyon Review 30 (1968): 274-281.

Atkinson, Brooks. "The Big White Fog." In Beckerman, Bernard, and Howard Siegman, On Stage: Selected Theatre Reviews from the New York Times, 1920-1970 (New York: Arno, 1973), p. 225.

_____. Broadway, rev. ed. New York: Macmillan, 1974.

_____. "Mulatto." In Beckerman and Siegman, On Stage, pp. 168-169.

_____. "Raisin in the Sun." In Beckerman and Siegman, On Stage, pp. 402-403.

_____, and Albert Hirschfeld. The Lively Years: 1920-1973. New York: Association Press, 1973.

"AUDELCO Recognition Awards Spotlight the Starts of Black Theatre." (N.Y.) Amsterdam News, 27 November 1976, D-10-11.

Austin, Elsie. Blood Doesn't Tell: A Play About Blood Plasma and Blood Donors. New York: Woman's Press, 1945.

Austin, William. "Blacks, 'the Great White Way.'" (N.Y.) Amsterdam News, 9 October 1976, D-11.

_____. "Controlled Chaos Dramatized" (Rehearsal). (N.Y.) Amsterdam News, 13 November 1976, D-9.

_____. "'The Defense' Dramatizes Survivor's Offense." (N.Y.) Amsterdam News, 20 November 1976, D-12.

_____. "New Musical at the Billie Holiday" (Music Magic). (N.Y.) Amsterdam News, 1 January 1977, D-7.

"Author Fills History Gap of Black Actors" (D. Bogle). In Nykoruk, Barbara, ed., Authors in the News, vol. 1 (Detroit: Gale Research, 1976), p. 51.

"Avante Theater Presents 'Blues' for Mr. Charlie'." Philadelphia Tribune, 18 February 1975; in Newsbank--Performing Arts, January-February 1975, 13:B 12.

Ayers, Vivian. Hawk. Houston: Hawk Press, 1957.

Azenberg, Emanuel. "An Interview: Van Peebles--Producer of Broadway Musicals." Yale/Theatre 4 (Summer 1973): 99-101.

"B.A./W. Scores with 'Dance' (Slow Dance on a Killing Ground). Seattle Times, 17 January 1977; in Newsbank--Performing Arts, January-February 1977, 11:G 13.

"'Babylon II' Has Cast of 50 Kids." (N.Y.) Amsterdam News, 13 November 1976, D-15.

Bach, Bert C., and Gordon Browning. Drama for Composition. Glenview, Ill.: Scott, Foresman, 1973.

Bailey, Peter. "The Importance of Being Black." Newsweek 73 (24 February 1969): 102-103.

_____. "'Raisin': Loraine Hansberry's Award Winning Play Becomes Musical Hit on Broadway." Ebony 29 (May 1974): 74-76, 78, 80.

_____. "'Woodie King, Jr.' Renaissance Man of Black Theater." Black World 24 (April 1975): 4-10.

Bain, Carl E.; Jerome Beaty and J. Paul Hunter. The Norton Introduction to Literature, 2nd ed. (A Son, Come Home). New York: Norton, 1977.

Baird, Keith E. "A Movie Review: 'Countdown at Kusini.'" Freedomways 16 (4th quarter 1976): 251-252.

Baldwin, James. Blues für Mr. Charlie. Trans. [Reinbek bei Hamburg, 1971].

_____. Blues para Mister Charlie. Drama en Tres Actos. Trans. Andres Bosch. Barcelona: Editorial Lumen, 1966.

_____. "Sweet Lorraine." Esquire 72 (November 1969): 139-140.

Ballet, Arthur. "The Theater of Middle America." In Theatre 4: The American Theatre, 1970-1971 (New York: Scribner's, 1972), pp. 73-81.

Balliet, Whitney. "Jazz: New York" (Me and Bessie). New Yorker 51 (10 November 1975): 151-152.

Bambara, Toni Cade. "'For Colored Girls'--and White Girls Too." Ms. 5 (September 1976): 36, 38.

Banks, Phyllis M., and Virginia M. Burke, eds. Black Americans:

Images in Conflict. New York: Bobbs-Merrill, 1970.

Baraka, Imamu Amiri. "For Maulana Karenga and Pharoah Saunders." Black Theatre no. 4 (April 1970): 7.

_____. "Jim Brown on the Screen." Black Theatre no. 4 (April 1970): 32.

"Barbara Ann Teer and the National Black Theatre." Ifco News 4 (January-February 1972): I

Barbour, Floyd B., ed. The Black Seventies. Boston: Sargent, 1970.

Barnes, Clive. "Ceremonies in Dark Old Men at the St. Marks." In Beckerman, Bernard, and Howard Siegman, On Stage: Selected Theatre Reviews from the New York Times, 1920-1970 (New York: Arno, 1973), pp. 433-35.

_____. "Off-Broadway" (Dream on Monkey Mountain). In Theatre 4: The American Theatre, 1970-1971 (New York: Scribner's, 1972), p. 34.

_____. "Off-Broadway and Off-Off, 1969-70." In Theatre 3: The American Theatre, 1969-1970 (New York: Scribner's, 1971), pp. 63-75.

Barnett, Douglas Q. "Annual Round-Up: Black Theater in America-- Seattle: Black Arts/West." Black World 25 (April 1976): 86-89.

Barranger, M. S., and Daniel B. Dodson, eds. Generations: An Introduction to Drama. New York: Harcourt Brace Jovanovich, 1971.

Barrett, Virginia; Dorothy Evans, Lorraine Henry, Jennifer Jordon and Vattel T. Rose. "An Annual Bibliography of Afro-American Literature, 1975, with Selected Bibliographies of African and Caribbean Literature." CLA Journal 20 (September 1976): 94-131.

Barrow, William. "Man of Many Faces: Frank Silvera." Negro Digest 12 (September 1963): 40-43.

Bartley, F. Fitz. "Soul Stirrin' Theatre: 'Aint Supposed to Die a Natural Death.'" Soul Illustrated 3 (Spring 1972): 19.

Batdorf, Emerson. "Black Play Has Ring of Truth." (Ceremonies in Dark Old Men). (Cleveland) Plain Dealer, 20 February 1975; in Newsbank--Performing Arts, January-February 1975, 13:E 1.

_____. "Karamu's 'Choice' Is Fresh, Funny Play." (Cleveland) Plain Dealer, 1 February 1975; in Newsbank--Performing Arts, 1975, 13:E 1.

Bates, Delores A. "A Comment on Culture." Freedomways 14 (1st quarter 1974): 53-58.

Bayete, Cynthia Cotten. "Annual Round-up: Black Theater in America--Los Angeles." Black World 25 (April 1976): 75-82.

Beckerman, Bernard, and Howard Siegman. On Stage: Selected Theater Reviews from the New York Times, 1920-1970. New York: Arno, 1973.

Bell, Bernard W. "Jean Toomer's 'Cane'." Black World 23 (September 1974): 4-19, 92-97.

Bell, Roseann Pope. "'For Colored Girls Who Have Considered Suicide/When the Rainbow Is Enuf.'" The Black Collegian 7 (May-June 1977): 48-49.

Bellamy, Peter. "Allen Stages Black Melodrama." (Cleveland) Plain Dealer, 3 July 1975; in Newsbank--Performing Arts, July-August 1975, 54:B 4.

_____. "'The Wiz' Musical a Whiz of a Show." (Cleveland) Plain Dealer, 25 May 1975; in Newsbank--Performing Arts, May-June 1975, 38:G 8.

Bender, William. "Scott Joplin: From Rags to Opera." Time 106 (15 September 1976): 85-86.

Benston, Kimberly W. Baraka: The Renegade and the Mask. New Haven, Conn.: Yale University Press, 1976.

_____. "'Cities in Bezique': Adrienne Kennedy's Expressionistic Vision." CLA Journal 20 (December 1976): 235-244.

Bentley, Eric. Theatre of War: Comments on 32 Occasions. New York: Viking, 1972.

_____. "White Plague and Black Terror." In his Theatre of War, pp. 404-405.

Berkvist, Robert. "New Face: Hector Jaime Mercado: The Ailey Disciple Who Portrays Judas." New York Times, 7 October 1977, C 3.

Berman, Sanford. "Getting to It; A Guest Editorial" (Black Writings). American Libraries 8 (February 1977): 77

Bermel, Albert. Contradictory Characters: An Interpretation of the Modern Theatre. New York: Dutton, 1973.

_____. "'Dutchman,' or the Black Stranger in America." Arts in Society 9 (Winter 1972): 423-34.

Bernard, Audrey J. "Harlem Writers Pay Tribute to Citizens."
(N.Y.) Amsterdam News: New Horizons, 5 February 1977,
D-14.

Beutel, P. "Talented Cast Transforms 'Don't Bother Me' Into a
Hit." (Austin) American Statesman, 24 November 1975; in
Newsbank--Performing Arts, November-December 1975, 83:A 11.

Bibliographic Guide to Black Studies: 1975. Boston: G. K. Hall,
1976.

"Bicentennial Assignment." Black World 24 (April 1975): 49.

Bigsby, C. W. E. Confrontation and Commitment: A Study of Contemporary American Drama, 1959-66. Columbia: University
of Missouri Press, 1968.

"Bill Gunn's Play a 'Mental Trip'; No 'Sounder' or 'Jane Pittman.'"
In Nykoruk, Barbara, ed., Authors in the News, vol. 1 (Detroit:
Gale Research, 1976).

Billingsley, Ronald G. "The Burden of the Hero in Modern Afro-
American Fiction." Black World 25 (December 1975): 38-45,
66-73.

"Billy Dee Williams as King Opens on Broadway." (N.Y.) Amsterdam News, 7 August 1976, D-4.

"Billy Dee Williams Opens in 'Dream.'" (N.Y.) Amsterdam News,
18 September 1976, D-18.

Birmingham, Stephen. Certain People. New York: Little, Brown,
and Co., 1977.

"Birthday Party" (Eubie Blake). New Yorker 52 (8 March 1976):
30-32.

Black, Doris. "James Earl Jones: Finest Serious Black Actor
Confounded by His Success." Sepia 25 (August 1976): 24-32.

"Black Actor Becomes U of M Summa Cum Laude Graduate" (First
Breeze of Summer). Minneapolis Spokesman, 2 June 1977, p. 1.

The Black Bibliography. Marriott Library, University of Utah, Salt
Lake City, n.d.

Black Comedy, Including White Lies; Two Plays. New York: Stein
and Day, 1969.

"Black Fury at Lincoln Center." (Black Picture Show). New York
Post, 7 January 1975; in Newsbank--Performing Arts, January-
February 1975, 13:G 8.

"Black Man's Burden" (The Education of Sonny Carson). Time 104 (16 September 1974): 6+.

"Black Picture Show." New York Theatre Critics' Reviews--1975 36 (13 January 1975): 386-89; containing:
    Barnes, Clive, "'Black Picture Show' a Tale of Corruption," New York Times, 7 January 1975.
    Watt, Douglas, "'Black Picture Show' Rates No Stars," (N.Y.) Daily News, 7 January 1975.
    Gottfried, Martin, "Black Fury at Lincoln Center," New York Post, 7 January 1975.
    Ettore, Barbara, "Black Picture Show," Women's Wear Daily, 8 January 1975.
    Kalem, T. E., "The Black Game," Time, 20 January 1975.
    Kroll, Jack, "Black and White Picture," Newsweek, 20 January 1975.
    Sanders, Kevin, WABC-TV, 6 January 1975.

"Black Playwrights Get a Break." Sepia 17 (November 1968): 20-23.

"The Black Revolution--'The Slave.'" In Dukore, Bernard, Documents for Drama and Revolution (New York: Holt, Rinehart and Winston, 1971).

"The Black Scholar Reviews: 'And Still I Rise!' by Maya Angelou." Black Scholar 8 (September 1976): 50-51.

"Black Theatre: A Big for Cultural Identity." Black Enterprise 2 (September 1971): 30-34, 44.

"Black Theater--An Evolving Force." In Goldstein, Roda L., Black Life and Culture in the U.S. (New York: Crowell, 1971).

"Black Theatre in the Black Colleges." Tuesday Magazine 7 (August 1972): 10.

"Black Theater Workshop at O.U." (Oklahoma City) Black Dispatch, 1 April 1976; in Newsbank--Performing Arts, March-Arpil 1976, 31:F 14.

"Black Theatres in the Black World." Black Theatre no. 6 (1972): 52-53.

Blackburn, Tom. "'Tambourine's Brings Players Glory." Trenton Times, 1 March 1976; in Newsbank--Performing Arts, March-April 1976, 30:G 12.

Blackman, Brandon R., IV. "Black Hope of Broadway." Sepia 24 (December 1975): 62-68.

"Blackstone Musical Puts Fun into Old-Time Religion." Chicago

Sun Times, 10 April 1976; in Newsbank--Performing Arts, March-April 1976, 27:G 6.

Blake, Richard A. "Humanity Against Itself." America 136 (15 January 1977): 34-35.

Bloom, Arthur W. "The Theatre of Non-Mimetic Propaganda: Critical Criteria." Xavier University Studies 11 (No. 1): 29-36.

Bloom, Samuel William. "A Social Psychological Study of Motion Picture Audience Behavior. A Case Study of the Negro Image in Mass Communication." Ph.D. Dissertation, Sociology, Wisconsin, 1956.

Blum, Daniel, and John Willis, eds. A Pictorial History of the American Theatre: 1860-1976, 4th ed. New York: Crown, 1977.

"Boatright Speaks Out for Blacks." Columbus (Ohio) Evening Dispatch, 7 March 1976; in Newsbank--Performing Arts, March-April 1976, 29:C 10, 11.

Bogle, Donald. "A Look at the Movies by Baldwin." Freedomways 16 (2nd quarter 1976): 103-108.

_____. "'Uptown Saturday Night': A Look at Its Place in Black Film History." Freedomways 14 (4th quarter 1974): 320-330.

Bond, Frederick W. "The Direct and Indirect Contribution Which the American Negro Has Made to the Drama and the Legitimate Stage, with the Underlying Conditions Responsible." Ph.D. Dissertation, English, New York University, 1938.

Bond, Jean Carey. "For Colored Girls Who Have Considered Suicide." Freedomways 16 (3rd quarter 1976): 187-91.

_____. "Reader's Forum: The Media Image of Black Women." Freedomways 15 (1st quarter 1975): 34-37.

Bondy, François. Gespräche mit James Baldwin, Carl J. Burckhardt, Mary McCarthy, E. M. Cioran, Witold Gombrowicz, Eugene Ionesco, Karl Jaspers--. Vienna: Europa, 1972.

Bonin, Jane F. Major Themes in Prize-Winning American Drama. Metuchen, N.J.: Scarecrow Press, 1975.

_____. Prize-Winning American Drama: A Bibliographical and Descriptive Guide. Metuchen, N.J.: Scarecrow Press, 1973.

Bontemps, Alex. "'Bubbling Brown Sugar': A Musical About Harlem Tells the History of Black Entertainment." Ebony 31 (February 1976): 124-26; 128-31.

_____. "Culture." Ebony 30 (August 1975): 105-115.

Bourne, Kay. "Melba Moore Speaks of Effects of Success."
(Boston) Bay State Banner, 25 March 1976; in Newsbank--Per-
forming Arts, March-April 1976, 22:D 9-10.

Bovosco, Carole. "Discovering Foremothers." Ms. 6 (September
1977): 56-59.

Brady, Owen E. "Baraka's 'Experimental Death Unit #1': Plan
for (R)evolution." Negro American Literature Forum 9 (Summer 1975): 59-61.

_____. "Cultural Conflict and Cult Ritual in LeRoi Jones's
'The Toilet.'" Educational Theatre Journal 28 (March 1976):
69-77.

Branch, William Blackwell. "Marketing the Products of American
Negro Writers." In The American Negro Writer and His Roots:
Selected Papers (New York: American Society of African Cul-
ture, 1960), 46-50.

"The Brass Medallion." Theatre News 8 (March 1976): 2-3.

"Breaking New Ground: Ford Foundation Grant to Establish Negro
Ensemble Company." Newsweek 69 (29 May 1967): 90.

Breitenfeld, Frederick, Jr. "Speeding Down the Wrong Track"
(Minority TV Programming). TV Guide 23 (25 January 1975):
22+.

Bright, Daniel. "An Emmy Award for Cicely" (The Autobiography
of Miss Jane Pittman). Sepia 23 (April 1974): 16-20.

Brockett, Oscar G. The Theatre: An Introduction, 2nd ed. New
York: Holt, Rinehart and Winston, 1969.

Brooks, Mary Ellen. "The Pro-Imperialist Career of LeRoi Jones."
Literature and Ideology (Montreal) no. 11 (1972): 37-48.

_____. "Reactionary Trends in Recent Black Drama." Litera-
ture and Ideology (Montreal) no. 10 (1970): 41-48.

Brown, Deming. Soviet Attitudes Toward American Writing.
Princeton, N.J.: Princeton University Press, 1962.

Brown, Lloyd L. "Paul Robeson: Now He Belongs to the Future."
Freedomways 16 (1st quarter 1976): 11-14.

Brown, Lloyd W. "The Cultural Revolution in Black Theatre."
Negro American Literature Forum 8 (Spring 1974): 159-
164.

_____ . "Dreamers and Slaves: The Ethos of Revolution in Derek Walcott and LeRoi Jones." Caribbean Quarterly 16 (September 1971): 36-44.

_____ . "Lorraine Hansberry as Ironist: A Reappraisal of 'A Raisin in the Sun.'" Journal of Black Studies 4 (March 1974): 237-247.

_____ . "West Indian Drama in English: A Select Bibliography." Studies in Black Literature 6 (Summer 1975): 14-16.

Brown, Lorraine A. "'For the Characters Are Myself': Adrienne Kennedy's 'Funnyhouse of a Negro.'" Negro American Literature Forum 9 (Fall 1975): 86-88.

Brown, Marcia L. "Review: 'One Is a Crown.'" Soul Illustrated 3 (Winter 1971): 10.

"'Brown Sugar' Is Sweeter for the Eyes and the Ears." (Newark, N.J.) Star-Ledger, 14 March 1976; in Newsbank--Performing Arts, March-April 1976, 28:A 12.

"'Brown Sugar's' Sparkling Return." Washington Post, 22 January 1976; in Newsbank--Performing Arts, January-February 1976, 12:A 11.

Brownfeld, Allan C. "New Films Degrade Blacks, Stimulate Violence." Human Events 34 (2 March 1974): 17.

"The Brownsville Raid." New York Theatre Critics' Reviews 37 (31 December 1976): 76-79; containing:
    Barnes, Clive, "Stage: 'The Brownsville Raid'," New York Times, 6 December 1976.
    Watt, Douglas, "An Honorable 'Raid'," (N.Y.) Daily News, 6 December 1976.
    Gottfried, Martin, "A Powerful Play in 'Brownsville'," New York Post, 6 December 1976.
    Sharp, Christopher, "The Brownsville Raid," Women's Wear Daily, 6 December 1976.
    Beaufort, John, "The Brownsville Raid," Christian Science Monitor, 10 December 1976.
    Kalem, T. E., "Blind Injustice," Time, 20 December 1976.

Brukenfeld, Dick. "Black Picture Show." Village Voice 20 (3 February 1975): 85.

_____ . "A Fresh Look at Black Manhood" (Charles Fuller). Village Voice 19 (13 June 1974): 81.

_____ . "Off-Off Broadway." In Theatre 4: The American Theatre, 1970-1971. New York: Scribner's, 1972, pp. 38-55.

_____. "Off-Off Broadway: Profile Rising" (Goin' a Buffalo, Don't Bother Me I Can't Cope, and El Hajj Malik). In Theatre 5: The American Theatre, 1971-1972 (New York: Scribner's, 1973), pp. 47-61.

_____. "The Unfortunate Sag." Village Voice 19 (18 July 1974): 57.

Brüning, Eberhard. "'The Black Liberation Movement' und das amerikanische Drama." Zeitschrift für Anglistik und Amerikanistik 20 (1972): 46-58.

Brustein, Robert S. "The Negro Revolution." In his The Third Theatre, pp. 107-51.

_____. The Third Theatre. New York: Knopf, 1969.

"Bubbling Brown Sugar." The Afro-American (Baltimore), 17-21 May 1977, p. 15.

"Bubbling Brown Sugar." Ebony 31 (February 1976): 124-126, 128-131.

"Bubbling Brown Sugar." New York Theatre Critics' Reviews--1976 37 (23 February 1976): 352-356; containing:
    Watts, Douglas, "Take the 'A' Train Quick," (N.Y.) Daily News, 3 March 1976.
    Barnes, Clive, "'Bubbling Brown Sugar' Boils at ANTA," New York Times, 3 March 1976.
    Gottfried, Martin, "'Sugar': How Sweet It Is!" New York Post, 3 March 1976.
    Kissel, Howard, "'Bubbling Brown Sugar' at the ANTA," Women's Wear Daily, 3 March 1976.
    Wilson, Edwin. "When Swing Was King in Harlem," Wall Street Journal, 3 March 1976.
    Beaufort, John, "Review," Christian Science Monitor, 11 March 1976.
    Kalem, T. E., "Doing the Harlem Hop," Time, 22 March 1976.
    Probst, Leonard, "Bubbling Brown Sugar," NBC, 2 March 1976.
    Sanders, Kevin, "Bubbling Brown Sugar," WABC-TV, 2 March 1976.

"'Bubbling Brown Sugar' Has 3 Matinees." (N.Y.) Amsterdam News: Arts and Entertainment, 6 August 1977, D-11.

Buck, Richard M. "Review: Ed Bullins. The New Lafayette Theatre Presents." Library Journal 99 (1 May 1974): 1322.

Buck, Richard M. "Review: Ed Bullins'--'The Theme Is Blackness.'" Library Journal 98 (15 January 1973): 180-81.

Bullins, Ed. "Black Revolutionary Commercial." Drama Review 13 (Summer 1969): 144-45.

_____, ed. "Black Theatre Groups: A Directory." Drama Review 4 (Summer 1968): 172-75.

_____. "Introduction: The Black Revolutionary Commercial." In his The Theme Is Blackness, pp. 127-130.

_____. "Introduction: Black Theater: The '70's--Evolutionary Changes." In his The Theme Is Blackness, pp. 1-15.

_____. "It Bees Dat Way: A Confrontation Ritual." In Theatre 2: The American Theatre, 1968-1969 (New York: International Theatre Institute of the United States, 1970), pp. 120-125.

_____. The New Lafayette Theatre Presents: Plays with Aesthetic Comments by 6 Black Playwrights. New York: Anchor Press/Doubleday, 1974.

_____. The Theme Is Blackness. New York: Morrow, 1973.

Burke, Lee Williams. "The Presentation of the American Negro in Hollywood Films, 1946-1961. Analysis of a Selected Sample of Feature Films." Ph.D. Dissertation, Speech and Drama, Northwestern, 1965.

Burman, Howard, and Joseph Hanreddy. "The Activist Theatre of the Thirties." Theatre Studies (Ohio State University) 18 (1971-1972): 55-64.

Burns, Ben. "The Creative Wizardry of Gordon Parks." Sepia 25 (April 1976): 36-40, 44-46.

"Bush Mama" (review). Tricontinental Film Center: 1977-78. Berkeley, Calif.: Tricontinental, 1977, p. 44.

Byrne, Bridget. "Laugh Dimension Makes Good 'Buy.'" (Buy the Bi and By). Los Angeles (Calif.) Herald Examiner, 14 January 1976; in Newsbank--Performing Arts, January-February 1976, 14:C 3.

"Caesar at DeLys" (Square Root of Soul). (N.Y.) Amsterdam News: Arts and Entertainment, 2 July 1977, D-11.

"'Caged Bird' Authoress Writes Script for Film." Jet (26 August 1971): 57.

Calloway, Earl. "Kamal as the Wiz Is Electrifying." Chicago Daily Defender, 7 June 1977, p. 20.

_____. "'Raisin' Explodes with Cool Intensity." Chicago Daily Defender, 30 March 1976; in Newsbank--Performing Arts, March-April 1976, 27:E 13.

_____. "'Sugar' Bubbles with Style." Chicago Daily Defender, 8 October 1975; in Newsbank--Performing Arts, September-October 1975, 66:G 13.

_____. "X-Boy Showcases Drama with Moving Pathos" (Warn the Wicked). Chicago Daily Defender, 8 January 1975; in Newsbank--Performing Arts, January-February 1975, 13:G 14.

Cameron, Kenneth M., and Theodore J. C. Hoffman. A Guide to Theatre Study. New York: Macmillan, 1974.

"Cannonball Adderley Medal." (N.Y.) Amsterdam News, 7 August 1976, D-2.

Carr, Chrystal. Ebony Jewels: A Selected Bibliography of Books By and About Black Women. Inglewood, Calif.: Crenshaw-Imperial Branch Library, 1975.

Carter, Art. "Shep Allen Calls It Quits: Manager of Old Howard Theatre." The Afro-American: Dawn Magazine (Baltimore), 9 July 1977, p. 10.

Cashman, Marc. Bibliography of American Ethnology. Rye, N.Y.: Todd, 1976.

Cassady, Marshall, and Pat Cassady, eds. An Introduction to Theatre and Drama. Skokie, Ill.: National Textbook, 1975.

"Cast of 'Slave Ship' Quits Stage After Protests About Conditions." New York Times, 24 January 1970, p. 24.

"Ceremonies in Dark Old Men." (N.Y.) Amsterdam News: Arts and Entertainment, 14 May 1977, D-2.

"'Ceremonies' of Laughter with Something Missing." (Chicago) Sun-Times, 28 February 1975; in Newsbank--Performing Arts, January-February 1975, 29:C 5.

Cerf, Bennett, ed. Four Contemporary American Plays. New York: Random, 1961.

Charters, Ann. Nobody: The Story of Bert Williams. New York: Macmillan, 1970.

Chernin, Donna. "Karamu 'Wedding Band' Has Vivid Memories." (Cleveland) Plain Dealer, 26 May 1975; in Newsbank--Performing Arts, May-June 1975, 39:G 10.

_____. "Ruby Dee with Ossie Davis Is Poetry in Motion."

(Cleveland) Plain Dealer, 29 October 1975; in Newsbank--Performing Arts, September-October 1975, 71:B 13.

Childress, Alice. When the Rattlesnake Sounds. New York: Coward, McCann, & Geoghegan, 1975.

Chintok, Jo Jo. "Lennox Brown: A Black Canadian Dramatist." Black Collegian 1 (January 1972): 28-29.

Chrisman, Robert. "The Black Scholar Reviews: 'Look! What a Wonder!'" Black Scholar 8 (September 1976): 53.

"Cicely Tyson." Miami (Fla.) Herald, 6 June 1976, in Newsbank--Film and Television, May-June 1976, 44:A 9, 10, 11.

"Cicely Tyson Is Dr. King's Wife in NBC-TV Drama." Chicago Daily Defender, 26 May 1977, p. 32.

Clarke, Sebastian. "Black Theatre." Plays and Players 22 (August 1975): 33-34.

_____. "Magic/al Delight(s)." Black Theatre no. 5 (1971): 54-55.

"Claudia McNeil Won Fame the Hard Way." The Afro-American (Baltimore), 15-19 March 1977, p. 1.

Clayborne, Jon L. "Modern Black Drama and the Gay Image." College English 36 (November 1974): 381-384.

Clayes, Stanley A. Drama and Discussion, 2nd ed. Chicago: Loyola University, 1978.

"Cleavon Little Has Got to Be 'Gooood.'" New York Post, 3 January 1977; in Newsbank--Performing Arts, January-February 1977, 5:G 1.

Cline, Julia. "Rise of the American Stage Negro." The Drama Magazine 21 (January 1931): n.p.

Clurman, Harold. "Je Seme Partout." In Theatre 1: The American Theatre, 1967-1968 (New York: International Theatre Institute of the United States, 1969), pp. 58-59.

_____. "New Playwrights: Boys and Girls on the Burning Deck." In Theatre 4: The American Theatre, 1970-1971 (New York: Scribner's, 1972), pp. 166-177.

_____. "Theatre"* (Black Picture Show, and The Wiz). Nation 220 (25 January 1975): 94.

---

*The following 30 or so reviews are ordered alphabetically by play reviewed; most were titled "Theatre: ...."

_____. : Black Terror. Nation 213 (29 November 1971): 572-574.

_____. : Black Visions: Harris, Sanchez, and Wesley. Nation 214 (17 April 1972): 508-509.

_____. : The Breakout; The Past Is the Past. Nation 220 (17 May 1975): 604-606.

_____. : The Brownsville Raid. Nation 223 (25 December 1976): 701-702.

_____. : Bubbling Brown Sugar. Nation 222 (27 March 1976): 381-382.

_____. ___: Bullins. Nation 206 (25 March 1968): 420-421.

_____. ___: Charles Russell, Ron Stewart and Neal Tate, Joseph Walker, LeRoi Jones. Nation 210 (2 February 1970): 124-125.

_____. ___: Cop and Blow. Nation 214 (17 April 1972): 508-509.

_____. ___: The Duplex. Nation 214 (27 March 1972): 411-412.

_____. ___: Eden. Nation 222 (27 March 1976): 381-82.

_____. ___: Every Night When the Sun Goes Down. Nation 222 (6 March 1976): 282-283.

_____. : First Breeze of Summer. Nation 220 (22 March 1975): 348-350.

_____. : Five on the Black Hand Side. Nation 210 (2 February 1970): 124.

_____. : For Colored Girls.... Nation 222 (1 May 1976): 541-542.

_____. ___: The Harangues. Nation 210 (2 February 1970): 124.

_____. ___: Les Blancs. Nation 211 (30 November 1970): 572-573.

_____. ___: Les Blancs. Nation 211 (7 December 1970): 605-606.

_____. ___: N. Harris. Nation 214 (17 April 1972): n.p.

_____. ___: My Sister, My Sister. Nation 218 (18 May 1974): 636-637.

_____. ____: The Pig Pen. <u>Nation</u> 210 (1 June 1970): 668-669.

_____. ____: A Recent Killing. <u>Nation</u> 216 (12 February 1973): 218-219.

_____. ____: Sambo. <u>Nation</u> 210 (2 February 1970): 124.

_____. ____: Slave Ship. <u>Nation</u> 210 (2 February 1970): 124-125.

_____. ____: The Sty of the Blind Pig. <u>Nation</u> 213 (20 December 1971): 668-670.

_____. ____: The Taking of Miss Janie. <u>Nation</u> 220 (5 April 1975): 414.

_____. ____: Wedding Band. <u>Nation</u> 215 (13 November 1972): 474-476.

_____. ____: What the Winesellers Buy. <u>Nation</u> 218 (9 March 1974): 315-316.

_____. ____: Your Arms Too Short to Box with God. <u>Nation</u> 224 (15 January 1977): 61.

_____. "Theatre and Films" (Black Girl). <u>Nation</u> 213 (1 November 1971): 443-446.

Cocks, Jay. "City Slickers" (Cooley High). <u>Time</u> 106 (1 September 1975): 45.

_____. "'Leadbelly'." <u>Time</u> 107 (24 May 1976): 76, 78.

_____. "Quick Cuts" (Thomasine and Bushrod). <u>Time</u> 103 (6 May 1974): 91.

Coe, Richard L. "'The Brass Medallion' of Manhood." <u>Washington Post</u>, 14 April 1976; in <u>Newsbank--Performing Arts</u>, March-April 1976, 29:F 6.

_____. "Midnight Special." <u>Washington Post</u>, 5 March 1976; in <u>Newsbank--Performing Arts</u>, March-April 1976, 31:D 11.

_____. "Poignant, Polished 'Medal'." <u>Washington Post</u>, 27 January 1976; in <u>Newsbank--Performing Arts</u>, January-February 1976, 13:C 11.

Cohn, Ruby. <u>Dialogue in American Drama</u>. Bloomington: Indiana University Press, 1971.

_____. "Theatre in Review" (Bullins). <u>Educational Theatre Journal</u> 28 (October 1976): 406.

Coleman, Larry. "Reviews: 'Black Terror'." Black Theatre no. 6 (1972): 36-37.

Colle, Royal. "Negro Image and the Mass Media." Ph.D. Dissertation, Cornell University, 1967.

Collier, Eugenia. "'Black' Shows for White Viewers." Freedomways 14 (3rd quarter 1974): 209-217.

Collins, John D. "American Drama in Anti-Slavery Agitation." Ph.D. Dissertation, State University of Iowa, 1963.

Collins, Leslie M. "A Song, a Dance, and a Play--An Interpretive Study of Three American Artists" (on Negro Performers). Ph.D. Dissertation, Fine Arts, Western Reserve University, 1945.

"'Come Laugh and Cry with Langston Hughes'." (N.Y.) Amsterdam News: New Horizons, 5 February 1977, D-10.

"Comedy on Sex Staged for Writer's Conference" (Alice Browning). Chicago Daily Defender, 20 June 1977, p. 19.

"Community Keynotes" (Armegeddon). (N.Y.) Amsterdam News: Arts and Entertainment, 11 June 1977, D-17.

Considine, Shawn. "British Theatre Had Its Angry Young Men, Off-Broadway Savors Its First Furious Woman, Ntozake Shange." People 6 (5 July 1976): 68-69.

Contee, Clarence G. "A Crucial Friendship Begins; Du Bois and Nkrumah: 1935-1945." Crisis 78 (August 1971): 181-185.

Cook, Mercer, and Stephen E. Henderson. The Militant Black Writer. Madison: University of Wisconsin Press, 1969.

Cooke, Michael. "The Descent into the Underworld of Modern Black Writers." Iowa Review vol. 5, pp. 77-90.

Cooper, Arthur. "Education in Blood" (The Education of Sonny Carson). Newsweek 84 (12 August 1974): 74.

Cooper, Grace C. "Joseph A. Walker: Evolution of a Playwright." New Directions: The Howard University Magazine 2 (October 1974): 10-13.

Corbin, Richard, and Miriam Balf, eds. Twelve American Plays. New York: Scribner's, 1973.

Cosby, Dennis. "Levar Burton: Prince of the Television Overnight Sensations." The Black Collegian 7 (May-June 1977): 36-37.

Cosford, Bill. "The Blues Are Gospel to 'Bessie' Star." Miami Herald, 10 February 1977; in Newsbank--Performing Arts, January-February 1977, 2:D 6.

_____. "Linda as 'Bessie' Sends Shivers Down the Spine." Miami Herald, 3 February 1977; in Newsbank--Performing Arts, January-February 1977, 10:B 11.

Cosgrove, William. "Strategies of Survival: The Gimmick Motif in Black Literature." Studies in the Twentieth Century no. 15 (Spring 1975): 109-127.

Coulthard, Gabriel R., ed. Caribbean Literature: An Anthology. London: University of London Press, 1966.

"'Countdown at Kusini'." Ebony 31 (April 1976): 90-94.

"'Crab Quadrille' A Social Satire." (N.Y.) Amsterdam News, 25 December 1976, D-16.

Craig, Randall. "Plays in Performance: Experimental." Drama 118 (Autumn 1975): 69-74.

"Creative Directions." Essence 3 (May 1972): 76.

Crew, Louie. "What You See Is What You Get. Black as Victim." Empirical Research in Theatre (Summer 1974): 35-43.

Cripps, Thomas R. "'The Birth of a Race' Company: An Early Stride Toward a Black Cinema." Journal of Negro History 59 (January 1974): 28-37.

_____. "The Death of Rastus: Negroes in American Films Since 1945." Phylon 28 (Fall 1967): 267-275.

_____. "The Noble Black Savage: A Problem in the Politics of Television Art." Journal of Popular Culture 8 (Spring 1975): 687-95.

_____. "Paul Robeson and Black Identity in American Movies." Massachusetts Review 11 (Summer 1970): 468-485.

_____. Slow Fade to Black. New York: Oxford University Press, 1977.

Crist, Judith. "Astaire, Kelly, and MGM" (Leadbelly). Saturday Review 3 (29 May 1976): 46-48.

_____. "Home-Grown Horror" (Uptown Saturday Night). New York 7 (24 June 1974): 58-59.

_____. "Sink or Swim in Watergate: The Year's Ten Best and

Worst" (The Spook Who Sat by the Door). New York 7 (14 January 1974): 75.

_____. "This Week's Movies: 'Uptown Saturday Night'." TV Guide (3-9 December 1977): A-21.

Crosby, Harry Lillis "Bing." 'What Show Business Owes the Negro." Black World (August 1951): 3-6.

Crowther, Hal. "Triumphant 'Sty' a Fresh Start." Buffalo (N.Y.) Evening News, 25 March 1975; in Newsbank--Performing Arts, March-April 1977, 25:A 13.

'''The Crucificado': Review." Black Creation 5 (Fall 1973): 45.

Curb, Rosemary Keefe. "The Idea of the American Dream in Afro-American Plays of the Nineteen Sixties." Ph.D. Dissertation, University of Arkansas, 1977.

Current Biography (Ed Bullins) 38 (May 1977): 15-18.

_____ (Douglas Turner Ward), 37 (1976): 417-421.

Current, Gloster B. "'Love You Madly'--Duke Ellington." Crisis 81 (June-July 1974): 196-200.

_____. "Noble Sissle." Crisis 83 (March 1976): 84-87.

_____. "Scott Joplin." Crisis 82 (June-July 1975): 219-221.

Cuthbert, David. "Dashiki 'Blind Pig' Eerie, Effective." (New Orleans) Times-Picayune, 16 July 1975; in Newsbank--Performing Arts, July-August 1975, 55:D 1.

_____. "Dashiki 'Contraband'." (New Orleans) Times-Picayune, 2 February 1975; in Newsbank--Performing Arts, January-February 1975, 13:D 12.

_____. "Violent 'Comedy' at Dashiki." (New Orleans) Times-Picayune, 18 September 1975; in Newsbank--Performing Arts, September-October 1975, 69:C 4.

Dace, Letitia. LeRoi Jones: A Checklist of Works by and about Him. London: Nether Press, 1971.

_____, and Wallace Dace. The Theatre Student: Modern Theatre and Drama. New York: Richards Rosen, 1973.

Dace, Tish. "LeRoi Jones/Amiri Baraka: From Muse to Malcolm to Mao." Village Voice 22 (1 August 1977): 12-14.

Dagnall, Cynthia. "Melba Moore's Cinderella Life" (Purlie). Chicago Tribune, 17 February 1977; in Newsbank--Performing Arts, January-February 1977, 6:B 2, 3.

Dance, Darrell. "Contemporary Militant Black Humor." Negro American Literature Forum 8 (Summer 1974): 217-222.

Dance, Daryl C. "You Can't Go Home Again: James Baldwin and the South." CLA Journal 18 (September 1974): 81-90.

Daughtry, Willia A. "A Quarter Century of the Black Experience in the Fine Arts, 1950-1974." The Negro Educational Review 27 (January 1976): 24-33.

David, Jay, ed. Black Joy. Chicago, Ill.: Cowles (Subsidiary of Regnery), 1971.

Davis, Arthur P. From the Dark Tower: Afro-American Writers 1900 to 1960. Washington, D.C.: Howard University Press, 1974.

_____. "Trends in Negro American Literature." In Altenbernd, Lynn, Exploring Literature (New York: Macmillan, 1970).

_____ and Michael W. Peplow, eds. The New Negro Renaissance, an Anthology. New York: Holt, Rinehart and Winston, 1975.

Davis, Curt. "Bill Cobbs: The Death of a Salesman, The Birth of an Artist." Encore 6 (17 January 1977): 33-34.

_____. "Earle Hyman Is Running the Other Race." Encore 6 (4 April 1977): 35.

_____. "The Ever-Flying 'Dutchman'." Encore 6 (4 April 1977): 40.

_____. "Getting It Together with Shauneille Perry." Encore 6 (5 July 1977): 41-42.

_____. "'Godsong' Is Godless." Encore 6 (21 February 1977): 41.

_____. "The Inner Voice of Louis Gossett." Encore 6 (6 June 1977): 28-31.

_____. "Isabel Is a Belly Laugh." Encore 6 (6 June 1977): 32-33.

_____. "It's Happening for Mabel King." Encore 6 (20 June 1977): 51-52.

_____. "Ken Page Is Doing Nicely-Nicely, Thanks." Encore 6 (7 February 1977): 35.

_____. "'The Last Street Play' Is First-Rate Wesley." Encore 6 (5 July 1977): 44.

_____. "'The Long Black Block' Alternate Side-of-the-Street Goodness." Encore 6 (18 April 1977): 40.

_____. "No Great Good in 'MacDaddy'." Encore 6 (23 May 1977): 40.

_____. "People in the News: 'Almos' a Man'." Encore 6 (9 May 1977): 30.

_____. "People in the News" (Bullins). Encore 6 (23 May 1977): 31.

_____. "People in the News" (Haley). Encore 6 (20 June 1977): 49.

_____. "People in the News--'Southern Fried'." Encore 6 (6 June 1977): 26.

_____. "People in the News" (Walker). Encore 6 (20 June 1977): 49.

_____. "People in the News--'Wiz'." Encore 6 (7 February 1977): 26.

_____. "Set Your Watch 'On Toby Time'." Encore 6 (7 March 1977): 36-37.

_____. "Smyrl Locks Up 'Lock-In'." Encore 6 (20 June 1977): 53.

_____. "Sound Taps for 'Brownsville Raid'." Encore 6 (3 January 1977): 33-34.

_____. "Welcome 'Arms'." Encore 6 (17 January 1977): 36.

Davis, (Brother) Joseph Morgan. "A Compilation and Analysis Concerning the Contributions of the Negro to the American Theatre in 1950-1960." Master's Thesis, Catholic University, 1962.

Davis, Ossie. "The English Language Is My Enemy." Negro History Bulletin 30 (April 1967): 18.

_____. "The Power of Black Movies." Freedomways 14 (3rd quarter 1974): 230-232.

Dawson, Cheryl. "An Inside Look at Alvin Childress." Black Stars (July 1975): 64-66.

"'Defense' Opens at New Federal." (N.Y.) Amsterdam News, 6 November 1976, D-15.

Delaunoy, Didier. "Black Picture Show." Encore 4 (17 March 1975): 4.

Dent, Thomas C. "Beyond Rhetoric Toward a Black Southern Theatre." Black World 20 (April 1971): 14-24.

_____. "Black Theater in the South: Report and Reflections." Freedomways 14 (3rd quarter 1974): 247-54.

DeRamus, Betty. "A Man Who Captures Detroit ... And Life." In Authors in the News, vol. 1 (Detroit: Gale Research, 1976), p. 348.

DeSchauensee, Max. "Black Cast Scores Big Success in 'Aida'." (Philadelphia) Evening Bulletin, 2 April 1976; in Newsbank--Performing Arts, March-April 1976, 28:G 13.

DeVine, Laurence. "A Four Year Run and Still Coping." Detroit Free Press, 19 June 1975; in Newsbank--Performing Arts, May-June 1975, 38:D 4.

_____. "'I Can't Cope' Keeps Coping with a Rhythmic Message." Detroit Free Press, 5 June 1975; in Newsbank--Performing Arts, May-June 1975, 38:D 5.

_____. "New York Is Still Where It's At, as Broadway Hits the Upbeat." Detroit Free Press, 17 March 1975; in Newsbank--Performing Arts, March-April 1975, 28:D 4.

Dickinson, Donald C. A Bio-Bibliography of Langston Hughes, 1902-1967, 2nd ed. Hamden, Conn.: Archon, 1972.

Dickstein, M. "Black Aesthetic in White America." Partisan Review 38 (Winter 1971-1972): 376-395.

Dictionary Catalog of the Schomburg Collection of Negro Literature and History, comp. by New York Public Library, vols. 1-9. Boston: G. K. Hall, 1962.

_____, 1st Supplement, vols. 1-2. Boston: G. K. Hall, 1967.

_____, 2nd Supplement, vols. 1-4. Boston: G. K. Hall, 1972.

_____, Supplement 1974. Boston: G. K. Hall, 1976.

"Digging It: Washington's DIG-IT Troupe." Newsweek 75 (27 April 1970): 64+.

Distler, Paul Antonie. "The Rise and Fall of the Racial Comics in American Vaudeville." Ph.D. Dissertation, Speech and Drama, Tulane, 1963.

Dodds, Richard. "Dashiki '76 Finale." (New Orleans) Times-

Picayune 8 January 1977; in Newsbank--Performing Arts, January-February 1977, 11:E 11.

_____. "A Welcome 'First Breeze'." (New Orleans) Times-Picayune, 19 April 1977; in Newsbank--Performing Arts, March-April 1977, 25: E 1.

Doll, Bill. "'Past', 'Changes', Boast Good Scripts at Karamu." (Cleveland) Plain Dealer, 11 October 1975; in Newsbank--Performing Arts, September-October 1975, 31:F 14.

"Dorothy Dandridge, 1950's Screen Siren." Encore 6 (21 February 1977): 3.

Dougherty, Jim. "'Blues for Mr. Charlie'." Edge no. 5 (Fall 1966): 116-120.

Douglas, Carlyle C. "Paul Robeson: Farewell to a Fighter." Ebony 31 (April 1976): 33-42.

_____. "The Whiz Behind 'The Wiz'." Ebony 30 (October 1975): 114-116+.

Downs, Joan. "Upbeat Blues" (Me and Bessie). Time 106 (3 November 1975): 66.

"Drama in Black Colleges: Black Faces or White Masks?" The Black Collegian (January-February 1972); (March-April 1972): 29-30, 51.

Drew, Michael H. "Critics Seem Unkind to Theater in Uneven Season." Milwaukee Journal, 26 February 1976; in Newsbank--Performing Arts, January-February 1976, 13:A 5.

Dreyfuss, Joel. "Marvelous Music and Dancing, But the Plot's No Revelation" (Your Arms Too Short to Box with God). Washington Post, 6 November 1975; in Newsbank--Performing Arts, November-December 1975, 83:A 5.

Driver, Tom. "Blues for Mr. Charlie: The Review That Was Too True to Be Published." Negro Digest 13 (September 1964): 34-40.

Dubois, John. "Family Finally Accepts His Decision." (Philadelphia) Evening Bulletin, 2 March 1975; in Newsbank--Performing Arts, March-April 1975, 30:B 13.

Du Bois, W. E. B. An ABC of Color: Selections From Over a Half Century of the Writings of W. E. B. Du Bois. Berlin: Seven Seas, 1963; Bell Press, 1964.

_____. "Dubois' Review of 'Nigger Heaven'." In Davis, Arthur

P., and Michael W. Peplow, eds., The New Negro Renaissance: An Anthology (New York: Holt, Rinehart and Winston, 1975), pp. 193-194.

Duckett, Alfred. "The Birth of a Screenwriter" (Wesley). Sepia 26 (January 1977): 62-70.

Dukore, Bernard. Documents for Drama and Revolution. New York: Holt, Rinehart and Winston, 1971.

Durdin, Glenda. "The Theme of Black Matriarchy in 'A Raisin in the Sun'." In Lester, James D., Writing the Research Papers (Glenview, Ill.: Scott Foresman, 1976), pp. 75-92; passim, 36-74.

Durrah, James W. "How Sweet It Is: 'Bubbling Brown Sugar'." (N.Y.) Amsterdam News: Arts and Entertainment, 25 June 1977, D-10, 11.

_____. "'Season's Reasons: Pretty Sound." (N.Y.) Amsterdam News: Arts and Entertainment, 23 July 1977, D-14.

_____. "'The Smile and Wonder Cycle': Production and Audience Suffer." (N.Y.) Amsterdam News: Arts and Entertainment, 14 May 1977, D-7.

_____. "Tony Stokes Stars in City College 'Roots'." (N.Y.) Amsterdam News: Arts and Entertainment, 28 May 1977, D-5.

Dyson, Dierdra. "Annual Round-up: Black Theater in America-- Chicago." Black World 24 (April 1975): 26-33.

_____. _____. Black World 25 (April 1976): 71-74.

Eaton, Gregory S. "Black Theatre and Drama in America to Baldwin." Ph.D. Dissertation, Washington, 1977.

Eckstein, George. "The New Black Theater." Dissent 20 (Winter 1973): 110-113.

_____. "Softened Voices in the Black Theater." Dissent 23 (Summer 1976): 306-308.

Edding, Cynthia. "'Essence Woman' Alice C. Browning." Essence 8 (May 1977): 6.

Eddy, Bill. "4 Directors on Criticism." Drama Review 18 (September 1974): 24-33.

Edelin, Ramona. "Shirley Graham Du Bois." First World 1 (May/

June 1977): 36-38.

"Eden." New York Theatre Critics' Reviews--1976 37 (5 May
1976): 278-280; containing:
    Watt, Douglas, "Black on Black in '27 N.Y.," (N.Y.) Daily
    News, 4 March 1972.
    Gussow, Mel, "Negro Ensemble Stages 'Eden', a Black
    'Hester Street'," New York Times, 4 March 1976.
    Gottfried, Martin, "Romeo and Juliet in 'Eden?'" New York
    Post, 4 March 1976.
    Beaufort, John, "Eden," Christian Science Monitor, 11
    March 1976.

Eder, Richard. "New Elaine Jackson Play Takes Old Drama Route."
New York Times, 17 October 1977, L 39.

_____. "Stage: The Lost Stir 'Rum an' Coca-Cola'." New
York Times, 27 October 1977, C 17.

Edmonds, Randolph. 'The Blacks in the American Theatre, 1700-
1969." The Pan-African Journal 7 (Winter 1974): 297-322.

"'The Education of Sonny Carson'." Ebony 29 (August 1974): 157-59.

Edwards, Flora Mancuso. "The Theater of the Black Diaspora:
A Comparative Study of Black Drama in Brazil, Cuba, and the
United States." Ph.D. Dissertation, New York University, 1975.

Eichelbaum, Stanley. "ACT Workshop for Blacks." San Francisco
Examiner, 28 September 1975; in Newsbank--Performing Arts,
September-October 1975, 68:D 13.

_____. "Onward with the 'Blues'." San Francisco Examiner,
16 September 1975; in Newsbank--Performing Arts, September-
October 1975, 67:A 3.

_____. "'Uncle Tom's Cabin' Open for Inspection." San Fran-
cisco Examiner, 24 February 1976; in Newsbank--Performing
Arts, January-February 1976, 14:G 9.

Eikleberry, Burton. "The Negro Actor's Participation and the
Negro Image on the New York Stage, 1954-1964." Master's
Thesis, University of Kansas, 1965.

Elbert, Alan. "Inside Cicely." Essence 3 (February 1973): 40-41,
74, 80.

Elder, Lonne, III. "Comment." Black Creation 4 (Summer 1973):
48.

"'The Electronic Nigger'." Cue (23 March 1968).

Elkind, Samuel, et al. Thirty-Two Scenes for Acting Practice. Glenview, Ill.: Scott, Foresman, 1972.

_____. Twenty-Eight Scenes for Acting Practice. Glenview, Ill.: Scott-Foresman, 1971.

Elwood, P. "The Evolution of 'Evolution'." San Francisco Examiner, 17 June 1975; in Newsbank--Performing Arts, May-June 1975, 38:G 12.

Emerson, Sally. "Rum an' Coca-Cola." Plays and Players 24 (January 1977): 32.

Emeruwa, Leatrice W. "Annual Round up: Black Theater in America--Cleveland." Black World 25 (April 1976): 62-70.

"'Emily T' Opens." (N.Y.) Amsterdam News, 16 October 1976, D-8.

"Emmy Show Stars 'Roots'." Milwaukee Journal, 13 September 1977, part 2, p. 3.

Engel, Lehman. The Critics. New York: Macmillan, 1976.

Engstrom, Karen. "A Story of Sin on a Stage Full of Kin" (In De Beginnin'). Chicago Tribune, 19 November 1977, 2: 12.

Enser, A. G. S. Filmed Books and Plays, rev. ed. London: Andre Deutsch, 1975.

Erdman, Richard. "'Purlie' Mostly Fun at Bonfils' Theatre." (Denver) Rocky Mountain News, 10 January 1976; in Newsbank--Performing Arts, January-February 1976, 11:E 8.

Erzsébet, Zombori. "LeRoi Jones: A Négerek Mozgalmának Drámairója." Nagyvilóg (Budapest), 15 (December 1970).

"Ethiopian Directs" (Bush Mama). (N.Y.) Amsterdam News, 13 November 1976, D-15.

Evans, Donald T. "Bring It All Back Home." Black World 20 (February 1971): 41-45.

_____. "Playwrights of the Fifties: Bring It All Back Home." Black World 20 (February 1971): 45.

_____. "The Theatre of Confrontation: Ed Bullins, Up Against the Wall." Black World 23 (April 1974): 14-18.

_____. "'Who's Got His Own' at Cheyney." Black World 19 (April 1970): 43-48, 97-98.

Everett, Chestyn. "'Tradition' in Afro-American Literature." Black World 25 (December 1975): 20-35.

"Every Night When the Sun Goes Down." New York Theatre Critics' Reviews--1976 37 (1 March 1976): 338-340; containing:
Barnes, Clive, "The Stage: 'Every Night When the Sun Goes Down'," New York Times, 16 February 1976.
Watt, Douglas, "Symbol Banging," (N.Y.) Daily News, 16 February 1976.
Gottfried, Martin, "Play's Problem: Too Many Ideas," New York Post, 16 February 1976.
Sharp, Christopher, "Every Night When the Sun Goes Down," Women's Wear Daily, 17 February 1976.
Beaufort, John, Christian Science Monitor, 23 February 1976.

F.H.K. "Carolina Negro Theatre: In Retrospect." The Carolina Play Book 8 (June 1935): 45-47.

Fabre, Michel. "Black Literature in France." Studies in Black Literature 4 (Autumn 1973): 9-14.

"'The Fabulous Miss Marie' Opens at the Locust." Philadelphia Tribune 22 March 1975; in Newsbank--Performing Arts, March-April 1975, 29:A 3.

Facts on File. New York: Facts on File, 1976.

Faia, M. P. "Straight with No Cop-Outs." (Guess Who's Coming to Dinner and A Patch of Blue). Social Problems 16 (Spring 1969): 525-527.

Falb, Lewis W. American Drama in Paris: 1945-1970. Chapel Hill: University of North Carolina Press, 1973.

Farber, Stephen. "'Cotton Comes to Harlem'." Hudson Review 23 (Winter 1970-1971): 692-96.

Farrell, Edmund J., et al. Upstage/Downstage: A Theatre Festival. Glenview, Ill.: Scott, Foresman, 1976.

Farrison, W. Edward. "The Kidnapped Clergyman and Brown's Experience." CLA Journal 18 (June 1975): 507-515.

Farrow, Charles. "'Music Is' Witty and Colorful Adaptation of 'Twelfth Night'." The Afro-American (Baltimore), 30 November-4 December 1976, p. 11.

_____. "Scott Joplin's 'Treemonisha' A Real Musical Jewel." The Afro-American (Baltimore), 16-20 September 1975, in Newsbank--Performing Arts, September-October 1975, 67:D 1.

Fauchereau, Serge, trans. "Des Figures Interesantes Rien de Plus" (Entretien avec M. L. Rosenthal). Quinzaine Littéraire no. 126 (1-15 October 1971): 9-11.

Fehrenback, Robert J. "William Easton's 'Dessalines': A Nineteenth Century Drama of Black Pride." CLA Journal 19 (September 1975): 75-89.

Feingold, Michael. "'Bubbling Brown Sugar'." Village Voice 21 (15 March 1976): 139.

_____. "Cases Alter Circumstances." Village Voice 19 (9 May 1974): 00.

_____. "Down to Rock Bottom" (The Sirens). Village Voice 19 (23 May 1974): 89.

_____. "It All Adds Up to Zero" (Les Femmes Noires). Village Voice 19 (21 March 1974): 64.

Felgar, Robert. "Black Content, White Form." Studies in Black Literature 5 (Winter 1974): 28-31.

"Felton Perry Minus All Labels." Los Angeles Herald Examiner, 29 January 1976; in Newsbank--Performing Arts, January-February 1976, 14:C 2.

Fenderson, Lewis H. "The New Breed of Black Writers and Their Jaundiced View of Tradition." CLA Journal 15 (September 1971): 18-24.

Fife, Marilyn Diane. "Black Image in American TV: The First Two Decades." Black Scholar 6 (November 1974): 7-15.

"The First Breeze of Summer." New York Theatre Critics' Reviews--1975 36 (16 June 1975): 228-231; containing:
    Barnes, Clive, "Theater: 'First Breeze of Summer'," New York Times, 3 March 1975.
    Watt, Douglas, "To a Matriarch with Love," New York Daily News, 4 March 1975.
    Gottfried, Martin, "Negro Company Premiere," New York Post, 3 March 1975.
    Mancini, Joseph, "The 'Breeze' and Eye Draws Tears," New York Post, 19 June 1975.
    Wilson, Edwin, "Family Life in a Black Household," Wall Street Journal, 13 June 1975.
    Sharp, Christopher, "The First Breeze of Summer," Women's Wear Daily, 12
    Beaufort, John, "The First Breeze of Summer," Christian Science Monitor, 10 March 1970.

Fisher, Titus. "'River Niger' Is Portrait of Life." Omaha World

Herald, 3 March 1975; in Newsbank--Performing Arts, March-April 1975, 31:C 5.

"'Five on the Black Hand Side'." Ebony 29 (May 1974): 96-102.

Fleckenstein, Joan S. "Theatre in Review--The 'Estate'." Educational Theatre Journal 28 (October 1976): 409-410.

Fletcher, Leah. "Black Theatre Alive and Struggling Hard." (Boston) Bay State Banner, 20 March 1975; in Newsbank--Performing Arts, March-April 1975, 28:G 1.

Flippo, Chet. "Broadway Rock: 'The Wiz' and the Worst." Rolling Stone 187 (22 May 1975): 18.

"For Colored Girls Who Have Considered Suicide/When the Rainbow Is Enuf." New York Theatre Critics' Reviews--1976 37 (27 September 1976): 199-202; containing:
  Watt, Douglas, "Here's to the Ladies Again," (N.Y.) Daily News, 16 September 1976.
  Wilson, Edwin, The Wall Street Journal, 21 September 1976.
  Gussow, Mel, "Stage: 'Colored Girls' on Broadway," New York Times, 16 September 1976.
  Kalem, T. E., "He Done Her Wrong," Time, 14 June 1976.
  Gottfried, Martin, "'Rainbow' Over Broadway," New York Post, 16 September 1976.
  Kroll, Jack, "Women's Rites," Newsweek, 14 June 1976.
  Beaufort, John, "For Colored Girls," Christian Science Monitor, 24 September 1976.
  Sanders, Kevin, "For Colored Girls...," WABC-TV, 19 September 1976.
  Probst, Leonard, NBC-TV, 15 September 1976.

Forbes, Cheryl. "Black 'Box' Is Best." Christianity Today 20 (30 January 1976): 16-17.

Fowler, Giles M. "Theatre in Mid-America." Kansas City (Mo.) Star, 9 February 1977; in Newsbank--Performing Arts, January-February 1977, 10:A 4.

Fox, Terry Curtis. "The Con Man In the Mirror" (Daddy). Village Voice 22 (20 June 1977): 71-72.

Franklin, J. E. Black Girl: From Genesis to Revelation. Washington D.C.: Howard University Press, 1976.

Freedman, Morris. American Drama in Social Context. Carbondale: Southern Illinois University Press, 1971.

Frenz, Horst, ed. American Playwrights on Drama. New York: Hill and Wang, 1965.

"From Warp to Wiz ... by Way of Mars." Chicago Tribune: Arts and Fun, 7 November 1976, 6:3-4.

Frye, Charles A. "Archetypes and Truth: Spiritual Hierarchies--
Another Look at the Movement." Black Images 3 (Autumn
1974): 30-33.

Fuller, Hoyt W. "Black World Interviews Woody King, Jr." Black
World 24 (April 1975): 12-17.

_____. "My Involvement with the Festival: HWF," (on the
Second World Black and African Festival of Arts and Culture)
Black World 24 (January 1975): 81-82.

Gaffney, Floyd. "Black Theatre: The Moral Function of Imamu
Amiri Baraka." Players 50 (Summer 1975): 122-31.

_____. "A Hand Is on the Gate in Athens." Educational Theatre
Journal 21 (May 1969): 196-201.

Gagey, Edmond M. Revolution in American Drama. New York:
Columbia University Press, 1947.

Gant, Lisbeth. "Ain't Beulah Dead Yet, Or Images of Black Women
in Film." Essence 4 (May 1973): 60-61, 72-75.

_____. "'Middle Class! Black?' at the Bed-Stuy Theatre."
Black Theatre 5 (1971): 52.

_____. "The New Lafayette Theatre." Drama Review 16 (De-
cember 1972): 46-55.

Gardiner, R. H. "Joplin's Only Opera Has Its Points." (Baltimore)
Sun, 8 September 1975; in Newsbank--Performing Arts, September-October 1975, 67:C 14.

Gardner, Bettye, and Bettye Thomas. "The Cultural Impact of the
Howard Theatre on the Black Community." The Journal of
Negro History 55 (October 1970): 253-265.

Gardner, R. H. "Play Still Needs Work" (First Breeze of Summer).
(Baltimore) Sun, 17 March 1977; in Newsbank--Performing Arts,
March-April 1977, 25:E 2.

Garland, Phyl. "The Prize Winners." Ebony 25 (July 1970): 29-37.

Garnett, Bernard. "Black Drama Finds New Audience." Race Relations Reporter 3 (7 February 1972): 4-6.

Gassner, John, and Bernard F. Dukore. A Treasury of the Theatre.
4th ed. vol. 2. New York: Simon and Shuster, 1970.

Gates, H. L. "Portraits in Black: From Amos 'n' Andy to Coonskin." Harper 252 (June 1976): 16-19+.

Gayle, Addison, Jr. "The Black Aesthetic 10 Years Later." Black World 23 (September 1974): 20-29.

"Gay's 'Survival' Staged at Kenwood High." Chicago Daily Defender, 22 June 1977, p. 24.

Geisinger, Marion, ed. Plays, Players, & Playwrights. New York: Hart, Inc., 1975.

George, Nelson. "Black Spectrum Theatre in Its Ninth Year." (N.Y.) Amsterdam News: Arts and Entertainment, 23 July 1977, D-8.

_____. "Is Hollywood Changing Its View of Black Men?" (River Niger). (N.Y.) Amsterdam News: Arts and Entertainment, 2 July 1977, D-8, 9.

_____. "Ms. Carroll Brings Black Richness to the Stage." (N.Y.) Amsterdam News: Arts and Entertainment, 5 March 1977, D-9.

Ghent, Henri. "Black Creativity in Quest of an Audience." Arts in America 58 (May 1970): 35.

Gibbs, Vernon. "Melba Moore in Touch with the Good Things" (Purlie). Essence 7 (November 1976): 42.

Gibson, Emily F. "Must a Black Actor Play Henri Christophe?" Sepia 23 (March 1974): 22-26.

Giddings, Paula. "'Raisin' Revisited." Encore 4 (7-14 July 1975): 28-31.

Giddins, Gary. "Doctored Jazz." New York 8 (10 March 1975): 69.

Giffin, Glenn. "Joplin Entrancing with 'Treemonisha'." Denver Press, 3 October 1975; in Newsbank--Performing Arts, September-October 1975, 67:C 10.

Gilbert, Ruth, ed. "In and Around Town: Off-Broadway" (Young, Gifted and Broke). New York 10 (8 August 1977): 16.

_____. "In and Around Town: Off and Off-Off Broadway" (Absurdities in Black). New York 10 (15 August 1977): 19.

_____. "In and Around Town: On Broadway; Off Broadway" (Bubbling Brown Sugar, For Colored Girls..., Wiz, Your Arms Too Short...). New York 10 (2 May 1977): 19-22 through 10 (5 September 1977): 21.

Gilder, Rosamond, et al. Theatre Arts Anthology. New York: Theatre Arts Books, 1934.

_____. "Theatre As People: Book Report." In Theatre 4: The American Theatre, 1970-1971 (New York: Scribner's, 1972), pp. 179-89.

Gill, Brendan. "Off Broadway: The Second Time Around" (The Prodigal Sister). New Yorker 50 (9 December 1974): 69-70.

_____. "The Theatre: Armageddon" (What the Winesellers Buy). New Yorker 50 (25 February 1974): 83.

_____. "The Theatre: The Good Old Days" (Bubbling Brown Sugar). New Yorker 52 (15 March 1976): 51.

_____. "The Theatre: Having a Good Time" (Your Arms Too Short to Box With God). New Yorker 52 (3 January 1977): 60.

_____. "The Theatre: Open for Business" (I Have a Dream). New Yorker 52 (4 October 1976): 75-78.

_____. "The Theatre: Things Go Wrong" (Les Blancs). New Yorker 46 (21 November 1970): 103-104.

_____. "The Theatre: Writing About Writing." New Yorker 51 (20 January 1975): 61-02.

Gilliam, Dorothy. "Last Goodbyes to Paul Robeson." Washington Post, 29 January 1976; in Newsbank--Performing Arts, January-February 1976, 11, A 7, 8.

Gilliat, Penelope. "The Current Cinema: Brilliant Bunglers" (Uptown Saturday Night). New Yorker 50 (17 June 1974): 88-91.

_____. "Current Cinema Retorts to 'The Birth of a Nation'." New Yorker 52 (29 March 1976): 88-91.

Gilman, Richard. "White Standards and Negro Writing." New Republic CLXVIII (March 1969): 25.

Giral, Sergio. "Cuban Cinema and the Afro-Cuban Heritage: An Interview with Sergio Giral." Black Scholar 8 (Summer 1977): 63-72.

Glackin, William C. "America--More or Less Out of Focus." Sacramento Bee, 1 May 1976; in Newsbank--Performing Arts, May-June 1976, 40:E 1.

Gobbins, Dennis. "The Education of Theodore Ward." New Masses 28 (October 1947): 10-14.

Goddard, Bob. "'Brown Sugar' Swings at American Theatre." St.

Louis Globe-Democrat, 5 January 1977; in Newsbank--Performing Arts, January-February 1977, 10:B 10.

"Goings on About Town: A Triple Bill by Bullins, Goss, and Wesley." New Yorker 53 (25 July 1977): 2.

Goldsmith, Sheilah. "Richard Wesley." Black Creation 6 (Annual, 1974-1975): 29-30.

Goldstein, Malcom. The Political Stage. New York: Oxford University Press, 1974.

Gorney, Carole. "Black Revue Excites Popejoy Hall Crowd." Albuquerque Journal, 20 November 1975; in Newsbank--Performing Arts, November-December 1975, 83:A 10.

"Gospel Truth" (Your Arms Too Short to Box With God). Newsweek 89 (10 January 1977): 66.

Goss, Clay. Home Cookin': Five Plays. Washington, D.C.: Howard University Press, 1974.

Gottfried, Martin. "Broadway" (Les Blancs). In Theatre 4: The American Theatre, 1970-1971 (New York: Scribner's, 1972), p. 22.

_____. "'Cold Storage' Defrosts into Lukewarm Theatre." New York Post, 17 April 1977; in Newsbank--Performing Arts, March-April 1977, 26:A 12.

_____. "How Sweet It Is." New York Post, 3 March 1976; in Newsbank--Performing Arts, March-April 1976, 28:A 13.

_____. "'Lock-In' Pleasant Due to Good Vibes." New York Post, 28 April 1977; in Newsbank--Performing Arts, March-April 1977, 23:F 6.

_____. "The New Ethnic Theater." New York Post, 4 October 1975; in Newsbank--Performing Arts, September-October 1975, 68:B 3-4.

_____. "Play's Problems: Too Many Ideas" (Every Night When the Sun Goes Down). New York Post, 16 February 1976; in Newsbank--Performing Arts, January-February 1976, 13:D 2.

_____. "Profile of a Hero" (I Have a Dream). New York Post, 29 March 1976; in Newsbank--Performing Arts, March-April 1976, 30:C 9.

_____. "Ribman Out on a Limb" (The Poison Tree). New York Post, 9 January 1976; in Newsbank--Performing Arts, January-February 1976, 14:D 7.

_____. "This 'MacDaddy' Is Not So Great." New York Post, 14 April 1977; in Newsbank--Performing Arts, March-April 1977, 23:D 10.

Gounard, Jean-François. "Richard Wright as a Black American Writer in Exile." CLA Journal 17 (March 1974): 307-317.

Gray, Bill. "Black Theatre in Transition, Playwright Says." In Nykoruk, Barbara, ed., Authors in the News, vol. 1 (Detroit: Gale Research, 1976), p. 348.

Gredsmith, Sheilah. "Richard Wesley." Black Creation 6 (Annual 1974-1975): 29-30.

Green, Dan S. "Resurrection of the Writings of an American Scholar." Crisis 79 (November 1972): 311-13.

Green, Jean G. "T. S. Young to Direct Play." The Afro-American (Baltimore), 22-26 March 1977, p. 15.

Greer, Edward G. "Broadway--On and Off" (Bullins). Drama 112 (Spring 1974): 54.

_____. "On and Off-Broadway, Spring 1975." Drama 117 (Summer 1975): 32-36.

Gresham, Jewell Handy. "James Baldwin Comes Home." Essence 7 (June 1976): 55, 80+.

Griffin, John C. "Jean Toomer: A Bibliography." The South Carolina Review 7 (April 1975): 61-64.

Griffith, Francis, and Joseph Mersand, eds. Eight American Ethnic Plays. New York: Scribner's, 1974.

Grimes, Nikki. "'Babylon II': A Triumph." (N.Y.) Amsterdam News, 27 November 1976, D-8.

_____. "'The Brownsville Raid' Saunters into Town." (N.Y.) Amsterdam News, 1 January 1977, D-7.

_____. "'Community Kitchen': A Showcase." (N.Y.) Amsterdam News, 20 November 1976, D-8.

_____. "'Ghetto 1999': Long on Message; Short on Plot." (N.Y.) Amsterdam News, 27 November 1976, D-8.

_____. "'Night Shift'." (N.Y.) Amsterdam News, 4 December 1976, D-3.

Grossman, Samuel L. "Trends in the Avant-Garde Theatre of the United States During the 1960's." Ph.D. Dissertation, University of Minnesota, 1974.

Grun, Bernard. The Timetables of History. New York: Simon and Schuster, 1975.

Groves, Cy, ed. Plays on a Human Theme. Toronto: McGraw-Hill Ryerson, 1967.

"Growing Theatre, Inc., Is Born at St. Philip's Church." (N.Y.) Amsterdam News, 21 August 1976, D-15.

Guernsey, Otis L., Jr., ed. The Best Plays of 1974-1975. New York: Dodd, Mead, 1975.

_____. The Best Plays of 1975-1976. New York: Dodd, Mead, 1976.

_____. Playwrights, Lyricists, Composers, on Theater. New York: Dodd, Mead, 1974.

Gussow, Mel. "Theatre East" (No Place to Be Somebody). In Theatre 5: The American Theatre, 1971-1972 (New York: Scribner's, 1973), pp. 67-73.

"Haile Gerima Discusses 'Bush Mama'." Tricontinental Film Center: 1977-78, p. 44.

Hairston, Loyle. "The Black Film--'Supernigger' as Folk Hero." Freedomways (3rd Quarter 1974): 218-22.

Haiti, Our Neighbor. Brooklyn: The Haitian Publishing Co., 1944.

Haley, Elsie Galbreath. "The Black Revolutionary Theatre: LeRoi Jones, Ed Bullins, and Minor Playwrights." Ph.D. Dissertation, University of Denver, 1971.

"Haley Receives Spingarn." Minneapolis Spokesman, 23 June 1977, p. 7.

"Haley Receives Spingarn." Twin Cities Courier (Minneapolis/St. Paul) 2 June 1977, p. 5.

Hall, Frederick Douglass. "The Black Theater in New York from 1960-1969." Ed.D. Dissertation, Columbia University, 1973, Part I.

Hall, Johnson. "James Baldwin." Transatlantic Review nos. 37-38 (Autumn-Winter 1970-1971): n.p.

Halliburton, Warren. "The Social Implication of Humor as Portrayed in the Contemporary Black Theatre." Ph.D. Dissertation, Teacher's College, Columbia, 1975.

"Hamlet Jones." (Cleveland) Call and Post, 27 September 1975; in Newsbank--Performing Arts, September-October 1975, 66:D 11.

Hanan, D. "Ghetto Theatre: Vital Drama or Social Therapy." Community 26 (April 1970): 7-10.

"Hansberry Drama Premieres at Park." Chicago Daily Defender, 5 July 1977, p. 21.

Hardwick, Mary R. "The Nature of the Negro Hero in Serious American Drama, 1910-1964." Ph.D. Dissertation, Michigan State University, 1968.

"Harlem, U.S.A." (Dubbling Brown Sugar). (N.Y.) Amsterdam News: New Horizons, 5 February 1977, D-16.

Harris, Jessica B. "'For Colored Girls' ... from Ntozake to Broadway." (N.Y.) Amsterdam News, 9 October 1976, D-10, 11.

_____. "Harper a Show Biz 'Wiz'." (N.Y.) Amsterdam News, 29 March 1975; in Newsbank--Performing Arts, March-April 1975, 29:F 2.

_____. "The New Lafayette: 'Nothing Lasts Forever'." Black Creation 4 (Summer 1973): 8-10.

_____. "The Women Who Arc the Rainbow." Essence 7 (November 1976): 87-89, 102+.

Harris, Leonard. "Broadway" (Ain't Supposed to Die a Natural Death). In Theater 5: The American Theatre, 1971-1972 (New York: Scribner's, 1973), pp. 22-30.

Harris, Robert R. "The Hollywood Connection" (Childress). Bookviews 1 (November 1977): 30-31.

Hartnoll, Phyllis, ed. The Oxford Companion to the Theatre, 3rd ed. London: Oxford University Press, 1972.

Haskell, Molly. "Here Come the Killer Dames" (Black Actresses). New York 8 (19 May 1975): 46+.

Haslam, Gerald W. "Two Traditions in Afro-American Literature." Research Studies 37 (September 1969): 183-93.

Hatch, James. "Speak to Me in Those Old Words, You Know, Those La-La Words, Those Tung-Tung Sounds (Some African Influences on the Afro American Theatre)." Yale/Theatre 8 (Fall 1976): 25-34.

_____. "Theodore Ward: Black American Playwright." Freedomways 15 (1st Quarter 1975): 37-41.

Hatch, James Vernon, and Omanii Abdullah. The Black Play-wright, 1823-1977: An Annotated Bibliography of Plays. New York: Bowker, 1977.

"Hatch-Billops Archives Interviews with Playwrights." Negro American Literature Forum 10 (Summer 1976): 64-65.

Hatch/Billops Collection: Archives of Black American Cultural History. New York: Hatch/Billops, 1971.

Haun, Harry. "Everyone's 'Breeze'." New York Daily News, 15 July 1975; in Newsbank--Performing Arts, July-August 1975, 54:A 5.

Haverstraw, Jack. "The Making of a Good Movie Star." Sepia 24 (May 1975): 44-52.

Hay, Samuel A. "African-American Drama, 1950-1970." Negro History Bulletin 36 (January 1973): 5-8.

_____. "Alain Locke and Black Drama." Black World 21 (April 1972): 8-14.

Haynes, Howard. "Grace Bumbry: International Opera's Super Star." Sepia 23 (June 1974): 46, 52.

_____. "Off-Screen Lovers Finally United in Movie." Sepia 23 (April 1974): 40-44.

Hazziezah. "Black Theatre Alliance Touring Companies...." (N.Y.) Amsterdam News, 7 August 1976, D-11.

_____. "'Infirmity Is Running': Uneven Black Family Love." (N.Y.) Amsterdam News, 30 October 1976, D-8.

_____. "Inversions." (Just An Old Sweet Song). (N.Y.) Amsterdam News, 16 October 1976, D-17.

"Heaven and Hell's Agreement." New Yorker 50 (22 April 1974): 103.

Hedley, Leslie Woolf. "Art vs. Society?" Arts in Society 9 (Winter 1972): 387-92.

Henderson, Archibald, ed. Pioneering a People's Theatre. Chapel Hill: University of North Carolina Press, 1945.

Henderson, Lenneal J., Jr. "W. E. B. Du Bois: Black Scholar and Prophet." The Black Scholar 1 (January-February 1970): 47-57.

Heston, Lilla, ed. Man in the Dramatic Mode. 6 vols. Evanston, Ill.: McDougal, Littell Co., 1970.

Hewes, Henry. "Black Hopes: Presentations in New York City." Saturday Review 53 (14 February 1970): 30.

_____. "Public Joy and Private Terror." Saturday Review 55 (8 January 1972): 38.

_____. "Theater: Brief Chronicles" (The Taking of Miss Janie). Saturday Review 2 (17 May 1975): 52.

_____. "To 'Disneyland' and Back" (Medal of Honor Rag). Saturday Review 3 (17 April 1976): 48-49.

Hicks, James. "Alex Haley Still Modest Despite Fame and Fortune." (N.Y.) Amsterdam News: New Horizons, 5 February 1977, D-9.

Hieronymus, Clara. "'The Wiz' a Wiz of a Show." (Nashville) Tennessean, 31 October 1975; in Newsbank--Performing Arts, September-October 1975, 66:G 4, 5.

Higgins, Chester. "People Are Talking About: Maya Angelou." Yes (21 October 1971): 45.

Higginsen, Vy. "Oh, Yeah." Essence 5 (November 1974): 12.

Hill, Edward Steven. "A Thematic Study of Selected Plays Produced by the Negro Ensemble Company." Ph.D. Dissertation, Bowling Green State University, 1975.

Hill, Errol. "LeRoi Jones." In Vinson, James, ed., Contemporary Dramatists (New York: St. Martin's Press, 1973), pp. 421-27.

_____. The Trinidad Carnival: Mandate for a National Theatre. Austin: University of Texas Press, 1972.

Hill, Karen. "Who Laughs at Racial Comedies on TV?" Essence 5 (May 1974): 8.

Hilliard, Connie. "Black Arts Festival." Africa 39 (November 1974): 63.

Hilliard, R. L. "The Integration of the Negro Actor on the New York Stage." Educational Theatre Journal 8 (May 1956): 97-108.

Hinton, J. L., et al. "Tokenism and Improving Imagery of Blacks in TV Drama and Comedy: 1973." Journal of Broadcasting 18 (Fall 1974): 423-32.

Hirsch, Foster. "No Place to Be Somebody." In Vinson, James, ed., Contemporary Dramatists (New York: St. Martin's Press, 1973), pp. 299-300.

Hirsch, Samuel. "The O'Neill Experience." In Theatre 5: The

American Theatre, 1971-1972. New York: Scribner's, 1973, pp. 145-151.

"Historical Precis: The New Lafayette Theatre." Black Theatre no. 6 (1972): 21.

Hobson, Harold, ed. International Theatre Annual: No. 4. New York: Grove Press, 1959.

Hobson, Sheila Smith. "The Rise and Fall of Blacks in Serious Television." Freedomways 14 (3rd quarter 1974): 185-199.

Hodenfield, Jan. "Vivian Reed: All of a Sudden She Bubbled to Stardom." New York Post, 12 March 1976; in Newsbank--Performing Arts, March-April 1976, 28:B 9.

Hoffman, William M., ed. New American Plays. Vol. 2, New York: Hill and Wang, 1968; vol. 3, 1970; vol. 4, 1975.

Hoggard, Bishop J. Clinton. "Don't Mourn For Me--But Live for Freedom's Cause" (Paul Robeson). Freedomways, 16 (1st quarter 1976): 15-18.

Holly, Ellen. "Where Are the Films About Real Black Men and Women?" Freedomways 14 (3rd quarter 1974): 270-73 [reprinted from The New York Times, 2 June 1974].

Holmes, Paul C., and Anita J. Lehman, eds. Keys to Understanding: Receiving and Sending [Drama]. New York: Harper and Row, 1970.

Hord, Fred. "Power in the Blood? or 'But We Need More'." Black Books Bulletin 21 (1974): 10-14.

Horton, Rod W., and Herbert W. Edwards. Backgrounds of American Literary Thought, 3rd ed. Englewood Cliffs, N.J.: Prentice-Hall, 1974.

Houghton, Norris. Advance from Broadway. Freeport, N.Y.: Books for Libraries Press, 1969.

_____. The Exploding Stage. New York: Weybright and Talley, 1971.

Hudson, Theodore R. From LeRoi Jones to Amiri Baraka. Durham, N.C.: Duke University Press, 1973.

Huggins, Nathan. Harlem Renaissance. New York: Oxford University Press, 1971.

Hughes, Catharine. "Bi-Centennial Reflections." America 135 (24 July 1976): 30-33.

_____. "Broadway Roundup." America 133 (6 December 1975): 408-409.

_____. "Broadway Roundup" (Your Arms Too Short to Box with God). America 136 (22 January 1977): 60.

_____. "New York" (What the Winesellers Buy). Plays and Players 21 (April 1974): 52-53.

_____. "Of Harlem and Verona." America 125 (18 December 1971): 534-35.

_____. "Other Cities" (What the Winesellers Buy). America 130 (9 March 1974): 175.

_____. "Theatre--'Black Terror'." America 136 (11 June 1977): 529.

_____. "Theatre: 'I'm Laughin' But I Ain't Tickled'." America 134 (12 June 1976): 519.

_____. "Theatre--'The Last Street Play'." America 136 (11 June 1977): 529.

_____. "Three New Musicals." America 135 (27 November 1976): 373.

_____. "Troy Traduced: Newark Revisited" (Last Street Play). America 136 (11 June 1977): 528-29.

_____. "Two Black Plays" (For Colored Girls ... and I Have a Dream). America 135 (9 October 1976): 214.

_____. "White on Black" (The Taking of Miss Janie). America 132 (31 May 1975): 427.

"Hughes at Columbia." New Yorker 43 (30 December 1967): 21-23.

Hurst, John V. "Purlie: Prolonged but Pleasant." Sacramento Bee, 30 May 1976; in Newsbank--Performing Arts, May-June 1976, 40: B 13.

"I Have a Dream." New York Theatre Critics' Reviews--1976 37 (27 September 1976): 186-190; containing:
    Watt, Douglas, "Blurry 'Dream' with Songs" (N.Y.) Daily News, 21 September 1976.
    Barnes, Clive, "'I Have a Dream' Plays Tribute on Stage to Martin Luther King," New York Times, 21 September 1976.
    Gottfried, Martin, "Some Dreams Don't Come True," New York Post, 21 September 1976.

Wilson, Edwin, "The Black Experience," Wall Street Journal, 21 September 1976.

Beaufort, John, "Martin Luther King on Stage," Christian Science Monitor, 23 September 1976.

Sharp, Christopher, "I Have a Dream," Women's Wear Daily, 21 September 1976.

Kroll, Jack. "Theater: 'I Have a Dream'," Newsweek, 4 October 1976.

Kalem, T. E., "A King in Darkness," Time, 4 October 1976.

Sanders, Kevin, "I Have a Dream," WABC-TV, 20 September 1976.

"The Image of Black Folk in American Literature." Black Scholar 6 (June 1975): 45-52.

"Images of the Eye" (St. Claire Bourne). Soul Illustrated 3 (Fall 1971): 22-23.

"'In De Beginnin' Opens August 3." Chicago Daily Defender, 28 July 1977, p. 13.

"Independence Day" (Bush Mama). In Tricontinental Film Center: 1977-1978 (Berkeley, Calif.: The Center, 1977), p. 45.

Inge, M. Thomas. "James Baldwin's Blues." Notes on Contemporary Literature 2 (September 1972): 8-11.

Jackson, Blyden. The Waiting Years: Essays on American Negro Literature. Baton Rouge: Louisiana State University, 1976.

Jackson, Esther M. "Le Roi Jones (Imamu Amiri Baraka): Form and the Progression of Consciousness." CLA Journal 17 (September 1973): 33-56.

Jackson, J. "'Slow Dance' Role a Dream for 'Line'." Boston (Mass.) Globe, 7 April 1976; in Newsbank--Performing Arts, March-April 1976, 32:F 3.

Jackson, Kennell, Jr. "Notes on the Works of Ed Bullins and 'The Hungered One'." CLA Journal 18 (December 1974): 292-99.

"James Earl Jones in 'Exorcist II: The Heretic'." The Afro-American: Afro Magazine (Baltimore, Md.), 31 May-4 June 1977, p. 13.

Jarrett, Vernon. "A Vicious Lynching Delights Audience." Chicago Tribune, 1 January 1978, 1:19.

"Jean Pace Checks Out Gay's 'Survival' at AAP." Chicago Daily Defender, 9 June 1977, p. 17.

Jefferson, D. W., ed. The Morality of Art. London: Routledge and Kegan Paul, 1969, New York: Barnes and Noble, 1969.

Jennings, Robert. "MSU's 'Glory' Is Refreshing." (Memphis) Commercial Appeal, 12 April 1975; in Newsbank--Performing Arts, March-April 1975, 29:F 10.

Jerome, Victor Jeremy. The Negro in Hollywood Films. New York: Masses and Mainstream, 1950.

"'Jesus Christ, Lawd Today'." Washington Star, 11 June 1976; in Newsbank--Performing Arts, May-June 1976, 40:B 3.

Jeyifous, Abiodun. "Black Critics on Black Theatre in America." Drama Review 18 (September 1974): 34-45.

_____. "Theatre and Drama and the Black Physical and Cultural Presence in America: Essays in Interpretation." Ph.D. Dissertation, New York University, 1975.

Johnson, Helen. "Stereotypes of the Black Man in American Drama." Master's Thesis, Jackson State, 1971.

Johnson, Malcom L. "HSC Obscures Walcott's 'Dream on Monkey Mountain'." Hartford (Conn.) Courant, 21 March 1976; in Newsbank--Performing Arts, March-April 1976, 32:E 1, 2.

Jones, Charles E. "Soul Stirrin' Theatre" (Baraka). Soul Illustrated, 2 (July 1970): 18.

Jones, John Henry. "Great Themes for Black Plays and Films." Freedomways 14 (3rd Quarter 1974): 255-65.

Jones, LeRoi (Imamu Amiri Baraka). "Black (Art) Drama Is the Same as Black Life." Ebony 25 (February 1971): 74-76.

_____. "The Revolutionary Theatre." In Dukore, Documents for Drama and Revolution (New York: Holt, Rinehart and Winston, 1971), pp. 206-07.

Jones, Martha. "Theater Southern Style: The FST." Black Creation 4 (Fall 1972): 12-13.

Jones, Norma R. "Sweetback: The Black Hero and Universal Myth." CLA Journal 19 (June 1976): 559-65.

Jones, R. "'Treemonisha' Return of a Lost Opera." New York Daily News, 28 September 1975; in Newsbank--Performing Arts, September-October 1975, 67:C 3, 4, 5.

Jones, Robert Earl. In Xeroxed Abstracts: Stage II. Video Educational Workshop, Inc., 54 E. 11th St., New York 10003.

Jordan, Casper L., ed. "Consortium List of African-American Materials." Central University, Durham, N.C., 1974.

Jouffray, Alain. "LeRoi Jones, le Théâtre de la Révolution Noire." Cahiers Renauld-Barrault 63 (October 1967): 44-53.

Junker, H. "No Miracles: Black Quartet." Newsweek 74 (11 August 1969): 82.

K., F. H. see F. H. K.

Kaiser, Ernest. "Black Images in Mass Media: A Bibliography." Freedomways 14 (3rd Quarter 1974): 274-287.

"Kaleidoscope" (Wesley). Black Creation 6 (Annual 1974-1975): 29-30.

Kalem, T. E. "Black on Black" (Black Visions: Harris, Sanchez, and Wesley). Time 99 (1 May 1972): 53.

_____. "The Blame Game" (Black Picture Show). Time 105 (20 January 1975): 76.

_____. "Blind Injustice." Time 108 (20 December 1976): 58.

_____. "Consecration." Time 98 (6 December 1971): 81.

_____. "Doing the Harlem Hop." Time 107 (22 March 1976): 79.

_____. "He Done Her Wrong" (For Colored Girls ...). Time 107 (14 June 1976): 74.

_____. "A King in Darkness" (I Have a Dream). Time 108 (4 October 1976): 100.

_____. "Off-Broadway: Play v Players" (God Is a Guess What?). Time 92 (27 December 1968): 47.

_____. "Oh, When the Saints ..." (Your Arms Too Short to Box with God). Time 109 (24 January 1977): 55.

Kane, George. "Brilliant Cast of 'Raisin' Makes It a Musical Joy." (Denver) Rocky Mountain News, 19 March 1976; in Newsbank-- Performing Arts, March-April 1976, 27:E 10.

Kauffmann, Stanley. "Arts and Lives: Stanley Kauffmann on Theater: Suite and Sour." New Republic 174 (3 & 10 July 1976): 20-21.

_____. "Now and Also Then" (The Taking of Miss Janie). New Republic 172 (7 June 1975): 20.

_____. "On Theatre" (What the Winesellers Buy). New Republic 170 (9 March 1974): 24-33.

_____. "Stanley Kauffmann on Theatre." New Republic 172 (8 February 1975): 22, 34.

_____. "Stanley Kauffmann Show" (The Wedding Band). New Republic 167 (25 November 1972): 22, 36.

Keller, Joseph. "Black Writing and the White Critic." Negro American Literature Forum 3 (Winter 1970): 103-110.

Kelly, Kevin. "'Slow Dance' Comes Back with Sharpened Edges." Boston Globe, 9 April 1976; in Newsbank--Performing Arts, March-April 1976, 30:F 9.

Kelly, Martin P. "'Man in the Family' a Play About Black Society." (Albany, N.Y.) Times-Union, 18 April 1977; in Newsbank-- Performing Arts, March-April 1977, 25:D 2.

Kent, George P. "Outstanding Works in Black Literature During 1972." Phylon 34 (December 1973): 307-29.

Kessler, J. "Keep to Ourselves." Saturday Review 53 (2 May 1970): 36.

Keyssar-Franke, Helene. "Afro-American Drama and Its Criticism, 1960-1972: An Annotated Checklist with Appendices." Bulletin of the New York Public Library 78 (Spring 1975): 276-346.

_____. "Strategies in Black Drama." Ph.D. Dissertation, University of Iowa, 1974.

Killens, John O. "Hollywood in Black and White." In Banks, Phyllis, and Virginia M. Burke, eds., Black Americans: Images in Conflict (New York: Bobbs-Merrill, 1970), pp. 31-34.

_____. "The Image of Black Folk in American Literature." Black Scholar 6 (June 1975): 45-52.

Kimball, Robert, and William Bolcom. Reminiscing with Sissle and Blake. New York: Viking, 1973.

King, Woodie, Jr. "Directing 'Winesellers'." Black World 25 (April 1976): 20+.

"'King Heroin': Harlem Play on the Destructive Effects of Dope Addiction in the Black Community." Ebony 26 (June 1971): 56-58.

Kinnamon, Keneth. "The Political Dimension of Afro-American Literature." Soundings 28 (Spring 1975): 130-144.

Klinkowitz, Jerome. "LeRoi Jones (Imamu Amiri Baraka):

'Dutchman' as Drama." Negro American Literature Forum 7 (Winter 1973): 123-26.

Klotman, Phyllis R. Another Man Gone: The Black Runner in Contemporary Afro-American Literature. Port Washington, N.Y.: Kennikat, 1977.

_____. "Langston Hughes's Jess B. Semple and the Blues." Phylon 36 (March 1975): 68-77.

Knight, Etheridge, et al. Black Voices from Prison. New York: Pathfinder Press, 1970.

Koiner, Bruce. "Ragtime Revival" (Scott Joplin). Commentary 61 (March 1976): 57-60.

_____. "Ragtime Revival" (Treemonisha). Commentary 61 (March 1976): 57-60.

Kraus, Ted M. "Critical Thoughts." Critical Digest 21 (2 February 1970): 35.

Kroll, Jack. "Between Negro and Black" (The Sty of the Blind Pig). Newsweek 78 (6 December 1971): 121-22.

_____. "Between Two Worlds" (Les Blancs). Newsweek 76 (30 November 1970): 98.

_____. "Black Mood" (Bullins). Newsweek 71 (18 March 1968): 110.

_____. "Caught in the Web." Newsweek 77 (28 June 1971): 85.

_____. "Dark Voyage" (Slave Ship). Newsweek 74 (1 December 1969): 86.

_____. "Hopes, Dreams, Fantasies" (Baraka, Dean, Walker). Newsweek 81 (19 February 1973): 75.

_____. "In Black America" (The Duplex). Newsweek 79 (20 March 1972): 98-99.

_____. "Public Affairs" (The Black Terror). Newsweek 78 (29 November 1971): 109-110.

_____. "Women's Rites" (For Colored Girls ...). Newsweek 84 (14 June 1976): 99.

Kupa, Kushauri. "Black Art at the Kuumba House, Newark." Black Theatre no. 5 (1971): 52-53.

_____. "Closeup: The New York Scene--Black Theatre in New York, 1970-1971." Black Theatre no. 6 (1972): 38-51.

"Kuumba Dancers Perform in Plaza." Chicago Daily Defender, 3 August 1977, p. 23.

"Kuumba Stages Special Show." Chicago Daily Defender, 27 June 1977, p. 19.

Ladvig, Ronald V. "The Black Black Comedy of Ben Caldwell." Players 51 (February/March 1976): 88-91.

"Lafayette Theatre's Reaction to 'Bombers'." Black Theatre 1 (April 1970): 16-25.

Lahr, John. "America: The Collapsing Underground." Gambit: An International Drama Quarterly 17: 65-69.

_____. Astonish Me. New York: Viking, 1973.

_____. "The Deli: Off Broadway and Off, '68-'69." In Theatre 2: The American Theatre, 1968-1969 (New York: International Theatre Institute of the United States, 1970), pp. 46-57.

_____, ed. Grove Press Modern Drama: Six Plays by Baraka, Brecht, Feiffer, Genet, Ionesco, and Mrozek. New York: Grove Press, 1975.

Lamb, Margaret. "Feminist Criticism" (Black Girl). Drama Review 18 (September 1974): 46-50.

Lambert, J. W. "Plays in Performance." Drama 112 (Spring 1974): 22-23.

Lamele, Nina. "'After the Rain'." (Boston) Bay State Banner, 10 July 1975; in Newsbank--Performing Arts, July-August 1975, 53:D 2,3

Larson, Charles R. "African-Afro-American Literary Relations: Basic Parallels: Omnipresent Negritude?" Negro Digest 19 (December 1969): 35-41.

Latour, Martine, ed. "Ntozake Shange: Driven Poet/Playwright; Interview." Mademoiselle 82 (September 1976): 182+.

Laufe, Abe. Anatomy of a Hit. New York: Hawthorn, 1966.

Lazier, Gil. "The Next Stage: Youth Theatre for the Ghetto." Record 69 (February 1968): 465-67.

Leab, Daniel J. "'All-Colored'--But Not Much Different: Films Made for Negro Ghetto Audiences, 1913-1928." Phylon 36 (September 1975): 321-339.

Lee, Dorothy. "Three Black Plays: Alienation and Paths to Recovery." Modern Drama 19 (December 1976): 397-404.

Lee, Maryat. "Street Theatre." In Theatre 4: The American Theatre, 1970-1971, pp. 150-157.

Lemons, J. Stanley. "Black Stereotypes As Reflected in Popular Culture, 1880-1920." American Quarterly 29 (Spring 1977): 102-116.

"Length of Run of American Plays in Paris." In Falb, Lewis W., American Drama in Paris: 1945-1970 (Chapel Hill: University of North Carolina Press, 1973), p. 166.

Leogrande, Ernest. "'Waiting for Mongo' Arrives." New York Daily News, 20 May 1975; in Newsbank--Performing Arts, May-June 1975, 40:E 3.

Lester, James D. Writing Research Papers (Raisin in the Sun). Glenview, Ill.: Scott Foresman, 1976.

Levine, Lawrence W. Black Culture and Black Consciousness. New York: Oxford University Press, 1977.

Lewis, Barbara. "Actress Ethel Ayler" (Eden). (N.Y.) Amsterdam News, 17 July 1976, D-2.

_____. "Black Theatre's Summer Festival of Talent." (N.Y.) Amsterdam News, 7 August, 1976, D-10, 11.

_____. "Black Writers Too Conservative According to Richard Wesley." (N.Y.) Amsterdam News: Arts and Entertainment, 23 July 1977, D-7.

_____. "Mini-Wiz Captivates Riker's Audience." (N.Y.) Amsterdam News: Arts and Entertainment, 30 April 1977, D-5.

_____. "New Lafayette Founder Makes Gold Comeback Bid." (N.Y.) Amsterdam News: Arts and Entertainment, 28 May 1977, D-2.

_____. "The Poet" (Ntozake Shange). Essence 7 (November 1976): 86, 119-20.

_____. "Smyrl and 'On the Goddam Lock-In'." (N.Y.) Amsterdam News, 23 October 1976, D-8.

Lewis, Claude. "Black Theatre (The New Theatre)." Tuesday Magazine (February 1969): 6-8, 10, 23.

Lewis, Theophilus. "'God Is a (Guess What?)'." America 120 (11 January 1969): 50.

_____. "Negro Actors in Dramatic Roles." America 115 (17 September 1966): 298-300.

_____. "Social Protest in 'A Raisin in the Sun'." Catholic World 190 (October 1959): 31-35.

"Lights Up on Black Women" (Emily T). (N.Y.) Amsterdam News, 14 August 1976, D-16.

"Lights Up on Black Women" (Transcendental Blues). (N.Y.) Amsterdam News, 14 August 1976, D-16.

Lindberg, John. "'Dutchman' and 'The Slave': Companions in Revolution." Black Academy Review 2 (Spring-Summer 1971): 101-108.

_____. "'Dutchman' and 'The Slave': Companions in Revolution." In Dr. S. Okechukwu Mezu, ed., Modern Black Literature (Buffalo, N.Y.: Black Academy Press, 1971), pp. 101-7.

Literary Guild of America. Works in Progess, No. 5. New York: Doubleday, 1972.

Littlejohn, David. Black on White: A Critical Survey of Writing by American Negroes. New York: Viking, 1966.

Lloyd, Llana. "Hollywood's 'Hottest' New Black Movie Director" (Monte). Sepia 25 (November 1976): 26-34.

"Lorraine Hansberry: The Black Experience in the Creation of Drama" (Narration by L. Hansberry and Claudia McNeil; excerpts from plays). Films for the Humanities, 16 mm., 35 min.; Video Cassette, F F H 128.

"Lorraine Hansberry's Play Returns a Smash Musical: 'Raisin'." Sepia 23 (April 1974): 32-39.

Los Angeles County. Superintendant of Schools. "Portraits: The Literature of Minorities: An Annotated Bibliography of Literature by and about Four Ethnic Groups in the U.S. for Grades 7-12." Los Angeles, 1970.

Lowery, Raymond. "Old-Fashioned In Some Ways, 'Treemonisha' Has Good Music." (Raleigh, N.C.) News and Observor, 2 May 1976; in Newsbank--Performing Arts, May-June 1976, 41:B 4.

Loynd, Ray. "'Raisin' Opens at the Shubert." Los Angeles Herald Examiner, 23 January 1976; in Newsbank--Performing Arts, January-February 1976, 11:E 9.

Lucas, Bob. "A 'Salt Pork and Collard Greens' TV Show" (Good Times). Ebony 29 (June 1974): 50-53.

_____. "Super Tall Super Sleuth in 'Cleopatra Jones'." Sepia 22 (September 1973): 38-45.

"M L K Players on RCA" (We Heard from Martin). (N.Y.) Amsterdam News: Arts and Entertainment, 14 May 1977, D-15.

McCabe, Jane A., comp. Black Entertainers and the Entertainment Industry. Published by the Indiana University Libraries and Focus: Black America Summer, 1969.

McClintock, Ernie. "Perspective on Black Acting." Black World 23 (May 1974): 79-85.

McElroy, Hilda Njoki. "Books Noted." Black World 24 (April 1975): 51-52, 80-83.

McGinty, Robin. "'... It's About a Sister Who's Been Hurt a Lot'." The Afro-American (Baltimore), 5-9 June 1977, p. 11.

McGraw-Hill Encyclopedia of World Drama. New York: McGraw-Hill, 1972. 4 vols.

Mackay, Barbara. "Black Musical 'Cope' Lights Up Stage." Denver Post, 15 April 1977; in Newsbank--Performing Arts, March-April 1977, 23:G 7.

_____. "Dancer Washington Takes 'Brooklyn Act' Nationwide" (Bubbling Brown Sugar). Denver Post, in Newsbank--Performing Arts, January-February 1977, 10:B 1.

_____. "Off-Beat Off-Broadway Musicals" (Micki Grant). Saturday Review 2 (22 March 1975): 39-40.

_____. "Off-Beat Off-Broadway Musicals" (The Ups and Downs of Theophilus Maitland). Saturday Review 2 (22 March 1975): 40.

_____. "Studies in Black and White." Saturday Review 2 (12 July 1975): 52.

McKenzie, Vashti. "The McKenzie Report 'The Wiz' Was a WOW ... Won Seven Tonys." The Afro American (Baltimore), 22 April 1975; in Newsbank--Performing Arts, March-April 1975, 31:D 12, 13.

_____. "D'Urville Martin, Actor-Producer Came Up 'Hard Way'." The Afro-American: Dawn Magazine (Baltimore), 14 May 1977, pp, 10, 14.

"The McKenzie Report Exclusive AFRO Interview with James Earl Jones." The Afro-American (Baltimore), 4 March 1975; in

Newsbank--Performing Arts, March-April 1975, 29:G 11, 12; 15 March 1975, 29:G 13, 14.

McLellan, J. "Something Splendid, Something New; A Dazzling Magical Opera." Washington Post, 7 September 1975; in Newsbank--Performing Arts, September-October 1975, 67:C 12, 13.

McMorrow, Tom. "Broadway Expects a Championship Season." New York Daily News, 7 September 1975; in Newsbank--Performing Arts, January-February 1975, 68:C 14-D1.

McNally, Owen. "Improvising 'Treemonisha'." Hartford Courant, 25 April 1976; in Newsbank--Performing Arts, March-April 1976, 22: G 7.

McWhirter, W. A. "Parting Shots: After Years of Futility Baldwin Explodes Again." Life 71 (30 July 1971): 63.

Mahoney, John C. "Free Southern Group Performs." Los Angeles Times, 10 December 1975; in Newsbank--Performing Arts, November-December 1975, 85:D 6.

Malitz, Joan. "Joplin Opera Super Entertainment." (Cleveland) Call and Post, 29 October 1975; in Newsbank--Performing Arts, September-October 1975, 67:C 9.

Mancini, Joseph. "Bullins' 'Miss Marie' Brings Cliches to Life." New York Post, 14 March 1975; in Newsbank--Performing Arts, March-April 1975, 29:A 4.

_____. "A Wiz." New York Post, 26 April 1975; in Newsbank--Performing Arts, March-April 1975, 27:A 4, 5.

Mandel, Oscar. "Notes on Ethical Deprivation in the Avant-Garde Drama." Antigonish Review (Nova Scotia) 8 (Winter 1972): 43-48.

Margrave, W. "'Treemonisha': A Crowd Pleaser." Washington Star-News, 5 September 1975; in Newsbank--Performing Arts, September-October 1975, 67:C 11.

Markholt, Otillie. "'Blues for Mister Charlie' Reconsidered: White Critic, Playwright: Water and Fire." Negro Digest 16 (April 1967): 54-60.

Marowitz, Charles; Tom Milne; and Owen Hole. The Encore Reader. New York: Methuen, 1965; New York: DBS Publications, 1971.

Marshall, Herbert, and Mildred Stock. Ira Aldridge--The Negro Tragedian. London: Rockliff, 1958; New York: Macmillan, 1958.

Martin, Sharon Stockard. "Bring It Down Front: The Tanning of Oz--Reflections on the Usurpation of a Myth." Essence 6 (September 1975): 32, 35.

_____. "David Langston Smyrl Is Making It All Real" ("On the Goddamn Lock-In"). Encore 6 (3 January 1977):36.

Marvin X. "The Black Ritual Theatre: An Interview with Robert Macbeth." Black Theatre no. 3 (1969): 20-24.

_____. "Everything's Cool: An Interview with LeRoi Jones." Black Theatre no. 1 (1968): 16-23.

_____. "Manifesto: The Black Educational Theatre of San Francisco." Black Theatre no. 6 (1972): 30-35.

_____. "Reviews: Moon on a Rainbow Shawl." Black Theatre no. 1 (1968): 30-31.

_____, and Faruk. "Islam and Black Art: An Interview with LeRoi Jones." Negro Digest 18 (January 1969): 4-10.

Maslin, Janet. "Home on the Porch" (Part 2, Sounder). Newsweek 88 (8 November 1976): 107-08.

Mason, B. J. "Bring It Down Front: Hollywood's New Bitch Goddess." Essence 5 (September 1974): 28, 109-110.

Massaquoi, Hans I. "Alex Haley: The Man Behind Roots." Ebony 32 (April 1977): 33-41.

Mathews, Les. "That's Showbiz ..." (Comments). (N.Y.) Amsterdam News: Arts and Entertainment, 7 May 1977, D-11.

Matthews, Geraldine O., et al., comps. Black American Writers, 1773-1949: A Bibliography and Union List. Boston: G. K. Hall, 1970.

Maynard, Richard A. The Black Man on Film: Racial Stereotyping. New York: Hayden, 1974.

"Me and Bessie." New York Theatre Critics' Reviews 36 (20 October 1975): 184-87; containing:
    Watt, Douglas, "Linda Sings Bessie Smith," (N.Y.) Daily News, 23 October 1975.
    Barnes, Clive, "'Me and Bessie' Is All Heart and Soul," New York Times, 23 October 1975.
    Gottfried, Martin, "Linda 'and Bessie' Are Special." New York Post, 23 October 1975.
    Wilson, Edwin, "Me and Bessie," Wall Street Journal, 28 October 1975.
    "Broadway Stages Life of Legendary Singer," Christian Science Monitor, 30 October 1975.

Ettore, Barbara, "Me and Bessie," Women's Wear Daily, 23 October 1975.

Sanders, Kevin. "Me and Bessie," WABC-TV, 26 October 1975.

Downs, Joan, "Up Beat Blues," Time (3 November 1975).

Meade, James. "Big Man Brings Elegance Back." San Diego Union, 26 October 1975; in Newsbank--Performing Arts, September-October 1975, 69:C 12.

"The Medal of Honor Rag." New York Theatre Critics' Reviews-- 1976 37 (5 May 1976): 271-274; containing:

Barnes, Clive, "'Medal of Honor Rag' Relives Trauma of Vietnam," New York Times, 29 March 1976.

Gottfried, Martin, "Profile of a Hero," New York Post, 29 March 1976.

Watt, Douglas, "Taut Duel of Wits," Daily News, 29 March 1976.

Kalem, T. E., "Living with Defeat," Time 12 April 1976.

Beaufort, John, Christian Science Monitor, 6 April 1976.

Kissell, Howard, "Medal of Honor Rag," Women's Wear Daily, 29 March 1976.

Wilson, Edwin, "The Personal Anguish of Vietnam," Wall Street Journal, 31 March 1976.

Probst, Leonard, "Medal of Honor Rag," NBC, 29 March 1976.

Melchinger, Siegfried. The Concise Encyclopedia of Modern Drama. New York: Horizon, 1964.

Menchise, Don N. "LeRoi Jones and a Case of Shifting Identities." CLA Journal 20 (December 1976): 232-34.

Mendelson, Phyllis Carmel, and Dedria Bryfonski, eds. Contemporary Literary Criticism, vol. 7. Detroit: Gale Research, 1977.

Meserve, Walter J. "Black Drama." In Albert J. Robbins, American Literary Scholarship--1970 (Durham, N.C.: Duke University Press, 1972), pp. 343-344.

_____. "Black Drama." In Albert J. Robbins, American Literary Scholarship: 1972 (Durham, N.C.: Duke University, 1974), pp. 368-369.

_____. "Black Drama." In James Woodress, ed., American Literary Scholarship: 1973 (Durham, N.C.: Duke University Press, 1975), pp. 380-381.

Mezu, Dr. S. Okechukwu, ed. Modern Black Literature. Buffalo, N.Y.: Black Academy Press, 1971.

Michelman, Frederic. "American and African Blacks: A Review of

Alain Ricard's Théâtre et Nationalisme: Wole Soyinka et Leroi Jones." Negro American Literature Forum 8 (Winter 1974): 282-283.

Michelson, Herb. "'Heavy' Stuff, Without Any Weight." Sacramento Bee, 19 June 1976; in Newsbank--Performing Arts, May-June 1976, 40:E 3.

_____. "'Raisin' Has Problems--Songs, Stage." Sacramento Bee, 6 March 1976, in Newsbank--Performing Arts, March-April 1976, 27:E 9.

Micklin, Bob. "'Treemonisha' Makes a Disappointment." Newsday (Long Island, N.Y.), 22 October 1975, n. p.

Mikell, C. A. "Hollywood and Black Women--The Way We Were." Mademoiselle 82 (November 1976): 62+.

Miller, Adam David. "A Report from San Francisco." Black Theatre no. 1 (1968): 3.

Miller, Barter R. "'A Mere Poem': 'Daybreak in Alabama,' A Resolution of Langston Hughes's Theme of Music and Art." Obsidian 2 (Summer 1976): 30-37.

Miller, Edwin. "From the Heart: Actresses Sally Struthers, Cicely Tyson Let It All Out." Seventeen 32 (February 1973): 106-07.

Miller, Jeanne-Marie A. "Annual Round-up: Black Theater in America--Washington, D.C." Black World 24 (April 1975): 34-38.

_____. "Annual Round-up: Black Theater in America--Washington, D.C." Black World 25 (April 1976): 83-86.

_____. "'Can't Cope'--Soft, Biting." San Francisco Examiner, 16 June 1976; in Newsbank--Performing Arts, May-June 1976, 40:E 2.

_____. "Images of Black Women in Plays by Black Playwrights." CLA Journal 20 (June 1977): 498-507.

Miller, Jordon Y. "Black Theatre." In James Woodress, ed., American Literary Scholarship: 1974 (Durham, N.C.: Duke University Press, 1976), p. 385.

"Millie Brown." Chicago Daily Defender, 23 June 1977, p. 17.

Mills, James. "Bonfils' Satire 'Purlie' No Pearl with Its Dated Material." Denver Post, 9 January 1976; in Newsbank--Performing Arts, January-February 1976, 11:E 7.

_____. "'Raisin' Can't Match Old Play's Wrinkles." Denver

Post, 18 March 1976; in Newsbank--Performing Arts, March-April 1976, 27:E 11.

Mills, Jon, II. "Bring It Down Front: Blackness in Televisionland." Essence 6 (April 1976): 15.

Milner, Arthur. "Live from the Library" (Joplin). American Libraries 8 (February 1977): 75-76.

Mitchell, Loften. "Black Theatre: Then and Now." (N.Y.) Amsterdam News: Black Academy of Arts and Letters Supplement, 18 September 1971, pp. D-11, 12.

_____. "The Negro in the American Theatre." In Hartnoll, The Oxford Companion to the Theatre, 3rd ed., pp. 679-81.

_____. Voices of the Black Theatre. Clifton, N.J.: James T. White and Co., 1975.

"Mixed Blood Theatre Co. --'Mother April's'." Twin Cities Courier (Minneapolis/St. Paul), 4 August 1977, p. 2.

"Mixed Blood Theatre Co. Opens Summer Session" (To Be Young, Gifted and Black). Minneapolis Spokesman, 30 June 1977, p. 6.

Molette, Barbara. "Black Women Playwrights. They Speak: Who Listens?" Black World 25 (April 1976): 28-34.

_____. "The First Afro-American Theatre." Black World 19 (April 1970): 4.

_____. "Manifesto for a Revolutionary Theatre." Encore 12 (1969): 44.

_____. "Our Theatre: Los Angeles." Encore 12 (1969): 55.

Monroe, Arthur. "Festac 77--The Second World Black and African Festival of Arts and Culture: Lagos, Nigeria." Black Scholar 9 (September 1977): 34-37.

Moore, Bob. "D'Urville Martin: Actor, Producer, Angry Black Man." Sepia 22 (October 1973): 69-80.

Moore, Honor, ed. The New Women's Theatre: 10 Plays by Contemporary Women. New York: Vintage, 1977.

_____. "Theatre Will Never Be the Same." Ms. 6 (December 1977): 36-39, 74-75.

Moore, Jacqueline. "Alice C. Browning: Realizes Deferred Writing Dream." Chicago Daily Defender: Joy, 20 June 1977, p. 11.

Moore, Marie. "Weeksville United Actors, Co., An Alternative

Education." (N.Y.) Amsterdam News, 23 October 1976, D-10, 11.

Mootz, William. "'Don't Bother Me' Is Black, Bold, and Brilliant." (Louisville) Courier-Journal, 8 October 1975; in Newsbank--Performing Arts, September-October 1975, 66:G 14.

Morgan, Geri. "Haley Wins Harlemites in Speech on Roots." (N.Y.) Amsterdam News: New Horizons, 5 February 1977, D-9.

Morris, Al. "Livin' Is a Hard Way to Die." (N.Y.) Amsterdam News: Arts and Entertainment, 16 July 1977, D-5.

Morrow, Lance. "Black People's Time" (The Great MacDaddy). Time 103 (25 February 1974): 69.

_____. "Ghetto Chayefsky" (Milner). Time 103 (25 February 1974): 69.

Morrow, Tom. "Broadway Expects a Championship Season." New York Daily News, 7 September 1975; in Newsbank--Performing Arts, September-October 1975, 68:C 14; 68:D 1, 2.

Moser, Norman. "A Revolutionary Art: LeRoi Jones, Ed Bullins, and the Black Revolution." December 12 (1970): 180-190.

Moses, Gilbert. "Hubert Humphrey Is to Politics...." In Theatre 2: The American Theatre, 1968-1969 (New York: International Theatre Institute of the United States, 1970), pp. 108-113.

_____. "Theatre Piece in Seven Moods." In Theatre 4: The American Theatre, 1970-1971 (New York: Scribner's, 1972), pp. 112-115.

Moss, Robert F. "The Arts in Black America." Saturday Review 3 (15 November 1975): 12-19.

_____. "Four Portraits: Douglas Turner Ward." Saturday Review 3 (15 November 1975): 18.

"Movies" (The Education of Sonny Carson). New Times 3 (8 August 1974): 62-63.

"Movies" (The Education of Sonny Carson [Mwina Imiri Abubadika]). Playboy 21 (October 1974): 26.

"Movies" (River Niger). Playboy 23 (June 1976): 34, 36.

"Movies" (Wesley). New Times 3 (12 July 1974): 63.

Munro, C. Lynn. "LeRoi Jones: A Man in Transition." CLA Journal 17 (September 1973): 57-78.

Murphy, Frederick D. "Melba Moore's Mystical, Magical Music" (Purlie). Encore 6 (7 February 1977): 32-33.

Murphy, Gloria Sewell. "Annual Round-up: Black Theater in America--San Francisco-Oakland Bay Area." Black World 25 (April 1976): 89-94.

Murphy, Ray. "Black Repertory Stages 'River Niger'." Boston Globe, 13 February 1976; in Newsbank--Performing Arts, January-February 1976, 15:A 6.

_____. "Play Celebrates Crispus Attucks." Boston Globe, 13 March 1976; in Newsbank--Performing Arts, March-April 1976, 32:D 8.

Murray, James P. "Blacks Invade Broadway in a Big Way ... With Soul, Cheers and Society Bows." St. Louis Argus, 17 April 1975; in Newsbank--Performing Arts, March-April 1975, 28:D 8, 9, 10.

_____. "Broadway Show Is ... on the Road with A." (N.Y.) Amsterdam News, 20 August 1975; in Newsbank--Performing Arts, September-October 1975, 71D

_____. "Running with Sweetback." Black Creation 3 (Fall 1971): 10 12.

_____. To Find An Image: Black Films from Uncle Tom to Superfly. Indianapolis: Bobbs-Merrill, 1974.

"'Music Magic' Opens at Billie Holiday." (N.Y.) Amsterdam News, 20 November 1976, D-9.

"My Sister! My Sister" (review). Milwaukee Journal, 25 April 1976, 2:14.

Myers, Walter Dean. "Gordon Parks: John Henry with a Camera." Black Scholar 7 (January-February 1976): 27-30.

"NBT 'Soljourney' Embarks August 12." (N.Y.) Amsterdam News, 14 August 1976, D-14.

Nachman, Gerald. "Who's Afraid of the Broadway Critics?" More 7 (July/August 1977): 18-22.

Nascimento, Abdias Do. "The Negro Theatre in Brazil." In Dr. S. Okechukwu Mezu, ed., Modern Black Literature (Buffalo, N.Y.: Black Academy Press, 1971), pp. 157-175.

National Black Theatre. "We Are Liberators Not Actors" (Interview-- B. A. Teer). Essence 1 (March 1971): 56-59.

"Negro Theatre at the Theatre of Nations." World Theatre 9 (Winter 1960): 344-351.

Nellhous, Arlynn. "Robert Nemiroff and Lorraine Hansberry." In Nykoruk, Barbara, ed., Authors in the News, vol. 2. (Detroit: Gale Research, 1976), p. 211.

Nelson, Natalie. More Things That Happen to Us: A Children's Play. New York: New Dimensions, 1970.

_____. Things That Happen to Us: A Children's Play. New York: New Dimensions, 1970.

Nesbitt, George B. "W. E. B. DuBois: An Apostle of Blackness." Crisis 79 (June-July 1972): 194-197.

Ness, David E. "Review: 'Les Blancs'." Freedomways 12 (3rd quarter 1972): 245-248.

Neville, John. "Theatre 3 'Purlie' Is a Joy." Dallas Morning News, 19 April 1975; in Newsbank--Performing Arts, March-April 1975, 26:G 8.

"New ACTF Award." Theatre News 8 (May 1976): 9.

"New Bread Theatre Producer." The Afro-American (Baltimore), 12-16 April 1977, p. 11.

"New Bubbling Brown Sugar." The Afro-American (Baltimore), 26-30 April 1977, p. 11.

Newman, Jill. "The Player's the Thing at Clay Stevenson's Players Workshop." Encore 6 (21 February 1977): 35-36, 39.

Nicholas, Denise. "Blacks in Television." Black World 25 (April 1976): 36-42.

Nicholas, Xavier, and Addison Gayle, Jr. "Two Views of ... 'Winesellers'...." Black World 25 (April 1976): 95-97.

No Crystal Stair: A Bibliography of Black Literature. New York Public Library, Office of Adult Services, 1971.

Norman, Shirley. "Television's First Mixed Marriage." Sepia 25 (December 1976): 66-78.

Novick, Julius. "In Search of the New Consensus" (The Wiz). Saturday Review 3 (3 April 1976): 42.

_____. "A Man for All Reasons" (Milner). Village Voice 22 (1 August 1977): 63.

_____. "Old Legend, New Version" (The Great MacDaddy).

Village Voice 19 (21 February 1974): 55.

"Ntozake Shange: Interview." New Yorker 52 (2 August 1976): 17-19.

"Ntozake Shange Interviews Herself." Ms. 6 (December 1977): 34-35, 70, 72.

Nykoruk, Barbara, ed. Authors in the News, vols. 1, 2. Detroit: Gale Research, 1976.

O'Brien, John, ed. Interviews with Black Writers. New York: Liveright, 1974.

O'Connor, John J. "TV's Venturesome 'Visions'." New York Times, 6 October 1977, C: 26.

Odubato, Robert. "A History of the Negro Units of Federal Theatre (WPA) in New York City and New Jersey from 1935-1939." Ph.D. Dissertation, New York University, 1977.

Ognibene, E. R. "Black Literature Revisited: Sonny's Blues." English Journal 60 (January 1971): 36-37.

Ogunbiyi, Yemi. "New Black Playwrights in America, 1960-1975." Ph.D. Dissertation, New York University, 1976.

O'Haire, P. "Bullins: A Philadelphia Story." New York Daily News, 7 June 1975; in Newsbank--Performing Arts, May-June 1975, 39:G 8.

_____. "One Man's Family History." New York Daily News, 9 April 1976; in Newsbank--Performing Arts, March-April 1976, 30:1 C.

_____. "White Lightning in Harlem." New York Daily News, 11 March 1976; in Newsbank--Performing Arts, March-April 1976, 28:B 8.

O'Hara, Frank Hurburt, and Marqueritte Harmon Bro. Invitation to the Theatre. New York: Harper, 1951.

Okpaku, Joseph O. New African Literature and the Arts, 3 vols. New York: Third Press, 1974.

Oliver, Edith. "The Comic View: Performance of R. McIver's 'God Is a (Guess What?)' by Negro Ensemble Company." New Yorker 44 (28 December 1968): 50-51.

_____. "In New England Winter'." New Yorker 46 (6 February 1971): 72.

_____. "Off Broadway: At Home with the Edwardses" (The First Breeze of Summer). New Yorker 51 (17 March 1975): 94-95.

_____. _____ (Baraka and Dean). New Yorker 48 (10 February 1973): 75.

_____. _____ (Black Girl). New Yorker 47 (26 June 1971): 76.

_____. _____: Twice Hail (Black Terror). New Yorker 47 (20 November 1971): 114, 119-20.

_____. _____ (Black Visions; Harris, Sanchez, Wesley). New Yorker 48 (8 April 1972): 97-99.

_____. _____ 'The Breakout'. New Yorker 51 (12 May 1975): 109.

_____. _____ (The Brownsville Raid). New Yorker 52 (20 December 1976): 84.

_____. _____: Change and Decay in All Around I See. New Yorker 52 (25 October 1976): 61-62, 64.

_____. _____ (Charles Fuller). New Yorker 50 (17 June 1974): 84.

_____. _____ (Contribution). New Yorker 45 (12 April 1969): 131.

_____. _____ (Daddy). New Yorker 53 (20 June 1977): 89.

_____. _____ (Davis and White). New Yorker 50 (April 1974): 52.

_____. _____ (Defense). New Yorker 52 (22 November 1976): 110-11.

_____. _____ (The Duplex). New Yorker 48 (18 March 1972): 85.

_____. _____ (Every Night When the Sun Goes Down). New Yorker 52 (1 March 1976): 77-79.

_____. _____ (Going Thru the Changes and The Past Is the Past). New Yorker 49 (28 January 1974): 69.

_____. _____: Happy Day Is Here Again (Brotherhood and Day of Absence). New Yorker 46 (28 March 1970): 84-88.

_____. _____: A Hard Night's Sleep (Goin' a Buffalo). New Yorker 48 (4 March 1972): 83.

_____. _____ : Hero (The Medal of Honor Rag). New Yorker 52 (12 April 1976): 101-102.

_____. _____ (Home Boy). New Yorker 52 (11 October 1976): 81.

_____. _____ (I Am Lucy Terry). New Yorker 52 (23 February 1976): 82, 84.

_____. _____ (In the Deepest Part of Sleep). New Yorker 50 (17 June 1974): 84.

_____. _____ : Superior Vintage (In the Wine Time). New Yorker 52 (10 May 1976): 104-105.

_____. _____ (Jo Anne). New Yorker 52 (25 October 1976): 62+.

_____. _____ : Joan of Washington Square (El Hajj Malik). New Yorker 47 (11 December 1971): 101-102.

_____. _____ (The Last Street Play). New Yorker 53 (30 May 1977): 84-87.

_____. _____ (Les Femmes Noires). New Yorker 50 (1 April 1974): 52.

_____. _____ (Liberty Call). New Yorker 51 (12 May 1975): 109.

_____. _____ : Life on the Edge (Neil Harris). New Yorker 52 (7 June 1976): 79-80.

_____. _____ (Malcochon). New Yorker 45 (12 April 1969): 131.

_____. _____ : The Newark Story. New Yorker 50 (27 May 1974): 64-66.

_____. _____ : O Bold New Prospero (The Great MacDaddy). New Yorker 50 (25 February 1974): 83-85.

_____. _____ (On the Lock-In). New Yorker 53 (9 May 1977): 59.

_____. _____ (Oyamo). New Yorker 51 (12 May 1975): 109.

_____. _____ (The Past Is the Past). New Yorker 51 (12 May 1975): 109.

_____. _____ : Portrait of the Artist as a Young Husband (The Last Street Play). New Yorker 53 (30 May 1977): 84, 86-87.

_____. _____ (A Recent Killing). New Yorker 48 (10 February 1973): 75.

_____. _____: Rejoice. New Yorker 46 (30 May 1970): 70-73.

_____. _____'s Revue by Voices, Inc.: 'The Believers'. New Yorker 44 (May 1968): 75.

_____. _____: The Seamstress and the Baker (The Wedding Band). New Yorker 48 (4 November 1972): 105, 106, 108.

_____. _____ (Sister Son/ji). New Yorker 48 (8 April 1972): 97-99.

_____. _____ (Square Root of Soul). New Yorker 53 (27 June 1977): 54.

_____. _____ (The Sty of the Blind Pig). New Yorker 47 (4 December 1971): 131.

_____. _____: Three to Get Ready (Carter, Gaines, Johnson). New Yorker 50 (22 April 1974): 103-04.

_____. _____: Twice Hail. New Yorker 47 (20 November 1971): [114,] 119-120.

_____. "Report from 137th Street." In Theatre 5: The American Theatre, 1971-1972. New York: Scribner's, 1973, pp. 129-133.

_____. "'String'." New Yorker 45 (12 April 1969): 131.

Olivia, L. J. "Ira Aldridge and Theophile Gautier." Journal of Negro History 48 (July 1963): 229-231.

"On the Lock-In." New York Theatre Critics' Reviews 38 (5 September 1977): 225-227; containing:
    Watt, Douglas, "With This, Even Audience Does Time," (N.Y.) Daily News, 28 April 1977.
    Gussow, Mel, "Stage: Musical Inmates with Dream," New York Times, 28 April 1977.
    Ettore, Barbara, "On--'the Lock-In'" [sic], Women's Wear Daily, 28 April 1977.
    Gottfried, Martin, "'Lock-In' Pleasant Due to Good Vibes," New York Post, 28 April 1977.
    Beaufort, John, "On the Lock-In," Christian Science Monitor, 28 April 1977.
    Lape, Bob, "On the Lock-In," WABC-TV, 27 April 1977.

O'Neal, Mary. "Tricked by Flicks" (Blaxploitation Movies). Essence 5 (October 1974): 17.

O'Neal, Regina. And Then the Harvest: Three Television Plays. Detroit: Broadside Press, n.d.

"Opera Named from Medgar Evers Words Praised." Jet (21 May 1970): 54-55.

"Opera--South's 'Jubilee' Played Before Sell-Out Audience." The Afro-American (Baltimore), 30 November-4 December 1976, p. 6.

Orman, Roscoe. "The New Lafayette Theatre." Black Theatre no. 5 (1971): 12-13.

Osborne, Eddie. "Miami's Theatre of Afro Arts." Black Creation 4 (Summer 1973): 38-39.

Osborne, Gwendolyn E. "Report from Aisle C: 'Bubbling Brown Sugar'." Crisis 84 (January 1977): 34.

"Oscar Brown, Jr. Home Again a Stronger Man." Chicago Daily News, 25 January 1975; in Newsbank--Performing Arts, January-February 1975, 13:C 1, 2.

"Ossie Davis Quits 'Cotton' Sequel; Mark Warren Takes Over." Jet (3 February 1972): 60.

"'Out of Site': Review." Black Theatre no. 4 (April 1970): 28-31.

Owens, Rochelle, ed. Spontaneous Combustion: Eight New American Plays. New York: Winter House, 1972.

Pacheco, Patrick. "'Bubbling Brown Sugar'." After Dark 9 (May 1976): 58-63.

Pantovic, Stan. "The Making of a Black Movie." Sepia 22 (December 1973): 54-62.

Papier, Deboran. "'Dreams' a Tribute to Two Poets" (L. Hughes and G. Brooks). Washington Star-News, 30 September 1975; in Newsbank--Performing Arts, September-October 1975, 66: C 9.

Parker, John, comp. Who's Who In the Theatre, 15th ed. London: Pitman & Sons, 1972.

Parks, Carole A. "The National Black Writers Convention." Black World 24 (January 1975): 86-92.

_____. "Perspectives: J. E. Franklin, Playwright." Black World 21 (April 1972): 49-50.

"Parks: Success by Fright." In Nykoruk, Barbara, ed., Authors in the News, vol. 2 (Detroit: Gale Research, 1976), p. 215.

Parone, Ed., ed. Collision Course. New York: Random House, 1968.

Pasquarillo, Nicholas. "Oscar Williams." Action 9 (September-October 1974): 18-21.

Patterson, Lindsay, ed. Anthology of the American Negro in the Theatre. Washington, D.C.: Associated Negro Universities Press, 1967.

_____. Black Films and Film-Makers: A Comprehensive Anthology from Stereotype to Superhero. New York: Dodd, Mead, 1975.

_____. "Black Theatre: The Search Goes On." Freedomways (3rd Quarter 1974): 242-46.

_____. "The Negro in the Performing Arts." In Patricia W. Romero, ed., Black America 1968: The Year of Awakening (Washington, D.C.: United Publishing Co., 1969), pp. 304-315.

_____. "New Home, New Troupe, New Play: 'In the Wine Time' on Off Broadway Theatre" [reprint], Negro History Bulletin 32 (April 1969): 18-19.

_____. "On the Aisle--Focus on Clarence Muse." Essence 7 (April 1977): 17, 103.

Pawley, Thomas D. "Dunbar As Playwright." Black World 26 (April 1975): 70-79.

Peel, Marie. "Power and Pattern v Morality 1: Poetry and Drama." Books and Bookmen 18 (October 1972): 38-42 (Part 1).

Peeples, Kenneth. "Baraka Dramatizes Senate Bill." (N.Y.) Amsterdam News, 14 August 1976, D-7.

Pennington-Jones, Paulette. "From Brother LeRoi Jones Through 'The System of Dante's Hell' to Imamu Ameer Baraka." Journal of Black Studies 4 (December 1973): 195-214.

Perkins, Hull D. "Wallace Thurman: Renaissance 'Renegade'?" Black World 25 (February 1976): 29-35.

Perrier. Paulette. "Review: The Black Magicians." Black Theatre no. 5 (1971): 51-52.

_____. "The Yard Theatre: Jamaica." Black Theatre no. 5 (1971): 9-10.

Peters, Ida. "'First Breeze of Summer' Unlocks Family--Leslie Lee ... the Playwrights." The Afro-American (Baltimore), 22-26 March 1977, p. 11.

_____. "King of Ragtime (Eubie Blake)." The Afro-American (Baltimore), 12-16 July 1977, p. 11.

_____. "Welcome Home Avon Long." The Afro-American (Baltimore), 28 June-2 July 1977, p. 11.

Peterson, Bernard L., Jr. "An Evaluation, Willis Richardson: Pioneer Playwright." Black World 24 (April 1975): 40-48, 86-88.

_____. "Shirley Graham DuBois: Composer and Playwright." The Crisis 84 (May 1977): 177-179.

_____. "Willis Richardson: Pioneer Playwright." Black World 26 (April 1975): 40-48, 86-88.

Peterson, Maurice. "Being About Ossie Davis." Essence 3 (February 1973): 20.

_____. "Black Imagery on the Silver Screen." Essence 3 (December 1972): 34.

_____. "Gilbert Moses: Repaving the Yellow Brick Road." Essence 5 (December 1974): 26.

_____. "Movies: Movies That Hit Home and Strike Out." Essence 5 (November 1974): 19.

_____. _____: They're Just in for Laughs (Uptown Saturday Night). Essence 5 (October 1974): 12.

_____. _____: Willie Dynamite, Blazing Saddles and Others (Purlie). Essence 5 (May 1974): 16.

_____. "On the Aisle: 'Bubbling Brown Sugar'." Essence 6 (January 1976): 28.

_____. _____ (Ceremonies in Dark Old Men). Essence 5 (January 1975): 25.

_____. _____ Part II: Deltas Go Hollywood. Essence 6 (May 1975): 30, 32, 77.

_____. _____ (Divine Comedy). Essence 8 (May 1977): 14.

_____. _____ (Dodson). Essence 8 (May 1977): 14.

_____. _____ (The Education of Sonny Carson and Raisin in the Sun). Essence 5 (November 1974): 19.

_____. _____: Focus on Avon Long. Essence 6 (January 1976): 28.

_____. _____: Focus on Marge Eliot. Essence 6 (May 1975): 12.

_____. _____ (For Colored Girls ...). Essence 7 (October 1976): 48.

_____. _____ (Hopkins). Essence 6 (February 1976): 31.

_____. _____ (The Long Night). Essence 7 (July 1976): 7.

_____. _____: New Place for Black Faces. Essence 7 (September 1976): 18.

_____. _____: Spotlight on Barbara Ann Teer. Essence 6 (August 1975): 19.

_____. _____: Spotlight on Betty Allen. Essence 6 (February 1976): 31.

_____. _____: Spotlight on Dianne oyama Dixon. Essence 7 (November 1975): 39.

_____. _____: Spotlight on Leslie Lee. Essence 6 (October 1975): 9.

_____. _____: Spotlight on Linda Hopkins. Essence 7 (June 1976): 45.

_____. _____: Spotlight on Stephanie Mills. Essence 6 (April 1976): 8.

_____. _____: Spotlight on Vinette Carroll. Essence 7 (March 1977): 8.

_____. _____ (The Taking of Miss Janie). Essence 6 (July 1975): 19.

_____. _____: Theater and Film (Walker and Aranha). Essence 5 (September 1974): 24.

_____. _____: Theater and Film (What the Winesellers Buy). Essence 5 (September 1974): 24.

_____. "On the Road with The Winesellers." Essence 6 (November 1975): 66-67, 84+.

_____. "Rising Stars." Essence 7 (December 1976): 52-53, 78+.

_____. "Taking Off with Joseph Walker." Essence 4 (April 1974): 54+.

_____. "Today's Films: For Reel or Reality." Essence 5 (July 1974): 25.

_____. "The Wiz's Wizzes: Ken Harper and Geoffrey Holder." Essence 6 (September 1975): 54-5, 83-4, 87.

Pettit, Paul B. "The Important American Dramatic Types to 1900. A Study of the Yankee, Negro, Indian and Frontiersman." Ph.D. Dissertation, English Dept., Cornell University, 1949.

Philp, Richard. "'Bubbling Brown Sugar'." Dance Magazine 50 (June 1976): 45-46.

_____. "Revivals" (Your Arms Too Short to Box with God). Dance Magazine 51 (May 1977): 36-40.

Pitts, Ethel Louise. "The American Negro Theatre: 1940-1949." Ph.D. Dissertation, University of Missouri--Columbia, 1975.

"Playboy After Hours--Movies: Leadbelly." Playboy 23 (March 1976): 22-24.

"[Black] Playwright Lab." Twin Cities Courier (Minneapolis), 14 July 1977, p. 2.

"Playwright's Conference Spotlights 12 New Dramas" (G. R. Point). (N.Y.) Amsterdam News, 14 August 1976, D-14.

Ploski, Harry A., and Warren Marr, II, eds./comps. The Negro Almanac: The Afro-American 1776 Bicentennial Edition--1976. New York: Bellwether, 1976.

Poag, Thomas E. "The First Negro Characters in American Drama and Theatre." Encore 17 (1974): 19-23.

"The Poison Tree." Facts on File. 1976, 1-8, 1014B 3.

_____. New York Theatre Critics' Reviews 37 (12 January 1976): 394-97; containing:
    Watt, Douglas, "Undigested Prison Thriller," (N.Y.) Daily News, 9 January 1976.
    Barnes, Clive, "'Poison Tree' Portrays Men in Cages," New York Times, 9 January 1976.
    Kissell, Howard, "The Poison Tree," Women's Wear Daily, 9 January 1976.
    Kroll, Jack, "Locking the Door," Newsweek (19 January 1976).
    Gottfried, Martin, "Ribman Out on a Limb," New York Post, 9 January 1976.
    Beaufort, John, "The Poison Tree," Christian Science Monitor, 16 January 1976.
    Probst, Leonard, "The Poison Tree," NBC, 8 January 1976.
    Sanders, Kevin. "The Poison Tree," WABC-TV, 8 January 1976.

Poland, Gilbert, and Bruce Mailman, eds. The Off Off Broadway Book. New York: Bobbs-Merrill, 1972.

Pollack, Joe. "'Bubbling Brown Sugar' Opens at American." St. Louis Post-Dispatch, 5 January 1977; in Newsbank--Performing Arts, January-February 1977, 10:B 8.

Porter, Curtiss E. "This Here Child Is Naked and Free as a Bird." Black Lines 2 (Spring 1973): 22-31, 34-45.

Potter, Vilma. "Baldwin and Odets: The High Cost of 'Crossing'." California English Journal I (1965): 37-41.

_____. "New Politics, New Mothers in Black Drama." CLA Journal 16 (December 1972): 247-255.

Poussaint, Alvin F. "Blaxploitation Movies: Cheap Thrills That Degrade Blacks." Psychology Today 7 (February 1974): 22+.

Powell, Charles. "Bibliography--Studies in Afro-American Literature." Obsidian 1 (Winter 1975): 100-127.

Powers, Ann, ed. Blacks in American Movies: A Selected Bibliography. Metuchen, N.J.: Scarecrow Press, 1974.

Proffer, Carl R., ed. and trans. Soviet Criticism of American Literature in the Sixties. Ann Arbor, Mich.: Ardis, 1972.

"Profile of Four Black Women Renewing Experience." (Little Rock) Arkansas Gazette, 22 March 1976; in Newsbank--Performing Arts, March-April 1976, 29:D 11, 12.

"'Purlie': Spirited Good Fun." Washington Post, 5 June 1975; in Newsbank--Performing Arts, May-June 1975, 38:F 10.

Pyatt, Richard I. "Will Moses Gunn Shoot Down Father Time?" Encore 6 (3 January 1977): 29.

"Queen of the B's: Pam Grier." Newsweek 87 (2 February 1976): 67.

Quick, Paula N. "Black Theatre." Black Creation 2 (April 1971): 54.

Quinn, Arthur Hobson. A History of the American Drama. New York: Harper, 1927.

Radford-Hill, Sheila. "The Role of Drama Criticism." First World 1 (May-June 1977): 48-49.

Raidy, William A. "'Bubbling Brown Sugar' Pure Joy." Long

Island (N.Y.) Press, 3 March 1976; in Newsbank--Performing Arts, March-April 1976, 28:B 2.

_____. "'Eden': Riveting Theater." Long Island (N.Y.) Press, 4 March 1976; in Newsbank--Performing Arts, March-April 1976, 30:C 2.

_____. "Linda Hopkins." (Newark, N.J.) Star-Ledger, 23 November 1975; in Newsbank--Performing Arts, November-December 1975, 83:B 1.

Raines, Robert A., ed. Modern Drama and Social Change. Englewood Cliffs, N.J.: Prentice-Hall, 1972.

"'Raisin' Is Exciting Theatre Experience." Seattle Times, 23 March 1977; in Newsbank--Performing Arts, March-April 1977, 23:F 7.

Rambeau, David. "Concept East and the Struggle Against Racism." Negro Digest 16 (April 1967): 22-27ff.

Rampersak, Arnold. The Art and Imagination of W. E. B. Du Bois. Cambridge, Mass.: Harvard University Press, 1977.

Ramsey, Alvin. "Through a Glass Whitely: The Televised Rape of 'Miss Jane Pittman'." Black World 23 (August 1974): 31-36.

Ray, David, and Robert M. Farnsworth, eds. Richard Wright: Impressions and Perspectives. Ann Arbor: University of Michigan Press, 1974.

Reavy, Charles D. "Myth, Magic, and Manhood in LeRoi Jones" (Madheart). Studies in Black Literature 1 (Summer 1970): 12-20.

Redding, Saunders. "The Black Arts Movement: A Modest Dissent." Crisis 84 (February 1977): 50-52.

Redmond, Eugene. "The Black Scholar Reviews: 'And Still I Rise' by Maya Angelou." Black Scholar 8 (September 1976): 50-51.

_____. "A Review of Maya Angelou's 'And Still I Rise'." 83 Crisis (September 1976): 50-51.

Reed, Ishmael. "Ishmael Reed on Ishmael Reed." Black World 23 (June 1974): 20-34.

_____. The Yardbird Reader, vol. 4, Berkeley, Calif.: Yardbird, 1975; and vol. 5, 1976.

Reed, Rex. "Vogue-Rated Tip-Offs" (Leadbelly). Vogue 166 (January 1976): 33.

Rehin, G. F. "Darker Image: American Negro Minstrelsy Through the Historian's Lens." Journal of American Studies 9 (December 1975): 365-73.

Reilly, John M. "Jean Toomer: An Annotated Checklist of Criticism." Resources for American Literary Study 4 (Spring 1974): 27-54.

Rendle, A. "Review: 'Electronic Nigger' and Other Plays." Drama 157 (Winter 1970): 70.

"Review: 'Cinderella Everafter'." (N.Y.) Amsterdam News: Arts and Entertainment, 7 May 1977, D-5.

"Review: 'Come Laugh and Cry with Langston Hughes'." (N.Y.) Amsterdam News: New Horizons, 5 February 1977, D-10.

"Review: Ed Bullins. 'The New Lafayette Theatre Presents'." Booklist 70 (15 March 1974): 769-70.

"Review: Ed Bullins. 'The New Lafayette Theatre Presents'." Choice 11 (May 1974): 436.

"Review: Ed Bullins. 'The New Lafayette Theatre Presents'." Book World 24 (April 1975): 51.

"Review: Ed Bullins. 'The New Lafayette Theatre Presents'." Publishers Weekly 204 (17 December 1973): 39.

"Review: Ed Bullins. 'The Theme Is Blackness: "The Corner" and Other Plays'." Book List 69 (15 April 1973): 787.

"Review: Ed Bullins. 'The Theme Is Blackness: "The Corner" and Other Plays'." Choice 10 (May 1973): 452.

"Review: 'Treemonisha'." New York Review of Books 22 (22 January 1976): 34+.

"'Revolution of Reform' Ongoing at Camden's Black Community Theatre." Philadelphia Tribune, 22 June 1976; in Newsbank-- Performing Arts, May-June 1976, 41:F 13.

Ribowsky, Mark. "'Father' of the Black Theater Boom." Sepia, 25 (November 1976): 66-78.

_____. "Is Ben Vereen Finally Ready to Become a Superstar?" Sepia 26 (April 1977): 46-54.

_____. "A Poetess Scores a Hit with 'What's Wrong with Black Men'." Sepia 25 (December 1976): 42-46.

Ricard, Alain. Théâtre et nationalisme: Wole Soyinka et Leroi Jones. Paris: Présence Africaine, 1972.

Rich, Alan. "Broadway's Senior Musicals--A Tourist's Guide." New York 10 (27 June 1977): 114.

_____. "'Bubbling Brown Sugar'." New York 9 (22 March 1976): 64-66.

_____. "For Audiences of Any Color When 'Rex' Is Not Enuf." New York 9 (14 June 1976): 62.

_____. "The King and Almost Everybody Else." New York 10 (11 July 1977): 77-78.

_____. "Singers Sweet, Singers Sour." New York 8 (10 November 1975): 84.

_____. "Theatre: A Coal Barge Named Desire" (The Great MacDaddy). New York 10 (2 May 1977): 68-69.

_____. "Why Did They Do It on the Road?" (Bubbling Brown Sugar). New York 9 (22 March 1976): 64-66.

Richards, David. "ACTF--Virtues in Brass." Washington Star-News, 13 April 1976; in Newsbank--Performing Arts, March-April 1976, 29:F 5.

_____. "'Brown Sugar' is Sweeter." Washington Star-News, 21 January 1976; in Newsbank--Performing Arts, January-February 1976, 12:A 10.

_____. "James Earl Jones Gets the Classic Roles by Default." Washington Star-News, 2 March 1975; in Newsbank--Performing Arts, March-April 1975, 30:A 1.

_____. "James Earl Jones Shows Us What 'Larger than Life' Means." Washington Star-News, 13 March 1975; in Newsbank--Performing Arts, March-April 1975, 31:B 5, 6.

_____. "'The Medal of Honor's' Psychological Burden." Washington Star-News, 26 January 1976; in Newsbank--Performing Arts, January-February 1976, 13:C 12.

_____. "'Midnight Special' a Slice of Grimy Life in Harlem." Washington Star-News, 4 March 1976; in Newsbank--Performing Arts, March-April 1976, 31:D 10.

_____. "A Musical in Touch with the Spirit." Washington Star-News, 5 November 1975; in Newsbank--Performing Arts, November-December 1976, 83:A 6.

_____. "Rambling Rather than Swinging." Washington Star-News, 14 November 1975; in Newsbank--Performing Arts, November-December 1975, 84:F 5.

_____. "Ron Milner's Upbeat View of the Ghetto." In Authors in the News, vol. 1 (Detroit: Gale Research, 1976), p. 349.

Richards, Stanley, ed. America on Stage: Ten Great Plays of American History. New York: Doubleday, 1976.

_____. The Best Short Plays 1971. Radnor, Pa.: Chilton, 1971.

_____. The Best Short Plays 1975. Radnor, Pa.: Chilton, 1975.

Richardson, Thomas. Place: America (A Theatre Piece). New York: NAACP, 1940.

Riley, Clayton. "The Black Critic--Theatre and Film." (N.Y.) Amsterdam News: Black Academy of Arts and Letters Supplement, 18 September 1971, p. D-18.

_____. "Black Theatre." In Theatre 5: The American Theatre, 1971-1972. New York: Scribner's, 1973, pp. 61-65.

_____. "A New Black Magic--And They Weave It Well" (Melvin Van Peebles). New York Times: Arts and Leisure, 7 November 1971, pp, 1, 13.

_____. "We Thought It Was Magic: Harlem's Apollo Theater." New York Times Magazine, 7 November 1976, 36-8+.

Ritter, Charles, C. Masterpieces of the Theatre. Columbus, Ohio: Collegiate Publishing, 1976.

"'River Niger' at Music Hall Tomorrow Night." (Memphis) Commercial Appeal, 16 March 1975; in Newsbank--Performing Arts, March-April 1975, 31:C 2.

"'River Niger' Yields Fine Performances." Birmingham News, 10 March 1975; in Newsbank--Performing Arts, March-April 1975, 31:C 3.

"Riverside Has 'Bread and Roses'." (N.Y.) Amsterdam News, 27 November 1976, D-4.

Robbins, Albert J. American Literary Scholarship: 1968. Durham, N.C.: Duke University Press, 1970.

_____. American Literary Scholarship: 1970. Durham, N.C.: Duke University Press, 1972.

_____. American Literary Scholarship: 1971. Durham, N.C.: Duke University Press, 1973.

_____. American Literary Scholarship: 1972. Durham, N.C.: Duke University Press, 1974.

Roberts, Susan O. "Tony Winner Delores Hall Thanks God for Success." (N.Y.) Amsterdam News: Arts and Entertainment, 9 July 1977, D-2.

Robeson, Paul, Jr. "Paul Robeson: A Home Is That Rock." Freedomways 16 (1st quarter 1976): 8-10.

Robinson, Le Roy. "Black Theatre: A Need for the Seventies." Soul Illustrated 2 (February 1970): 39, 57, 64.

_____. "New Images for the Black Actor." Soul Illustrated 1 (August 1969): 14-18, 65.

_____. "Soul Stirrin' Theatre: 'Two Plays for L.A.' and 'Murderous Angels'." Soul Illustrated 2 (July 1970): 15-16, 63.

Robinson, Louie. "Bad Times on the 'Good Times' Set." Ebony 30 (September 1975): 33-42.

_____. "Cicely Tyson: A Very Unlikely Movie Star." Ebony 29 (May 1974): 33-40.

_____. "Have Blacks Really Made It in Hollywood?" Ebony 30 (June 1975): 33-42.

_____. "Le Var Burton's Rise to Fame: College Drama Student Uses 'Roots' as Spring Board to Success." Ebony 32 (October 1977): 146-148, 150.

Robinson, Major. "Invisible Stars Twinkle." (N.Y.) Amsterdam News: Arts and Entertainment, 25 June 1977, D-15.

Rockwell, John. "Scott Joplin's 'Treemonisha'." Rolling Stone 202 (18 December 1975): 110.

Rodgers, Curtis E. "'Car Wash': Chuckless, Stupid!" (N.Y.) Amsterdam News, 30 October 1976, D-5.

Rodriguez, Juan. Why We Lost the Series. New York: New Dimensions, 1970.

Rogers, Curtis E. "Black Men View 'For Colored Girls': Good Theatre but Poor Sociological Statement." (N.Y.) Amsterdam News, 9 October 1976, D-11.

Rojas, Don. "Roots Captivates Millions of T.V. Viewers" (Haley). (N.Y.) Amsterdam News: New Horizons, 5 February 1977, D-8.

"Rolling Thunder" (Moss Gunn). Time 95 (6 April 1970): 62-63.

Rollins, Charlemae Hill. Famous Negro Entertainers of Stage, Screen, and T.V. New York: Dodd, Mead, 1967.

Ronan, Margaret. "Films: 'Cooley High'." Senior Scholastic 107 (23 September 1975): 40.

_____. "Films: 'Leadbelly'." Senior Scholastic 108 (23 March 1976): 38.

_____. "Films: 'Part 2, Sounder'." Senior Scholastic 109 (16 December 1976): 23.

"'Roots' Gets 37 Emmy Award Nominations." St. Louis Post Dispatch, 4 August 1977, p. 16C.

Ross, Lillian, and Helen Ross. The Player and a Profile of an Art. New York: Simon & Schuster, 1962.

Ross, R. "Role of Blacks in the Federal Theatre, 1935-1939." Journal of Negro History 59 (January 1974): 38-50.

Roth, Phillip. "Channel X: Two Plays on the Race Conflict" (Blues for Mr. Charlie and Dutchman). New York Review of Books 2 (28 May 1964): 10-13.

Rowe, Billy. "Black Actors Impact on American Culture." (N.Y.) Amsterdam News, 13 November 1976, D-10, D-11.

Rowell, Charles H. "Studies in Afro-American Literature: An Annual Annotated Bibliography, 1974." Obsidian 1 (Winter 1975): 100-27.

_____. "Teaching Black American Literature: A Review." Negro American Literature Forum 7 (Spring 1973): 16-18, 31.

Rowland, Mabel, ed. Bert Williams: Son of Laughter--A Symposium of Tribute to the Man and His Work. New York: English Crafters, 1923.

Rubin, Louis D., Jr., ed. "A Bibliographical Guide to the Study of Southern Literature." Louisiana State University, Baton Rouge, 1969.

"Ruby Dee Looks to Drama as a Medium for Messages." St. Louis Post Dispatch, 1 April 1975; in Newsbank--Performing Arts, March-April 1975, 29:B 10.

Rush, Sheila A. "Introduction: Drama and Ideology." In Ward, Douglas Turner, Two Plays: Happy Ending and Day of Absence (New York: Third Press, 1966).

Rush, Theressa G.; Carol F. Myers; and Esther S. Arata. Black American Writers Past and Present: A Biographical and Bibliographical Dictionary, 2 vols. Metuchen, N.J.: Scarecrow Press, 1975.

Russell, Candice. "Local Talent Abounds in 'Raisin'." Miami Herald, 5 April 1976; in Newsbank--Performing Arts, March-April 1976, 27:E 12.

_____. "Patti Jo Returns in 'Purlie' Role; 'Won't Let Up'." Miami Herald, 6 April 1975; in Newsbank--Performing Arts, March-April 1975, 27:A 9, 10.

Ryan, Barbara Haddad. "'Bubbling Brown Sugar' a Sassy Musical." (Denver) Rocky Mountain News, 20 January 1977; in Newsbank-- Performing Arts, January-February 1977, 10:B 14.

_____. "'I Can't Copy' Belies Title--With Pride, Wit." (Denver) Rocky Mountain News, 16 April 1977; in Newsbank--Performing Arts, March-April 1977, 23:G 8.

Ryan, Pat M., comp. Black Writing in the U.S.A.: A Bibliographic Guide. Brockport, N.Y.: Drake Memorial Library, 1969.

Saddler, Jeanne E. "On the Aisle: Ron Milner--The People's Playwright." Essence 5 (November 1974): 20.

Sader, Marion. Comprehensive Index to English-Language Little Magazines: 1890-1970, 2 vols. New York: Kraus-Thomson, 1976.

Saggittarus. I Am Ishmael, Son of the Blackamoor. Washington, D.C.: Nuclassics and Science Publishing Co., 1975.

Sainer, Arthur. "Making It All the Way" (What the Winesellers Buy). Village Voice 19 (28 February 1974): 58.

_____. "Somebody Do Something!" (Wesley). Village Voice 19 (25 January 1974): 70, 76.

Salaam, Kalamu ya. "James Earl Jones: A Great Black Hope." The Black Collegian 7 (January-February 1977): 32, 62-63.

_____. "Making the Image Real." The Black Collegian 7 (March-April 1977): 54-60.

Salaam, Yusef Abdul. "Van Peebles' Warm and Sensitive Song" (Just An Old Sweet Song). (N.Y.) Amsterdam News, 2 October 1976, D-17.

Salem, James M. A Guide to Critical Reviews. Part I: American

Drama, 1909-1969. Metuchen, N.J.: Scarecrow Press, 1973.

Salvo, Patrick. "'It Takes a Hell of a Man to Put Up with Me'....
Denise Nichols." Sepia 24 (February 1975): 36-44.

_____. "John Amos: Will He Be First Black Producer of
Movies Glorifying Black Heroes of History?" Sepia 25 (March
1976): 24-32.

_____, and Barbara Salvo. "Gregg Morris Speaks Out on Black-
ness and Movies." Sepia 22 (December 1973): 46-52.

_____, and _____. "TV/Movie Star Jayne Kennedy Tells:
Why a Girl Needs a Husband in Hollywood." Sepia 24 (April
1975): 36-44.

Sandle, Floyd L. "A History of the Development of the Educational
Theatre in the Negro Colleges and Universities, 1911-1959."
Ph.D. Dissertation, English Dept., Louisiana State University,
1959.

_____. The Negro in the American Educational Theatre. Ann
Arbor, Mich.: Edwards Brothers, 1964.

"Sara Fabio Webster Presents: A Tribute to Owen's Song." Black
World 24 (July 1975): 76-87.

Savory, Jerold J. "Descent and Baptism in Native Son, Invisible
Man, Dutchman." Christian Scholar's Review 3 (1973): 33-37.

Sayre, Nora. "New York's Black Theatre." New Statesman 76
(25 October 1968): 556.

Schatt, Stanley. "Bibliography Contemporary Afro-American Drama."
West Coast Review 8 (October 1973): 41-44.

Schatz, Walter. Directory of Afro-American Resources. New
York: R. R. Bowker, 1970.

Schechner, Richard. Public Domain. Indianapolis: Bobbs-Merrill,
1969.

Scheller, Bernhard. "Die Gestalt des Farbigen bie Williams, Albee, und Baldwin und ihre szenische Realistierung in DDR-
Aufführungen" [The Concept of the Colored Races in Williams,
Albee, and Baldwin and Its Scenic Realization in D.D.R. Pro-
ductions]. Zietschrift für Anglistik und Amerikanistik 20: 2
(1972): 137-157.

Schier, Ernest. "Van Peebles' Musical Has Good Intentions."
Philadelphia Evening Bulletin, 16 May 1975; in Newsbank--Per-
forming Arts, May-June 1975, 38:D 6.

Schmuhl, Robert. "Treating the Harlem Human Condition." Negro History Bulletin 37 (January 1974): 196-97.

Schneider, Elisabeth W.; Albert L. Walker; and Herbert E. Childs, eds. The Range of Literature, 3rd ed. New York: Van Nostrand, 1973.

Schorer, Mark. The Literature of America: Twentieth Century. New York: McGraw-Hill, 1970.

Scott, Johnie. "The Ceremony of the Land." Arts in Society 10 (Fall-Winter 1973): 33-39.

"'Selma' Folds." The Afro-American (Baltimore), 8-12 March 1977, p. 11.

Senelick, Laurence. "The Boston Theatre Season." New Boston Review 2 (Winter Issue: January 1977): 23-24.

Setrakian, Edward. "The Acting of James Earl Jones." Ph.D. Dissertation, New York University, 1976.

"Setting Basketball to Music." San Francisco Examiner, 7 September 1975; in Newsbank--Performing Arts, September-October 1975, 66:F 14.

Shafer, Yvonne. "Black Actors in the Nineteenth Century American Theatre." CLA Journal 20 (March 1977): 387-400.

Shange, Ntozake. For Colored Girls Who Have Considered Suicide/ When the Rainbow Is Enuf: A Choreopoem. New York: Macmillan, 1977.

"Shaw Players Slate 'The Sistuhs' Here." The Afro-American (Baltimore), 8-12 March 1977, p. 6.

Shere, Charles. "Baldwin's 'Blues for Mr. Charlie' a Grabber." Oakland (Calif.) Tribune, 6 October 1975; in Newsbank--Performing Arts, September-October 1975, 68:E 7.

Sherman, Jimmie. "From the Ashes." Antioch Review 27 (Fall 1967): 285-93.

Shipley, W. Maurice. "Reaching to Glory: Comparative Sketches in the 'Dreams' of W. B. Yeats and W. E. B. Du Bois." Crisis 83 (January 1976): 195-201.

"Shirley Graham Du Bois 1907-1977: Biographer, Playwright-Composer, Stage Director." The Afro-American (Baltimore), 12-16 April 1977, p. 14.

Shockley, Ann Allen. "Joseph S. Cotter, Sr.: Biographical Sketch of a Black Louisville Bard." CLA Journal 18 (March 1975): 327-340.

_____. "Pauline Elizabeth Hopkins: A Biographical Excursion into Obscurity." Phylon 33 (Spring 1972): 22-26.

Shuck, Barry. "The Afro-American Thespians of Philadelphia." Black Theatre no. 1 (1968): 3.

_____. "Philadelphia's Black Drama Season, 67-68." Black Theatre no. 2 (1969): 34-35.

Silva, Candelaria. "'Raisin': Capitalizing on an Overplayed Theme." (Boston) Bay State Banner, 1 January 1976; in Newsbank--Performing Arts, January-February 1976, 11:E 10.

Silver, Reuben. "A History of the Karamu Theatre of Karamu House, 1915-1960." Ph.D. Dissertation, Ohio State Univeristy, 1961.

Simmons, Bill. "The Last Poets" (Brother Cain). Black Theatre 2 (1969): 32-33.

_____. "Review: The Last Poets" (Epitaph to a Coagulated Trinity). Black Theatre 2 (1969): 32-33.

_____. "Some Impressions of The Amen Corner." Black Theatre no. 2 (1969): 32-33.

_____. "Third World Revelationist." Black Theatre no. 4 (April 1970): 39-40.

Simon, John. "Black Picture Show." New York 8 (27 January 1975): 51.

_____. "Black Plays/White Reviewers." In Singularities: Essays on the Theatre, 1964-1973 (New York: Random House, 1975), pp. 213-215.

_____. "Don't Let's Be Beastly to the Nuns." New York 8 (19 May 1975): 93.

_____. "A Dull House" (The First Breeze of Summer). New York 8 (24 March 1975): 78-79.

_____. "Improbable Extremists." New York 9 (26 April 1976): 72-73.

_____. "Mad, Bad, Sad, and Glad" (The Prodigal Sister). New York 7 (16 December 1974): 96.

_____. "Music of the Squares." New York 8 (27 January 1975): 51.

_____. "New Soap, Old Bubbles" (What the Winesellers Buy). New York 7 (4 March 1974): 62.

_____. "Ripe or Merely Ready?" New York 7 (13 May 1974): 98.

_____. Uneasy Stages: A Chronicle of the New York Theatre, 1963-1973. New York: Random House, 1975.

Simonds, P. Muñoz. "Medal of Honor Rag." Educational Theatre Journal 28 (October 1976): 412-413.

Siskel, Gene. "Van Peebles: A Man Who Keeps on Popping Up." Chicago Tribune, 27 July 1975; in Newsbank--Performing Arts, July-August 1975, 54:G 12, 13.

"Sister Yvette Hawkins: An Interview with Black Theatre." Black Theatre no. 6 (1972): 28-29.

"'Slave Ship' Closed Again by 14 Actors." New York Times, 25 January 1970, p. 70.

"Slide Lecture Will Open Federal Theater Series." [Bread and Circuses: The Federal Theatre of the Thirties] Wisconsin State Journal, 10 September 1976, n.p.

Sloan, Margaret. "Film: Keeping the Black Woman in Her Place." Ms. 2 (January 1974): 30+.

"Slow Dance on a Killing Ground." (Boston) Bay State Banner, 22 April 1976; in Newsbank--Performing Arts, March-April 1976, 30:F 8.

Smiley, Sam. Playwrighting: The Structure of Action. Englewood Cliffs, N.J.: Prentice-Hall, 1971.

Smith, Agnes R. "'Bubbling Brown Sugar' Hits Town." (Chicago) Courier, 11 October 1975; in Newsbank--Performing Arts, September-October 1975, 66:C 2.

_____. "Superfly Has Flown Away." (Chicago) Courier, 6 September 1975; in Newsbank--Performing Arts, September-October 1975, 70:B 10, 11.

Smith, Alexis. "'I Have a Dream' a Powerful Emotion-Filled Drama." (N.Y.) Amsterdam News, 25 September 1976, D-9.

Smith, Angela E. "All-Black, All Soulful and Very Together." St. Louis Argus, 17 April 1975; in Newsbank--Performing Arts, March-April 1975, 27:A 6.

_____. "'J.D.'--Ghostly Thriller." (N.Y.) Amsterdam News, 4 September 1976, D-3.

Smith, Barbara. "Reader's Forum: Black Women in Film Symposium." Freedomways 14 (3rd quarter 1970): 266-269.

Smith, Donald. Harriet Tubman. New York: New Dimensions, 1970.

Smith, Ed. "Special Reports: The Performing Arts in Jamaica-Theater." Black World 23 (July 1974): 73.

Smith, Jessie Carney. "Special Collections of Black Literature in the Traditionally Black College." College & Research Libraries 35 (July 1974): 322-335.

Smith, Marian. "Black Theater Week Renews Basic Aim: Reflect Community." Chicago Sun-Times, 23 May 1976; in Newsbank--Performing Arts, May-June 1976, 41:G 6, G 7.

Smitherman, Geneva. "Everybody Wants to Know Why I Sing the Blues." Black World 23 (April 1974): 4-13.

_____. "'We Are the Music': Ron Milner, People's Playwright." Black World 25 (April 1976): 4-19.

Smythe, Mabel M., ed. The Black American Reference Book, rev. ed. Englewood Cliffs, N.J.: Prentice-Hall, 1976.

Sontag, Susan. Against Interpretation and Other Essays. New York: Farrar, Straus & Giroux, 1966.

Spinks, William C. "Bert Williams: Brokenhearted Comedian." Phylon 11 (1st quarter 1950): 59-65.

Sprecher, Daniel. Guide to Films About Negroes, 16mm. Alexandria, Va.: Serina, 1970.

"Stage, Screen and Black Hegemony: Black World Interviews Woodie King, Jr." Black World 26 (April 1975): 12-17.

Stamper, Sam. "Playwright [Bullins] in Residence for One Week." (Boston) Bay State Banner, 30 January 1975; in Newsbank--Performing Arts, January-February 1975, 13:C 4.

Standby, Fred L. "James Baldwin: The Crucial Situation." South Atlantic Quarterly 65 (1966): 371-381.

"Stanley Ramsey Featured in 'Bubbling Brown Sugar'." The Afro-American (Baltimore), 7-11 December 1976, p. 11.

Staples, Robert. "'Roots': Melodrama of the Black Experience." Black Scholar 8 (May 1977): 37.

Stasio, Marilyn. "Off-Broadway." In Theatre 5: The American Theatre, 1971-1972 (New York: Scribner's, 1973), pp. 33-45.

_____. "Review: 'In New England Winter'." Cue (6 February 1971): 8.

Steele, Mike. "Mixed Blood Theatre Opens with 'To Be Young, Gifted and Black'." Minneapolis Tribune, 9 July 1977, p. 7B.

_____. "'Sty of the Blind Pig' Presented by Mixed Blood Theatre Company." Minneapolis Tribune, 5 April 1977; in Newsbank-- Performing Arts, March-April 1977, 25:A 12.

Stein, Shifra. "Actress Brings Back Bessie and the Blues." Kansas City Star, 21 April 1977; in Newsbank--Performing Arts, March- April 1977, 23:G 9, G 10.

Stephenson, Oliver. "Culture Projected by Caribbean American Repertory Theatre" (A Fog Drifts in the Night; A Trinity of Four). (N.Y.) Amsterdam News, 18 September 1976, D-2.

Stevenson, Robert L. "The Image of the White Man as Seen in Plays by Representative Black American Dramatists, 1847- 1973." Ph.D. Dissertation, Indiana University, 1975.

Steverson, William. "Musical About Civil Rights Has Heart-Stopping Scenes." (Memphis) Commercial Appeal, 4 April 1977; in News- bank--Performing Arts, March-April 1977, 23:F 8.

Stewart, Fred. "Bill Gunn's 'Mental Trip' No 'Sounder' or 'Jane Pittman'." In Nykoruk, Barbara, ed., Authors in the News, vol. 1 (Detroit: Gale Research, 1976), p. 206.

Stewart, Tod. "Hollywood's Prettiest Black Star." Sepia 24 (January 1975): 36-44.

"Still Another" (Thomasine and Bushrod). New Yorker 50 (22 April 1974): 32-33.

Stone, Chuck. "'Roots': An Electronic Orgy in White Guilt." Black Scholar 8 (May 1977): 39-41.

Stone, Laurie. "Act 1 for Women Playwrights." Ms. 6 (August 1977): 37-38.

Stowe, William M., Jr. "Damned Funny: The Tragedy of Bert Williams." Journal of Popular Culture 10 (Summer 1976): 5-13.

"Street Theatre: A Way of Life" (Straight from the Ghetto). (N.Y.) Amsterdam News, 11 September 1976, D-11.

"'Sugar' in Star's Hometown." The Afro-American (Baltimore), 14- 18 June 1977, p. 11.

Sugg, R. S. "Heaven Bound." Southern Folklore Quarterly 27 (De- cember 1963): 249-266.

Sullivan, Dan. "Theatre West" (Don't Bother Me I Can't Cope). In Theatre 5: The American Theatre, 1971-1972 (New York: Scribner's, 1973), pp. 87-97.

Sullivan, Victoria, and James Hatch. Plays by and about Women. New York: Random House, 1973.

"Summer Schedule." (N.Y.) Amsterdam News: Arts and Entertainment, 23 July 1977, D-14.

Sumpter, Clyde S. "The Negro in the Twentieth Century American Drama: A Bibliography." Theatre Documentation 3 (Fall 1970 and Spring 1971): 3-28.

Sverdlik, Alan. "Joe Attles at 73 Living a Little of His Part Each Day." (N.Y.) Amsterdam News, 2 October 1976, D-2.

_____. "Queens Drama about Worn Soles and Souls." (N.Y.) Amsterdam News, 31 July 1976, D-11.

Sweet, Jeff. "'Like a Goddess ... on that Stage'." (Long Island, N.Y.) Newsday, 26 October 1976; in Newsbank--Performing Arts, September-October 1975, 66:E 6, 7.

Swortzell, Lowell, ed. All the World's a Stage: Modern Plays for Young People. New York: Delacorte Press, 1972.

Taggart, P. "'River Niger' Tribute to Humanity." (Austin) American Statesman, 10 March 1975; in Newsbank--Performing Arts, March-April 1975, 31:C 6.

Taki. "'Zetta'--Alike or Dead (or Who Cares?)." (Chicago) Courier, 6 September 1975; in Newsbank--Performing Arts, September-October 1975, 66:G 11, 12.

"The Taking of Miss Janie" (Ed Bullins). The New York Theatre Critics' Reviews--1975 36 (2 June 1975): 243-247, containing:
   Barnes, Clive, "Bullins' Race Play Is at Mitzi Playhouse," New York Times, 5 May 1975.
   Watt, Douglas, "'Miss Janie' Is a Stunner," New York Daily News, 5 May 1975.
   Gottfried, Martin, "A Radical Idea," New York Post, 5 May 1975.
   Wilson, Edwin. "The Topsy-Turvy Sixties," Wall Street Journal, 9 May 1975.
   Beaufort, John, "Harsh, Brilliant 'Miss Janie'," Christian Science Monitor, 12 May 1975.
   Sharp, Christopher, "The Taking of Miss Janie," Women's Wear Daily, 5 May 1975.
   Kalem, T. E., "Requiem for the 60's," Time (19 May 1975).

Tapley, Mel. "Abcodun Oyewole's 'Comments' Answer 'For Colored Girls' Applauded." (N.Y.) Amsterdam News: Arts and Entertainment, 14 May 1977, D-14.

_____. "Black Theatre Exhibit" (Jamaica Arts Center, N.Y.). (N.Y.) Amsterdam News, 30 October 1976, D-7.

_____. "Chet French's Problem: Second Baseman or Movie Star." (N.Y.) Amsterdam News, 18 December 1976, D-12.

_____. "Did 'Bugsy Malone' Rip Off Mini Marvin?" (N.Y.) Amsterdam News, 18 December 1976, D-13.

_____. "Long Island 'Scarecrow' Gets Broadway Break." (N.Y.) Amsterdam News, 11 September 1976, D-2.

_____. "MLK Players' Director Changes His Name" (Salim). (N.Y.) Amsterdam News, 28 August 1976, D-9.

_____. "New College Musical Captivates, Charms Audience." (N.Y.) Amsterdam News: Arts and Entertainment, 2 July 1977, D-11.

_____. "Prison Workshops Breed Professional Theatre Groups." (N.Y.) Amsterdam News, 3 July 1976, D-10, D-11.

_____. "Trazana, Delores, and Diane Win Tonys." (N.Y.) Amsterdam News: Arts and Entertainment, 11 June 1977, D-2.

Taubman, Howard. The Making of the American Theatre. New York: McCann, 1965.

_____. "Ossie Davis Stars in His Play at Cort--'Purlie Victorious'." In Beckerman and Siegman, On Stage: Selected Theatre Reviews from the New York Times, 1920-1970 (New York: Arno, 1973), pp. 433-35.

_____. "'The Slave' and 'The Toilet' by LeRoi Opens." In Beckerman and Siegman, On Stage, pp. 472-73.

Taylor, Cassandra. "'Square Root of Soul'." (N.Y.) Amsterdam News: Arts and Entertainment, 16 July 1977, D-7.

Taylor, Clarke. "Fortune Smiles on Broadway's Gypsies." Essence 7 (August 1976): 78.

_____. "In the Theater of Soul." Essence 5 (April 1975): 48-49, 70-72.

Taylor, Clyde. "'Roots': A Modern Minstrel Show." Black Scholar 8 (May 1977): 37-38.

Taylor, J. Chesley, and G. R. Thompson. Ritual, Realism, and

Revolt; Major Traditions in the Drama. New York: Scribner's, 1972.

Taylor, Willene P. "The Fall of Man Theme in Imamu Amiri Baraka's Dutchman." Negro American Literature Forum 7 (Winter 1973): 127-30.

_____. "The Reversal of the Tainted Blood Theme in the Works of Writers of the Black Revolutionary Theatre." Negro American Literature Forum 10 (Fall 1976): 88-92.

Tedesco, John L. "Blues for Mister Charlie: The Rhetorical Dimension." Players 50 (Fall/Winter 1975): 20-23.

_____. "The White Image as Second 'Persona' in Black Drama, 1955-1970." Ph.D. Dissertation, University of Iowa, 1974.

Teer, Barbara Ann. "We Are Liberators Not Actors." Essence 1 (March 1971): 56-59.

Tener, Robert L. "The Corrupted Warrior Heroes: Amiri Baraka's The Toilet." Modern Drama 17 (June 1974): 207-215.

_____. "Pandora's Box: A Study of Ed Bullins' Dramas." CLA Journal 19 (June 1976): 533-44.

_____. "Role Playing as a Dutchman." Studies in Black Literature 3 (Autumn 1972): 17-21.

_____. "Theatre of Identity: Adrienne Kennedy's Portrait of the Black Woman" (The Owl Answers). Studies in Black Literature 6 (Summer 1975): 1-5.

Thayer, C. G. "Scott Joplin's 'Treemonisha'." The Ohio Review 18 (Winter 1977): 112-114.

Theatre 1: The American Theatre, 1967-1968. New York: International Theatre Institute of the United States, 1969.

Theatre 2: The American Theatre, 1968-1969. New York: International Theatre Institute of the United States, 1970.

Theatre 3: The American Theatre, 1969-1970. New York: Scribner's, 1971.

Theatre 4: The American Theatre, 1970-1971. New York: Scribner's, 1972.

Theatre 5: The American Theatre, 1971-1972. New York: Scribner's, 1973.

"Thelma Houston to Play Movie 'Bessie Smith'." The Afro-American (Baltimore), 30 November-4 December 1976, p. 11.

Thimmesch, Nick. "NAACP Zeroes In on Black Exploitation of Blacks." Human Events 34 (16 March 1974): 22.

Thingvall, Joel. "Simple Story of 'Sounder'." Twin Cities Courier (Minneapolis/St. Paul), 9 December 1976, p. 2.

Thom, Rose Anne. "The Gypsy Camp" (Raisin). Dance Magazine 49 (April 1975): 89-91.

Thomas, Barbara. "Opening Night Troubled." Atlanta Journal, 28 October 1975; in Newsbank--Performing Arts, September-October 1975, 69:C 3.

_____. "'River Niger' Angry Play on Poverty." Atlanta Journal, 12 March 1975; in Newsbank--Performing Arts, March-April 1975, 31:C 4.

_____. "'Wedding Band' Brimming with Emotion." Atlanta Journal, 22 August 1975; in Newsbank--Performing Arts, July-August 1975, 53:D 11.

Thomas, Bob. "Black Actor Is 'Still Not My Master'." (St. Paul) Pioneer Press: TV Tab, 27 February 1977, n.p.

Thompson, Sister Francesca. "Final Curtain for Anita Bush." Black World 23 (July 1974): 60-61.

_____. "The Lafayette Players, 1915-1932: America's First Dramatic Stock Co." Ph.D. Dissertation, University of Michigan, 1972.

_____. "The Lafayette Players, 1915-1932." Paper Presented at the Midwest Modern Language Association Meeting, Chicago, 3 November 1973.

Thompson, Larry. "The Black Image in Early American Drama." Black World 24 (April 1975): 68.

_____. "Black Writing if It Is Not Going to Disappear." Yale Literary Magazine 138 (September 1969): 4-6.

_____. "Jean Toomer as Modern Man." Renaissance 2 Issue one (1971): 7-10.

Thurston, Chuck. "For Black and White: A Change." Detroit Free Press, 1 January 1977; in Newsbank--Performing Arts, January-February 1977, 12:E 1.

_____. "There's a Message Here in All the Talk" (The Sign in Sidney Bruestein's Window). Detroit Free Press, 28 April 1976; in Newsbank--Performing Arts, March-April 1976, 30:F 10.

Todd, George. "Alonzo Players' New Comedy Applauded" (Beaulah

Johnson). (N.Y.) Amsterdam News: Arts and Entertainment, 25 June 1977, D-17.

Toll, Robert C. The Blacking Up. New York: Oxford University Press, 1974.

Toure, Askia Muhammad. "The Crises in Black Culture." Black Theatre no. 1 (1968): 11-15.

"Treemonisha." New York Theatre Critics' Reviews--1975 36 (20 October 1975): 189-193; containing:
    Henahan, D., "'Treemonisha,' a Legend Arrives," New York Times, 22 October 1975.
    Gottfried, Martin, "Joplin Tried, But 'Treemonisha' Fails as Good Theater," New York Post, 22 October 1975.
    Watt, Douglas, "An Endearing 'Treemonisha'," (N.Y.) Daily News, 22 October 1975.
    Wilson, Edwin, "Scott Joplin's Final Vindication," Wall Street Journal, 23 October 1975.
    Beaufort, John. "Scott Joplin's Rag Opera," Christian Science Monitor, 22 October 1975.
    Kissel, Howard, "Treemonisha," Women's Wear Daily, 21 October 1975.
    Sanders, Kevin, WABC-TV, 21 October 1975.
    Probst, Leonard, NBC-TV, 21 October 1975.

"'Treemonisha': Review." New York Review of Books 22 (22 January 1976): 34+.

Trescott, Jacqueline. "A Revival of 'Jesus Christ--Lawd Today'." Washington Post, 12 June 1976; in Newsbank--Performing Arts, May-June 1976, 40:B 4.

_____. "Robert Guillame: The Leading Guy." Washington Post, 6 May 1976; in Newsbank--Performing Arts, May-June 1976, 40:D 5-D 6.

"Tributes to Paul Robeson." Freedomways 16 (1st quarter 1976): 8-24.

Tricontinental Film Center: 1977-78. Berkeley, Calif.: Tricontinental Film Center, 1977.

Troesch, Helen D. "The Negro in English Dramatic Literature on the Stage, and a Bibliography of Plays with Negro Characters." Ph.D. Dissertation, Western Reserve University, 1940.

Troupe, Quincy. "I Mimic No One--Roscoe Lee Brown." Essence 7 (December 1976): 55, 57, 92-94, 112.

Trubo, Richard. "The Black Star Who Won't Act in Black Movies." Sepia 24 (September 1975): 32-39.

_____. "A Cinderella Story for a Hollywood Writer" (Sanford and Son). Sepia 23 (December 1974): 30+.

_____. "TV Genius Who Ended the Blackout on Blacks." Sepia 24 (June 1974): 27-34.

True, Warren R. "Ed Bullins, Anton Chekov, and the 'Drama Mood'." CLA Journal 20 (June 1977): 521-532.

Trumbo, Dalton. "Blackface, Hollywood Style." Crisis 50 (December 1943): 365-67, 378.

Turner, Alice K., comp. "What Your Favorite Authors Are Working On" (Maya Angelou). Ms. 6 (December 1977): 108.

Turner, Darwin T. "Afro-American Literary Critics." Black World 19 (July 1970): 54.

_____. "The Failure of a Playwright." CLA Journal 10 (June 1967): 308-318.

_____. "An Intersection of Paths: Correspondence Between Jean Toomer and Sherwood Anderson." CLA Journal 17 (June 1974): 455-67.

_____. "Lonne Elder III." In Vinson, James, ed., Contemporary Dramatists (New York: St. Martin's Press, 1973), pp. 233-34.

_____. "Visions of Love and Manliness in a Blackening World: Dramas of Black Life Since 1953." Iowa Review 6 (Spring 1975): 82-98.

_____. "W. E. B. Du Bois and the Theory of a Black Aesthetic." Studies in Literary Imagination 7 (Fall 1974): 1-21.

Twining, Mary Arnold. "Heaven Bound or The Devil Play: A Note on Dichotomus Predicates." CLA Journal 19 (March 1976): 347-51.

"Two Afro-American Plays Featured at Kuumba." Chicago Daily Defender, 14 July 1977, p. 18.

Tynan, Kenneth. Curtains: Selections from the Drama Criticism and Related Writings. New York: Atheneum, 1961.

"Tyson: Lady of Many Roles." Chicago Daily Defender, 21 July 1977, p. 19.

"'Uptown Saturday Night': A Comedy Featuring Largest Black All-Star Cast." Ebony 29 (July 1974): 52-57.

Unwen, Nathan. Martin Luther King, Jr. New York: New Dimensions, 1970.

Vacha, J. E. "Black Man on the Great White Way." Journal of Popular Culture 7 (Fall 1973): 288-301.

Van Atta, Jean. "'Matters of Choice', a Timely Drama at Karamu." Call and Post (Cincinnati), 8 February 1975; in Newsbank--Performing Arts, January-February 1975, 13:E 6.

Velde, Paul. "LeRoi Jones II: Pursued by the Furies." Commonweal 88 (28 June 1968): 440-41.

"The Victim's Revenge: Broadway Reviews the Critics." More 7 (July/August 1977): 30-31.

Vincent, Chas. "His Theater Is of Blacks, for Blacks." Detroit Free Press, 17 October 1975; in Newsbank--Performing Arts, September-October 1975, 68:B 6.

Vinson, James, ed. Contemporary Dramatists. New York: St. Martin's Press, 1973.

"Vonetta McGee's Own Story: Hollywood's Daring Mixed Romance Movie." Sepia 24 (March 1975): 28-38.

Wadud, Ali. "Don't Bother to 'Lock-In'." (N.Y.) Amsterdam News: Arts and Entertainment, 16 July 1977, D-7.

_____. "Great MacDaddy." (N.Y.) Amsterdam News: Arts and Entertainment, 7 May 1977, D-11.

_____. "Winti-Train." (N.Y.) Amsterdam News: Arts and Entertainment, 19 March 1977, D-13.

_____. "'Young, Gifted and Broke' Rich in Music." (N.Y.) Amsterdam News: Arts and Entertainment, 11 June 1977, D-7.

Walcott, Derek. Dream on Monkey Mountain and Other Plays. New York: Farrar, Straus & Giroux, 1970.

_____. "What the Twilight Says: An Overture." In his Dream on Monkey Mountain, pp. 3-40.

Walker, George H. "The Negro on the American Stage." Colored American Magazine 11 (October 1906): 243-48.

Walker, Jesse H. "And Now a Word ..." (Me and Bessie). The Afro-American (Baltimore), 19-23 July 1977, p. 11.

Wall, Cheryl A. "Paris and Harlem: Two Culture Capitols." Phylon 35 (March 1974): 64-73.

Wallace, Karl, ed. A History of Speech Education in America. New York: Appleton-Century-Crofts, 1954.

Wallach, Allan. "Hate Behind the Bars" (The Poison Tree). (Long Island, N.Y.) Newsday, 9 January 1976; in Newsbank--Performing Arts, January-February 1976, 14:D 8.

_____. "'Treemonisha' Naiveté...." (Long Island, N.Y.) Newsday, 22 October 1975; in Newsbank--Performing Arts, September-October 1975, 67:C 6.

Walsh, Elizabeth, and Diane Bowers. "WPA Federal Theatre Project." Theatre News 8 (April 1976): 1-3.

Wander, Brandon. "Black Dreams: The Fantasy and Ritual of Black Films." Film Quarterly 29 (Fall 1975): 2-11.

Wansley, Joy, and Lois Armstrong. "Alex Haley's Search for 'Roots'...." People 6 (18 October 1976): 84-91.

Ward, Douglas T. "Black Answers to White Questions." In Theatre 1: American Theatre, 1967-1968 (New York: International Theatre Institute of the United States, 1969).

_____. Two Plays (Day of Absence and Happy Endings). New York: Third World, 1971.

Ward, Francis. "Black Male Images in Films." Freedomways 14 (3rd quarter 1974): 223-29.

Ward, Renée. "Black Films, White Profits." Black Scholar 7 (May 1976): 13-24.

Warner, R. Stephen. "The Hero, the Sambo, and the Operator: Three Characterizations of the Oppressed." Urban Life and Culture 2 (April 1973): n.p.

Waters, H. F., and V. E. Smith. "One Man's Family: Filming 12-Part Serialization of Alex Haley's 'Roots'." Newsweek 87 (21 June 1976): 73.

Watkins, Mel. Black Review: No. 1. New York: Morrow, 1977.

Watt, Douglas. "A Black Odyssey." New York Daily News, 15 April 1977; in Newsbank--Performing Arts, March-April 1977, 23:D 9.

_____. "A Bubbling Song for Every Light on Broadway." New York Daily News, 14 March 1976; in Newsbank--Performing Arts, March-April 1976, 28:A 14; B 1.

_____. "It's Lively But Crude." New York Daily News, 1 May 1975; in Newsbank--Performing Arts, May-June 1975, 40:G 12.

_____. "'Miss Janie' Is a Stunner." New York Daily News, 6 May 1975; in Newsbank--Performing Arts, May-June 1975, 39: G 9.

_____. "Poems Slow Songfest." New York Daily News, 19 May 1976; in Newsbank--Performing Arts, May-June 1976, 40:E 6.

_____. "An Undigested Prison Thriller" (The Poison Tree). New York Daily News, 10 January 1976; in Newsbank--Performing Arts, January-February 1976, 14: D-9.

Weales, Gerald. "Birthday Mutterings." Modern Drama 19 (December 1976): 417-421.

_____. "The Day LeRoi Jones Spoke on the Penn Campus, What Were the Blacks Doing in the Balcony?" New York Times Magazine (4 May 1969): 38-40+.

_____. "Losing the Playwright." Catholic World 90 (5 September 1969): 542-543.

Weathers, Diane. "Fantasy in Black Theatre: A New Kind of Freedom." Encore 4 (21 April 1975): 28, 32-34.

Weaver, Harold D., Jr. "Paul Robeson and Film: Racism and Anti-Racism in Communications." Negro History Bulletin 37 (January 1974): 204-206.

"Welcome to the Great Black Way." Time 108 (1 November 1976): 72-75.

West, Hollie, I. "James Earl Jones: Expanding Horizons." Washington Post, 21 March 1975; in Newsbank--Performing Arts, March-April 1975, 30:A 3.

Westerbrook, Colin L., Jr. "The Screen." Commonweal 101 (18 October 1974): 65-66.

Wetzsteon, Ross. "A Season for All Seasons." Village Voice 22 (6 June 1977): 91, 93.

"What Ever Happened to ... the 'Amos 'n Andy' Cast?" Ebony 28 (July 1973): 138.

"Where Talent Abounds: Dance Theater of Harlem." Ebony 29 (June 1974): 106-113.

White, Jean M. "The Center and Blacks." Washington Post, 9 February 1977; in Newsbank--Performing Arts, January-February 1977, 11:A 6.

White, Melvin, and Frank M. Whiting. Playreader's Repertory Drama on Stage. Glenview, Ill.: Scott, Foresman, 1970.

Whitlow, Roger. "Black Literature and American Innocence." Studies in Black Literature 5 (Summer 1974): 1-4.

Wilkins, Patricia. "Reflections on One Black Experience" (The Last Chord). (N.Y.) Amsterdam News, 28 August 1976, D-14.

Williams, Mance Raymond. "The Aesthetics of the Black Theatre Movement in America, 1960-1970." Ph.D. Dissertation, University of Missouri (Columbia), 1977.

Willis, John. Theatre World: 1973-1974 Season, vol. 30. New York: Crown, 1975.

_____. Theatre World: 1974-1975 Season, vol. 31. New York: Crown, 1976.

Willis, Robert. "Anger and Contemporary Black Theatre." Negro American Literature Forum 8 (Summer 1974): 213-215.

Willis, Thomas. "Musical Mergers Miss the Vinyl Mark" (Joplin). Chicago Tribune: Arts & Fun, 4 April 1977, pp. 6-7.

Wilmer, Valerie. "The Sound in Europe." Soul Illustrated 2 (October 1969): 30-32, 45.

Wilson, John M. "Making It As a Screenwriter." 1978 Writer's Yearbook no. 49 (annual--1978): 18.

Wilson, Robert Jerome. "The Black Theatre Alliance: A History of Its Founding Members." Ph.D. Dissertation, New York University, 1974.

Winer, Linda. "Black Feminism Sparkles Under a Poetic Rainbow." Chicago Tribune: Arts & Fun/Books, 25 December 1977, 2, 5.

_____. "The Boom in Black Theatre: Growing Profit ... and Growing Pains." Chicago Tribune: Arts & Fun, 30 May 1976, 6: 2-3.

_____. "Here, It's Promises, Promises." Chicago Tribune: Arts & Fun/Books, 23 January 1977, p. 3.

_____. "Local Curtain Going Up for 10 Black Stage Troupes." Chicago Tribune: Arts & Fun, 30 May 1976, 6:3.

_____. "On Broadway ... Profits Earn Top Billing" (For Colored Girls ...). Chicago Tribune: Arts & Fun/Books, 23 January 1977, 2-3.

_____. "Over the Rainbow, Into the Shubert." Chicago

Tribune: Arts & Fun, 7 November 1976, 6: 3.

_____ . "... the Stage Is Set for a Hit Season" (Shange). Chicago Tribune: Arts & Fun, 26 June 1977, 6: 3, 12.

"Winning Playwright Seeks Film 'Angel'." (N.Y.) Amsterdam News, 4 September 1976, D-2.

Withers, Zachary. "The Negro and the Stage." Half-Century Magazine 4 (June 1918): 9, 13.

Witt, Linda. "Up Front" (Roots). People 7 (9 May 1977): 28-33.

"The Wiz" (W. F. Brown and C. Smalls). New York Theatre Critics' Reviews--1975 36 (13 January 1975): 390-394; containing:
  Watt, Douglas, "Fine Cast and Splendid Looking in 'Wiz'," (N.Y.) Daily News, 6 January 1975.
  Barnes, Clive, "Stage: 'The Wiz' of Oz," New York Times, 6 January 1975.
  Gottfried, Martin, "Black Wizard of Oz Musical," New York Post, 6 January 1975.
  Wilson, Edwin, "Jivey Dudes," Wall Street Journal, 9 January 1975.
  Kissel, Howard, "The Wiz," Women's Wear Daily, 6 January 1975.
  Beaufort, John, "Broadway's All-New, All Black Musical 'Wizard of Oz'," Christian Science Monitor, 10 January 1975.
  Kalem, T. E., "Jumping Jivernacular," Time (20 January 1975).
  Kroll, Jack, "Oz with Soul," Newsweek (20 January 1975).
  Probst, Leonard, "The Wiz," NBC, 6 January 1975.
  "The Wiz," WABC-TV, 5 January 1975.

Wolff, G. "Muffled Voices." Newsweek 77 (24 May 1971): 100ff.

Woodress, James, ed. American Literary Scholarship: 1973. Durham, N.C.: Duke University Press, 1975.

_____ . American Literary Scholarship: 1974. Durham, N.C.: Duke University Press, 1976.

Woods, Porter S. "The Negro on Broadway: Transition Years, 1920-1930." D.F.A. (Drama), Yale University, 1965.

Woolten, Dick. "Karamu Serves Up Tense Comedy." Cleveland Press, 31 January 1975; in Newsbank--Performing Arts, January-February 1975, 13:E 7.

"The Words of Abram Hill." In Mitchell, Loften, Voices of the Black Theatre (Clifton, N.J.: White, 1975), pp. 117-51.

"The Words of Dick Campbell." In Mitchell, Voices of the Black Theatre, pp. 91-109.

"The Words of Eddie Hunter." In Mitchell, Voices of the Black Theatre, pp. 35-57.

"The Words of Frederick O'Neal." In Mitchell, Voices of the Black Theatre, pp. 173-175.

"The Words of Paul Robeson." In Mitchell, Voices of the Black Theatre, pp. 155-163.

"The Words of Regina M. Andrews." In Mitchell, Voices of the Black Theatre, pp. 67-81.

"The Words of Vinnette Carroll." In Mitchell, Voices of the Black Theater, pp. 195-207.

"World Premiere of the Adderley's 'Big Man'." (N.Y.) Amsterdam News, 3 July 1976, D-6.

Wortis, Irving. "Review: Five Plays by Ed Bullins." Library Journal SCIV (July 1969): 2635.

"'A Wreath for Udomo' at Karamu." Jet (31 March 1960): 60.

"'A Wreath for Udomo'--Broadway Preparation." Jet (2 March 1961): 59.

Wren, Robert M. "Ola Rotimi: A Major New Talent." African Report 18 (September/October 1973): 29-31.

Wright, W. D. "The Cultural Thought and Leadership of Alain Locke." Freedomways 14 (1st quarter, 1974): 35-50.

Xeroxed Abstracts: Stage I; Stage II. Video Educational Workshop, Inc., 54 E. 11th St., New York, N.Y. 10003.

Yancey, Gloria Pauline White. "The Evolution of Black Drama." M.A., University of Louisville, 1974.

"Your Arms Are [sic] Too Short to Box with God." Milwaukee Journal, 24 December 1976, part 2, p. 2.

"Your Arms Too Short to Box with God." New York Theatre Critics' Reviews 37 (31 December 1976): 52-56; containing: Barnes, Clive, "Stage: Your Arms Too Short...," New York Times, 23 December 1976.

Gottfried, Martin, "'Arms' Short of Good Theater," New York Post, 23 December 1976.

Watt, Douglas, "A Show for All Seasons," New York Daily News, 23 December 1976.

Wilson, Edwin, "Your Arms Too Short to Box with God," Wall Street Journal, 23 December 1976.

Sharp, Christopher, "Your Arms Too Short to Box with God," Women's Wear Daily, 23 December 1976.

Beaufort, John, "Gospel Music," Christian Science Monitor, 27 December 1976.

Kroll, Jack, "Gospel Truth," Newsweek (10 January 1977).

Lape, Bob, "Your Arms...," WABC-TV, 6 January 1977.

Probst, Leonard, NBC, 22 December 1976.

Yvonne. "Cecily Tyson." Ms. 3 (August 1974): 45-47, 76-79.

Zanger, Jules. "The Minstrel Show as Theatre of Misrule." Quarterly Journal of Speech 60 (February 1974): 33-38.

Zastrow, Sylvia Virginia Horning. "Structure of Select Plays by American Women Playwrights: 1920-1970." Ph.D. Dissertation, Northwestern University, 1975.

Zatlin, Linda G. "Paying His Dues: Ritual in LeRoi Jones' Early Dramas." Obsidian 2 (Spring 1976): 21-31.

Zeisler, Peter. "The East Coast." In Theatre 4: The American Theatre, 1970-1971 (New York: Scribner's, 1972), pp. 57-71.

Zimmerman, Paul D. "Black Comedy" (Uptown Saturday Night). Newsweek 83 (24 June 1974): 80, 82.

Zyda, Joan. "William Warfield: 26 Years Later Just Keeps Rollin' Along." Chicago Tribune: Arts & Fun, 9 January 1977, pp. 6-7, section 6.

TITLE INDEX

The following symbols are used:
c children's play   + musical
* film script   x radio script
o television script

Aaron Asworth (Powell)
Absurdities in Black (Bullins
  and Rayden)
An Adaptation of Malcolm X's
  Autobiography* (Davis, O.)
The Adding Machine (Harrison)
Adjou Amissah (Angelou)
Africannus (Thompson, E. B.)
The Afrindi Aspect (Jones, S.)
After Hours (Richardson, V.)
After the Rain (Bowen)
After "Yuh, Mamma" (Seals)
Aid to Dependent Children
  (Hassen)
Ain't Supposed to Die a Natural
  Death+ (Van Peebles)
Ajax (Angelou)
Alice in Wonder (Davis, O.)
Alimony Rastus (Richardson, W.)
All for the Cause (Brown)
All Over Nuthin' (Lights)
Almos' a Man: An Adaptation
  (Lee)
Alonzo Jason Jefferson Jonesc
  (Berry, K. M.)
The Amateur Prostitute
  (Richardson, W.)
The Ambassadors (Acaz)
Amen Corner (Baldwin)
The American Flag Ritual
  (Bullins)
An American Night Cry (Dean)
Amistad (Dodson)
Ananse and the Rain Godc
  (Abdallah)

The Ancestor--A Street Play
  (Jones, G.)
And Now, Will the Real Bud
  Jones Please Stand Up
  (Brown, Wesley)
And Still I Rise! (Angelou)
And Then the Harvest: Three
  Television Plays (O'Neal,
  Regina)
And We Own the Night (Garrett)
Andrew (Goss)
Angelo Herndon Jones (Hughes,
  L.)
Antonio Maceo (Richardson,
  W.)
Appearances (Anderson, G.)
Are You Still in Your Cabin
  Uncle Tom? (McComas)
Arife and Pendabus (Owens)
Arm Yourself or Harm Your-
  self (Baraka)
Armageddon (Sahkoor)
As I Lay Dying a Victim of
  Spring (Lee, L.)
As Long As You're Happy,
  Barbara (Lasdun)
Attucks, the Martyr (Richard-
  son, W.)

B/C (Jackson, C. B.)
B. P. Chant (Baraka)
The Babbler (Everett)
Babylon IIc (Aremu)
Backstage (Felton)

307

ERRATA

The earlier volume, Black American Playwrights, 1800
to the Present, contains the following errors that look
correct but are not.

	page and location	error	change to
9	Baldwin, line 9	Phyllis	Phillip
89	Grainer [sic]	Grainer	Grainger
93	Hansberry, death date	1954	1965
187	Stewart, Fon [sic]	Fon	Ron
277	Black Picture Show	(Gern)	(Gunn)
142	Miller, May Plays Published in Anthologies: Graven Images, line 14, play was published in Richardson, Plays and Pageants.